Gentle Patriot

Gentle Patriot
A Political Biography of Walter Gordon
Denis Smith

Hurtig Publishers
Edmonton

To my parents

Hurtig Publishers
10560 105 Street
Edmonton, Alberta

ISBN 0-88830-074-3

Designed, typeset, printed and bound in Canada

Contents

Acknowledgements / 7
Introduction / 9
1   A Career in the Making, 1906 – 1955 / 15
2   "Shadowing Forth the Future" / 31
3   Into Politics / 51
4   Rebuilding the Party / 71
5   Round One: 1962 / 93
6   Round Two: 1963 / 107
7   Confidence / 134
8   Checkmate / 155
9   Pulling Apart or Pulling Together, 1963 – 1964 / 180
10 Slow Movement / 211
11 An Election of Convenience / 242
12 After the Fall / 268
13 On the Brink / 294
14 "The party is where it was; only Walter Gordon has lost his freedom" / 307
15 Last Days / 326
16 Discovering the National Interest / 348
Notes / 365
Appendices / 407
Index / 410

Acknowledgements

This book is an independent study of the political career of the Hon. Walter L. Gordon. I gratefully acknowledge the cooperation of the subject, who offered full access to his *Papers* and left me entirely free to draw my own conclusions. These were admirable acts of self-restraint by a politician in the presence of a contemporary historian. (I urge them on other politicians too.) He was generous in discussing his political life and answering my enquiries in the course of writing.

The primary sources were Walter Gordon's *Papers* (in the possession of Mr. Gordon), public documents, the press, and interviews and correspondence with friends and political colleagues of Walter Gordon. In addition, I have consulted the various drafts of an unpublished manuscript *Memoir* written by Walter Gordon during 1968 and 1969. Wherever possible I have gone beyond the *Memoir* to the original sources; in general I have used the *Memoir* as one retrospective account of recent events to be amplified, verified and balanced by the private and public record, interviews and correspondence. It has been useful as a summary review of Walter Gordon's political career as seen through his own eyes; but the perspective of this book is necessarily wider and less personal.

Mrs. Diana Murray was unfailingly helpful in guiding me into the Gordon *Papers*; my secretary, Mrs. Arlene Davis, performed her unstinting duties with the usual great skill; and Mr. Roy Maddocks worked most helpfully as my research assistant.

I am grateful to all the friends and political colleagues of Walter Gordon with whom I talked and corresponded; further acknowledgements to most of them appear by name in the footnotes. In particular, I record my appreciation for the helpfulness of the late Right Honourable Lester B. Pearson in answering many questions relating to his long and close political association with Walter Gordon. The course of that association is one of the inevitable themes of this book – it is, in fact, a study of Gordon and Pearson – and Mr. Pearson's frankness was indispensable.

The Canada Council awarded me a Leave Fellowship in 1971 – 1972, and a research grant throughout the period of my work on the book; without that assistance it would have been impossible to undertake. Trent University generously permitted me to take leave of absence beyond a period of sabbatical leave to complete the manuscript.

I am especially grateful to Abraham Rotstein, William Neville and John Stubbs for reading and commenting on the manuscript in draft. My wife Dawn has also, as always, been a thoughtful and patient source of advice, encouragement and support.

A work of contemporary history obviously cannot be an exhaustive account of the times. Too much of the record remains inaccessible, the sensitivities of living men must be taken into consideration, and the perspective is often too short to allow definitive judgments of men and events. Within those limitations, I have sought to tell the story of Walter Gordon's political career as fully and accurately as possible, and to document the sources. I have felt free, in particular, to examine the central events in Gordon's life in politics without inhibition. Occasionally confidential sources remain unacknowledged, and very occasionally I have not treated peripheral matters fully out of respect for privacy. I do not believe that the record has been seriously distorted as a result, and hope that the materials I have used will one day be available for judgment from the longer historical perspective. For the errors, omissions and possible misinterpretations that follow, I am alone responsible. I thank Bernard Levin for directing me (on the title page of his *The Pendulum Years: Britain and the Sixties*) to Sir Walter Raleigh's salutary warning that "who-so-ever, in writing a modern history, shall follow truth too near the heels, it may haply strike out his teeth."

Denis Smith
Champlain College, Trent University
April 15, 1973

Introduction

When Walter Gordon joined Lester Pearson in reorganizing the Liberal Party of Canada after the catastrophic defeat of 1958, he came to be regarded as something of a miracle man. By the time the party gained power in April, 1963 Gordon seemed to possess the golden touch. He was the architect of the Liberal party's reconstruction, the person most responsible for the party's reforming program and for its vigorous organization. He was admiringly compared (among less fastidious Liberals) to the strong man of the St. Laurent administration, Clarence Decatur Howe. He was confident; he was decisive; and he knew what he wanted to do. Even the party's opponents regarded his prospects with high expectation.

The awe in which Walter Gordon was held in 1963 could not be entirely explained by his role in the party's revival, or by the cool contrast he offered to the political hysteria and economic muddle of the Diefenbaker government. His practical talents were undoubted; but the deeper source of his reputation was symbolic. He was one of the Canadian business elite, a priest of the nation's materialist faith – and they did not normally enter parliamentary politics. To the Canadian business community, politics, like 'trade' to the gentry of Victorian England, was an undignified vocation indulged in by the socially inferior. The spread of the business ethos after the Second World War meant that this judgment was widely, although unconsciously, shared among Canadians; and in a certain sense it was encouraged by the Liberal governments of W. L. Mackenzie King and Louis St. Laurent. The period of postwar prosperity was regarded by the early 1950s as an era when politics had ceased. The Opposition parties in Parliament were weak and ineffective, and there was a widespread assumption, which was current not only among Liberals, that the Liberal party, under astute guidance, could remain in power forever. The country had come into its own: it was independent of the United Kingdom, it was a leading economic power thanks to the benefits of a distant war and a prudent leadership, and it existed beside a benevolent neighbour that offered permanent prosperity in return for the opportunity to extract the country's abundant natural resources. There was only one acceptable view of foreign policy, that Canada was a disinterested junior member of a liberal alliance led by the United States which would bring the benefits of collective security, peace and law to a generally grateful world. At home, the welfare state and Keynesian fine tuning of the economy promised stability and security for all. The realities were more subtle and more harsh than the myth, but the liberal political vision transcended them in utopian complacency. There was apparently no foundation and no need for political conflict. (The 'end of ideology' was a fact in Canada ten years before it was discovered in the United States.)

In place of politics was substituted the purer and tidier process of administration, managed by an efficient Cabinet with the aid of a small group of senior civil service advisers. These advisers (by common agreement that was discreetly promoted by the men themselves) were a body of outstandingly brilliant and altruistic mandarins, devoted only to the service of the country.

The wartime need to coordinate and control a vastly expanded manufacturing economy had been the major stimulus in creating this elite, and it had also brought the civil service into intimate association with the leaders of business and finance. The 'dollar-a-year men' who came to Ottawa to run the special agencies and divisions required for emergency operations were the link between the two Canadian mandarinates of Ottawa and Bay Street – St. James Street. The ties of friendship and mutual respect which developed through six years of war in the Department of Munitions and Supply, the Wartime Prices and Trade Board and the Bank of Canada were there to be maintained after 1945 when the administration of things had come to replace the government of men.

The separation between Cabinet ministers and their senior advisers grew indistinct as the Cabinet and the Liberal party came to depend increasingly on the mandarins for ideas and policies; and a career in the higher ranks of the federal civil service became one of the favoured paths into the federal Cabinet. The political process of general elections and parliamentary debate appeared less and less central to the real business of managing the country's affairs. Politics was a quaint and frequently tiresome ritual to be fulfilled, providing diversion for some members of the government who had it in their blood; but power and authority were to be acquired elsewhere.

The business community of English Canada has been little attracted to political life in this century; but the wartime experience of substantial cooperation with the federal administration opened a fresh and dignified path to political influence which bypassed the uncertain route through party politics. Walter Gordon was one of the heirs of the wartime experience, and from 1946 to 1954 he continued from time to time to accept commissions from Ottawa on a variety of subjects. Given the high place that efficient management was accorded in the Liberal scheme of things, it was natural that he should be seen in due course as a candidate for political office in the federal Cabinet. He had proved himself in his private practice of chartered accounting and management consulting, in his wartime service to the Bank of Canada and the Department of Finance, and in his more recent commission studies and advisory reports for the Cabinet. In 1954 Prime Minister St. Laurent invited Gordon to join his government; and if Gordon had been more attracted to politics than he was, he would probably have accepted the appointment on the assumption that he could spend his mature years in honourable, complacent and untroubled service on Canada's national board of directors.

It was not that Walter Gordon lacked ambition – his family had long prided itself in possessing that quality in sufficiency – or that he rejected the administrative route to the Cabinet. He was restrained by his attachment to a successful business career, by the traditional scepticism of his class toward politics (even at Cabinet level), and most significantly, by unease at the Cabinet's lack of foresight and imagination. He was particularly troubled about where the wide-open encouragement of Canadian development, financed by foreign equity capital, might eventually lead the country. But he was no political partisan, and his nascent dissatisfaction did not take the form of support for one of the Opposition parties. Instead, it was revealed in his determination only to accept a Cabinet appointment if it involved a senior portfolio such as Finance or Trade and Commerce, through which he might exercise a real influence on the government's direction. He had learned not to waste his opportunities, and took for granted that entry into the country's leadership would not be worthwhile unless he had something special to accomplish and the power to accomplish it. This was not quite the neutral commitment to efficient administration and the *status quo* that was Ottawa's ideal.

Prime Minister St. Laurent did not offer Gordon a senior portfolio, and he therefore declined the invitation. That decision marked a turning point in his life, because it led him, on reflection, not back to a private career but deliberately toward public life. He still saw his role as a consultant and administrator, not as a politician; but choice and circumstance over the next six years brought him at last into the political arena. His ideas about national policy began to emerge clearly during his chairmanship of the Royal Commission on Canada's Economic Prospects from 1955 to 1958. He would have preferred to see those ideas adopted without involving himself in partisan politics, and he saw the Royal Commission initially as a means of encouraging this. But in June, 1957 something totally unexpected occurred: Canadian politics came violently to life again under the inspiration of John Diefenbaker. The Liberal government was repudiated by the electorate, administration was rebuked, and politics – unpredictable, refreshing and exasperating – was once more triumphant.

The new Prime Minister was suspicious of both the senior civil service and the business community. In Opposition, he had hinted at support for Walter Gordon and the recommendations of the Royal Commission; but in office Diefenbaker rejected them scornfully as the Liberal proposals of a Liberal agent. In the literal sense this was unfair and untrue; in another sense it was revealing. The Liberal government had created the Cabinet-civil service-business axis, and propagated the view that the Liberal party was, not a partisan institution, but the legitimate embodiment of the national will. Only its opponents were partisan and factious. The unreflected acceptance of this belief smoothed the way for the integration of senior civil servants and businessmen into the Liberal national system: for they could play their cooperative roles without making any overt political commitment to the party. The degree of accommodation which they actually made to a particular view of the nation could be genuinely unconsidered – and could be made in good faith. But from the perspective of the Liberal party's political opponents, the government's loyal aides and advisers were tainted men; and in retrospect – once the party had been turned out of office – some of them (but decidedly not all) gradually discovered that they did possess an allegiance to the Liberal party. John Diefenbaker's suspicion, in a few cases, became self-fulfilling prophecy.

The reasons why the Diefenbaker government failed, ultimately, to win the active loyalty of the civil service and business elements of the old Liberal axis are complicated and various (and by no means adequately analyzed). The government's ineptitude in seeking reconciliation was one factor; its political obsession and economic confusions

12

were others. These were all considerations that influenced Walter Gordon. But for him, there were two overriding personal factors as well – his friendship with Mike Pearson, the new leader of the Liberal party; and his growing conviction that postwar Liberal policy had taken Canada in a direction it should not go.

Gordon took for granted after 1958 that the Conservative party of John Diefenbaker would not comprehend the essential mistake or alter direction; it was leading the country blindly and stumblingly down the same road as its predecessor. But the Liberal party might conceivably do so. It had been shattered in the general election of 1958, and most of its leading figures had retired or been defeated. Mike Pearson was open-minded and in need of assistance, and the party had to establish its claim to power anew. Pearson wanted Gordon's help, and Gordon found himself moving naturally and almost imperceptibly into politics.

If the Liberal party had somehow retained power but shed its old leadership in favour of Lester Pearson in 1957, Walter Gordon might possibly have moved directly into the Cabinet according to the efficient pattern of the 1940s and early 1950s, to carry out the program recommended in his *Report* of the Royal Commission on Canada's Economic Prospects. The Cabinet might have retained the comfortable illusion that it was not a political institution and that its members were not partisan politicians. Instead, if Gordon now wished to assert his influence, the defeats of 1957 and 1958 left him no alternative except to make an explicit political engagement. Cabinet posts were no longer within the Liberal dispensation. To help put Mike Pearson into power, Gordon would have to declare his partisan choice and demonstrate its value to a sceptical nation. This was what he did after 1959.

In making that deliberate choice, Walter Gordon began to reveal himself both as a distinctly unconventional Liberal and an unusual member of the business community. The choice was distinguished by its independence and its audacity. There were not many prominent Liberals or businessmen, after 1958, who were prepared to risk their careers in politics at the side of Mike Pearson. The belief was common (Pearson at first shared it himself) that he would spend a few unrewarding years in Opposition before giving place to another leader who might, after ten years, bring the party back to power. Gordon was not prepared to take this pessimistic assumption for granted. He measured the risks and opportunities, and then threw himself directly into the political battle. Meanwhile, some of the party's old guard fled the scene after 1957, preferring to follow their administrative careers in the security of business or commerce rather than joining the political contest in Opposition. A few of those who remained on the Liberal front bench were adept politicians, but they preferred the tactical intricacies of the game to any hard effort to reassess the party's policy or to revivify its organization. They did not appreciate the political lessons of defeat, and seemed to believe that the electorate had made a mistake which it would later rectify as a matter of course. The Opposition's role, according to this view, was simply to wait, to harass, to display one's innate superiority, and eventually to reassume the party's rightful place in power. Lester Pearson and Walter Gordon sensed that this complacency was bankrupt. They believed that the renewal of public confidence in the party would require a substantial effort to transform it, and they were undoubtedly right. With Pearson's encouragement, Gordon set out to transform it.

These circumstances made Walter Gordon's entry into politics notable. He brought with him the prestige of a highly successful chartered accountant and adviser to governments, with claims to authority both in Ottawa and on Bay Street. He symbolized the best qualities of both, and he demonstrated his willingness to undergo the risks of political life. He was immediately marked by the press as a politician beyond the ordinary. In the years of Liberal Opposition, the commentators were inclined to foresee his future in politics as a steady ascent onwards and upwards to the final rewards of glory. The party did nothing to discourage this flattering assessment of his prospects; where Walter Gordon went, the party would go too. No other destiny would fit the Liberal myth of Canada's progress. But the simple stereotype was deceptive. Walter Gordon was in fact setting out to challenge some of the most deeply held articles of his party's faith, and – given the peculiar axis which postwar Liberal governments had created – of the whole English Canadian establishment. His political career is the turbulent record of that challenge.

1   A Career in the Making, 1906 – 1955

There was little in Walter Gordon's early life to indicate the unusual course it would take in his fifties. His youth was unexceptional; he seemed to be a young man who would move capably and unobtrusively into a place in the expanding family accounting firm in Toronto. That company, Clarkson, Gordon & Dilworth, had grown since early in the century into Toronto's leading firm of chartered accountants.[1] When Walter Gordon entered it as a student of accountancy just before his twenty-first birthday in January, 1927 it had already begun to branch out into general management consultancy for business and government, and Gordon soon decided that it was in that side of the profession he wished to specialize. By the mid-1930s, when he became a partner, the firm had a national reputation and Walter Gordon himself was already demonstrating his initiative and entrepreneurial talents in various endeavours undertaken on behalf of the firm. His skills were those of a business and administrative consultant who had no personal interest in politics. He put his professional roots down in the depression years of the thirties, and his intellectual focus was very much on problems of organization and management rather than on the social and political turmoil of the interwar period. According to the temper of the time, he was a nationalist who favoured Canadian independence from Great Britain, and an isolationist who did not wish to see Canada involved in another European war; but at home he had no politics. He was not particularly attracted by the novelty or excitement of radicalism on the right or the left; he found it easy and natural, as a member of a consulting firm which regularly offered its services to both Liberal and Conservative governments in Ottawa and

Toronto, to maintain his political neutrality. His political convictions, which revealed themselves increasingly after 1955, were the product of long and direct personal experience of business and public administration rather than of abstract reflection. He was a practical man, concerned with measurable achievement – which befitted his Scots ancestry.

He was a second generation Canadian on his father's side, and a third generation Canadian on his mother's side. His paternal grandfather, W. H. Lockhart Gordon, emigrated to Toronto from Scotland in 1868, a graduate of Trinity College, Cambridge and a student of law in the Inns of Court. In Toronto, he soon settled comfortably, if not aggressively, into the legal community.

Gordon's father, Harry Duncan Lockhart Gordon, was the firstborn, in 1873, of a family of nine children. He grew up in the modestly affluent surroundings of Toronto's rising middle class, attended Upper Canada College and the Royal Military College at Kingston, and in 1896 entered his articles as a chartered accountant in the unpaid employment of Messrs. Cooper Brothers & Co. in London, England. In 1898 he returned to Toronto, was awarded the degree of Chartered Accountant by the recently organized Ontario Institute of Chartered Accountants, and joined the firm of Clarkson & Cross as an employee.[2]

Early in 1905 he married Kathleen Hamilton Cassels, the daughter of Walter Cassels, another Scot whose family had come to Toronto by way of Quebec City in the mid-nineteenth century. Walter Cassels was a partner in the prominent Toronto law firm of Blake, Anglin & Cassels, and soon after was appointed a member of the Exchequer Court of Canada.[3] On the occasion of his marriage, Harry Gordon left Clarkson & Cross to establish his own accounting firm. The practice prospered, Gordon took on an assistant who shortly became his partner, and in 1913 his previous employers invited both of them to join in full partnership as Clarkson, Gordon & Dilworth. From this time on, the private fortunes of the Gordon family were fused with the expanding destinies of the consultancy and accounting firm. For this Scots family of probity and good reputation, business and private life complemented rather than contrasted with one another in their lessons and requirements, each demanding similar standards of loyalty, discretion, honesty, and application to duty. The firm itself had the character of a family in its closely-knit solidarity and continuity, and in its self-imposed standards of professional conduct. It soon became one of the leading institutions of post-Edwardian Toronto, a source of initiative and change in the business community as well as a servant to it.

Walter Lockhart Gordon was the first son of Kathleen Gordon, born on January 27, 1906. His brothers Hugh and Duncan were born in 1908 and 1914, and his sisters Isabelle and Kathleen in 1910 and 1912. The three Gordon boys grew up under the vigorous influence of their father as he advanced with sureness and integrity in his profession and established his place in the public life of the community. H. D. L. Gordon was an officer in the militia, and in August, 1914, on the declaration of war, was Colonel in command of the Mississauga Horse. He went on active service at once as commander of a squadron of the newly amalgamated 4th Canadian Mounted Rifle Regiment. The unit went overseas to the western front, and in 1916 Colonel Gordon assumed command of the Regiment, which he retained until he was invalided home in 1918 bearing the Distinguished Service Order and the Volunteer Officer's Decoration. Two of his brothers died in France.

By the 1920s Colonel Gordon was a leader of the Toronto business community, a member of the executive of the Ontario Institute of Chartered Accountants, and an active layman in the affairs of St. James Anglican Cathedral and the Order of St. John of Jerusalem.

In the emerging Canadian nationality, there was still much formlessness and confusion of manners; but the Toronto business class (like that of Montreal) had already defined itself with some precision. It was an open class, but with its own firm patterns of social acceptability. Walter Gordon was an easy and observant pupil of his own community. He accepted its code of good manners, and added to it the spice of independence and irreverence given to him by his Scottish ancestry. Like his father, he attended Upper Canada College and the Royal Military College, where he demonstrated his athletic prowess as captain of the football team and a regular participant in track and boxing. His upbringing was conventional, his path was direct: and on January 2, 1927 he began his apprenticeship with Clarkson, Gordon & Dilworth, the first of the three brothers to enter the firm, as the Clarksons, too, were doing on their side. As one of his closest political advisers later said, Walter Gordon was "an old Toronto WASP . . . born with a silver adding machine in his hands."[4]

This privileged upbringing offered Walter Gordon shelter, standards and opportunities; beyond that, it awarded no special advantages which had not been earned. He began his studentship in the firm at a salary of $60 per month, and hours that regularly stretched, during the winter months, over six days and more than seventy hours per week.[5]

His first extended experience of general consultancy occurred when Clarkson, Gordon & Co. were engaged by the federal Royal Commission on Customs and Excise in 1927 to assist in examining the accounts and records of many business enterprises. Gordon accompanied the Commission across the country for its public hearings in the role of "glorified office boy," gaining valuable experience of Canadian business operations, the mechanisms of a public enquiry, and Canadian public personalities.

During his four years as a student, Gordon's salary rose gradually to $150 a month – an amount, in the depression year of 1931, which satisfied a single person living at home. But on receiving his qualification Gordon was restless. He took a few weeks' leave from the firm to make pilgrimage to New York City, to investigate the opportunities for accountants there. Most of the firms he saw offered him jobs. But for Gordon as for other Canadians, the exposure to New York at a crucial period in his life helped him to define himself as a Canadian. After ten days, he decided to return to Canada, quietly determined to demonstrate the competence of the Canadian profession. On the advice of his father that he might be earning $10,000 a year by the age of thirty, he made his commitment to Clarkson, Gordon & Dilworth.[6]

In October, 1932 he married Elizabeth Counsell, the daughter of J. L. Counsell, Q.C., of Hamilton.[7] The familiar work continued, while Gordon increasingly devoted himself to the general consultancy side of the practice. In 1934, for almost a full year, he concentrated upon work for the House of Commons Committee (and later the Royal Commission) on Price Spreads and Mass Buying. This investigation had been established by the House on the motion of Prime Minister Bennett in February, 1934 as one means of confronting the confusions and misfortunes of the great depression. Its moving spirit and chairman (until his resignation in October) was the prickly Minister of Trade and Commerce, the Hon. H. H. Stevens. The committee's concern was to examine the purported abuses of retail pricing and their effects on wages and working conditions in industry – a task of muckraking that attracted avid public curiosity. Stevens led the enquiry with a pugnacious sense of publicity and an aggressive satisfaction at the embarrassments he caused to the business community.[8]

In June, 1934, after months of preparation, Walter Gordon appeared before the committee with other members of the Clarkson, Gordon firm in the role of "investigating auditors" examining the operations of the T. Eaton Company. Their testimony about the company's wage and piecework rates, executive salaries and profits was a highlight of the committee's extravagantly publicized hearings. Gordon returned later in the year to the witness stand to offer testimony on the agricultural implement industry.

In the later stages of the investigation, when the House committee had been translated to the status of a royal commission, Prime Minister Bennett arranged for the appointment as secretary to the Commission of L. B. Pearson, a promising young member of the Department of External Affairs. Pearson's assignment was to organize and complete the work of the enquiry as quickly as possible. Walter Gordon and Lester Pearson thus met for the first time, admired each other's work, and became close friends. In Gordon's judgment, Pearson accomplished his task for the commission "with the good humour, hard work and tact for which he was already becoming known – and with a minimum of fuss."[9]

One result of Gordon's prominent role in the investigations of the Stevens committee, coupled with the accounts that he was already bringing to Clarkson, Gordon & Co., was an invitation to become a partner. J. Grant Glassco, another young employee, received a similar invitation, and they both accepted partnerships in 1935. Together they took the lead in expanding and consolidating the business of the firm.

Walter Gordon took more and more initiatives on his own behalf and that of the company. In 1938 the ingenious entrepreneur and the patriot in him combined to react to the growing trend of takeovers of Canadian businesses by American ones.

> It seemed to me this trend could be offset by forming a Canadian holding company with adequate capital which would be available as an alternative purchaser. In those days, the shares of Canadian companies, especially family-owned companies, were usually valued at much lower prices, relatively speaking, than they are today. . . . Moreover, many of the companies that were available to purchase had accumulated large cash balances which a holding company could withdraw without incurring any liability for tax. It was possible in this way for a holding company to acquire an existing corporation and to use the surplus cash accumulated by it to pay for the substantial proportion of the purchase price.[10]

With "an imposing list" of Canadian companies available for purchase, the goodwill of his father and G. T. Clarkson (the senior partners), and the friendly support of two leading Canadian industrialists,[11] Gordon set off for England in search of capital. There, after several months, he was able to obtain commitments for £5 million, a substantial sum well beyond what he had initially expected to raise. He prepared to launch a holding company "which might have become very big indeed" and to devote much of his time to the new venture.

But the shadows of a European war were already descending, and the Bank of England discouraged the underwriters from carrying through this transfer of capital to Canada. "Thus collapsed," Gordon recalled wistfully, "an early attempt by private interests to offset the encroachment of American financial control of Canadian business enterprises and Canadian resources."[12]

*

The outbreak of the European war, and Canada's independent declaration of war on September 7, 1939 marked the conversion of many Canadian isolationists to the Allied cause. Walter Gordon was one of them. As a former platoon commander in the militia of the 48th Highlanders of Canada, he would have gone into the army in September; but chronic gout prevented it. Instead, Gordon found himself in Ottawa within a few days of the outbreak of war, responding to a request from the governor of the Bank of Canada, Graham Towers, for assistance in creating the Foreign Exchange Control Board. Here Gordon's emerging flair for brilliantly improvised administration, and his qualities of independence and self-confidence, made themselves evident to his associates.

Installed in an unfinished room under the eaves at the Bank of Canada, he was given the task by Graham Towers of establishing the initial machinery and procedures of wartime trade and financial controls. The need was urgent: the Order-in-Council creating the Foreign Exchange Control Board had laid down that every subsequent import and export transaction required a Control Board permit. The young chartered accountant did not await the careful definition of his duties, but used the telephone and the telegraph to bring a preliminary staff to Ottawa almost overnight, to grant quick clearance for many international transactions, and to design a simplified system of monthly reporting for trade and financial exchanges which avoided unnecessary administration. Businessmen were impressed by the Board's efficiency.

By January, 1940 the work of creating the Board was completed, and under pressure from his firm, Gordon returned to Toronto to assist in organizing the consulting business to withstand the disruptions of a long war.[13] The senior partners were now elderly; Grant Glassco had left the firm in 1939; many other staff members were enlisting (116 employees served in the Canadian forces during the war); and as a result "things were in something of a mess."[14] Soon afterwards Glassco returned to the partnership, and under Gordon's and Glassco's joint direction Clarkson, Gordon & Co. maintained its practice for five years with a largely temporary staff, and kept in touch with its former employees in the armed forces, most of whom eventually returned to the business.

The uncertainties of war brought Gordon back to Ottawa within a few months. After the fall of France in June, 1940 Gordon joined two officers of the Bank of Canada in thinking privately about the economic and administrative implications for Canada of a possible British defeat; but this project was happily suspended before the end of the year.[15] By that time Gordon was engaged in occasional conversations about wartime economic policy with the Minister of Finance, J. L. Ilsley, a friend since 1934 when Ilsley had served as a member of the Price Spreads committee. These led to a meeting with the Deputy Minister, Dr. W. C. Clark, and Gordon's appointment in December, 1940 as a special assistant to the Deputy Minister. His duties were not clearly defined, but this potential source of frustration was compensated for by the association with Clark and the other senior assistants he had brought together in the Department of Finance. Gordon found Clark himself especially stimulating:

> He was always interested in any new idea and generated more of them himself than the rest of us put together. Intellectually speaking, he was the most exciting man I have ever worked for. And his contribution in terms of proposals for social security legislation – family allowances, old age pensions, hospital insurance and so on – have made a lasting impression on this country.[16]

Gordon's other close associates in Finance were W. A. Mackintosh, R. B. Bryce and John Deutsch. (Later Mitchell Sharp joined the Department too in a more junior capacity.)

Prime Minister W. L. Mackenzie King, a cautious politician at the best of times, was anxious in the autumn of 1940 and the spring of 1941 about the possible duration of the war and Canada's ability to maintain the burdens she was assuming. "I feel," he recorded in his diary in October, "that the time may come when England will have to look to us to supply her needs for war material and that, to save the Empire itself, we must make every possible outlay."[17] But King's (not very reliable) economic instincts made him balk at this spectre. In the Cabinet War Committee, King warned that the war might last three or four years. Unless expenditures could be tightly controlled, he feared that there might be "a financial panic or collapse before the war is over."[18] For reassurance, Clifford Clark was invited to the War Committee to explain that the war effort could be financed out of an expanding national income; and in early 1941 Gordon accompanied Clark to a Cabinet meeting to discuss the first major wartime budget.

> It was my first experience before this august body and my main impression was the reluctance of all ministers to say anything in opposition to Mr. King. I was asked a question or two and soon found myself in the position of defending the budget proposals, much to the displeasure of the Prime Minister. In the end, he turned to Dr. Clark . . . and asked him whether in his opinion the proposed wartime budget was within the economic competence of the nation. He replied, "Yes, Mr. Prime Minister, I think we can do it." That was that.[19]

In the spring of 1940, meanwhile, the Rowell-Sirois Commission had produced its massive analysis of and prescription for the country's economic and constitutional ills. It called for the centralization of direct taxation in the hands of the federal government, and the redistribution of tax income to the provinces by Ottawa so as to assure a minimum common level of welfare and government services in all provinces, rich and poor. The need for special wartime economic measures complemented the report's centralist approach to policy-making, and strengthened Ottawa's approval of its major proposals. But the Royal Commission had been vilified during its hearings by three Premiers, Mitchell Hepburn of Ontario, Maurice Duplessis of Quebec and William Aberhart of Alberta; and the realistic prospect for dominion-provincial agreement on its recommendations was slight. Nevertheless Ottawa prepared to meet the provinces in January, 1941 to seek national agreement on the Rowell-Sirois constitutional plan. W. C. Clark was apparently confident that the provinces and Ottawa would reach agreement.

Walter Gordon, on the other hand, was convinced that Premier Hepburn would defy Prime Minister King at the conference and guarantee its collapse. He advised Ilsley that the meeting should be cancelled. When Clifford Clark invited his new assistant to attend the proceedings, Gordon provocatively declined on the ground that it would be a waste of his time. "Clark was furious at my attitude and assured me the conference could not be allowed to fail."[20]

But in two days it did so, in face of the predictably uncompromising attack on the federal scheme by Mitchell Hepburn, supported by the delegates of Quebec, Alberta and British Columbia. Gordon's realism had proved to be prophetic. Clifford Clark was piqued and depressed at the outcome, and in a fit of impatience suggested to Gordon "that as I had been so smart in predicting the failure of the conference, I could take on the job of finding an alternative solution to the problem of financing the war effort."[21] Gordon chose to treat the request seriously.

A few days later he approached Clark with a response designed to meet Ottawa's wartime financial needs while temporarily putting aside the social objectives of Rowell-Sirois.

> My premises were that as long as Hepburn was around, we should not expect cooperation from the provincial governments; that, however, a large majority of the people in English-speaking Canada was behind the federal government in the war effort and probably was prepared to accept some of the burden this implied; that if this public support was to be retained, the federal government must bounce back from its failure at the conference with tax proposals the provinces would have no option but accepting. I argued that the tax proposals should be confined simply to financing the war effort and not mixed up with social objectives no matter how overdue or desirable these might be. I suggested these social aims would have to be pursued after the war was over, although I acknowledged that a little something could be done to alleviate the financial difficulties of the poorer provinces in the plan I would put forward.[22]

Gordon's proposal was straightforward: Ottawa should impose the heavy direct taxes it had previously intended to impose. At the same time it should promise to give any province that agreed to suspend its own income, corporation and succession taxes an annual 'rental' payment at least equal to its previous annual tax revenues in these fields, with further benefits for the poorer provinces. This was a species of genteel blackmail, made legitimate by Hepburn's intransigence and the necessities of war. Agreement was to be voluntary, but the citizens of provinces failing to come to terms would face intolerable levels of double taxation, in some cases totalling more than one hundred percent of their income.

> ... I argued that would be the responsibility of the provincial government in question, not of Ottawa. It was my submission that a scheme along these lines would work and that every province would have to accept it if the federal government was firm enough. The situation would become chaotic, however, if the federal government were to get cold feet and start making special deals with individual provinces.[23]

Clifford Clark was enthusiastic. The scheme ran the departmental gauntlet to the Minister of Finance, who took it to Cabinet. One minister, P. J. A. Cardin, told Gordon:

> . . . I like your plan. It would be like playing poker with the provinces, but this time the federal government would have all the aces. I think a plan like this would work. But we in Ottawa must not waver. It will work but only if we remember that the strength is on our side.[24]

On March 26, 1941 the Cabinet adopted the proposal, and agreed with Prime Minister King that there should be no advance warning to the provinces; the announcement of the political gamble would be made for maximum effect in J. L. Ilsley's budget speech. Mackenzie King confided to his diary that night that the plan "is a bold and far-reaching policy but will, I believe, succeed."[25] He was duly impressed with its authors.

> Clark, the Deputy Minister of Finance, is doing exceedingly good work. His mind is very clear and far-seeing in financial affairs. Ilsley is a lucky man to have so able a group of advisers at his back.[26]

Thus Ottawa recovered the initiative it had lost in January and carried forward its program of wartime financing. Much of the credit was Walter Gordon's. One after another over the next twelve months the provinces signed tax rental agreements on these terms. Gordon supervised the detailed preparation of the agreements for Ottawa, and finally appeared at the table with J. L. Ilsley to present the conditions to Premier Hepburn, the last of the provincial leaders to capitulate. W. L. Morton concludes approvingly that:

> All this was the outcome of the necessities of total war, not of broad-visioned national planning as the Rowell-Sirois Report had intended. Another result, however, was that the national government had command of the tax yield of the growing volume of national product, and on this basis Ilsley and his advisers achieved a war revenue by taxation and borrowing which not only financed Canada's own war effort but made a major contribution in money and supplies to that of Britain and of Canada's allies other than the United States.[27]

Gordon's work in 1941 as special assistant to the Deputy Minister included visits to Washington for consultation over Canadian and American financial policy, and participation in the planning for more rigorous price and wage controls, which culminated in Prime Minister King's announcement of rigid price ceilings in October, and the subsequent appointment of Donald Gordon (a friend of Gordon's, but no relation) as chairman of the Wartime Prices and Trade Board. Walter Gordon became a director of the Board.

In the spring of 1942, when the tax rental agreements were near completion, Gordon (who was suffering again from incapacitating gout) retired from the Department of Finance and returned to Toronto. There he enlarged the management consultancy firm of J. D. Woods and Gordon Ltd. (which had become associated with Clarkson, Gordon on his initiative in 1939), and turned over its services on a non-profit basis to the Wartime Prices and Trade Board.[28]

For the remaining months of the war, Walter Gordon's major contribution to policy-making was an excursion into public controversy. By the summer of 1944, the Department of Finance was studying various alternatives for postwar tax reduction. Clifford Clark was inclined to favour an immediate and sharp decrease in corporation taxes, while Gordon and others believed that priority should be put upon the reduction of personal income tax and the corporate excess profits tax. (Personal income tax rates in Canada in 1944 were substantially higher than the equivalent American rates.) Gordon, with the knowledge and agreement of Clark, set out his views in an article on postwar taxation published in December, 1944.[29] The article touched off a national discussion in the business and financial community which generally supported the Gordon case, and "in the result, Clifford Clark and his officials ... modified their views, and ... placed the emphasis in postwar tax reductions on the personal rates. My campaign had been far more successful than I had dreamed of."[30]

The last consequence of Gordon's wartime association with Clifford Clark and the Department of Finance was an invitation from Clark in February, 1946 to chair a royal commission on salaries and staffing in the federal civil service. Gordon took this on reluctantly when Clark confessed to him that the Order-in-Council appointing him had already, inadvertently, been adopted by the Cabinet.[31] With carefully limited terms of reference and two other full-time commissioners, the Royal Commission on Administrative Classifications in the Public Service completed its work in four months. It recommended the sorting out of confused relations between the Civil Service Commission and the Treasury Board, and a new and simplified salary structure for senior civil servants.[32] The report, which was only twenty-eight pages in length, and the Commission's entire budget of $14,996.91, were examples of Walter Gordon's spare and economic managerial style. The administrative recommendations were ignored.

*

By June, 1946 Walter Gordon had reached forty years of age. He had achieved business success, economic security, a modest national reputation, a characteristic style, and a well-defined range of professional interests. Canada had been kind to him, and he had made the most of his chances. He was known by his friends and colleagues as a man of independent convictions, public spirit, irreverent wit, and an unbureaucratic devotion to action. He put high value upon personal friendships in his work, was not overawed by the vanities and pretensions of power, and moved easily in its obscure corridors. The somewhat stiff and entirely proper young man of the photographs revealed his sense of economy and precision, but concealed his more human qualities under a façade of propriety. His social conscience had been stimulated by Clifford Clark, and by 1945 he fully shared the liberal commitment to state intervention in economic life in the interest of full employment and the general public welfare. He saw public issues from the national perspective of Ottawa, was a centralist by habit, and (barring serious ill-health) could assume that the mature career which now stretched before him would bring him back, one way or another, to Parliament Hill.

*

By 1947, Louis St. Laurent had become the heir apparent to Prime Minister Mackenzie King. St. Laurent had entered the Cabinet reluctantly as King's Quebec lieutenant in 1942, and had always insisted that he would return to his private law practice in Quebec City after the war.[33] But a sense of duty and the persistent persuasion of King and his colleagues kept him in Ottawa; and in September, 1946 he took on new responsibilities as Secretary of State for External Affairs. The longer he remained, the more determined King became that St. Laurent should take the succession as the second French-Canadian Prime Minister. Through the spring and summer of 1947, while St. Laurent hesitated, King intensified his persuasion. Knowledge of King's imminent retirement was now general, and ministers, party associates and even political opponents added their voices to the chorus of support for St. Laurent. In this atmosphere, Walter Gordon called on St. Laurent in the autumn of 1947 to tell him that "as a relatively young man . . . from Ontario, I felt it would be a wonderful thing for Canada if he, a French Canadian, were to become Prime Minister."[34] St. Laurent replied with noncommittal grace. About the same time, Mackenzie King finally gained the impression from St. Laurent that he would accept nomination for the party leadership.

The succession was clear sailing in the Liberal party, and arrangements went forward for a national party convention to register the choice in August, 1948. St. Laurent's place of affection and respect in the party assured his victory, and Mackenzie King's unwavering management consolidated it. On August 7, 1948, without any kind of campaign, Louis St. Laurent was chosen leader of the Liberal party by the votes of 848 delegates, to 323 for James Gardiner and 56 for C. G. Power.[35] Walter Gordon attended the convention as a guest of Duncan MacTavish, the president of the National Liberal Federation, and watched with satisfaction as his candidate was confirmed.[36]

Lester Pearson's career was now linked closely to that of Louis St. Laurent. At the end of the Second World War, Pearson had been Canadian ambassador to Washington, where his genial personality and casual competence had made a notable mark.[37] When St. Laurent became Minister for External Affairs in 1946, Pearson was called home from Washington at once to become St. Laurent's under-secretary, and together they managed Canada's emergence as a sober and outward-looking middle power, active as a conciliator in the United Nations and then, in 1948, in the creation of the North Atlantic Treaty Organization.[38] St. Laurent and Pearson, writes Dale Thomson, "established a fruitful working relationship based on mutual trust and admiration. . . . So close was their cooperation that it was difficult to distinguish the contribution of each one to a particular decision."[39]

Just as he had assured himself of C. D. Howe's continuing presence in his new Cabinet as "a sort of general manager of the Canadian economy" before accepting the leadership, so St. Laurent now invited Lester Pearson to become his Minister for External Affairs, hoping to balance the domestic manager with a foreign one.[40] Pearson called his closest friend Walter Gordon to discuss the invitation, and the two met the next day for lunch.

The request was no surprise to Pearson, for Mackenzie King had been hinting strongly to him that he should enter politics; but Pearson had never possessed enough confidence in King to think of serving in his Cabinet. Louis St. Laurent's accession altered the matter. Pearson knew he could serve St. Laurent with complete faith; and his concern for the deteriorating world crisis made him reluctant to decline the invitation. But he had two doubts which he shared with his friend: was he tough enough to withstand the buffeting of a political career? And how could he be sure of sufficient financial security to permit a safe entry into politics?

Walter Gordon encouraged Pearson to enter the government, but offered his caution:

> I did not know how he would react under the kind of pressures one must expect in public life. While his wit and charm and friendliness would be great assets in any occupation, only he could guess how he would get along under attack, an experience he had not so far encountered.[41]

There was also, as Pearson had said, another reason for seeking Gordon's counsel. Pearson's anxiety over the financial risks of politics may have been sharpened by Louis St. Laurent's discouraging experience: St. Laurent had told Mackenzie King that he could not afford to remain in politics, and had finally agreed to accept the Prime Ministership only after a group of friends had offered him a private gift substantial enough to wipe out his debts and meet his needs for the future.[42] The humiliating pattern was a familiar one for Canada's leading politicians. And St. Laurent was a successful politician: what about the failures? Pearson's fears were understandable, and Gordon undertook at once to raise the funds for a modest annuity which would temper this source of hesitation.[43]

Pearson continued to advise Gordon about his deliberations, and soon announced his acceptance of the invitation. On September 10, 1948 he became Secretary of State for External Affairs. A safe seat was vacated for him in Algoma East, and he entered the House of Commons.

Meanwhile Walter Gordon's reputation among Ottawa politicians and senior civil servants continued to grow. In the autumn of 1948 he was engaged by the Minister of National Defence, Brooke Claxton, to assist in reorganizing the Department to meet Canada's new military responsibilities in NATO. After consultations in London and Washington (which included some tentative study of the question of unification of the three armed forces), Gordon submitted a report early in 1949 recommending the appointment of the Deputy Minister to ex-officio membership on the Chiefs of Staff committee, a general decentralization of authority in the Department, and the simplification of administrative procedures in the services. Claxton accepted and implemented the recommendations contained in the report.[44]

A few months later, in the spring of 1949, Prime Minister St. Laurent called his first general election. During a visit to Toronto at the beginning of the campaign, the Prime Minister invited Gordon to meet him, to suggest that Gordon should contest a Toronto seat for the Liberal party. Gordon declined the invitation.[45]

He preferred to remain in the political wings, a friend and adviser to politicians and governments but a publicly uncommitted one. In the spring of 1953 he was asked by Lester Pearson, apparently on behalf of the Prime Minister, if he would consider becoming Canadian ambassador in Washington. The idea intrigued him, but Gordon knew that Arnold Heeney (then Canadian ambassador in Paris) had already been offered and had accepted the post. Gordon was puzzled and disturbed by the incident, and told Pearson so, adding that "I would not consider the appointment in the circumstances."[46] He never learned the explanation for this affair.

Further chores and opportunities in Ottawa soon followed. Early in 1954 Prime Minister St. Laurent invited Gordon to advise him privately on the revision of senior civil service salaries; and for most of three months Gordon interviewed senior civil servants in Ottawa while preparing his recommendations. Later in the year Gordon reviewed the status of federal-provincial fiscal arrangements, at first on a joint brief from the Ontario and federal governments and then, when this division of responsibility proved awkward, for Ottawa alone.

Gordon was a member of the inner circle of consultants to the Liberal government, moving with ease between Wellington Street in Toronto and the East Block in Ottawa. In spite of the great expansion of government activities after 1940, that higher circle remained a small one. In the late spring of 1954, not unexpectedly, Gordon received another invitation to see the Prime Minister. He sensed by this time that he would be offered a Cabinet appointment, and sought the advice of Mike Pearson before his interview with Prime Minister St. Laurent. Pearson

> . . . agreed that Mr. St. Laurent might be about to ask me to join the government, and he seemed to agree also with my reservations about doing so. The Liberals had been in power since 1935 and the government was showing signs of getting old and tired. I felt it was becoming increasingly cautious, increasingly disinclined to re-examine its own policies or to subscribe to new ones. Mr. St. Laurent was seventy-two, Mr. Howe was sixty-eight, and the departure of Abbott, Claxton and Chevrier [in 1953] had been severe blows. I presumed it was hoped I might be able to fill one

of these holes, at least to some extent, but as I pointed out to Pearson it would mean giving up a great deal. Ours was the largest professional firm in Canada, and my own practice was interesting and varied. I did not want to give this up for a junior position in a government that gave every appearance of being well set in its ways. . . .

After a long discussion with Pearson, we agreed I should very seriously consider an offer to accept one of the senior portfolios, specifically Finance or Trade and Commerce, but that I should decline anything else. Mike did not seem to think this would be in any way presumptuous on my part, only realistic. After all, he would not have joined the government himself more than five years before this except as foreign minister.[47]

St. Laurent did invite Gordon to join his Cabinet. He told Gordon that a minister from Toronto was "badly needed," but did not offer a senior portfolio on Gordon's prearranged terms.

I felt rather relieved about this, as it permitted me to decline his invitation without any doubts or reservations.[48]

Before he did so, however, St. Laurent asked Gordon to chat with C. D. Howe.

I found Mr. Howe ready to receive me and after a few preliminaries I asked him what he liked about his experience in politics. He replied: "Where else could I get as big a job?" It was as simple as that. He could not seem to understand why I was hesitating. I tried to explain that I had a rather independent turn of mind, that I was my own boss more or less, and I was not at all sure what my position would be if I joined the government. I said, "If, for example, Mr. Howe, you were to bring a proposal to Cabinet and as a new member I questioned it, what would your reaction be?" His reply was one of astonishment: "You'd do *what*, young man?" I had all the answer I required. Mr. Howe, who was nearly seventy, was not going to change, and neither was the government.[49]

Gordon declined the invitation, but with regret which stemmed from his admiration for the Prime Minister. However immobile the government might have become, that respect for Louis St. Laurent remained intact.

2   "Shadowing Forth the Future"

The invitation to join the Cabinet was a compliment and a source of stimulus to Walter Gordon. It indicated that his political opinions might carry weight with the St. Laurent government. But in rejecting the Prime Minister's invitation, Gordon had foregone the chance to use his influence at the Cabinet table. He was quite content, unless the terms were right, to remain in his professional career. If he had also been satisfied with the trend of government policy, the decision to stay out of politics might have had no further consequences for him. As his remarks to Lester Pearson and his insouciant question to C. D. Howe had implied, however, he was not satisfied. "For some time during the late 1940s and early 1950s," he wrote, "I had been worrying about the government's economic policies, and particularly the complacency with which Canadians were witnessing the sell-out of our resources and business enterprises to Americans and other enterprising foreigners."[1]

Under the paternal guidance of the Minister of Trade and Commerce, Canada was going all-out for economic expansion, especially in the resource industries, and this expansion was being financed and directed largely from abroad.[2] C. D. Howe's unquestioned policy was that of the open door. Gordon believed in economic growth, but his entrepreneurial sense was offended by the increasing foreign role in the Canadian economy, as it had been when he sought to promote a Canadian holding company in 1938. Beyond this businessman's concern, he now had a vague premonition that the country's political independence might someday be undermined by a foreign-dominated economy. The sense was inchoate and could not easily be articulated; and it rested on a further assumption that Canadian and American interests in the world were not – or would not always be – necessarily identical.

While Canadian politicians paid lip-service to the independence of Canadian interests, this notion was unconventional in 1955 for some-one close to the Liberal party. All federal political parties were loyal adherents of the Western alliance with its Cold War assumptions and its presumption of American righteousness. The progress of mankind, and Canada, was almost universally seen to rest with the unimpeded leadership of the American colossus. Within that mental framework, it was difficult to conceive of separate Canadian interests. Canadian resources were needed to fire the furnaces of the American economy; the exploitation of these resources would bring prosperity to Canada; expanding American economic power was needed to hold the frontiers of the Free World; and Canadians, among others, were all citizens in that Free World. A thousand speeches since 1948 had reminded Cana-dians of their privileged position in that scheme of things.[3] If Canada were to adopt an independent stance in relation to the United States, it would have to be within the very narrow margins allowed by this overriding community of interest recognized by all parties. For the Liberal party, with its continental economic perspective, the margin for manoeuvre seemed even smaller. In 1955, there were rhetorical stirrings of nationalism among Progressive Conservative and CCF members of Parliament dissatisfied with the free-wheeling resource-development policy of the Liberal Cabinet, hints that the Canadian interest was not being protected by a government with that continental perspective. But the complaints tended to be vague and emotional rather than carefully reasoned ones, and the government in its compla-cency chose to ignore them.

Walter Gordon's concerns about the failings of Liberal economic policy increased after his refusal to join the government. "Subcon-sciously, perhaps, I felt this might have been a chance for me to influ-ence policy and opinion in this matter, though hardly in a Cabinet which included C. D. Howe."[4] The result was a decision to provoke debate on the subject, and, at best, to convince the government to change its policies. Gordon had a feeling that some fresh policies were needed for their own sakes, but he was a friend of the Liberal party and would not object if the party gained new momentum by taking up his suggestions. In an article drafted for publication in the *Interna-tional Journal*,[5] he questioned some aspects of Canadian economic policy – especially the unrestricted sale of Canadian enterprises abroad – and advocated the creation of a royal commission 'to examine thoroughly the various issues that had been raised in the context of a forecast of the probable future growth of Canada's population and national output."[6]

Before publication, Gordon sent a copy of the article to K. W. Taylor, the Deputy Minister of Finance, asking if the article might embarrass the Department. Three weeks later, Gordon telephoned Taylor, who said he supported the proposal for a royal commission and had discussed the article with the Minister, who had himself consulted the Prime Minister. Gordon could expect to hear soon from the Minister, the Hon. Walter Harris.

Harris spoke to Gordon within a few days,

> ... to ask if I would mind very much if the government took over my idea. He said he would like to put forward the proposal for a royal commission in his forthcoming budget speech but this would mean I would have to forego the original plan of publishing the article. Naturally I agreed to this suggestion with alacrity. Instead of having to prod the government into taking action, they had been convinced by the draft article. My objective had been achieved with a minimum of effort, or so I thought.[7]

Walter Harris announced the creation of the Royal Commission on Canada's Economic Prospects in his budget speech in April, 1955. The economy was coming out of a mild recession, and the Commission was proposed in a speech which also offered direct incentives to economic expansion; it made up part of a package intended to gain political credit for the Liberal government.

The initiative shown on the subject of the Royal Commission was, as Gordon knew, that of Walter Harris and the Department of Finance. It reflected a relative growth in the influence of Harris as opposed to C. D. Howe within the Cabinet. (There were other concurrent signs of this changing balance of influence as well.)[8] The Cabinet decision to establish the Royal Commission was taken, according to Gordon, in the absence of C. D. Howe; and Howe opposed the enquiry from the beginning. In a retrospective review written in April, 1958, Tom Kent, the editor of the Winnipeg *Free Press*, said of the Commission:

> The way it was jokingly put in Ottawa at the time was that an investigation of the Canadian economy was, in Mr. Howe's view, an investigation of C. D. Howe; and he saw no need for that. It was one of the silly tricks of the men he called the "Junior Leaguers" — Harris, Pickersgill, et al.[9]

Walter Gordon saw the enquiry from the other side of the fence, but in similar terms: it was undertaken in the hope of deflecting the Cabinet from some of the policies of Mr. Howe. But the old autocrat was not exhausted yet, and the study therefore faced a stalwart and powerful antagonist within the Cabinet from the outset.

The Commission was thus born in the most intensely political circumstances: it represented the desire of a faction in the Cabinet to refresh an old and increasingly inflexible government. Tom Kent further described the Commission:

> Its avowed purpose was to take stock of Canada's economic prospects. That was perfectly genuine. But it soon became an open "secret" in Ottawa that the sponsors of the idea had another purpose too. They were conscious that after twenty years, as it then was, in office, the Liberal party was getting a bit stale. It needed an injection of new ideas, perhaps the shuffling off of some ideas that had become outdated.
>
> There was nothing illegitimate, in itself, about this second purpose. Indeed it surely should be counted for virtue in political leaders that, in seeking new ideas as politicians should, they were prepared to see what the thoughtful procedures of a royal commission had to offer.[10]

W. L. Morton described the situation more sardonically.

> ... the Liberals did not doubt of victory in the general election of 1957. With fine exuberance, they appointed a royal commission under Walter L. Gordon, a distinguished Toronto accountant, to study Canada's economic prospects and provide a new program of Liberal legislation. Rarely, if ever, had the great instrument of the royal inquisition been used to shadow forth the future and usurp the prerogative of the fortune-teller, or a party made a more revealing admission of intellectual insolvency.[11]

Soon after Harris's budget speech, he conveyed Louis St. Laurent's invitation to Walter Gordon to become chairman of the Commission; this understanding had obviously accompanied the Cabinet's acceptance of the proposal. Gordon modestly and routinely demurred, suggesting Graham Towers or W. A. Mackintosh as "better qualified" commissioners than he, but then accepted the appointment. He was joined by four other commissioners, Omer Lussier, A. E. Grauer, Andrew Stewart, and Raymond Gushue.[12] For the key position of secretary and director of research, Gordon sought and obtained the agreement of L. B. Pearson to the appointment of Douglas V. LePan, then minister counsellor in the Canadian embassy in Washington.[13] The Order-in-Council establishing the Royal Commission was approved on June 17, 1955.[14]

In his expeditious manner, Walter Gordon indicated that he intended to complete the Commission's work and report by the end of 1956. This timetable was politically appropriate because, as Tom Kent asserted, it was "the timing required to serve the political purpose of providing ideas for the Liberal party. The next election was expected in the spring of 1957."[15] But Gordon also considered this to be a reasonable timetable for a sufficiently thorough investigation to be done: his whole record and experience as a consultant had already demonstrated his organizing talents and his preference for economy and despatch in his work; and he was unwilling to spend longer than eighteen months away from his firm. Even without any element of political calculation, he was firmly inclined to set a tight schedule. Gordon knew fairly clearly what matters he wished to study and, in part at least, what conclusions he wished to reach.[16] But almost inevitably the timetable became a subject of controversy and misunderstanding in Ottawa.

The research staff for the Commission was recruited during the summer of 1955, and under the direction of Gordon and LePan, close to five months was occupied in carefully planning the subjects to be studied by the enquiry. Gordon considered this preliminary work of boundary-setting and definition to be essential.

> We settled on the main subjects to be covered, and decided on the various studies that should be undertaken for the Commission, some by its own staff and some, we hoped, to be contributed by independent organizations. The scope of each of them was determined in advance and in considerable detail before the work was started. . . .
>
> In addition to the studies, the Commission received some 330 separate briefs. While those submitting briefs were free to cover any points they wished, the Commission wrote to most of them beforehand indicating the kind of information and opinions on which it wished to be enlightened.[17]

And further:

> The first few months spent in detailed planning proved to be of

35

great importance. Because of it, everyone concerned with the work was made familiar with what the Commission intended to cover, and conversely what it did not intend to do. It meant in effect that almost all the data collected and the opinions expressed in the briefs submitted at the public hearings fitted into some section of a great, predetermined blueprint. Without this detailed advance planning, it would have been quite impossible to complete the work within the self-imposed target dates which the commissioners set themselves.[18]

This planning and targetting signalled the commissioners' intentions: they would produce a precisely delimited study of certain prospects for and problems of Canadian economic development. But these intentions conflicted with the vague expectations, the pace and the sense of propriety of many of those affected by the commissioners' work. There were complaints from provincial governments and other bodies intending to testify before the Commission that too little time had been allowed to prepare briefs before public hearings commenced in the autumn of 1955.

The shortness of time allowed made people outside Ottawa think that the Commission was really interested only in its own research and was treating the outside submissions as an unavoidable formality. That impression was not altogether fair. The Commission wanted outside briefs quickly, but it proposed to get its own research done hardly less quickly.[19]

Nationwide public hearings commenced on October 18, 1955 and continued with short interruptions until March 9, 1956; and there were further tours by the commissioners to the western Arctic in August, 1955 and to Newfoundland and Labrador in July, 1956.

The volume of evidence and the scale of research begun on behalf of the Commission soon made the terminal date of December, 1956 appear unrealistic. Many of the research studies would only be completed by late 1956 or 1957. The Commission accepted that the *Final Report* could not be completed within the original timetable. Walter Gordon did not wish to rush Douglas LePan in producing the document; but neither did he consider it realistic to delay publication of the Commission's conclusions once they had been agreed upon.[20] In the late summer of 1956, the chairman presented a memorandum of conclusions and recommendations to the commissioners for discussion, and after several meetings, this memorandum, with minor amendments, was approved.

In between the meetings, at least one of the commissioners tended to shift his ground on some of the points previously agreed to. . . . I was afraid that if the discussions were prolonged or if we waited until the *Final Report* could be completed, some of the commissioners might wish to change their minds again. . . . While there was a fair amount of discussion about the pros and cons of producing a preliminary report, I think the other members of the Commission felt as I did that having agreed upon the conclusions, the sooner these were published, the better, both to avoid changes of heart and also to avoid leaks.[21]

The commissioners agreed reluctantly with the chairman to produce a *Preliminary Report.*

Now, too, after the battering of the trans-Canada pipeline debate in May and June, 1956, the government was in difficulty. C. D. Howe had rammed the pipeline Bill through the House of Commons under closure, in the face of bitter criticism, leaving the impression of a weak and spiritless Prime Minister intimidated by the strongman in Trade and Commerce. There was more reason than ever to give the government a new face. In September, from his summer home on the St. Lawrence River, the Prime Minister made plans to refresh his party through new policies and his own reasserted initiative.[22] He welcomed Walter Gordon's request to see him to discuss the Royal Commission's progress, and "seemed interested and excited about the new ideas for policy which I expounded. . . . "[23] Gordon told St. Laurent that the Commission could provide the government with a *Preliminary Report* summarizing its conclusions before Christmas,[24] and Gordon left the meeting optimistic that the government would welcome and act upon the Commission's recommendations. "My recollection is that I told him I felt Mr. Howe would not like some of the proposals. . . . Mr. St. Laurent told me not to worry; he could take care of that."[25] Mike Pearson, whom Gordon also briefed in advance about the *Preliminary Report*, told Gordon "that he thought the changes and proposals contained in it were desirable and that the report should serve a useful purpose."[26] These initial reactions, from a tired Prime Minister and a Minister of External Affairs who was little concerned with domestic policy, could not be taken as the fixed word of the government; but Walter Gordon was encouraged.

The decision to produce a *Preliminary Report* reinforced the scepticism toward the Commission of some senior civil servants in Ottawa, notably in the Department of Trade and Commerce. Tom Kent spoke for them in his *Free Press* review:

The civil servants were professionally bound to disapprove of the Commission's method of working. They are the regular advisers to the government; in appointing a royal commission, a government is in effect saying "this matter needs deeper and broader consideration than our regular advisers will give it." In other words, the justification for a royal commission, in the civil servants' eyes, must be that it can devote much more study and thought to an issue than the civil servants have time for. The preliminary report ran entirely counter to this concept of a royal commission. The senior civil servants all knew that the Commission had tried to get its research done too fast and been determined to reach its conclusions anyway.[27]

C. D. Howe's opposition sprang from the very creation of the Royal Commission, and was probably unalterable; but that of the civil servants was more complicated. The Commission initially met with support at that level, certainly in the Department of Finance. But like C. D. Howe, the government's advisers would be sensitive to any criticism of its major policies. They had become intimately associated with the Liberal government during its long reign, were the fellow architects of much of its program, and identified themselves with its approach.[28] They would undoubtedly wish, for the sake of their own self-esteem, to apply unusually critical standards to any report which challenged that approach. And if they rejected the Commission's recommendations, they would exercise a decisive influence on the Cabinet's own response. A great deal now rested on the ability of the Commission to argue its case convincingly in the *Preliminary Report*. Yet for Walter Gordon the case had already been received warmly in his meeting with Mr. St. Laurent. The Prime Minister's general enthusiasm may have obscured the need for further, more public, persuasion in the *Preliminary Report*.

The *Preliminary Report*, a document of 142 printed pages and nineteen short chapters, was presented to the Cabinet at the beginning of December, 1956. It made clear, according to the American economist Jacob Viner, that when the Royal Commission had completed its work it would have "added lustre to a great tradition" of public enquiries.[29] The *Preliminary Report* took for granted the maintenance of "a flexible market economy" and continuing public commitment to high employment as the bases of policy, and assumed for the sake of its projections that there would be no global war, no economic depression like that of the 1930s, no long period of mass unemployment, and no radical changes in government policy bearing on economic development.[30]

The *Report* commenced with a series of forecasts of population, output and per capita income for Canada from 1956 to 1980 which, while hedged with statistical cautions, demonstrated the prospect of very substantial economic growth for the country in the succeeding twenty-five years. The emphasis on forecasting prompted a wry comment from Jacob Viner:

> This marks somewhat of a red-letter day in the history of economic forecasting; never before, I am sure, in the history of mankind since the time of Joseph has economic prophesying been performed on so exalted a level.[31]

These " 'opinions' expressed in statistical terms" were doubtfully reliable, and the Commission recognized and warned of this; but the impact of the first chapters was nevertheless "gloriously optimistic."[32] This part of the *Preliminary Report*, in its apparently statistically neutral manner, reinforced the strong conventional belief in the country's long-term economic growth, and was therefore politically uncontroversial. In its optimism, it could be accepted by the Cabinet as a reassuring statement of the conditions of Canadian existence and of the basic wisdom and benevolence of its Liberal governors.[33] (The statistics provided the Prime Minister with the material for many tedious recitals of Canada's material good fortune on the hustings in 1957.) The Opposition would not wish to cavil at this good fortune, and could only challenge the implied claim that prosperity would depend on the maintenance in power of the Liberal party. "The main purpose of the government in setting up this Commission and in having it make its report just before a general election," complained George Hees in the House of Commons in January, "is to attempt to create in the minds of the public the idea that all the good things which the report forecasts will take place in the next twenty-five years . . . only if this government is returned to office." "It is the only way," responded Jean Lesage from the government front bench.[34]

Within the framework of general prosperity set out by the Commission, the *Preliminary Report* went on to make policy recommendations in the fields of national energy policy, tariff and commercial policy, wheat marketing, capital needs and foreign investment policy, Atlantic provinces development, and manpower and educational policy. Here the *Preliminary Report* entered the realm of controversy. It favoured a greater degree of national economic planning than had been the Liberal habit since 1945; and it sketched an outline of policies intended to define and assert, in moderate terms, a national policy favouring domestic investment and management of the economy. This was the guiding theme of the *Report's* prescriptions. In its mild preoccupation, the *Preliminary Report* also accepted a stable tariff policy which would not involve any decisive move toward free trade, and questioned the usefulness of strict anti-monopoly legislation in the Canadian situation of a small domestic market.

None of the Commission's proposals was radical, except perhaps the suggestion for export licensing of natural resources; many were eventually shown to be sensible ones which became government policy under the succeeding administrations of John Diefenbaker and Lester Pearson. But the *Report's* approach to wheat marketing, the tariff, energy and foreign investment policies did offer mild challenges to the *status quo* and its representatives. The reputation of the *Preliminary Report* among the politicians and the mandarins depended on the coherence – and perhaps the diplomatic skill – of its arguments for these changes in policy: it was, after all, the prospect of criticism and the possibility of change which made them sensitive to the Commission in the first place. And here the *Preliminary Report* was inadequate. Too often it did not elaborate the evidence for its recommendations, nor argue the case for them; it simply stated them, as though they were matters of common sense which would be evident to any reasonable man. If this was difficult to avoid within the confines of a short *Preliminary Report*, it demonstrated the risks to the Commission's influence which were inherent in that device.

The discussion of foreign investment policy was typical of the *Preliminary Report*, and crucial, because in Walter Gordon's mind the subject was already becoming the central issue of Canadian politics. His concern was obvious from the chapter devoted to the subject.[35] But the concern remained tentative, polite, impressionist, and non-technical; it was expressed with extreme caution, in a tone almost of apology.

The chapter noted that Canada had always welcomed foreign investment and would continue to benefit from it. Foreign funds offered an important source of capital, experience and market connections for large, long-term projects involving substantial risk and no early return. But the quantity of direct investment, and its concentration in certain parts of the economy, had aroused the anxiety of "many Canadians" about the resulting transfer of economic decision-making into the hands of non-residents. The *Preliminary Report* conceded that the companies concerned were subject to Canadian laws, and that there was "little evidence" that they were in fact acting against Canada's best interests (the document itself offered no evidence that they were); but it added that "it is not axiomatic that this will always be the case."[36]

Companies by their nature must act in the interests of their entire operations and their shareholders; and international companies might be ignorant of local Canadian conditions and the opinions of the Canadian public. The hypothetical prospect was immediately balanced by a reassurance.

> It would, however, be both unfair and ungenerous to suggest that Canada has been hurt so far in these or other ways, as a result of the foreign capital which has been invested in this country.[37]

This brief assertion of good will from the Commission did not appear to distill the results of any research. In its brevity and sweeping character it left an impression of casualness and inexactitude equalling that of the reference to the "many Canadians" who were worried about the subject. It had in fact been discussed at length during the Commission's hearings, and there was considerable evidence in the record of those hearings to sustain Canadian anxiety. One of the most obvious sources of concern was that private companies (including wholly-owned subsidiaries of foreign companies) were not required to disclose their financial operations in Canada. This meant that much of the evidence for public judgment was simply not available. The spokesmen for major foreign-owned companies tended to assert, without supporting argument, that policy decisions made in their companies' interests were automatically in the national interest as well. Without access to their records such claims could not be assessed. The questions raised by prolonged discussion in the hearings, and later in the Commission's research studies, however, could not be fully treated in the brief *Preliminary Report*.[38]

The chapter foresaw a continuing trend toward foreign control in the economy, and went on to even less firmly based political speculation. If the trend continued,

> ... it seems probable that this will continue to cause concern in this country. And conceivably, if this proves to be the case, it could lead to actions of an extreme kind being taken at some future time. This is the problem – the question is what can or should be done about it?[39]

On this tenuous thread hung the whole case for government initiative in the field of foreign investment. The chapter contained no analysis, and made reference to none. It merely expressed a concern, and a warning that the subject might someday have political consequences.

This was not the stuff to galvanize democratic politicians into a change of policy. Critics considered that the reference to distant political consequences was introduced to bolster a case that could not stand on its own merits in the present; but the device was politically weak, because politicians looking forward to the next election are rarely worried by distant possibilities.

The remedies proposed in the *Preliminary Report* were mild, as suited the case when the diagnosis had pronounced the patient still healthy. The Commission recommended that foreign-owned companies should, where possible, employ Canadians in technical and senior management positions and make their purchases in Canada; that they should make "full disclosure" of their Canadian operations in their published financial statements; that the larger Canadian subsidiaries should sell "an appreciable interest (perhaps twenty percent to twenty-five percent) in their equity stock to Canadian investors and should include on their boards of directors a number of independent Canadians"; and that Canadian control of the chartered banks and life insurance companies should be provided for by law.[40] The purpose was to assure that Canadian interests would be considered and served. No compulsion was recommended to ensure the employment of Canadians and the publication of financial information; but certain revisions in the tax laws to provide "material incentives" were suggested to accomplish the sale of equity stocks in Canada and the appointment of Canadians to boards of directors.

The recommendations were mostly unexceptionable. They did not, for that very reason, strike a note of urgency; and like the previous expression of concern, they made an unconvincing case to an audience which thought little about the more detailed background and was habituated to complacency in the matter. The situation and the essential case remained unexamined in any detail. The common sense and the prophetic character of the concern expressed in the chapter were thus discounted and made to appear insignificant through the chapter's own manner of presentation. The Commission's anxiety was unlikely to be taken seriously by the sceptical Mr. Howe or his critical civil servants. The nationalist aspects of the *Report* were largely neglected by an unobservant press; only the Montreal *Star* and *Le Devoir* commented favourably.[41]

What was worse for the immediate fate of the *Preliminary Report*, however, was that its concern played into the hands of the parliamentary opposition. More and more, since the pipeline debate, Conservatives and CCFers had emphasized the theme of Liberal collusion in the American takeover of the economy. John G. Diefenbaker, the new leader of the Progressive Conservative party, raised the question provocatively when the *Preliminary Report* was tabled in January, 1957. He asked

> ... whether it is the intention of the government to bring in any measures to encourage Canadian companies in business to compete successfully with foreign companies, such as by special tax concessions and the like, as recommended by the Commission?[42]

When the Prime Minister replied that the Cabinet had made no decisions on the *Report*, Mr. Diefenbaker began to twist the knife. "Some of the recommendations do not coincide with government views?" he asked.[43] A month later, he made his major attack in the House, pointing out that a Conservative motion of July, 1956 had anticipated a number of the proposals now made by the Royal Commission. Why did the government disregard the *Report*? Was it because the Commission had "given support to almost every one of the points raised by this party in July of 1956 and back through the years to 1952"?[44] He made full use of the opportunity to hoist the government on its own petard. The Conservative party wanted a national development plan, he said:

> ... not a policy of nationalism but one whereby Canada in the days ahead will remain an independent Canada and will not inexorably drift into economic continentalism; one whereby Canada will maintain her economic independence and her sovereignty; a policy that will provide national development for a greater Canada in which growth and prosperity will not be purchased at the expense of our economic independence and our effective national sovereignty.[45]

When the Conservative party said this in the past, the government had been contemptuous.

> Today as one reads the Gordon report one can only conclude that Mr. Gordon and the outstanding group associated with him found that there was a solid basis for the amendments which we moved and the courses we suggested.[46]

Mr. Diefenbaker taunted Mr. Howe. The Conservative party had called for foreign firms to sell equity interests in Canada, to appoint Canadians to their boards, to develop their Canadian character, to process more raw materials in Canada; and C. D. Howe had called these views "some of the greatest rot he had ever heard."[47] John Diefenbaker challenged the government to say now what its attitude was to the *Report's* recommendations for serving the national interest. But the government was silent.

The Commission was caught in the squeeze. A Cabinet which retained Mr. Howe in it was unlikely to take up the *Report's* nationalist proposals anyway; but action was made more unlikely by John Diefenbaker's probing. A confident Cabinet completely untroubled by its opponents might conceivably reverse itself by stealth; it would not do so under the wagging finger of the leader of the Opposition. The Royal Commission had provided ammunition for Mr. Diefenbaker, and the cautious and complacent Cabinet saw no choice but to close ranks behind Mr. Howe.

Walter Gordon's retrospective judgment was that

> It was particularly unfortunate that the government was unwilling or unable to take immediate action on the Commission's proposals for reversing the trend under which the control of so much of Canadian industry was being acquired by foreigners. A great opportunity to safeguard Canada's independence was allowed to slip by, and a few months later, in June, 1957, the government went down to defeat.[48]

This judgment cannot quite stand. It is doubtful that the Commission's modest proposals would have "reversed the trend" unless they had been only the first steps in a comprehensive new program which was still largely unarticulated; and it is problematic who had let the opportunity slip by. Those in the Cabinet who might have been sympathetic were not provided with the evidence or the arguments to carry the case against Mr. Howe; and he was never likely to let it go by default. At most, the Commission had made a hesitant contribution to a growing public debate. No immediate government action could be expected from that.

In its discussion of the economic condition of the Atlantic provinces, the *Preliminary Report* provided more incendiary (and unexpected) fuel for public controversy. After a few pages urging, in the most general terms, the reduction of the regional income differential through "a positive and comprehensive approach to the problems" of the area and the assistance of Canada in achieving that object, the following paragraph appeared:

If it should turn out that there is not the necessary combination of resources in sufficient quantities to permit a substantial rise in living standards in the Atlantic region, generous assistance should be given to those people who might wish to move to other parts of Canada where there may be greater opportunities. But even if assistance is provided for those people who might be willing to move elsewhere, many people undoubtedly would prefer to remain where they are, despite the handicaps referred to. People who so choose should at the same time be prepared to accept a different kind of life, or certainly life at a different tempo, and lower levels of income, though not necessarily a lower standard of living in its broadest sense, than people in certain other parts of Canada.[49]

These awkward remarks were political dynamite. They were drawn out of the *Preliminary Report* as a sensation, given banner headlines in the Maritimes, and provided the basis for widespread editorial and public castigation of the Royal Commission. The Commission, it was charged, wished to depopulate the region by fiat.[50] Clarie Gillis, the combative socialist MP from Cape Breton, sang the chorus of discontent.

He says to move out. We have been moving out for the last fifty years, and there is nothing in the report that would suggest that there is any future development for the Maritime provinces.[51]

A few rather thoughtlessly phrased remarks had stimulated the Maritimes' reflex of distrust and obscured the Commission's positive recommendations for the region. This spontaneous public reaction was not the sort to be greeted eagerly by politicians preparing to face an early general election. It was another factor affecting the St. Laurent Cabinet's response to the *Preliminary Report* once it had been made public: and its effect was inhibiting. Later, from the political safety of their scholars' chairs, Jacob Viner described these words as "both a courageous and a wise position to take"[52] and Harry G. Johnson applauded their "healthy emphasis" upon migration as opposed to subsidized inefficiency.[53] But the political damage had been done.

In its other sections the *Preliminary Report* was equally spare in its analysis and argument. As a result, it provoked reactions varying "from bitter hostility to indifference" in Liberal Ottawa.[54] The most severe critic in the Cabinet was reported – predictably – to be C. D. Howe, who took strong exception, according to Grant Dexter, to the *Report's* proposals on wheat marketing, freight rates and energy resources. He was supported by James Gardiner, while other ministers described the

Preliminary Report vaguely as "disappointing." The common reaction of senior officials was apparently based as much on form as on substance: the *Report* was called "half-baked" because it did not offer adequate argument for its recommendations.[55]

> Men with long experience of the policy problems of government declared themselves unable to trace the logic and the economic analysis that the Commission had used to reach its conclusions. The Commission's case was not argued in a way that commanded understanding, let alone agreement, among the men best qualified to understand an adequate case.[56]

Some of these critics, presumably, were not hostile to the Commission's role; rather, they were disappointed that the *Preliminary Report* failed to provide them with more convincing arguments to confront the complacency of the Cabinet. Others, out of their liberal internationalism, could not concede the legitimacy of the nationalist perspective which was implied rather than argued in the *Report*.

The outcome was disappointing for the Commission. Ottawa would not rush into any program of action proposed in the *Preliminary Report*. The Prime Minister could only be drawn to make one testy comment after tabling the *Preliminary Report* in the House of Commons.

> The government has nothing to announce on this matter and it may very well be that some of the projects that the government will place before Parliament will – not because of the report but because of the consideration that had been given to the matters previously – coincide with recommendations of the report. . . . [57]

The dismissal was abrupt and excessive, because the Commission had not brought quite the political benefit to the Liberal government which its proponents had foretold, and which Louis St. Laurent himself seemed to expect after his September interview with Walter Gordon.

In the budget speech in March, Walter Harris made his duty reference to the *Preliminary Report*. Its picture of Canada in 1980, he asserted, was "most stimulating." One major purpose of the Royal Commission had been accomplished in the hearings and the preparation of briefs: "large numbers of Canadians have been thinking more imaginatively and more precisely about our longer term prospects and problems." But as for its controversial elements, he implied, who would expect a government to deal with them?

Whether the particular views or particular questions developed in these briefs and reports prove to be completely accurate or valid is in one sense a secondary matter.

On the preliminary report itself I do not propose to comment at length, except to say that many of the views it expresses will command general assent, and that on the other hand it does not avoid a number of controversial questions on which differences of opinion are to be expected.[58]

The government would pick up a few crumbs beneath the Commission's table. It had anticipated the Commission the previous autumn, said Mr. Harris, by increasing aid to universities and technical colleges; it would launch a comprehensive study of Maritime transport as recommended; it would increase at once its subventions for Atlantic region freight rates by $2 million; and it was examining the high cost of electric power in the region. "But on most of the major issues we shall await the final and detailed report before reaching such definite conclusions as may be required."[59] The only immediate benefit afforded to the government by the Commission was its promise of continuing economic growth; for a government content to stand on its record and unconcerned about new policy, that perhaps was benefit enough. It felt no need to take positions on the contentious parts of the *Preliminary Report.*

Perhaps in Walter Gordon the members of the government had misjudged their man. They had taken a risk without fully comprehending it, and it had not entirely paid off. Gordon had, as he told C. D. Howe in 1955, "a rather independent turn of mind" and would recommend what he wished to recommend, whether or not it coincided with the momentary sentiments of the ministry. He hoped, certainly, to be able to serve their interests; but how that could best be done was a matter of political judgment on which he and the Cabinet might or might not agree. Perhaps he, too, had misjudged his audience. His patrons were divided, they did not share some of his concerns, they were politically wary, and they were not to be moved. Chiefly, they were not to be moved. Their self-satisfaction and imperviousness to criticism were greater than Walter Gordon had anticipated.

If that result was likely, then the Commission's appeal, to be effective in the short-run, would have to be made over the heads of the government to the Opposition parties and to the public. In that too the Commission failed – or produced a result it had not intended. Walter Gordon had always thought of the Commission as an aid to the Liberal administration. This was not so much out of any conscious partisan spirit – which he lacked – as out of an assumption that the other federal parties did not count. Gordon had almost reckoned without the possibility of party politics, and had not foreseen the complications of a party battle over his proposals. Since the summer of 1956, however, the political battle had been engaged, and now the Opposition was led by a master of the game, John Diefenbaker. In the intense atmosphere before the 1957 general election, when the first real contest since 1935 was taking shape, the Gordon *Report* served as election fodder. For the Opposition the Commission was politically tainted and did not have to be judged coolly. It was labelled as a Liberal instrument, and at the same time held up as a challenge to an immobile government. Ironically, the public consequence of the *Preliminary Report* was to strengthen the feeling "that there was indeed something wrong but the Liberal leaders could not or would not do anything about it; that the government had gone stale, needed new ideas, but wouldn't accept them."[60]

The major work of the Commission continued. Its compensations were that the studies might assist intelligent long-range economic planning, and that some of the specific recommendations for action might commend themselves later to governments when the controversy of the day had been forgotten.

After the publication of the *Preliminary Report*, Walter Gordon returned to Toronto while Douglas LePan wrote the manuscript of the *Final Report* and supervised the completion of the Commission's research. LePan had written the first eight chapters in his distinctive and elegant prose when he became seriously ill in the late spring of 1957 and had to give up the task.[61] At that point Walter Gordon returned to Ottawa to direct the completion of the *Report*. It was duly presented to the new government of John G. Diefenbaker in November, 1957, but remained unpublished until April, 1958. The new Prime Minister then released it and pointedly ignored it.

Only after the work of the Commission had been brushed aside by Liberal and Conservative governments in turn did it become possible for reasonable consideration to be given to the message of the Commission.

The *Final Report* did not suffer from the incompleteness of the *Preliminary Report*. Contrary to the impression created when the *Preliminary Report* was published, the *Final Report* demonstrated the Commission's caution and reluctance to offer alternative visions of the future. Its clarity of presentation, particularly in the first eight chapters, made evident the very conventional perspective through which the Commission viewed Canada's economic future. The *Report*, said Tom Kent,

. . . discusses Canada over twenty-five years on the assumption that we will get better off but otherwise we and our problems will change very little. The range of variation in policies that is considered is, at most points in the discussion, very narrow indeed. It would hardly be an exaggeration to say that, so far as major political issues are concerned, not since China behind the Great Wall has a society been so static as, in many ways, the Commission seems to think that Canada will be between now and 1980. Whether or not that would be desirable, it is certainly unrealistic.[62]

The *Report* foresaw continuing economic growth and rising standards of living for the country, within a framework of government economic policy that would remain basically unchanged. The *Preliminary Report's* projections of growth were presented in greatly expanded form; the recommendations of that report were repeated and explained more fully and satisfactorily; and the offensive reference to the Atlantic provinces was made more cosmetic. The unifying perspective was economic nationalist, but its exposition was always muted. There was no fundamental speculation about national goals or public values, there were no sensations and no startling insights. As Harry Johnson had noted in the case of the *Preliminary Report*,[63] the *Final Report* too lacked any explicit framework of philosophic or economic theory: it was persistently empirical, sticking closely to things as they were or had been. Various proposals for further study, for the rationalization of aspects of the economy, and for the minimization of some of the discomforts of existing trends, were made. But the Commission neither foresaw nor desired a different kind of community. If it had pressed the nationalist case further, the potential for novelty in its approach might have been clearer. Instead, the *Final Report* was a moderate testament to the economy of growth, reflecting rather than repudiating the complacent materialism of the St. Laurent era but seeking to appropriate its benefits more definitely for Canadians.[64] The currents of that materialism were still running strong, and were represented in all the political parties and most elements of Canadian society; but the Commission missed any premonition of the dissatisfactions and turbulence that were to come in the 1960s as the logic of the existing style of economic growth continued to work itself out. The public rejection of the Liberal party in June, 1957 had already given veiled notice of a more complicated Canadian mood, and in the face of that change the *Final Report* left a peculiarly flat impression.

The work of the Gordon Commission, in the end as in the beginning, reflected Walter L. Gordon's own closeness to the Liberal party, his lean and empirical outlook on politics, his experience as a business consultant and accountant, and his growing nationalist instincts. The disappointment of Ottawa in the *Preliminary Report* was the result, partly, of misplaced expectations. What was expected was not quite clear; but it was some utopian elixir that Walter Gordon had never intended to deliver. When the *Final Report* appeared, it made much less impact because its limited purposes were more evident, and because for the moment politics had passed it by. The *Final Report* would set no prairie fires, but it might still have some role to play in the Liberal party as the foundations of Canadian politics shifted. Under Louis St. Laurent the party had spurned Walter Gordon's advice, and had disintegrated in the general election of 1957 while still carrying the banner of C. D. Howe. Perhaps at some level Walter Gordon had expected this to happen, and had not been averse to assisting the process. Now that combination of circumstances was to give him fresh ambition and fresh opportunity to influence the party in its defeat and disarray.

3   Into Politics

The indifference of the St. Laurent government to the recommendations of the Gordon Commission was one among many signs of the Cabinet's deeply entrenched self-satisfaction. The instinct for renewal which led to the creation of the Royal Commission in 1955 could not survive the smugness and intellectual poverty of an administration twenty-two years in office. Louis St. Laurent himself was tired and unable to invigorate the Liberal party as it approached the general election of June, 1957; in the House of Commons he displayed an increasingly irascible nature. The course of the pipeline debate had been unfortunate for the government, but by the autumn of 1956 no one in authority felt it necessary to acknowledge the Cabinet's errors of tactics and principle or to act decisively to erase the public's memory of May and June. The government would stand on its long record, and expected the electorate to be grateful, as it had been in 1949 and 1953. Symptoms of political discontent in the Maritimes, the prairies, in the provincial governments, and among special interest groups like the pensioners, were treated with indifference, disdain or condescension; the Cabinet had lost its ability to read the political temperature of the nation. It was not helped by the Liberal party organization, which had been allowed to wither on the assumption that an obedient electoral organization could be aroused automatically every four years. The centralism of the Cabinet had deprived the party of any role in policy-making.[1] "No one," wrote W. L. Morton, "had yet recognized that in fact the government was old, weary, and brittle, and subtly arrogant from the conviction that it was indispensable."[2]

But the voters were on the point of making that independent

judgment, and the English-Canadian electorate's newly critical and energetic mood was caught by John Diefenbaker. He applied his limitless energy to the exploitation of every public dissatisfaction in the country. During the general election campaign of May and June, 1957, the Liberal government found itself more and more alienated from the public. In its desperate attempts to adjust to the restless mood, it became awkward and inept, and conducted a disastrous campaign. On June 10, 1957, the invincible government fell, and eleven days later John G. Diefenbaker became Prime Minister of Canada with the support of the largest minority group in the new House of Commons.

C. D. Howe, Walter Harris and Robert Winters were among the victims of the anti-Liberal tide. Louis St. Laurent was returned to Parliament, but he was exhausted and dispirited, and could offer no further leadership to his party. In September, he announced his intention to resign, and sat through the autumn session of the new House in silence.

With Walter Harris defeated, only Paul Martin and Lester Pearson remained in the House of Commons as plausible candidates for the succession.[3] There was no doubt that Martin sought the leadership, and he shortly began a campaign of speechmaking to establish his claim. But Pearson clearly possessed greater support among both party and public. As Secretary of State for External Affairs, he had gained an international reputation as a statesman; his skilful initiative in the Suez crisis the previous autumn had led to the creation of the United Nations Emergency Force and the ceasefire, and subsequently, in the fall of 1957, to his receipt of the Nobel prize for peace. Pearson had remained aloof from domestic politics, and almost alone among members of the St. Laurent Cabinet his reputation was undamaged in the Liberal decline. He was reluctant to seek the party leadership, but was persuaded to do so under pressure, out of obligation to the party that had given him the occasion for international leadership.

The pressure for Lester Pearson to become leader came from the grass roots as well as from the party hierarchy. The candidate himself made it known "that he was not seeking the job and would not make any strenuous efforts to obtain it,"[4] and his supporters saw no need to organize a formal pre-convention campaign in his name. By the standards of the leadership contests of the 1960s, this one was nonexistent. Only one event set the stage for the convention – and its purpose was not exclusively promotional. This was a testimonial dinner for Mr. Pearson in Toronto following his acceptance of the Nobel prize in Oslo in November, 1957. The dinner was sponsored by the Canadian Institute of International Affairs and the United Nations

Association, but its promoters (Walter Gordon among them) could not deny that there was political advantage for Lester Pearson in the occasion. Over one thousand persons attended; and Paul Martin made what use he could of the evening to greet the guests personally and to shake one thousand hands.

With some slight anxiety over Martin's conspicuous campaigning in the month that followed, Walter Gordon telephoned Lester Pearson early in January, 1958 (one week before the leadership convention) to ask what preparations he was making for the convention.

> He replied that he had not thought it would be necessary to do any campaigning and asked what I thought should be done. I told him I expected he would win the leadership anyway, but that if he did so by a narrow margin he would not have the authority he would need to rebuild the Liberal party. I added that, while I was a complete neophyte in such matters, I would go to Ottawa immediately and would see him first thing next morning. It was in this way that I became a sort of self-appointed campaign manager for Mike Pearson at the 1958 convention. It was agreed that I should remain anonymous and should keep in the background. This objective was achieved largely, I suppose, because I had no experience with political conventions and knew absolutely nothing about the techniques that have been developed subsequently.[5]

About the same time a young Liberal from Toronto, Keith Davey, called Gordon to offer his support for Pearson. Gordon encouraged him to take the initiative as he himself had done, and Davey enthusiastically rounded up ninety percent of the votes of Toronto delegates for Pearson.[6] Other supporters from elsewhere in the country made similar contact when they reached Ottawa and visited the Pearson campaign suite in the Chateau Laurier; but the organization was never more than rudimentary. "We never did solve the money problem," Walter Gordon wrote, "but we managed to keep the total cost down to about $3,000 by the simple expedient of being anything but generous with our hospitality."[7] Pearson, Gordon, Robert Fowler, Pearson's executive assistant Mary Macdonald, and the band of last minute volunteers conducted four days of disorganized lobbying, and were rewarded on the first ballot with a vote of 1,074 for Pearson to 305 for Martin.[8]

> It was an impressive victory. I felt that our combined efforts in the four days before the voting had swung about 150 votes to Pearson that might have gone the other way. In that case, his victory would

have been somewhat less impressive. Another, and perhaps even more important factor in his win, was the decision of the Quebec caucus that they should support an English-speaking Protestant against Paul Martin on the grounds that Mr. St. Laurent, a French-Canadian Catholic, had been Prime Minister for nine years. If the tradition in the Liberal party of switching alternatively from an English-speaking to a French-speaking leader was to be continued, it was the turn this time for an English-speaking Protestant to get the nod.[9]

Lester Pearson's accession offered the Liberal party the first prospect of restoring its public standing after the defeat of 1957. But the party had not noticeably absorbed the lessons of that defeat, and would undergo further painful scourging before it could foresee a return to office. The humility that had been lost before 1957 was still not evident at the leadership convention. "Except for the acceptance speech by the new leader and Martin's moving nomination address," reported Peter C. Newman, "the convention was notable mainly for the bad-mannered exaggerations by former Liberal ministers."[10]

On the Monday after the convention, the new leader was to make his debut in the House of Commons to move an Opposition amendment to a supply motion. Pearson's uncertainty in the new role was shown by his difficulty in deciding upon the appropriate wording for the amendment. His advisers were divided on the question. An unambiguous want of confidence motion might have been supported by the minor parties and carried; Pearson rejected this because its adoption would bring an immediate general election. But on the advice of J. W. Pickersgill he also rejected a motion of conditional support for the government, and accepted Pickersgill's draft calling for the resignation of the Diefenbaker Cabinet. Louis St. Laurent and C. D. Howe, too, urged this course on the reluctant leader.

Apart from Pickersgill and Mr. St. Laurent, not even a handful of Liberals knew what was coming, and the new leader made no mention of his plan when he met the Liberal parliamentary caucus on the morning of the great debate. Pickersgill, however, who enjoys his own jokes so hugely that he finds it impossible not to share them with others, had leaked the word that he had devised a motion critizing the government in terms which the CCF could not support.[11]

Walter Gordon learned of the proposed amendment by telephone on the weekend, and felt that it was a mistake.

On reflection, however, I realized that I knew nothing about parliamentary practices and felt diffident about venturing an opinion in a field in which I was so ignorant. Pearson told me later that he also had had his doubts about the proposed resolution, but that he was exhausted after getting practically no sleep for three or four nights and was not in a position to think clearly. He said that, if I had called him, it would have given him just enough encouragement to reconsider the matter. He added that if on any other occasion I ever had even the beginnings of a doubt about a proposed course of action, he hoped I would not hesitate to let him know.[12]

On January 20 Pearson moved the amendment, offering to form a new Liberal administration dedicated to "getting this country back on the Liberal highway of progress" if Mr. Diefenbaker would comply and offer his resignation. The Prime Minister replied scornfully that the Liberal government had ignored the Trade and Commerce Department's warning of economic decline in 1957, and had misled the public during the election campaign by predicting continuing economic growth. With all his theatrical flourish, he threw Lester Pearson's charge of economic mismanagement back at the Liberal party, and added to it the accusation of duplicity. The speech was dramatically studded with quotations from a confidential report on Canada's economic outlook prepared in March, 1957 and signed by Mitchell Sharp, the Deputy Minister of Trade and Commerce.[13] For two hours the Prime Minister mercilessly dissected the record and pretensions of the Liberal party, completely overshadowing the leader of the Opposition as Diefenbaker prepared his case for an early dissolution and general election. Walter Gordon believed that "Mike Pearson never quite recovered from the tongue-lashing Diefenbaker gave him on this occasion. He knew he was no match for Diefenbaker when it came to oratory, and for years afterwards, he gave the impression in the House of Commons that he was secretly a bit afraid of his opponent."[14]

John Diefenbaker's ferocious display was only the prelude to two months of misfortune for the Liberal party. On February 1, the Prime Minister took the next step by advising the Governor General to dissolve the House and issue writs for an election on March 31. The signs in that campaign all pointed to a rout: the Conservative organization flourished while those of the Opposition parties collapsed; funds flowed easily to the party in power while the Opposition was starved; in Quebec Union Nationale organizers threw their considerable weight behind the Conservative candidates. Mr. Diefenbaker continued to press home his advantage ruthlessly from every platform, and consolidated his specific claims with an appeal to national faith:

Catch the vision! Catch the vision of the kind of Canada this can be! ... I've seen this vision; I've seen this future of Canada. I ask you to have faith in this land and faith in our people.[15]

The public was in a mood to 'Follow John' and against this secular John the Baptist the Pearson campaign floundered. With no alternative vision beyond the claim that prosperity could be restored by the Liberals, the party made scant impact. Beyond the Conservative momentum and panache, John Diefenbaker in 1958 personified a view of Canada which transcended material progress; and this the Liberal party of the 1950s could not match. The Conservative appeal was beguiling but also precarious, for the party could only be maintained in office by satisfying the great range of obscure expectations it had aroused.

But at the end of March, 1958, that consolation was too distant to comfort the Liberal party in distress. It had little more than Lester Pearson's buoyancy for reassurance. When the devastating results came in on the evening of March 31, Walter and Liz Gordon were waiting nervously with the Pearsons at the Chateau Laurier. The returns from the Atlantic provinces set the pattern, and Lester Pearson foresaw the rout. He soon went to Liberal headquarters in Ottawa to "see if we can cheer them up," and maintained a stoic façade throughout the long evening,[16] as Conservative victories mounted beyond two hundred and the Liberal phalanx fell to forty-eight.

Walter Gordon had resisted the party leader's hints that he should contest a Toronto seat in that campaign.

I did not believe that in the current climate of opinion I could be elected, assuming I were successful in obtaining a Liberal nomination. I pointed out that, if I ran and lost, my potential usefulness to the Liberal party would be finished. I offered, however, to help Pearson unofficially with some of his policy speeches on subjects that I was conversant with through the work of the Royal Commission on Canada's Economic Prospects. This I did do.[17]

Gordon was edging ever closer to an open political role, but was still hesitant to make the final commitment.

In the meantime, there was another public enquiry to see through. During the 1958 campaign, Premier Frost of Ontario invited Gordon to become chairman of a committee on the organization of government in Ontario. Gordon declined to take such an appointment from the Conservative government in the course of the federal campaign, because of his closeness to Lester Pearson; but Frost offered to delay the undertaking until after the election. On this understanding Gordon accepted the appointment, and the committee was created by provincial Order-in-Council on June 12, 1958. The investigation occupied more than a year, and concerned particularly the status of boards and commissions, which had proliferated in Ontario since 1945. The report, submitted in September, 1959, acknowledged the need for these semi-independent agencies, but emphasized the importance of ministerial responsibility and financial accountability to the legislature for their operations, the grouping of related functions and the right of appeal from the decisions of executive and quasi-judicial agencies. Few of the committee's recommendations for reform were implemented.

*

From the nadir of March 31, 1958, Lester Pearson slowly began the work of making the shattered Liberal parliamentary party into an effective Opposition. Two economists, Maurice Lamontagne of Laval University and Allan MacEachen of St. Francis Xavier University in Nova Scotia, joined Mr. Pearson's staff in 1958 as research assistants. The parliamentary battle was conducted largely by the four remaining front-bench veterans of the St. Laurent Cabinet, Pearson, Martin, Pickersgill, and Lionel Chevrier. For more than a year after the election, Pearson concentrated patiently on the uneven parliamentary contest, ignoring temporarily the more general problems of policy and organization which would have to be dealt with before another general election. The party organization remained moribund and its finances in disorder.

In the late summer of 1959, Pearson turned to these matters, and invited Walter Gordon to review the state of the party organization for him. Gordon undertook the job with the directness and clinical despatch typical of his work as a business consultant and royal commissioner-at-large, interviewing the leading members of the party hierarchy and other prominent Liberals. His report took the form of a long letter and separate memorandum to Lester Pearson dated November 5, 1959, in which Gordon assessed "the general opinion about Pearson's leadership" as well as reviewing the condition of the party's organization and finances.

The letter began candidly:

> ... As far as I could ascertain from the conversations I have had, everyone likes you, holds you in the highest respect and is fundamentally loyal to you. You have immense prestige and your power within the party is more or less unlimited. You can make any decision you want to make without any fear of opposition. In fact, the more decisions you make the stronger you are likely to be.

However, even some of your most ardent supporters have been influenced by the subtle propaganda that you have not the necessary toughness to be a successful Prime Minister or the necessary desire and decisiveness to do all the unpleasant things necessary to win the election. In addition, a few people have the impression that you may allow yourself to be lured away to some international job prior to the election which, of course, would leave everyone here in quite a spot.

I have no doubts about your ability to do the job if you and Maryon decide that this is what you want to do or rather that this is what you ought to do. But both of you will have to make up your minds about this one way or the other very soon indeed. If the answer is yes, then there are some things that you will have to face up to right away. To begin with, Maryon will have to make up her mind to do a great many things that she dislikes.[18]

This was the tough, confidential advice of a close friend. Gordon sensed the need for this kind of frankness and recognized that no one else was in a position to offer it to Mike Pearson. Gordon's independence and relative aloofness from political life meant that at this stage he had no obvious personal interest to promote. He could afford to be honest with his friend, and he knew Pearson well enough to expect that the comments would be respected.

Walter Gordon himself was not yet convinced of Pearson's commitment to the leadership. He knew that Pearson found the experience of domestic politics "grubby," and that his heart remained in foreign affairs. Gordon expected that Pearson would accept the Secretary-Generalship of the United Nations if it were offered to him, and believed also that he was interested in the post of NATO Secretary-General. Pearson's uncertainty seemed to convey itself to his supporters and the public, and Gordon felt that a resolution of his doubts, one way or the other, would be a vital step in restoring the sense of purpose and will of the Liberal party.

The "subtle propaganda that you have not the necessary toughness . . . or the necessary desire and decisiveness" hinted at the mediocre reputation for administration which had followed Pearson from his years in the Department of External Affairs.[19] After nearly two years in the leadership, evidence was accumulating in the Liberal party of the same weaknesses. Pearson had failed to appoint a new national organizer of the party, to dispense with party officers who were no longer assets after the defeats of 1957 and 1958, or to arrange for a sufficient and stable income for the party. Gordon went on to discuss these points in detail in the letter and memorandum. He recommended a new, "relatively young" executive assistant or private secretary for the party leader (implying a diminution of Mary Macdonald's influence in Pearson's office), the immediate appointment of a national organizer (James Scott was recommended), the possible appointment of an organization committee whose chairman might act as Pearson's deputy in all matters of organization, the dismissal of several members of the party headquarters staff, the retirement of Duncan MacTavish as president and national treasurer (MacTavish had suffered a heart attack and wished to retire), the preparation of a realistic party budget, and a fund-raising campaign to make the party solvent for the two-and-one-half years before the next general election.[20] Gordon wrote that "I have not anyone in mind yet – except myself – " as chairman of the proposed committee on organization, "but will hope to come up with a more satisfactory suggestion before I see you."[21] His tentative budget called for $75,000 to eliminate the deficit in party accounts, and an operating budget of $600,000 for thirty months from January, 1960 until June, 1962.

Finally, Gordon summarized his judgments of the political situation.

> My own view about the central issue is perhaps biased and over-simplified. By your own actions, you are not likely to beat Diefenbaker. He must be given every encouragement to defeat himself. At the same time people must be convinced that you can surround yourself with the necessary people to help you do it. And you must build an organization to take advantage of Diefenbaker's mistakes. My instinct would be to sharpen up and emphasize the contrast between you and him. Somewhere along the line you may have to take a strong stand on some domestic issue just to show that you can do so but I see no reason why you should hurry about this and certainly not until your public relations people have prepared the ground a bit.[23]

The letter was wryly signed: "With commiserations."

Gordon subsequently discussed his report with Pearson, and the leader agreed "with considerable reluctance" to do what Gordon had recommended.[24] Walter Gordon himself promised to assist in raising $200,000 for the party, and took a leading part in a successful campaign in December, 1959 and January, 1960. General A. Bruce Matthews of Toronto became president and treasurer of the National Liberal Federation at the same time.

Gordon's meetings with Pearson became more frequent, and his political advice more pointed. In February, 1960 Gordon wrote again to Pearson to comment on the leader's personal situation, "just in case" Pearson lacked the time for his own analysis. Gordon was still concerned that Pearson was not at ease in his role.

In the first place, it seems to me your present life must be a thoroughly frustrating one and to some extent this is beginning to be apparent to the public or some sections of the public which is not good.

I was pleased to see you take after Diefenbaker and, in fact, urged that you should do so. You have made it clear that you are quite capable of getting him angry and taking him on and, secondly, you have succeeded, I think, in bringing home to the public that the man is essentially dishonest intellectually. It is important, however, that this tactic should not be overplayed and, in particular, as you yourself mentioned, that you should not personally be made to seem petty or picayune in your criticism and interventions in the House. This is easier said than done . . . particularly so if you allow yourself to become overtired. If I was your oldest living relative therefore or your medical adviser . . . I would urge you not to spend as much time in the House as you have felt it necessary to do so far, not to accept any engagements to speak at noon when the House is in session and not to make any engagements for the weekends. Quite apart from the need, as I see it, for you to ease up on your present killing pace, I think you should have at least two days a week for thinking and meditation, both about long-term strategy and immediate Machiavellian tactics for the next few days. . . . I do suggest it is important for everyone, regardless of age or sex, to learn how to say no – occasionally.[25]

Gordon advised one or two more speeches "of the excellence and depth" of Pearson's recent effort in the throne debate, and suggested that Mitchell Sharp or John Deutsch might prepare drafts for a speech in the budget debate if they were asked to do so.

Lester Pearson was now urging Walter Gordon more firmly than ever to become openly associated with him in the Liberal party (and perhaps was growing impatient at his friend's hesitations); and Gordon's unofficial activities were identifying him more and more widely with Liberal fortunes. Gordon discussed his position with Mike Pearson a number of times over the winter. He had two related concerns, one professional, one a matter of policy. Gordon was genuinely attached to the varied life afforded him in the work of the firm – of which he had been the only senior partner since Grant Glassco's departure in 1957 – and was reluctant to give this up for a trial in politics. His scrupulous conception of business and political ethics required that if he entered active politics to seek a ministerial post, he would have to be ready to sever all his professional connections, in order to be as independent as possible.

But burning one's bridges was a serious matter, and did not seem justified without a certain kind of guarantee. The risk, if possible, should be measured and reasonable.

> ... I had no desire to become involved in partisan politics – much as I liked and respected Pearson and wished to help him – if my views on public policy, developed in the course of the work of the Royal Commission on Canada's Economic Prospects, were to prove embarrassing or unacceptable to him or to the Liberal party.[26]

Gordon therefore decided to make a number of speeches on policy in the spring of 1960 both to establish his own position and to seek a response from Lester Pearson: "and in order to avoid the possibility of future misunderstandings, I wrote a number of letters to Pearson about them."[27]

His first major speech was made to the Ontario Federation of Labour on February 13, 1960. Three parts of it were notable. The first contained a harsh and direct condemnation of the Diefenbaker government for countenancing the Bank of Canada's tight money policy beyond the period in 1958 and 1959 when, Gordon judged, high interest rates had been desirable. "It would be quite unfair," he said, "to blame the central bank authorities for this situation."

> Much of our present difficulty has resulted from a failure to coordinate and integrate monetary policy with policies in the fiscal, tax and debt management fields. This is not the fault of the Bank of Canada. The Prime Minister, on the other hand, who or whose ministerial colleagues might be expected to develop coordinated policies in these various fields, has refused to accept any responsibility for the present tight money policy. This to me seems quite nonsensical. If the Bank of Canada – or any other government agency for that matter – should at any time persist in a policy that the government of the day felt was contrary to the best interests of the country, then obviously the government and Parliament could not allow this to continue.[28]

This was Walter Gordon's first public statement on the developing controversy over the relationship of the Bank of Canada and its governor, James Coyne, to the government. While criticizing the policy of the Bank, Gordon was careful to specify that the central question was one of responsibility: and that, he insisted, rested with the Cabinet, which had recently been "unnecessarily crude and clumsy in [its] policies or lack of policies."

The second significant section of the speech, like the first, concerned Gordon's belief "that at the national level we are not managing our affairs these days either very skilfully or with much imagination." He suggested that the Canadian dollar was overvalued on the international market, and that this overvaluation – the result of the high rate of inflow of foreign capital rather than of a favourable balance of trade – was costing Canada export markets and an international indebtedness that would one day be a source of real economic difficulty. He therefore linked his call for lower interest rates with a recommendation "to reduce the present artificially high value of the Canadian dollar," that is, to devalue.

> I do not say this lightly. A policy to reduce the present artificially high price of the Canadian dollar to the extent that it resulted in some reduction of importations of consumer goods would tend to increase the cost of living at least to some extent. Furthermore, any restrictions upon the inflow of foreign capital would tend to moderate the rate at which the Canadian economy is developing – or the rate at which the provinces and municipalities can go ahead with many projects and services that we now think are both necessary and desirable. But surely to do nothing means only that we are putting off the evil day of reckoning. Surely we would be better off in the long run if by such moves we strengthened both our great export industries and also our secondary manufacturers – and at the same time brought our foreign trade into some sort of balance.[29]

Finally, Gordon saw Canada's economic destiny dependent upon two basic attitudes: "whether we are prepared to concede enough power to the federal government to influence the rate of economic activity throughout the country," and "the importance we place upon retaining our economic and political independence." He was an advocate of firm central intervention in the economic process not only on the Keynesian grounds of economic stability and full employment, but also on a ground which Keynes had been able to take more for granted: the integrity of national sovereignty in economic policy.

62

The pressures for a greater degree of integration with the United States are tempting, insidious, considerable and continuous. . . . The benefits obtained by Canadian subsidiaries of United States parent companies through their access to research facilities, technological and management know-how and, above all . . . assured markets in the United States simply cannot be exaggerated. But, understandably, we have had to pay a price for these advantages. This is reflected in the abrogation of some measure of control over day-to-day decisions in the economic field.

To even hint at this these days is to leave one open to the charge of narrow nationalism. Nevertheless, in no other industrialized nation in the world is so much of the basic industry of the country controlled by non-residents. . . .

The fact is, whether or not we are willing to admit it, Canada by degrees is losing a considerable measure both of her economic and her political independence. . . .

Canadians should face up to this question objectively and without emotion. We should make up our minds in which direction we would like to see this country go. . . . [30]

The appeal for an objective and unemotional choice was ironic: for despite leaving the question open as he ended his speech, there was no doubt that Walter Gordon himself chose the path of independence, and did so with intense, if well-controlled, emotional commitment. Here was a strong political attack upon the confusions of the Diefenbaker administration, and the outline of a national policy intended to end those confusions.

The Toronto *Star*, which was beginning to give prominent notice to Walter Gordon in its news pages,[31] reported the speech at length,[32] and a week later the *Financial Post* devoted its major editorial to the speech and its implications under the title "Walter Gordon, MP, The Next Step?"

Walter Gordon, of Royal Commission fame, is a responsible and knowledgeable private citizen. Many ordinary Canadians have learned to listen to and agree with him. But in view of what he had to say a few days ago to the Ontario Federation of Labour, it seems a pity that he hasn't a wider and more influential audience such as, for example, the House of Commons.

Indeed, there are political overtones in his speech that suggest that the House of Commons is where Mr. Gordon is heading. He leaves the impression that he is not unwilling to be the Minister of Finance when the Liberals next come to power. This is not to be deplored; we need men of Gordon's stamp in political life whatever the party. . . . [33]

Following the speech, on March 9, 1960 Gordon wrote to Lester Pearson "to analyse my own thoughts and situation because I think you are entitled to know where I stand and what my plans are."

To begin with, as I have said before, I would like to do anything I can to help you become Prime Minister in two or two and a half years' time if there is any practical chance of this becoming possible. To be honest, I am not sure there will be a chance of achieving this so soon. As I suggested to you last November, this will depend primarily on Diefenbaker and on the times. To a lesser extent, it will depend on you, the people you get around you, the enthusiasm that you and they inspire, the kind of program or platform the Liberals agree upon, the way it is presented and upon the kind of organization that can be developed and the kind of candidates that can be secured.

From a personal standpoint, I shall hope that the program will tend to be leftish, imaginative, reasonably clear cut and that it will discard as many as possible of the old theories and beliefs that are no longer relevant. If it does not do these things, I doubt if the Liberal party will regain power for some years to come despite the mistakes that Diefenbaker may make between now and the next election.

I can say without any reservation that I would like to serve under you as Minister of Finance. The job would intrigue me both because I would enjoy participating as a senior Minister in Canada's international negotiations and because I would like to help you tidy up our present domestic policies or lack of them. . . . However, all this is somewhat academic as there are two questions about which I still am very doubtful. The first one has to do with issues and the second with the not inconsiderable task of getting both me and the Liberal party elected.

I am still not sure that my views on freer trade, on integration with the United States, on the need for a greater degree of direction and control of the economy by Ottawa or on defence policy would be acceptable to most Liberals. I tried to spell out how I feel about the first subject in my speech to the Ontario Federation of Labour on February 13 – which was not very different from the views expressed in the report of the Royal Commission. I am against "high" tariffs but I think we shall need "more" not "less" secondary industry throughout all of Canada if we are going to lick chronic unemployment. To me, the objectives of reducing many of the "higher" tariff rates and, at the same time, of having more secondary industry are not necessarily incompatible. In fact, I believe just the opposite.

However, as I think you know, I would be very hesitant about a policy of all-out free trade – even on some regional basis like the North Atlantic Area – unless I was more certain than I now am of where it would lead and the extent of the disruptions that would be involved. . . . In certain circumstances, I can visualize a situation on the international scene that might justify, perhaps might force, a complete merging of the Canadian and United States economies but in this case I would hope there would be a political merger also. Such a merger of the two economies would, I believe, result in very great upheavals but if the international situation was sufficiently serious, we would just have to face up to this.

I am unhappy about the gradual economic and financial take-over by the United States, or rather by the owners of United States capital, that is taking place and if I were in public life I expect I would wish to urge some modest steps to counteract what is presently going on in this direction. As I have said at other times, I would prefer us to go in one direction or the other knowing what is happening and what we are trying to do about it. (Personally, I would have thought this could be made into a major political issue. But quite apart from that aspect of the matter, at the appropriate time I would like you and the Liberal party to be positive about it one way or the other.)

I doubt if the question of a strong central government is one on which there would be any serious differences of opinion. I might want to go farther and faster in this direction than some people but I expect this would be more a question of degree than one of principle.

On the question of defence policy, I am becoming more of the opinion that Canada should begin to take an independent line and should stop pouring money down the drain. I do not profess to know too much about this subject or all its implications, but I assume that this line of thinking might lead to the cancellation of the NORAD deal and thus to a full dress argument, or showdown, with the Americans. (This, again, could become a highly charged political issue, apart from the more serious aspects of the question. Again, at the appropriate time, I would like the Liberals to be positive about this in one way or the other.)

I dare say you will think the doubts that I have raised concerning the above issues are not so very different from the doubts that everyone has felt who has considered these matters seriously. This may be true about defence policy and the need for a strong central government. I think I am more concerned, however, about the trade question and integration with the United States where I lack the instinctive convictions that most people of the Liberal persuasion seem to have. More faith and less skepticism might be better for my soul in this and other matters but I am getting too old to change easily my habits of thought and meditation. . . .

So much for the issues that perturb me and which perhaps we shall be able to talk out satisfactorily. I now come to more immediate practical matters which I am afraid may be more difficult to rationalize.

I am a few years younger than you are – in a chronological sense, that is – and, naturally, if I went into things full out, I would worry to some extent about your probable successor in the event you decided to retire earlier than is customary for people who hold such exalted positions as you do now and the even more exalted one I hope you will hold later. Perhaps you will be quite able and willing to stay on – your energy and vigour continue to amaze me – but if, for one reason or another, you did drop out, it might be difficult for me to do likewise, at least immediately, without bad feeling. However, I do not mean to make too much of this point. It seems somewhat academic at this moment and, in any event, is far less important to me than what follows.

As I have mentioned to you before, I would plan to retire from my two firms if I decided to campaign in any election or to announce that I intended doing so. I would have no reservations about doing this if there was every prospect of becoming a senior Minister in a government you headed. But I would feel a fool if I were to do so as a gesture. I have had quite a hand in building our two firms into what they are today and if I should leave them, which I would do with considerable heart pangs, I would not want to go off like a damp firecracker. . . .

To get down to cases, as I am sure you will understand, I am not very partisan by nature – except possibly where Diefenbaker is concerned. I am told that I do not suffer fools gladly which, of course, I do not agree with and, in fact, consider to be libellous! But I must admit I have not the temperament or the personality or the interest, for that matter, for door-to-door electioneering. I am quite certain that I would not enjoy the proceedings in the House of

Commons especially in Opposition. In fact, it would drive me to distraction. The truth is that I am not very interested in the detail and personalities of politics. I think I would enjoy being a Minister, in developing policy and in implementing it. I could easily become interested in political strategy but I doubt if I could get worked up for long about the day-to-day tactics of political activity.

Furthermore, and I expect this is the crux of the matter, unless there should be a major swing to the Liberals during the next two years – which, of course, is not impossible although at this stage perhaps it may not appear too likely – I do not see how I could possibly be elected in Toronto even with months and months of hard electioneering. (And I would not be prepared to electioneer on such a scale just on the chance that I and also the Liberal party would be successful.) I have come to this conclusion – as I did in 1958 – after reviewing the voting records in the last three elections although, admittedly, without the benefit of any sampling of opinion or professional advice upon the matter.

All this leads me to the conclusion that it would be foolish for me to say now that I will run in the next election. As I have said, I do not see how I could be elected. Even if I were elected, it seems somewhat unlikely at this juncture that the Liberal party will be returned to power so soon. And even if I were elected and the Liberal party was returned, I might find myself in disagreement with you or with the party on one or more of the policy issues I have mentioned.

You may think I am being too cold and selfish in this analysis and perhaps I am. The truth is that while I would really like to help you to the very best of my ability I have a horror of doing something that would make me out a fool. . . .

I am prepared, of course, to give you first claim upon as much of my time as you would like until after the next election. If you wish, you may announce publicly that I will act as chairman of a committee to advise you personally on organization or any other matters. (I would prefer you to emphasize the personal angle of this relationship rather than to imply a formal obligation on my part to the party.) When the election comes, I will help in any way I can.

. . . I would like to talk to you about the various points that I have raised, particularly if you disagree with my conclusions. Because, if you can convince me I am wrong or can suggest ways of overcoming the difficulties mentioned, I shall be quite delighted.[34]

This honest and self-critical letter emphasized the unusually personal nature of Walter Gordon's political involvement: he was being drawn in out of his respect for and friendship with Mike Pearson. It drew renewed attention to the special importance of policy for Walter Gordon, and made evident (although in general terms) how far he wished the Liberal party to move from its conventional position of unquestioning alliance with the business community and the United States. If he entered active politics, he would do so with specific objectives, and the expectation of achieving them.

> I realized that I would have to be in a position of some authority if I were to influence public policy to the extent I felt to be important. The obvious post from which to accomplish this objective would be that of Minister of Finance. ... I would be going into politics primarily because of my interest in promoting policies which I believed would benefit the average Canadian, and help Canada to retain her independence and, hence, her influence in the world. And while my principal concern was not with titles or position, I wanted to be reasonably sure of being able to accomplish these objectives.[35]

There was no conclusive response to this letter. But Gordon continued, with Lester Pearson's support, to survey and pull together the pieces of the Liberal party organization according to the scheme of reorganization agreed upon the previous autumn. James Scott was appointed national organizer; Bruce Matthews, John Aird and Louis Gelinas persisted in their fund-raising; some pruning occurred in the staff of the national office; and, independent of Ottawa influence, there were signs of life at the local level of the party, particularly in Toronto and southern Ontario.[36] But there were still fatal deficiencies in the organization. Bruce Matthews was carrying too heavy a load in his joint role as president and treasurer of the party; James Scott became seriously ill in the spring of 1960 and took leave for several weeks; Gordon's proposed advisory committee on organization, with a senior chairman, was not created; the Quebec wing of the party was split in factional conflict; the advertising and public relations services of the party remained undeveloped; and there were not yet any prominent "new faces firmly identified with the party."[37] Gordon summarized the situation in a letter to the leader on July 8, 1960. In it he recommended that General Matthews should be enabled to concentrate upon his task as treasurer; that steps should be taken to defuse the Quebec conflict in the party; that the special advisory committee on organization should perhaps be created; and that the persons to be responsible for party policy should be designated quickly.[38] The brisk and comprehensive nature of this advice owed something to Gordon's increasingly optimistic judgment of the general political situation:

> ... the party's fortunes have improved enormously. I think the tremendous job that you have been doing in the House is beginning to get through to the public. Certainly the public seems to be, or is at least beginning to be, disillusioned with Diefenbaker and his lack of policy and fumbling over key issues. The recent Gallup poll would seem to substantiate this view. Apart from this, the Quebec and New Brunswick elections have given everyone a great lift. We should take advantage of this improved atmosphere and get on with the job of organizing for the next election. There is a tremendous amount to be done if we are to win it – and at long last, it looks as if you could have a real chance.[39]

But Gordon's own formal role in the party remained undecided. On July 12, 1960 he wrote again to Pearson enclosing copies of his three speeches of February, May and June, and the draft of a fourth to be delivered in August. Gordon was now pressing for some explicit sign of agreement with his views from the party leader:

> This material, plus the contents of the reports of the Royal Commission, covers practically everything on which I have any views that matter ... in the context of our discussions. In the last analysis, all this pretty well boils down to the points of policy raised in my letter to you of last March.
>
> I need not emphasize the importance of this whole subject to both of us. It is imperative that there should be no misunderstandings, and as I said on the telephone yesterday, I can easily go to Ottawa on Friday afternoon if you think a conversation would be useful. In any event, please call me when you have had a chance to look over this material.[40]

Pearson did so two days later, and Gordon recorded the result of that conversation in handwriting at the top of his copy of the letter to Pearson.

> Mike called to say he had read the attached draft and the copies of the other three speeches that I sent him. He said he agreed *completely* with my ideas. He repeated this two or three times saying

that this is exactly how he feels on these various issues with particular emphasis on the draft speech for August 29. In the circumstances, he suggested there is no point in me going down to see him tomorrow evening.   WLG 8 PM 14/7/60   41

The extended effort of reassurance seemed to have succeeded.

Nothing could have been more explicit than Pearson's remarks to me on the telephone on July 14 ... and any doubts I may have had about possible differences of opinion about policies were resolved. Because of this, shortly afterwards I agreed to his request that I become chairman of the Policy Committee at the rally of the Liberal party to be held the following January. I knew quite well that, if I did so, I would be identified in the public's mind as an acknowledged member of the Liberal party, and a prominent one, at that. There could be no turning back in this regard, even though this would not necessarily commit me officially to run in the next election whenever it was called.[42]

4   Rebuilding the Party

When Walter Gordon spoke in Vancouver on August 29, 1960 he did so with new assurance as Lester Pearson's chief adviser on policy and potential chief-of-staff. No longer was he testing his ideas on the party leader; the two men understood themselves to be in full agreement on the aims of policy. Gordon's missionary activity was now directed at the wider audience of the Liberal party and the Canadian electorate. His immediate purpose was to elaborate the reform program he had outlined in his recent speeches and letters to the party leader, and to have that program, or a substantial part of it, adopted as the policy of the Liberal party. From his position of trust close to Pearson, Walter Gordon could reasonably expect to achieve this goal. As the party very gradually recovered its confidence and equilibrium it clung loyally to the new leader; and Mr. Pearson's intellectual openness created an atmosphere in the party that encouraged departures in policy.

The Vancouver speech to which Lester Pearson had given his particular support was devoted to Gordon's "own personal views about what the broad objectives of Canadian policy should be," seen within the context of the economic trends forecast by the Gordon Commission.[1] In the core of the speech Gordon rejected the "continental approach" to the solution of Canada's economic problems.

> The fact is that in recent years, whether we like to admit it or not, Canada has been losing steadily a considerable measure of her independence, both economically and politically. If we are sensible, we should decide either to accelerate the pace of integration with

the United States, politically as well as economically, or alternatively, to take steps without delay to reverse the present trend. Either course, in my opinion, would entail difficulties and some unpleasantness.

Free trade with the United States, he warned, "would bring about a great disruption of Canadian industry and serious unemployment, certainly during an extended period of readjustment and probably for longer." Without an accompanying measure of political union, he feared, Canada would find her prosperity subject to the whims of another sovereign power. Gordon spurned that course, and hoped that "Canadians will choose to regain a greater measure of economic independence than we now have."

> To do nothing, to refuse to recognize the situation that confronts us or to admit its implications, will lead inevitably to our becoming a more or less helpless satellite of the United States. (The great majority of Canadians might never fully realize just when or how this happened.)[2]

But Gordon also warned that his choice would not be an easy one:

> ... we could not hope to reverse the present trend and to regain some of our lost independence without paying some sort of price in terms of a less rapid rise in our standard of living, though not, I think, of greater unemployment. (This is a price, incidentally, that Canadians have always been prepared to pay, ever since Canada became a nation, when the situation was explained to them.) Furthermore, we could not hope to accomplish our objective quickly. To be successful, we would have to work at it for many years and with great determination.[3]

Gordon did not specify the policies necessary to bring about the change, but the statement of faith was unmistakable.

The American military alliance was the subject of a growing undercurrent of criticism in Canada in 1960, given impetus by the publication of James M. Minifie's *Peacemaker or Powdermonkey*, in which Minifie called for Canadian withdrawal from the alliance through a declaration of neutrality, a "vivid and memorable act as readily recognizable as the Declaration of Independence."[4] Walter Gordon, too, was beginning to reconsider this aspect of Canada's relationship with the United States, as he demonstrated in the Vancouver speech. But he could not go as far as Minifie because "the Americans are our friends – our very best friends – even if at times we may find their attentions a little overpowering. And the Russian Communists are not our friends, let us remember." Canada should therefore remain a member of the NATO alliance. The matters of the NORAD agreement and the acquisition of nuclear weapons were different, however, because they placed Canada in a position of subservience to American command.

> Despite all the words – many of them contradictory – that have been uttered about the NORAD arrangement that was entered into so hurriedly and obviously without much serious consideration in the summer of 1957, it seems to boil down to the fact that Canada has contributed a few squadrons to the American Air Force. Much publicity has been given to the fact that a Canadian airman is deputy commander of the NORAD Force, and that both the president of the United States and some unspecified official of the Canadian government (possibly the Prime Minister) must give joint approval before any shots are fired in anger. I find these explanations unconvincing. To me, it seems farcical to suggest that, in a grave emergency, retaliatory measures would be delayed while the officials in question were located, the situations explained to them, and their approval given to repel attack.[5]

Gordon hinted at, but did not quite state, his desire for a Canadian withdrawal from the joint air defence command. On nuclear weapons, he was more explicit:

> Similarly, if Canadian defence forces are to be equipped with nuclear arms, including nuclear warheads for the Bomarc missile, I think a decision to use such arms and warheads should be made by the Canadian authorities and by them alone. I do not believe this should be contingent upon the approval of the American authorities, or jointly by the Americans and the Canadian Prime Minister. If these are the conditions, I would prefer to see us get along, at least for the time being, without weapons that are not within our control.[6]

The American insistence upon joint (and ultimately, American) control of nuclear weapons supplied from the U.S. arsenal was clear: it followed that Gordon opposed Canadian acquisition of nuclear arms.

The two major objectives of Canadian policy, Gordon told his student audience, should be full employment and the restoration of Canadian independence. It was evident that his justification for these goals went beyond the merely economic or utilitarian. His interest in economic efficiency came second to a concern for national dignity and a Galbraithean emphasis on amenities rather than the gross national product.

> I would hope that twenty years from now there may be less emphasis than there is today on material values. I am in favour of competition and I believe in the profit motive – but it should not be the only motive if our objective is a well-balanced, rounded, happy, and at the same time interesting and stimulating life for a people who can be proud of their accomplishments, their independence, and of their influence in the world for good. These are some of the things that seem to me important when we talk about Canadian development.[7]

The whole statement was couched in mild and cautious language, and the implications of its sentiments remained undeveloped in detail. But it established the ground for a nationalist program in economic and defence policy; and, most significantly, it bore the private approval of the leader of the Liberal party. August, 1960, however, was much too early in the remaking of the party to estimate the consequences of that approval.

The speech was prominently reported in Canada, and provoked editorial comment in half a dozen newspapers.[8] The Toronto *Star* was fully sympathetic. In the first of three editorials on the speech, it concluded: "Let Mr. Gordon and others who have defined the theme of a great national debate now propound the policies that can give substance to Canadian independence."[9] Two further editorial articles recommended policies intended for this purpose: a national development fund to "stimulate Canadian financing of economic growth"; tax incentives to promote Canadian representation on the boards of directors and Canadian participation in the ownership of foreign firms in Canada; more complete disclosure of the financial operations of Canadian subsidiary companies; and devaluation of the Canadian dollar. (These recommendations, which the *Star* "put forward tentatively, not as pat answers to a ramified and delicate problem," owed their inspiration almost entirely to earlier suggestions made by Mr. Gordon. The great national debate was not noticeably being fed from fresh sources.)

The Victoria *Times* shared the *Star's* sympathy and its desire for Mr. Gordon to indicate the means by which he would achieve Canada's independence.[10] The Toronto *Telegram* was approving but complacent. It recalled that "fear of a U.S. takeover was a factor in the Diefenbaker victories of 1957 and 1958," and reassured its readers that, just as the Diefenbaker government had legislated to maintain Canadian ownership of insurance companies, so "it is a reasonable expectation that it will take action to provide for Canadian participation and control in other forms of investment."[11] Other commentators were more sceptical. The Ottawa *Citizen*, too, was reminded of "some of the visions seen by Prime Minister Diefenbaker during the last two general elections," but added wryly that "with his electoral successes, however, the supposed American economic domination of Canada has seemed to be not all that grave a problem to the Prime Minister." There might be a need for specific legislation on limited matters, but there was no general problem of domination; that was "a bogey better suited to an election campaign."[12] The Hamilton *Spectator* complained that for years Mr. Gordon "has been intimating that something must be done, but has never been precise concerning what the something should be."[13] The Vancouver *Province* offered a bromide:

> By and large, Canada is doing the best she can to adapt herself to circumstances, the most important of which being that we live next door to the most powerful and wealthy nation in the world and that it is inevitable we come under its influence and protection.
>
> These are the circumstances to which we have adapted ourselves and we should at times kneel in thanksgiving that they are such pleasant circumstances, that the influence and protection under which we live is friendly and generous.
>
> Things could be a lot worse. As some of the Hungarians who have come among us could explain.[14]

This mixed response confirmed that Gordon had touched a live nerve. The subject was politically sensitive and could be exploited; it had not been exclusively appropriated by John Diefenbaker and the Conservative party. There were increasing signs, indeed, that the government was stumbling in confusion over the whole nationalist question.

The Liberal party now gave two substantial public demonstrations of its resilience and reviving spirits. In mid-September, the National Liberal Federation sponsored a Study Conference on National Problems at Queen's University in Kingston. The conference, which was originally planned for 1959 but postponed because of the prevailing anti-Liberal atmosphere, had been promoted by Lester Pearson as a means of drawing independent intellectual support and inspiration to the party. By 1960 the political atmosphere was right. The conference was organized by the former Deputy Minister of Trade and Commerce, Mitchell Sharp, who was then a vice-president of Brazilian Traction, Light and Power. It attracted two hundred politicians, academics, journalists, labour union officers, and businessmen, many of them not formally associated with the Liberal party. Mr. Sharp told the meeting that its purpose was neither to criticize the Conservative government nor to produce a program for the Liberal party, but rather

> ... to discover what a group of intelligent, liberally-minded Canadians from all walks of life and all parts of the country think ought to be done about some of the more serious national problems.[15]

The conference recalled Vincent Massey's 1933 Liberal study conference at Port Hope, held during the party's previous sojourn in the wilderness. It made the best of the party's involuntary absence from power to demonstrate its openness and alertness to new ideas. (Not all Mr. Pearson's front-bench associates welcomed such a dangerous flirtation.)

The papers read at Kingston indicated that the party's advisers and intellectual well-wishers hoped for a very moderate shift to the left for the Liberal party into support for a comprehensive system of welfare capitalism. Maurice Lamontagne and Tom Kent called for the completion and refinement of the postwar edifice of social security and anticyclical measures, including medical insurance, a prices review board, a council of economic advisers, tax incentives and public investment for depressed areas, retraining for the unemployed, massive investment in education, and the possible use of an advertising tax as a device of fiscal policy.[16] The dominating influence in the approach of these two papers was that of J. K. Galbraith's *The Affluent Society*.[17] The approach was emphatically liberal; but Lamontagne and Kent were criticized by prominent businessmen in the party for embracing socialism.[18] The seeds of mutual suspicion planted then bore fruit after the party came to power.

Michael Barkway of the Toronto *Star* led the conference into discussion of the national question with a severe criticism of the Liberal party's traditional *laissez-faire* attitude to foreign investment.[19] Shortly after Kingston, Barkway's arguments were reinforced by Lester Pearson himself, who devoted a major address to this issue. His remarks were based upon a letter and memorandum from Walter Gordon, in which Gordon examined in detail the tax advantages in

Canada for American corporate investors and their freedom from the normal restraints of Canadian monetary policy, and recommended a series of remedies.[20] Gordon carefully emphasized "the various qualifying phrases that should not be excluded if you decide to refer to any specific items in your speech,"[21] noting that "you should avoid, if possible, being accused of discrimination. This was the main criticism of the Commission's proposals."[22] The memorandum concluded:

> I would hope that you would end up on a mild note – in fact, I am sure you will take a mild line all the way through – preferably by recognizing that the members of all political parties, and the great majority of Canadians, feel the same way about this issue. You might say that, in view of this, it is not something that should ever be permitted to become a political issue. You could say that you are making these specific suggestions only because the present government has not apparently been able to come up with any concrete proposals for dealing with the subject. And also because you wish to make it clear that you and the Liberal party are determined that Canada shall remain free and independent – and that you have some specific ideas and suggestions in this regard.[23]

The party leader did emphasize his moderation on the question, and avoided detailed consideration of his friend's recommendations; but in spite of this, the speech appeared to mark a new and serious concern on the part of the Liberal party.

Soon after the Kingston Conference, on October 20, 1960, the party announced Walter Gordon's appointment as chairman of the policy committee of the National Liberal Rally to be held in Ottawa at the beginning of January.[24] Paul Hellyer, the chairman of the Rally, successfully proposed (with the support of Pearson and Gordon) that all the policy discussions should take place at open sessions in the presence of the press. "This was an excellent idea," wrote Gordon, "and one that was to give us a maximum amount of publicity." But this threw a special burden, as they saw it, on the organizers: "it called for a great deal of organizing and careful handling if approval of ill-considered or silly resolutions was to be avoided."[25] The policy committee was divided into twenty-one subcommittees, each with an appointed chairman and vice-chairman. While these subcommittees were to receive for consideration all the resolutions presented by provincial and constituency organizations, they were also provided with a framework of working papers and tentative resolutions prepared by a small group under Walter Gordon's supervision.[26] The resolutions emerging from the subcommittees were to be screened through the main policy committee before coming to the floor for approval by the plenary meeting.

The Rally attracted eighteen hundred delegates for three days of widely-reported meetings. Walter Gordon believed that his democratic centralist preparations had been rewarded: "because of the advance work on the working papers and the checks provided, the party produced a body of resolutions that were in the main consistent and non-contradictory in character."[27] As policy chairman, Gordon found the going "hectic" and saw many of the draft proposals altered or defeated. But on the two matters which chiefly concerned him – Canadian independence and Canadian defence policy – Gordon was satisfied that the Rally had endorsed his views. The resolution "for a strong and independent Canada" called for "greater Canadian participation in the ownership of Canadian enterprises" and a more clearly directed channelling of institutional investment funds into "more intensive development of our national resources." The resolution proposed tax incentives to encourage shared Canadian ownership and "the extension of the requirement that there be a majority of Canadians on the board of directors."[28] Finally, the resolution stated straightforwardly that chartered banks, life insurance companies and trust companies must be required to remain under Canadian control.

The resolution on defence policy (which was approved in advance by Lester Pearson) was somewhat more precise.

1. Any extension of the possession of nuclear weapons under national control will greatly increase the danger of accidental outbreak of nuclear war and also the difficulty of achieving disarmament. Membership in the nuclear club therefore should not be extended beyond the four countries which now possess such weapons. The objective should be not the extension of ownership of such weapons but their abolition before they destroy the world.

Canada cannot deny nuclear weapons to other nations and at the same time arm her own forces with them. A new Liberal government therefore should not acquire, manufacture or use such weapons either under separate Canadian control or under joint U.S.-Canadian control.

2. Canada should continue to play an important part in the defence policy of NATO which seeks security through collective action. However, NATO's objectives and the means of achieving them should be reconsidered in the light of the conditions of today, rather than those of twelve years ago. . . .

3.   Under a new Liberal government Canada will withdraw from NORAD insofar as its present interceptor role is concerned. Liberal policy would, however, provide for an appropriate Canadian contribution to continental defence in cooperation with the U.S.A. The Canadian role in such defence should be that of detection, identification and warning.

We would stop using our defence resources on interceptor fighter squadrons or on Bomarc missiles. For the U.S.A., with its vast resources and world responsibilities, these forms of defence may be necessary. There is no reason why Canada should participate in a role inappropriate to her circumstances.[29]

With this resolution the Liberal Rally sought to identify the party with the growing Canadian lobby opposing nuclear testing and the armament of Canadian forces with nuclear weapons. It thus allied itself with the faction of the Cabinet, under Howard Green, that gave first priority to disarmament. The decision of the Rally undoubtedly strengthened the inclination of the Prime Minister to temporize on the question of nuclear arms. There was still time to do so, since the weapons Canada had contracted for in 1959 would not be available for perhaps another eighteen months. The effect of the Liberal resolution was thus to point a contrast between the decisiveness and peaceful aims of the Opposition and the confusions of the government. For Walter Gordon, the contrast was both principled and politically expedient.

Gordon was pleased by the mood and results of the Rally. The party had suddenly, he believed, become "a credible alternative to the Diefenbaker government": it had gained an enthusiastic core of new supporters and had adopted "bold new policies on many issues."[30] Gordon had relished the experience of the Rally, and that had overcome any lingering hesitation about a political career.

> ... what pleased and reassured me most was the fact that the Liberal party in formal session had approved the kind of policies that I personally believed in and was prepared to fight for. From that time on, for all practical purposes, I was committed to the idea of seeking a seat in Parliament.[31]

In such political circumstances, adrenalin may affect the most seasoned political judgment. Where Walter Gordon saw a commitment to moderately left-wing nationalism, more weathered politicians saw only some convenient tacking with the political winds. Independent observers were not greatly impressed. Ramsay Cook wrote in the *Canadian Forum*:

> The one niggling question that remains after the tumult and the shouting at Ottawa have died is: what happened to all the strenuous thinking that went on at Kingston last autumn? Moreover, one wonders why two thousand delegates were brought all the way to Ottawa to draw up a platform which isn't a platform but a guide, and which contains nothing new.[32]

On unemployment, he suggested, the party stood squarely on the 1945 Green Book proposals for counter-cyclical financing; on health insurance it stood where it had, obscurely, since 1919; on dominion-provincial finances it stood with the St. Laurent government; on NORAD, the party "simply want to return to the position that existed before the Conservative victory in 1957 – Canada would take part in North American defence for purposes of detection, but not for purposes of interception"; on apartheid and South African membership in the Commonwealth it took no position; on China, "a Liberal government would agree to allow discussion of the question of Red China's admission to the U.N."

There was obviously a substantial gap of perception between Ramsay Cook's judgment that "at every stage of the proceedings (except on free education which is a provincial responsibility) the left-wing elements were silenced by defeat or compromise" and Walter Gordon's belief that the party "had approved the kind of policies that I personally believed in and was prepared to fight for." In emphasizing what the Rally had repeated from the past, Ramsay Cook tended to ignore the resolutions which reflected the reforming instincts of Gordon, Lamontagne, Kent, and Sauvé: those, for instance, dealing with an economic council, a municipal loan fund, and regional development policy. And he missed the potential significance (for internal party conflict if not for substantial change) of the foreign investment resolution. The party was no longer the docile, continentalist monolith that it had been under C. D. Howe. But the disenchanting prophecy with which Professor Cook ended his commentary offered a sobering dash of scepticism to the optimistic reformers in the party:

> The Liberals now have a guide for the future which is no more radical than Mr. Diefenbaker's promises, and less in tune with twentieth century liberalism than the program which John Kennedy offered to the American electorate last autumn. Clearly the new

Pearson is but the old King – with a dash of Walter Gordon. As a theme song the Rally might well have adopted that popular tune of the thirties, "Parliament will decide in the light of existing circumstances."[33]

Although there could be differences over the novelty and boldness of the new Liberal program, there was little doubt that the Rally had revived Liberal spirits, attracted much publicity for the party, and made it appear once again to be a force in the public life of the country. Strangely, however, Lester Pearson did not attempt to sustain the initiative the Rally had given him. For several months he made no overt effort to build on the enthusiasm of the persons who had organized the Rally. If this was a calculated matter of pacing the party, of allowing a period of calm to succeed the activity of the previous few months, it was not understood that way, and left some of the leader's advisers confused and disappointed. More likely, it was evidence of Lester Pearson's lack of elementary organizational sense. The leader did not communicate with Walter Gordon for more than two months after the Rally, and this apparent indifference led Gordon almost to the point of abandoning thought of a political career.[34] The episode left him with a nagging doubt about Pearson's ability to make use of political fortune for his own and the party's advantage.

The lapse, however, was temporary. By the end of March Gordon and Pearson were again in close communication over party organization and strategy.[35]

In the meantime, a small group of young activists (all of them supporters of L. B. Pearson in the leadership contest of 1958) had taken control of the previously stagnant Liberal organization in Ontario. By early 1961, as the result of a cooperative effort over three years, Keith Davey had become president of the Toronto and Yorks Liberal Association, Royce Frith was president of the Ontario Liberal Party, Daniel Lang was treasurer of the Ontario party, and Bruce Powe had become Ontario organizer.[36] Richard Stanbury, David Anderson and David Greenspan were associated with these four in a weekly dinner meeting at the Toronto Board of Trade, begun in 1959, which the members mockingly referred to as "Cell 13."[37] The informal group, which later became the nucleus of the Ontario Campaign Committee in the 1962 general election, had transformed the Toronto riding associations of the party into active bodies through a combination of purges, entertainments, advertising promotion, and practical political training.[38] All this occurred under the ebullient guidance of Keith Davey, an immensely energetic and high-spirited advertising man who was determined to modernize the party organization and provide Lester Pearson with the instruments he needed to come to power in Ottawa.

From the summer of 1960, Walter Gordon joined this genial group for their weekly dinner meetings. The interest was mutual: Davey and company were now hoping to make their mark on the national party, but believed that they needed more influence to do so; and Walter Gordon, from the national perspective, was on the lookout for promising supporters to man the national organization for the forthcoming general election. Keith Davey took the presence of Walter Gordon as an indication that the Toronto reformers had arrived:

> We were astounded. We never thought a guy with his prestige and standing would join us. Once Walter got involved things really began to move.[39]

Gordon's presence, in Davey's view, also involved a surprising bit of political education for this man of prestige.

> We were excited as well by him. We all 'Waltered' him, which was new for him. In his business, everyone had always called him 'Mr. Gordon.' We had a tremendous *esprit de corps*; it was a very witty group. It was the first time he realized that politics could be fun.[40]

Gordon, who had his own confident resource of wit, entered into these occasions wholeheartedly – and with more calculation than Keith Davey may have realized.

> They knew their stuff, but it seemed to me as an outsider that they spent too much time in wisecracking, and did not quite appreciate how big a task it would be to dislodge Mr. Diefenbaker from power and put Mike Pearson in. However, my first objective was to get their confidence – they were all younger than I, and I was a neophyte in politics – so I did not volunteer many suggestions to begin with.[41]

Gordon soon came to appreciate the special and exuberant talents of Keith Davey. When it became clear in the spring of 1961 that a new national director of the party would be needed to replace James Scott, Gordon took the lead in seeking a candidate, and discussed the matter with the Wednesday dining group. When Royce Frith suggested later to him that Keith Davey was the man for the job, Gordon agreed. He proposed Davey's name to Lester Pearson, and with the leader's support, offered the position to Davey. Aside from a formal meeting with Pearson early in April, 1961 to confirm the invitation, the negotiations for Davey's appointment were carried on entirely by Walter Gordon.[42] Davey became national director in May, 1961. With Lester Pearson's relatively passive acquiescence, Gordon had now effectively taken hold of the machinery of the party, outside any formal structure of command.

From the point of Davey's accession, that structure took shape rapidly, according to the design and preference of the prime movers, Gordon and Davey. An occasional meeting of Lester Pearson and his leading parliamentary and party colleagues was transformed into a regular strategic planning committee, the Leader's Advisory Committee, which met fortnightly. Pearson chaired the meetings, Davey acted as executive secretary, and Gordon, as vice-chairman, took executive control of the committee's work.[43] For a year, until the election campaign began in April, 1962, this committee served as the central party authority. Gordon and Davey planned the agendas and supervised the work assigned to subcommittees or individuals by the committee. Keith Davey admired Walter Gordon's leadership of the committee as "hard nosed, organized and precise." Gordon always knew what he wanted done, said so briefly and decisively, and had "a great sense of priorities" which kept members' attention on the important questions.[44] (At intervals in the meetings, Pearson and Davey indulged their common passion for baseball statistics, while Walter Gordon eyed the two of them dubiously.)

Later in 1961, as administrative planning for the campaign intensified, Gordon became chairman of the National Campaign Committee, with direct responsibility for the recruitment of candidates and the management and financing of the party's campaign.[45] This committee was, according to Gordon, "a fairly loose body which operated in a somewhat different way in each province,"[46] but whose effect was to lessen the power of provincial party presidents and to increase the degree of central control in the conduct of the campaign.[47] Provincial campaign chairmen were appointed to the committee by the party leader on the recommendation of Gordon and Davey, and this meant that, where they judged it desirable and possessed sufficient authority, the local party establishment could be bypassed. "We appointed people whom we thought could organize and do the job. It was much more efficient than relying upon the elected representatives."[48] The normal work of the National Campaign Committee was conducted, not in formal session, but through direct liaison between Gordon and Davey in Ottawa and the provincial chairmen across the country.[49] In

October, 1961 Tom Kent joined Mike Pearson's staff with the cumbersome title of "Special Consultant to the Leader of the Liberal Party and to the National Liberal Federation," charged with preparing the strategy papers, policy statements, campaign materials, and major speeches of the party leader for the 1962 campaign.[50]

In addition, Gordon and Davey retained their senior roles in the Ontario Campaign Committee under the chairmanship of Daniel Lang.[51] (The meetings of this committee in 1961 and 1962 frequently took place in Gordon's Toronto office.)

While there were, by mid-1961, a number of promising recruits to the national party organization and the provincial campaign committees, it had become clear that Walter Gordon and Keith Davey were the driving forces behind the Liberal party's revival. Gordon had acquired his authority gradually, as the party leader came to depend more and more upon his administrative talents and his suggestions for policy, and as Gordon cultivated his own public reputation through speeches and writings in criticism of the Diefenbaker government. Lester Pearson's trust in and dependence upon Walter Gordon gave Gordon a quite unusual range of initiative in the party. He used this initiative systematically in 1961 and 1962, with the enthusiastic cooperation of Keith Davey, to prepare the party's campaign in as orderly and thorough a way as his managerial instincts demanded. Together, Gordon and Davey did more than anyone to transform the methods of Canadian political campaigns from the intuitive and ad hoc devices of all previous federal elections to the highly managed, pseudo-scientific and promotional techniques of American presidential campaigns in the 1960s. The application of Gordon's organizational skills to the Liberal party's activities was as basic a novelty as was the influence of his ideas upon party policy.

The party and the country were now taking note of Walter Gordon's emerging political prominence, and Gordon himself appreciated that a new stage had been reached in his fledgling political career.

By the spring of 1961, I detected a feeling in the Ontario group that I should get the feel of the situation in the field – and incidentally show what I could do when I was away from the quiet and security of my own office. I agreed to make a four-day trip through southwestern Ontario to meet the local Liberals on the understanding that I would not be asked to make more than two speeches. The truth was I was nervous about speaking without a well-prepared text before me.[52]

Two invitations to speak were duly accepted, to the Rotary Club of Simcoe on June 5 and the Windsor Chamber of Commerce on June 8, and the journey was undertaken. Pegging his remarks on the forthcoming budget speech by the Minister of Finance, Gordon repeated his increasingly familiar catalogue of the government's economic failures, and his own program for economic recovery.[53] The Ottawa *Citizen* suggested innocently or sardonically that:

> If Mr. Fleming is not too obsessed with political considerations, such as winning the next election, he should pay some attention to it, for the man who headed the most exhaustive enquiry ever made into the Canadian economy has both experience and judgment. . . . It will be interesting to see whether Mr. Fleming heeds the sensible advice offered him. He might, of course, come to the same conclusions independently. Even a belated awakening will be welcome.[54]

Gordon was accompanied on the tour by the Ontario party organizer, Bruce Powe, and Vincent Barrie, mayor of St. Thomas and president of the Southwestern Ontario Liberal Association. They made certain that his first political tour would not be as restricted as he had hoped.

> Everywhere we went, Liberals turned out to see the new face, and I had to make two, three, or even four speeches each day. It was like a rehearsal for an election campaign, and I found that I enjoyed it.[55]

The excursion eventually took in Simcoe, Tillsonburg, St. Thomas, London, Ridgetown, Chatham, Leamington, and Windsor. In Windsor, while a noisy dance band played beyond a thin partition, Paul Martin introduced Gordon to a Liberal audience at the Sunnyside Tavern as a "real Canadian" like C. D. Howe, "who knew how to give leadership and provide jobs for Canadians."[56] Martin's compliments "were so exaggerated and so prolonged that after ten or fifteen minutes everyone was laughing. I had no choice but to abandon my prepared speech and talk about Paul in kind, always a good thing to do in Windsor."[57]

Press reports of Gordon's political activity were prominent and generally expansive, reflecting the party's own euphoria over his role.[58] As Lester Pearson's friend and close confidant, he was the most prominent and fascinating of the new recruits to the party. The potential differences of view and emphasis in the party arising from Gordon's attitudes on foreign investment were prudently ignored in the mood of admiration for his organizing talents and his constructive program for domestic economic revival. There was a nice irony – and perhaps also a source of danger – in Paul Martin's association of Gordon with C. D. Howe. This comparison, which centred on technique rather than the substance of policy, was taken up glibly by the press in the months that followed.[59] It helped to raise public expectations of what a new Liberal government might accomplish through determination and administrative efficiency. The contrast with Conservative bungling was too easily drawn to be entirely reliable.

The organizational effort for the coming election was rapidly gaining momentum. Walter Gordon told Lester Pearson that the party's planning would be based on the prospect of a general election in June, 1962; and in spite of periodic rumours about earlier dates, Gordon insisted that his deliberate timetable should be maintained. John Diefenbaker's timing coincided with Walter Gordon's: the election was called for June 18, 1962.

The Liberal party's strategic planning for the campaign developed out of the program adopted at the National Rally, the information gained from a series of public opinion surveys in 1961 and 1962, and the political instincts of Lester Pearson's senior advisers about how to relate and make use of the other two elements. The surveys, according to Gordon,

> ... indicated the state of opinion on various issues, on what the various parties stood for, the groups of people who traditionally supported the different parties, and the public's impressions of the characteristics of the several party leaders.[60]

The party's advertising agency, MacLaren Advertising (which had carried out two elementary surveys before the Niagara Falls and Peterborough by-elections in 1960) undertook some initial studies in 1961. But Gordon and Davey sought more highly specialized advice than the agency could provide.

> All of us, of course, read everything we could about John F. Kennedy's campaign in the 1960 presidential election and especially Theodore White's *The Making of the President, 1960.* We were, therefore, very much alive to and aware of the importance of public opinion polls and surveys. Our difficulty was to get them made in Canada quickly and by experienced people. It was at about this time that Robert Winters mentioned that a friend of his, Sam

Harris, the treasurer of the Democratic Party in the state of New York, had suggested that we should use the services of Louis Harris (no relation), who had been in charge of all the survey work for the Kennedy campaign committee.

I met Lou Harris in this way, and was immediately impressed with him. He talked to Keith Davey, Tom Kent and me on several occasions, and we determined that he was the man whose advice we had to have. He had a subsidiary company in Canada, or proceeded to establish one, and of course used Canadians for all the interviewing. The results were tabulated in Lou Harris's own office and, of greater importance, he interpreted them for us himself.[61]

Gordon's and Davey's instinct – to obtain the most professional advice available – overrode any possible feeling of incongruity about the appointment. For them, the use of a specialist to give technical advice could not conceivably involve any compromise of their nationalist principles. The matters were in quite separate categories.[62] There was, on the other hand, the potential political awkwardness of employing President Kennedy's chief pollster in the effort to overthrow Prime Minister Diefenbaker: by this time relations between the Prime Minister and the president were icy. The presence of Lou Harris in Canada as a Liberal consultant was likely to be interpreted by Mr. Diefenbaker and his party as a direct intervention by President Kennedy in Canadian politics. Technically, this was not so: the initiative had been entirely Canadian. There was enough sensitivity about appearances, however, that no announcement of Harris's appointment was made, and his role was not widely known in the party.[63]

The Harris surveys indicated that the public, in 1961, retained a high regard for Prime Minister Diefenbaker despite growing criticism of his government's record.[64] He was looked upon as an honest and direct, "clean living Christian gentleman." The Liberal party in Opposition was widely considered to be too partisan, and Lester Pearson had failed to convey any strong impression of his own character and program. His special interest in international policy was not reciprocated by the electorate; voters of other than British and French origin tended to be positively suspicious of his internationalism; and "he sometimes gave the impression that he was vacillating and indecisive." These judgments jolted Gordon and Davey.

Active Liberals, from Mike Pearson on down, found it almost

impossible to believe these estimates of Mr. Diefenbaker or to accept the obvious conclusion to be drawn – that the proper strategy for the Liberal party was to emphasize the positive aspects of the Liberal program in simple concrete terms, while attacking the Tory party for its weaknesses. It was clear that it would be a serious mistake to launch an assault on Mr. Diefenbaker himself. It was also clear that the Liberals should concentrate on a relatively few issues and explain what they would do about them. At the top of the list was the Liberal party's program for dealing with the unemployment problem and promoting industrial growth.[65]

The authority of the polls as interpreted by Lou Harris finally told, and the party's strategy was altered to reflect their influence. A few leading elements of the party program were emphasized; an effort was made to popularize the "image" of a newly determined but still decent and informal Mike Pearson; and special attention was focussed on the "Pearson Team" as a means both of drawing some attention away from the leader and of contrasting the Liberal collective style with the single-handed pyrotechnics of the Diefenbaker party.[66] In retrospect, it is a moot point whether this advice was any less occult, or any more reliable, than the impressionist judgments of political professionals might have been. But there were few professionals of reliable judgment in the party to depend upon, and the mood of fascination with American electoral techniques, in that short and blissful twilight of American optimism and grandeur sustained by John F. Kennedy, disarmed the critical spirit. Lou Harris was the Rainmaker and his advice was heeded.

Campaign organization, financing, policy-making, attunement with the trends of popular opinion: the strands were being carefully woven. The remaining element was to attract an impressive body of new candidates. The decimation of 1958 required it and made it possible. The two leading organizers did not leave the process to local initiative and the force of inertia. On July 7, 1961 Gordon wrote a memorandum to Pearson on the "difficulty in getting good men to stand for Parliament":

> We are confronted with a situation in Ontario, and the same thing may well be true in some other provinces, where the kind of men who would make good candidates are reluctant to go in for federal politics. There are many examples of good men who would prefer to run for the provincial legislature. The reasons are clear enough. A federal member must now expect to spend more than half the year in Ottawa, and be separated from his family and busi-

ness or professional practice for long periods at a time. For this, the ordinary member leads a frustrating life, and his indemnity is often insufficient to cover his expenses.

In view of this situation, it would seem desirable to agree upon a series of changes for the future that would make the prospects for a federal member of Parliament somewhat more attractive than they are at present. The following suggestions are put forward as a basis for discussion at the next meeting of your Advisory Committee:

a)   Indemnities to be increased after the next election.

b)   Perhaps a promise to review the whole question of members' pensions.

c)   An undertaking to make members' expenses in connection with their ridings deductible for tax purposes, up to some agreed amount.

d)   The House Rules to be drastically revised so as to make possible a reduction in the work week to four days – Tuesday, Wednesday, Thursday and Friday. Alternatively, the House to sit for ten days continuously (except Sunday), and then adjourn for eight days, to permit members to go home for one week out of three.

e)   More secretarial and research assistance to be provided for the ordinary member.

f)   Members to be given passes on the airlines, and compensated for travelling by automobile between Ottawa and their constituencies at the rate of ten cents per mile.

g)   A general promise or undertaking that, if you are elected, you will reshuffle your Cabinet and parliamentary assistants much more frequently than in the past, so that more members can look forward to advancement.

h)   Possibly a suggestion that the Senate will be reformed, so that vacancies will occur somewhat more frequently.

i)   A conscious effort to upgrade the standing of members generally.

j)   A firm promise to review the whole question of election expenses and the source of funds for this purpose.

No doubt you will have other suggestions to make in this connection. All I wish to do is point out that we shall find it very difficult to persuade the kind of men we want to stand unless we plan to make the prospects of life in Ottawa a little less unattractive for them.[67]

This memorandum signified a revolution in the nature of the Liberal parliamentary party. In the days of apparently permanent

Liberal power under King and St. Laurent, no similar concern was shown for the satisfactions of Liberal MPs. The perquisites of office were sufficient reward for the score of patrician MPs who formed the Cabinet; beyond that inner circle the quality of government backbenchers was a matter of indifference. The Cabinet could always be invigorated by appointments from the senior civil service or from provincial Liberal cabinets, and there seemed no point in catering to the dignity of backbenchers. They provided reliable votes for the majority party, and for that task self-respect and material comfort were unimportant – perhaps even dangerous. But now the Liberal party had to justify its claim to power and recruit a team that would command public confidence. There was no guarantee of Cabinet posts for the best candidates. The conditions of life in the House for all MPs had thus become a matter of concern, out of hard political necessity. Gordon sensed the situation shrewdly, and acted upon it.

The leader's response to these comprehensive suggestions was helpful: "Pearson agreed to implement most of these proposals if he were elected, and I was authorized to inform prospective candidates to this effect. This made a considerable difference to our recruiting efforts."[68]

Once the machinery of the national organization had been established, Keith Davey's major effort was concentrated on finding promising candidates. In addition, on Gordon's urging, Daniel Lang took two months' leave from his law practice at the end of 1961 to seek candidates. The background and presence of Gordon, Davey and Lang in Ontario meant that the most intensive search for new candidates occurred there; and this circumstance coincided with the more conscious decision to expend the party's energies in the 1962 campaign primarily in the metropolitan centres and southern Ontario where disillusionment with the Diefenbaker government seemed to be greatest.[69]

By the spring of 1962, as the party awaited the dissolution of Parliament, the search for candidates had paid impressive dividends. The Liberal team could be presented to the public with complete plausibility as an alternative government.[70]

During these months Walter Gordon's contribution to the Liberal build-up was also literary. In November, 1961 he published a short tract for the times, *Troubled Canada*,[71] which reviewed his criticisms of the Diefenbaker government, his concerns over foreign investment, and his specific recommendations for restoring buoyancy to the economy. These now included a proposal for "a National Development Corporation to sponsor and to invest in large economic undertakings that may not be expected to pay returns for a considerable period," a means of rallying domestic capital for projects previously accessible only to foreign development.[72] The discussion of foreign investment was prominent, but the dominant message of the book was that, if general prosperity and full employment were to be restored, Canada would need an expertise in government which it lacked under John Diefenbaker. The peroration concluded:

> To be successful, we shall have to manage our affairs with all possible skill and imagination. We shall need inspired and dedicated leadership. We shall need sound and consistent policies carried out with vigour and determination by expert and experienced administrators. Above all, we shall need a unity of purpose and a passionate belief that unemployment in Canada need not and must not be tolerated.[73]

The book was a piece of reasonable and calculatedly non-partisan polemic. It contained no explicit mention of the Liberal party, although its proposals coincided remarkably with those of the National Liberal Rally of the previous January. No one could be misled by the author's restraint. The "inspired and dedicated leadership" of "expert and experienced administrators" that he hoped for was that of the Pearson team. The Montreal *Star*, out of editorial scepticism, lamented that *Troubled Canada* seemed to be the Authorized Version, bearing the "approval, benediction, imprimatur" of Mr. Pearson.[74] Political reporters described *Troubled Canada* as "a potential handbook of Liberal campaigners"[75] and as "the new Liberal Bible."[76] Walter Gordon judged afterwards that the book had indeed served that purpose.

> *Troubled Canada* proved to be a handy guide for many Liberal candidates in the election campaign that was soon to be upon them. And it was one of the reasons why in that campaign, and to a large extent in the 1963 campaign as well, nearly all Liberals seemed to be saying the same things and preaching the same doctrine from coast to coast.[77]

Given Walter Gordon's growing reputation and his crucial role in making Liberal policy, an important element in attracting candidates to seek Liberal nominations would be his own willingness to enter Parliament. Gordon recognized this. Early in December, 1961, after consultation with Pearson and his former assistant Andrew Thompson (who now sat in the Ontario legislature as the Liberal MPP for Dovercourt), Gordon agreed to contest the nomination in Davenport, a west-central Toronto constituency of largely working class and immigrant population whose boundaries coincided with Thompson's provincial riding. To counter the charge of 'parachuting' into the constituency, a petition was organized by Thomson urging Gordon to stand for the nomination. It gained fifteen hundred signatures.[78] On January 22, 1962, Walter Gordon was nominated unopposed at a meeting attended by six hundred voters and the national leader, who promised that Gordon would have "a big part to play in the next Liberal administration."[79] The Conservative Toronto *Telegram* noted the lesson of this nomination for the party: "Mr. Gordon's acceptance of the invitation of the Liberal executive in Davenport riding serves as a guide to other good candidate material. He is the kind of man who, long interested in public affairs, should enter public life." And the editorial remarked on his pluck in doing so:

Mr. Gordon has not picked an easy seat for a Liberal candidate. Davenport is no pocket borough. . . . Its voters in 1957 repudiated Hon. Paul Hellyer, former Liberal minister, who had represented Davenport for two terms. The present Conservative member, M. D. Morton, had a plurality of 4,245 in 1958 and, in thousands, the seat divided roughly P.C. 12; LIB. 8; CCF 5.[80]

By January, 1962 that was the kind of challenge the once reluctant politician was eager to face in the contest to unseat Prime Minister Diefenbaker.

5   Round One: 1962

John Diefenbaker's nationalism was one of the sources of his great victory in 1958. He had promised to halt the growing appropriation of Canadian resources and industries by American investors; and he had promised to renew the ties of Commonwealth to counterbalance the dominant economic, cultural and foreign policy influences of the American colossus. But the task was beyond him. His government was never able to coordinate the separate strands of policy according to a clear nationalist pattern. "The decline and fall of the British Empire-Commonwealth," wrote Donald Creighton, "and the growth of a continentally organized North America were twin processes which had been going on now for over four decades and which successive Liberal governments in Canada had actively encouraged and assisted. To arrest these powerful tendencies at this late stage would require the invention of novel and daring policies designed to defend Canadian integrity and independence against continentalism."[1] No invention took place; instead the government fell victim, in its inexperience, to buffetings and pressures which it could not understand or respond to consistently. One of its first acts was to enter formally into the NORAD agreement negotiated but not signed by the St. Laurent administration, thus ratifying the subservience of Canada to the United States in North American defence. In the autumn of 1957 the government's promise to divert fifteen percent of Canada's trade from the United States to the United Kingdom was revealed to be a rash piece of bluffing when Canada brusquely rejected Britain's offer of free trade (an offer perhaps intended to call Canada's bluff at a time when Britain herself was considering how to come to terms with the European Common Market). Four years later, when Britain applied for entry to the Market, Canada was no better prepared for the British initiative than she had been in 1957, and responded with belligerence rather than sympathy.

In the face of large annual deficits in the balance of trade with the United States, the Diefenbaker government was disinclined to interfere with the flow of American capital into the country, because it served the convenient short-term purpose of balancing Canadian international payments. So the American takeover of the Canadian economy continued at an accelerating pace in the late 1950s and early 1960s.[2] The cancellation of the Avro Arrow interceptor project, which occurred essentially because Canada could find no market in the United States for the aircraft, was followed by agreements to purchase American Bomarc missiles and interceptor aircraft, and the signing of the Defence Production Sharing Agreements, which tied Canada ever more intimately to the American military system and defence economy.

In this record, the administration did manage to insert a handful of nationalist measures. The Board of Broadcast Governors, created in 1958, imposed new Canadian content limitations on Canadian radio and television stations; and legislation was adopted requiring Canadian control of insurance companies, fifty percent Canadian participation in oil companies operating in the Canadian Arctic, and compulsory Canadian participation in domestic energy-producing companies. Good intentions, but nothing more, were demonstrated in the appointment of the O'Leary Royal Commission on Publications. But these were peripheral measures which left the central problems of growing American economic penetration unresolved. The problems were never faced by the Diefenbaker government.

The nationalist failures of the government were, however, increasingly overshadowed by its general incompetence in domestic matters. As the 1962 election approached, Walter Gordon's nationalist proposals fell into the background of the Liberal program. There were more simple criticisms of the government to be made which suited the folk habits of the Liberal party better than the novel venture sponsored by Walter Gordon. For the continentalists in the party, the relative neglect of the Gordon program was a comfortable return to good sense; for the nationalists, it seemed a harmless expedient. Walter Gordon was not concerned by the shifting balance of priorities. The first task was to defeat John Diefenbaker. During the election campaign of 1962 commentators almost universally failed to notice the nationalist element in the Liberal program.[3]

After the energetic flourishes of its first two years in office, the

Diefenbaker government had gradually retreated into immobility before the complexities of economic decline, the American alliance, and the political awakening in Quebec. John Diefenbaker's docile majority in Parliament seemed, paradoxically, to paralyse his initiative rather than to liberate it. Power and the overwhelming electoral triumph of 1958 did not reinforce the self-confidence of the Prime Minister, but instead made him more than ever vulnerable to criticism. His friendly relations with the press soured rapidly as parliamentary reporters carped at the government's record. Parliament and the public remained transfixed by the Prime Minister's virtuoso performance in the House; but the object of the exercise grew more and more obscure. The performance itself, the daily conquest of the challenger across the aisle, appeared to be its own justification. Lester Pearson bore the daily humiliations with weary stoicism, and only occasionally wounded his opponent in return.

But the parliamentary show was just a diverting charade. The high expectations aroused in 1958 of a great and unifying national crusade led by John Diefenbaker had dissolved in disenchantment. The government stumbled in puzzlement over its inability to manage the economy, its role in the alliance, its relationship with Quebec, and even its own parliamentary timetable. Uncertainty soon took the place of euphoria in the national mood.

By the summer of 1960 the government's drift and confusion appeared endemic, and the *Globe and Mail* commented gloomily on the parliamentary session just adjourned:

> The Cabinet provided little leadership. Its members gave the impression of men baffled by the problems which confront them, unsure of their course, anxious to put off action in the hope that something would turn up. It is this impression of indecision and fumbling which probably accounts ... for the disquietude throughout the country.[4]

Rising unemployment and a persistent conflict between the expansionist budgeting of the Minister of Finance and the restrictionist policy of the Bank of Canada sharpened public criticism. When the government finally chose in 1961 to respond to critics on the Bank of Canada issue, it did so not by asserting the authority of the Minister over the governor of the Bank directly, but by seeking to dismiss the governor over the question of his pension. This was probably the watershed of toleration for the Diefenbaker government. The issue was human and political rather than economic. As Walter Gordon had made clear, the Liberal party accepted the ultimate pre-eminence of the Minister in any major policy dispute with the governor, and it favoured cheaper credit; the party had been urging the government to resolve the conflict with the governor on the Cabinet's terms, and would have supported it in doing so. Now the government handed the Opposition a major issue by the manner rather than the matter of its response. The Liberal party stung the government with its charges of ineptitude and unfairness in seeking to dismiss the governor of the Bank on a pretext without allowing him to defend himself before a House of Commons committee. Lester Pearson made skilful use of the Liberal majority in the Senate to allow James Coyne to testify for himself there, and to defeat the government's dismissal Bill. His honour sustained, Coyne then resigned. The Liberal party gained credit for its defence of a martyr against a vengeful and floundering administration, and the case came to symbolize the weaknesses of the Diefenbaker government.

The government, meanwhile, had consolidated its following in the West with its overseas grain sales, its farm support programs, and its rhetorical defence of the oppressed minorities of Eastern Europe (the high point of which was Mr. Diefenbaker's speech to the United Nations General Assembly in September, 1960). It kept the fences mended in the Maritimes with a number of measures of regional aid. But in Ontario the government's lack of grand strategy, and the Prime Minister's politics of delay and bombast, increasingly alienated urban voters, who were more and more cultivated by the Liberals and the New Democratic Party. In Quebec the vague hope of reconciliation between the two language communities was soon dissipated by the traditional indifference of the Conservative party to French Canada's special sensitivities.

In the House of Commons, the government demonstrated its profound administrative incompetence. The Estimates for 1961 – 1962 were not adopted during the fiscal year; the parliamentary timetable was clogged and incoherent. By the spring of 1962 the Prime Minister was claiming that systematic obstruction in the House had frustrated his government's intentions.

The parliamentary setting focussed attention upon the party leaders. Mr. Diefenbaker, by his public preening and belligerence and his private domination of the Cabinet, encouraged this concentration upon personalities, his own and Lester Pearson's. Pearson disliked this kind of lurid display as much as John Diefenbaker revelled in it; but the system and his opponent largely set the conditions of Pearson's life as challenger. Lou Harris might caution the Liberal campaign managers that the party should avoid attacks on the person of Mr. Diefenbaker;

but the advice simply emphasized the extraordinary role that the Prime Minister's personality played in Canadian politics in the 1960s. So did the attempt to diffuse public concentration on Lester Pearson by playing up the "Liberal Team"; for what this signalled was the relative lack of flamboyance of Mr. Pearson in contrast to John Diefenbaker. In the language of the hustings, it was an admission that Lester Pearson was no match for the Prime Minister, and that the party recognized this disability.

There was one remarkable departure from the Liberal party's general embargo on personal attacks on the Prime Minister. This came in the House of Commons on February 22, 1962 when a little-known Quebec backbencher, Lucien Cardin, blistered the chamber with an outpouring of anger at the Prime Minister's arrogance, malice, deviousness, bluster, and sophistry. The speech engaged the Prime Minister on his own rhetorical ground, excoriating him not for his government's policies but for his own contemptuous treatment of his political opponents and the House of Commons. Cardin condemned the Prime Minister for his insinuation that Lester Pearson had never sought to support the Ukrainians against Soviet oppression: this was "a Fascist lie with strong overtones of McCarthyism." The deputy Speaker required the withdrawal of the charge as a reflection on the integrity of a member of the House; but Cardin had registered his point, and persisted in the attack. The reason for the Prime Minister's malice toward Mr. Pearson, Cardin believed, was his jealousy of Pearson's international reputation. "In the deep recesses of his soul," asserted Cardin, "there burn the envious fires of the little green-eyed monster. . . . Perhaps the Prime Minister's otherwise inexplicable attitude toward the leader of the Opposition stems from the fact that the Prime Minister has never quite forgiven the leader of the Opposition for being awarded the Nobel peace prize in 1957."[5] Cardin ridiculed the political antics of the Prime Minister as those of "a silent film hero who overacts his performance. . . . The Prime Minister's speeches in the House, which should set the note for useful and constructive debates, degenerate into criminal court debating tactics filled with personal insinuations, half truths and sophistry such as will not be found in the records of *Hansard* of any former Prime Minister of Canada."[6] This was invective equal to the best of Mr. Diefenbaker and Mr. Fleming.

The speech caused a sensation in the House. "For a time," wrote Peter Dempson, "the House of Commons appeared stunned. Even Liberal MPs squirmed uncomfortably, having difficulty believing what was going on. Tory MPs began to interject, trying to drown out Cardin's words. But Cardin, a little wisp of a man, brushed aside all interruptions."[7] He spoke resentments that the normal decorum of the House left unrelieved; he exposed the bitterness and frustration that John Diefenbaker's overbearing style aroused in his opponents. Cardin had bearded the lion in its den, but he did not suffer politically for it in 1962. In the election campaign that followed, the Prime Minister spoke in Cardin's constituency of Richelieu-Verchères, but Cardin was easily re-elected.[8]

By the spring of 1962 all parties in the House of Commons were impatient to plunge into a general election campaign. The government's legislative program for the year possessed the limited coherence of a pre-election pastiche, with increases in old age pensions, a larger winter works program, greater acreage payments to prairie farmers, and additions to the Gaspé Railway. In the debate on the speech from the throne in January, Lester Pearson confidently challenged the Prime Minister to call an election at once on the government's record, but doubted that he would respond because "of course, we must remember that the Prime Minister has always placed great faith in the healing virtues of delay, as in the camouflaging magic of confusion."[9] The leader of the Opposition criticized the government's failure to stimulate economic growth or to reduce massive unemployment; its inability to react positively and coherently to the creation of the European Common Market and Britain's application for entry; and its failure "after two years of indecision and procrastination, confusion and contradiction," to produce any statement "of an intelligible Canadian defence policy, especially whether Canada is or is not to have nuclear arms."[10] In contrast to a Conservative government based on "political illusions [and] outmoded ideas," Mr. Pearson offered the electorate the choice of a Liberal government committed to "hard, fresh thinking" that would act upon "wise and planned policies."[11] The Liberal party's stated concern for coherence of policy, efficient administration, the restoration of economic growth, and decisiveness in government set it off clearly from the record of fumbling, hesitation and posturing of the Diefenbaker administration.

The Prime Minister demonstrated in reply that his contest with the Liberal party would be a reckless one. Bruce Macdonald reported in the *Globe and Mail* on January 25 that "If Prime Minister John Diefenbaker's performance in the throne speech debate . . . is any indication, the current election campaign seems likely to become rough, tough and nasty before it has finally run its course."[12] The Prime Minister dismissed the claim that the Liberal party offered anything new to the country; the evidence of the Kingston Conference and of Mr. Pearson's choice of advisers was that the party sought to put back the clock to an era of bureaucratic regimentation:

> I think of these people, I am not going to name them all, but most will be able to identify those who treated Parliament with patent and unconcealed contempt and deprived it of its rights, those men referred to as bureaucrats in a previous government. They were our masters. That is what we fought against year after year in this House of Commons. These are the men who want that power again and they have made it clear that they are ready to act in accordance with the statements they have made. These are the men who bypassed Parliament, the men who found it easier to rule by Order-in-Council under so-called emergency legislation. . . . These are the bright bureaucratic boys. These were the dictators who dominated Canada.[13]

Mr. Diefenbaker applied these strictures to four persons: Mitchell Sharp, C. M. Drury, Maurice Lamontagne and Tom Kent. Without hesitation the press added Walter Gordon to the list as one, presumably, who didn't need naming.[14] Two of the five, Sharp and Gordon, had held civil service posts in Ottawa during the war, Sharp permanently and Gordon temporarily; Lamontagne and Drury did so later. Kent had never done so, but he was a man of ideas and former editor of the Winnipeg *Free Press*, which came to much the same thing in John Diefenbaker's lexicon of abuse.

The Prime Minister attacked Lamontagne and Kent for their advocacy at the Kingston Conference of a prices board and an advertising tax. The implementation of these measures, he said, would require the use of rigid, socialist state controls. Lester Pearson's assurance that these proposals did not form part of the Liberal program was immaterial to Mr. Diefenbaker. Mr. Pearson's advisers had revealed their inclinations, and in John Diefenbaker's mind the leader of the Opposition was stuck with them.[15]

Mr. Diefenbaker continued to play upon the populist fear of the centralizing bureaucrats throughout the 1962 campaign. John Bird warned in the Toronto *Star* after this initial outburst that citizens might as well get to know these bogeymen at once "because, throughout the next election, your flesh will have to creep and you are to lie awake nights worrying about them."[16] The element of truth in the Prime Minister's alarmism, which permitted the exploitation of this issue, was that the Liberal policy-makers did desire a coherent set of national economic policies involving greater government intervention in the economy. Walter Gordon had said so many times. John Diefenbaker, on the other hand, was a *laissez-faire* liberal in economic matters who did not understand the machinery of economic management and instinctively suspected it. The state's economic role, for him, was not one of high direction but of piecemeal adjustment and compassionate assistance to the unfortunate.[17] For such a mind, the economic managers in the Liberal leadership, many of them former senior civil servants, were quite plausibly seen as dangerous bureaucrats intent upon invading the realm of private economic choice to impose their intellectual schemes. By taking the position he did on Mr. Pearson's economic advisers, Mr. Diefenbaker underlined the definition of his political constituency. His appeal in 1962 was to rural and small-town voters, primarily outside central Canada, who had uncomplicated views on economic matters and were congenitally suspicious of the central government. Given the trends of population movement and the growth in opportunities for higher education, this meant also that the Conservative appeal in 1962 was to age rather than youth.[18] The Liberal appeal, in contrast, was aimed at the very elements of the population that the Prime Minister chose to ignore: the urban, the skilled technical and professional, the mobile, the economically literate, the young, the central Canadian. Liberals and Conservatives spoke to two different Canadas. The members of these two distinct communities could be identified roughly in 1962 according to whether they admired or distrusted the dominating personality across the border, President John F. Kennedy. This polarization was manifested in many different words and acts, and neither party chose to counter it. In 1957 and 1958 the two parties made national appeals; in 1962 they did not.[19]

Late in January the Liberal party convened what it expected to be the immediate pre-election meetings of the National Council and the National Campaign Committee. Walter Gordon pronounced the campaign committee meeting "tremendously successful" and "very down to earth."[20] He revealed to the press afterwards that the party had conducted public opinion surveys of its own "using all the modern techniques and tools," but discreetly declined to indicate the results, or to say what kind of campaign the party would conduct.

> ... Mr. Gordon was keeping a few cards up his sleeve. He declined to say whether the campaign would be pitched mainly on the Liberal platform or on the personality and leadership of Lester Pearson.
> "I'd prefer not to answer that directly," he said. "That is the heart of our strategy."[21]

There was assurance in his remarks, sustained by the most recent Gallup poll results which showed the Liberal party to be leading the government substantially in public popularity.

The campaign chairman's revelation about the use of "all the modern techniques of 'motivation' research and surveys" prompted the Peterborough *Examiner* to reflect upon some of the dilemmas the party faced in interpreting the Harris polls.

> There are strong arguments in favour of selling political beliefs by the same method used to hawk deodorants and headache pills. For one thing, the methods apparently work. 'Research' has shown that a man who buys a red convertible is really taking himself a mistress! Most of those who smoke, this substitute for phrenology holds, are simply using cigarettes to compensate for the denial of breast feeding! Who knows what strange motives may lie in the unconscious of those who vote Liberal, Conservative or NDP?
>
> It will have to be decided by the party organizers what image their man should present on television. If surveys have shown that half the nation looks upon him as a father and the other half sees him as a lover, should he appear on television in a business suit with a waistcoat and fob watch, or with his manly chest bared?[22]

Fortunately, perhaps, for Mr. Pearson and the electorate, the guidance actually offered to the Liberal campaign committee was less Freudian than the *Examiner* imagined.

The election campaign proper occupied two gruelling months after the dissolution of Parliament on April 18. The Liberal program, based upon the resolutions of the 1961 policy convention, was published in a series of fourteen pamphlets containing seventy-five major proposals. Most of these involved federal spending, and in the course of the campaign Lester Pearson persisted in adding further promises to the list. On balance, observers concluded, the party did hold to its strategy of imitating the Kennedy campaign "by concentrating on a few major generalized issues: the economic slowdown and the need to get the country moving again; the Conservative bungling and mismanagement and the experienced Pearson team; and the loss of respect abroad."[23] But the existence of the larger party program, and the leader's readiness to add promises to it as he toured the country, sat discordantly with this limited strategic intention, for it suggested that the Liberal party, like the government, was too eager to bribe the electorate for its support. "Even the friends of the party," wrote John Saywell, "were sceptical of the wide range of promises made."[24] The Toronto *Globe and Mail* spoke bluntly for its enemies.

The basis of the Liberal campaign is a contradiction. Mr. Walter L. Gordon, chief financial critic of the Liberal party, again illustrated this fact in a speech in Sackville, New Brunswick. After painting a gloomy picture of the Canadian economy, Mr. Gordon said that one of the first things a new government must do is to restore confidence in the financial administration of our affairs. But he did not make a single suggestion as to what must be done to restore confidence. He did not repudiate one item in the Liberal spending program, whose effect on confidence is destructive, certainly on the confidence of our friends abroad.

Mr. Gordon's fellow financial expert in the Liberal party, Mr. Mitchell Sharp, has similarly ignored his party's promises of more spending. Instead he has attacked the Conservative Minister of Finance, Mr. Donald Fleming, as "the defender of extravagance and the leading exponent of living beyond one's means." His words might better have been applied to the Liberal program.

The Liberal party must choose between fulfilling its expensive seventy-five promises and providing Canada with a responsible fiscal policy. It cannot do both.

Do the Liberals plan to spend the nation into bankruptcy, or will they abandon the vote-catching subsidies, welfare schemes and special projects they have promised every interest group in the length and breadth of Canada?[25]

That was asking too much. The party was caught by the demands of a national election campaign. It could not explain the complicated fine print of its program in detail, but depended upon the general appeal of a few slogans and the particular appeal of local promises. The program that emerged during the campaign was thus not as coherent and responsible as Walter Gordon would have preferred it to be, and this perhaps reflected more inherent contradictions and inadequacies in the original program than the party leaders had appreciated. The *Globe and Mail* concluded that Walter Gordon's essential prescription amounted to "what the naive may mistake for a solution to all economic problems": a permanent economic advisory council.

Councils . . . planning . . . looking ahead . . . government machinery. This is the sum of Liberal economic theory. But this promise of so-called planning is not a policy. It should not be accepted as an excuse for failing to propose specific measures.

Why do not the Liberals tell the electorate now what strong medicine they would prescribe for the economy? Would they rather employ the vague and painless term, planning, to justify the measures they may have to adopt after the election?[26]

The party's general appeal came down, as election day approached, to a call for trust in the experience, poise and wisdom of the Pearson team, as opposed to the demonstrated incompetence in office of the Diefenbaker Cabinet. A Liberal administration would restore confidence and a high rate of growth, and this would permit the expansion of state welfare and aid programs. These axioms were not yet self-evident to many of the voters who had turned to John Diefenbaker in 1958, and the Pearson campaign somehow never gained complete conviction and authority. Partly this failure indicated public scepticism about the qualities of leadership of Lester Pearson: the same scepticism, in fact, which had been felt by Walter Gordon in 1959 and 1960. Partly, it reflected scepticism about the party program and the leader's team, which John Diefenbaker played upon assiduously in his attacks on the bureaucrats around Lester Pearson and their bureaucratic policies.[27] And partly, the failure simply reflected the unusual strength of the public commitment to John Diefenbaker made four years earlier. The Liberal party had a very long way to go in altering loyalties and votes to overcome his entrenched power. It would take a remarkable politician to unseat the man Donald Creighton described as "a novel and extraordinary phenomenon – a positive prodigy – in Canadian politics."[28] In 1962, Lester Pearson did not appear to be that politician. As the election campaign progressed, Gallup poll indications of support for the Liberal party fell from forty-four percent on May 26 to thirty-eight percent on June 13.

But this did not mean that the outlook for the government was hopeful. It was in difficulty throughout the campaign. Since January, a crisis of financial confidence had been developing, stimulated especially by the persistent budget deficits and the government's unrealistic exchange rate policy. (The Canadian dollar, while formally floating against the policy of the International Monetary Fund favouring fixed exchange rates, had since June, 1961 been 'manipulated' by the Bank of Canada to maintain a discount of about five cents on the dollar.) Public warnings came not only from domestic sources, but in February also from *Barron's Magazine*, the *Economist*, and *The Times*. The Minister of Finance defended the government's policy of supporting the dollar at ninety-five cents (U.S.) in his budget speech on April 10, but in the following weeks the Exchange Fund was forced into massive buying of Canadian dollars to offset the flight of speculative capital out of Canada. On May 2, Mr. Fleming announced a devaluation to ninety-two and one-half cents (U.S.) and the pegging of the exchange rate. "The very extensive financial resources available to the government," he said, "and its policies both domestic and international will be directed to maintaining the stability of our exchange rate at the definitive level."[29] A change in policy which might have been accomplished relatively calmly in more normal circumstances became a further source of uncertainty and misunderstanding when adopted unexpectedly in the midst of a general election campaign. The devaluation was generally welcomed as overdue; the adoption of a fixed exchange rate was criticized widely as being indefensible without the imposition of domestic controls; the timing was deplored. Walter Gordon commented that "Mr. Fleming would not have done this unless the situation was out of control,"[30] and the action inevitably strengthened the Liberal case that the government's economic policy was in disarray. For a short time, apparently, the pegging of the dollar stabilized Canadian foreign exchange reserves. But in June, in the face of continuing electoral uncertainty and further confusing statements by ministers, there were massive outflows of American dollars from the Exchange Fund. The evidence of economic confusion was an unexpected bonus for the Opposition; but it was also a dangerous issue to exploit. John Diefenbaker and Donald Fleming did everything they could to blame their critical opponents for undermining international confidence in Canada and thus creating the financial crisis.

The Prime Minister revealed his positive electoral program in his opening address of the campaign at London, Ontario on May 5, a "sixteen-point prosperity blueprint" which promised a wide range of measures of economic development and social welfare. The program was not contained in any explicit framework of general goals, but was an eclectic mixture of great development projects, porkbarrel public works, and vaguely nationalist schemes which owed much inspiration to Walter Gordon and the Liberal National Rally of 1961.[31]

With this program on the record, the Prime Minister too fell back familiarly upon his arsenal of slogans and catch-phrases, charged with elements of colour, wit and malice that the Liberal generalizations lacked. Mr. Pearson's brains trust was "a cacophony of paragons, pseudo-economists, economic centralizers and former bureaucrats";[32] they were "your potential masters, a conglomeration of hopeless and hopefuls, a veritable Cave of Addulam, where all the misfits in creation are collected together – a cacophony of jargon."[33] Mr. Pearson was "soft on Communism"; the Soviets wanted John Diefenbaker out because his government wasn't afraid to denounce Russian colonialism.[34] The Liberal party had expected this use of the Russian bogey against Mr. Pearson, and Pearson replied angrily that "I was fighting

Communism at the United Nations before John Diefenbaker ever heard of it."[35] But the charge complemented the Prime Minister's own long-cultivated appeal to Ukrainian voters on the prairies. It was therefore extraordinarily difficult to challenge, except before relatively internationalist Liberal audiences who did not need to be told that it was misleading demagogy. The Prime Minister embellished the picture of his government under siege by the great powers when he claimed on May 23 that the United States, too, desired a Liberal victory.[36] He was most at home in the role of underdog, and as the campaign progressed he benefited increasingly from his disadvantages. By the end of May disruptive audiences in Trail and Vancouver, B.C. and Chelmsford, Ontario had begun to draw public sympathy to this tribune of the people, harassed by all the forces of domestic and international power.

Walter Gordon meanwhile managed the Liberal party's high strategy in close consultation with Mike Pearson and Keith Davey. As he had planned, Gordon concentrated his efforts on the Ontario campaign, with secondary attention to the West and the Maritimes. From January to June, he made twenty-four formal speeches in British Columbia, Saskatchewan, Ontario, New Brunswick, and Nova Scotia, and innumerable informal addresses in Ontario. At the same time, with the assistance of Andrew Thompson and Joe Grittani, Gordon conducted his local campaign in Davenport riding against the sitting Conservative member, Douglas Morton, and William Sefton, the trade unionist candidate of the NDP. The riding had a high level of unemployment in 1962, "and many people had become almost desperate about it."[37] In spite of the substantial Conservative plurality of 1958, it was thus regarded as a marginal constituency in 1962. The NDP recognized this, and chose it as one of a few Toronto ridings where the party's local campaign should be concentrated. Gordon considered that "they were too aggressive, and I suspect they frightened many people off."[38] Strengthened by his national stature and his vigorous constituency organization, Walter Gordon was elected to the House of Commons on June 18, 1962 with forty-two percent of the vote.[39]

The national result was not nearly so encouraging, but it reflected accurately the party's preliminary assessment of its possibilities and the focus of its efforts. There were twenty-eight gains in Ontario, eleven in Quebec, six in the Maritimes, and four in British Columbia. The Liberal party returned 100 members to the Conservatives' 116, the NDP's 19, and Social Credit's 30. Urban Ontario's rejection of the Progressive Conservative party gave the Liberal party the gains it expected there, but rural Quebec's defection to Social Credit and British Columbia's endorsement of the NDP deprived Lester Pearson of victory.[40] On the prairies, where they had not expected to make inroads into John Diefenbaker's ranks, the party drew a virtual blank, with only two gains in Manitoba. A long but insufficient step had been taken back toward office, and the relative failure nevertheless offered the Liberal party reassurance.

> The Tories lost ninety-two seats and were far down in the percentage of the popular vote, from 53.7% in 1958 to 37.3%. The Liberals gained forty-one seats and were a fraction ahead of the Tories in the popular vote. . . . It was a tremendous victory for Mike Pearson, and no one expected that the new minority government of Mr. Diefenbaker would last for very long.[41]

The encouraging contrast with 1958, however, and the hope of victory in another early campaign, perhaps helped to conceal the limited social basis of the Liberal party's gains under the electoral management of Walter Gordon and Keith Davey. The hope of victory generated by the 1962 result was based more on a judgment of the government's shattered morale and its loss of momentum than it was on a careful analysis of the election results.[42] The Liberal party had made its appeal to urban Canada; John Diefenbaker had made his appeal to rural Canada; and the two constituencies had responded favourably to their separate calls. The minor parties sliced off segments of the vote which deprived either party of a majority. Both major parties ignored Quebec. Unless one of the major parties could somehow break out beyond its 1962 constituency, or undermine the third party appeal to that constituency, the prospect for continuing minority government seemed strong. Murray Beck drew this conclusion about Lester Pearson and the electoral divisions of June, 1962:

> Lester Pearson's role, it turned out, was to reinforce rather than reduce the cleavage that the Prime Minister had done so much to create. The Liberal leader could not communicate to the rural dweller in either English or French Canada. Urban Canada, which wanted nothing so much as business-like management in government, could see nothing wrong in Pearson's surrounding himself with a brains trust. But rural Canada was highly suspicious that he might rely excessively on experts and bureaucrats, especially since John Diefenbaker lambasted them so derisively. Seldom have two leaders been so antithetical in the images they have presented to different sections of the electorate; the outcome was a deeper rural-urban cleavage than the country had heretofore experienced.[43]

6   Round Two: 1963

The speeches of Lester Pearson, Walter Gordon and Mitchell Sharp in the closing days of the 1962 campaign reflected their anxiety that the country was now facing a severe short-term financial crisis in addition to the more deep-rooted economic failure which they had been calling attention to for months. The possibility that they would have to deal with this crisis if the party triumphed on June 18 stimulated a tone of marked caution and sobriety in their public remarks on the subject as the election campaign concluded. Without being specific, they hinted at the Liberal party's readiness to adopt severe economic remedies to overcome the emergency.

The inconclusive result of the election apparently intensified the financial crisis. Two days afterwards, Lester Pearson called on the government to meet Parliament at once to face "the developing emergency in the flight of capital." He telephoned Walter Gordon to tell him that the governor of the Bank of Canada, Louis Rasminsky, had met with him to seek his approval for a package of emergency measures proposed to Canada by the International Monetary Fund in return for international support of the dollar.[1] The Fund, through the intermediacy of the Bank, was asserting the influence it had acquired the previous month when it had persuaded the government to adopt a fixed exchange rate. Gordon was alarmed at the prospect of further dictation to Canada by the IMF, and feared that Rasminsky was attempting to make use of Pearson's influence to persuade the Prime Minister to accept the IMF proposals. "I knew that Pearson's response would be, 'Here's a proposal from a senior civil servant; of course we must accept it.' "[2] Gordon flew to Ottawa at once to discuss the situation at close hand, but by the time he arrived Pearson had given his support and the government had agreed to "what came close to being an ultimatum from the Bank of Canada and, indirectly, from the International Monetary Fund."[3] On Sunday, June 24, Prime Minister Diefenbaker appeared on national television and radio to review the government's measures to meet the crisis. They provided for credits to Canada of $1 billion from the IMF, the U.S. Federal Reserve Bank, the Bank of England, and the U.S. Export-Import Bank, in return for Canadian adoption of temporary tariff surcharges, the reduction of duty-free exemptions for Canadians travelling abroad, and a commitment to reduce government spending estimates by $250 million in the current fiscal year. Simultaneously the Bank of Canada imposed a high rediscount rate of interest of six percent. Mr. Diefenbaker promised that these temporary measures would be replaced "as soon as circumstances permit" by "longer-term measures of a positive, constructive nature." For the time being, he concluded, "until after a cooling-off period . . . for political passions to subside and be followed by calm reason," there would be no session of the new Parliament.

Walter Gordon believed that the government's course, adopted under duress, "had placed Canada in something of a strait jacket."

> I believed it was a serious mistake for Canada to have adopted a fixed exchange rate at the insistence of the IMF. I thought at the time it would be preferable to allow the Canadian dollar to find its own level even if it were to drop to eighty-five or even eighty cents for a short period rather than to accept direction from an international authority located in Washington. That authority might possibly be influenced, at least to some extent, by points of view that would tend to reduce Canada's room for manoeuvre and independence.[4]

Already Gordon's anxiety had been sustained, as Canada adopted a domestic austerity program dictated from abroad rather than adopted freely according to domestic judgments of priorities and timing. His common sense and nationalist approach to the exchange value of the dollar affronted international financial orthodoxy; Gordon would have to wait eight years before his belief in floating rates would gain national and international respectability.[5] But given the circumstances of emergency in which the austerity program had been imposed, and the consultation which had preceded it, the Opposition withheld its criticism.

Over the following six months, the emergency program succeeded in restoring Canada's currency reserves and an attitude of confidence about Canada in the international financial community. Interest rates fell steadily during the autumn, and some import surcharges were removed. By January, 1963 Canada had discharged all of its crisis borrowings except the $300 million loan from the IMF. The director of the International Monetary Fund noted the success of the austerity program at the Fund's meeting in September, while echoing the concern of the Bank of Canada that "there was a continuing need for long-run constructive measures to improve our basic international payments position."[6]

As the Liberal party's leading spokesman on financial affairs, Walter Gordon emphasized this fundamental aspect of the situation. In London, Ontario on August 31, 1962 he renewed his criticism of the Diefenbaker government.

> The foreign loans that were obtained have served their purpose in dealing with the immediate dollar crisis. What happens now? When the austerity program was imposed we were told it was to meet an emergency, and that "longer-term measures of a positive, constructive nature will be introduced to improve our current international accounts." More than two months have now elapsed and no indication has been given of any longer-term measures that are or may be contemplated. There seems to be no sense of urgency, and little if any appreciation of the seriousness of the difficulties we are faced with.[7]

Gordon reiterated his view that the primary objective of government policy must be to stimulate economic activity in order to restore a satisfactory annual growth rate and high levels of employment. The long-term policies required to meet this objective, he believed, fell into three categories:

1. Our finances must be put in order and the budget balanced.
2. Our transactions with other countries must be brought more nearly into balance.
3. Our financial policies must be designed to foster and encourage economic expansion throughout the country.[8]

The restrictive and protectionist approach of the austerity program put the burden of financial recovery, "in terms of higher prices and increased unemployment – on the people who are least able to afford it." This was unsatisfactory. The crisis had come about partly because there had been a series of large and uncontrolled budget deficits since 1957, unrelated to any effort to encourage economic growth. "Any system of permanent deficit financing," said Gordon, "can lead only to disaster as the run on the Canadian dollar showed." The restoration of confidence in Canada's financial stability now required a firm commitment to balance the federal budget. "I do not mean," he explained, "that the budget should be balanced in one fell sweep, within a year. It should be enough to show that realistic steps are being taken to bring it into balance over a two or three year period." This should not be done by reducing public works, raising tariffs, or cutting back social security programs. The alternatives were limited, and Gordon tried to be specific.

> This means that, if government expenditures are to be reduced appreciably without serious damage to the economy, we shall have to take a hard look at all unnecessary expenditures on defence and be prepared to cut them. We should stop spending money on obsolete weapons like the Bomarc missile which are imported and thus add to our balance of payments difficulties. And we should re-examine all other defence expenditures, especially those outside of Canada.[9]

This meant, in particular, that the maintenance of Canadian troops in Europe deserved review, and that "in our present circumstances we should concentrate more of our total effort here in Canada in connection with the defence of North America.[10]

His other suggestions for bringing the budget into balance were more conventional ones: the elimination of waste and inefficiency in government operations, the plugging of "loopholes and anomalies" in the tax laws, and the restoration of full employment as an indirect means of stimulating tax revenues. This, "together with the other proposals I have mentioned . . . would more than produce a balanced budget."

Gordon accepted the stabilization of the exchange value of the dollar at ninety-two and one-half cents (U.S.), and recommended efforts to balance Canada's international accounts to prevent any further fall in its value. The tariff surcharges, he asserted, should be discontinued because they might promote international reprisal; the major effort should be to promote rather than to reduce external trade. Tax policy should be used actively to encourage export sales abroad; government agencies should give preference in their purchases to domestic suppliers; the reduced tariff exemptions for Canadians returning home should be maintained. Domestic industry should be encouraged to modernize and rationalize through the creation of a new department of industry charged with "an industry by industry examination of our secondary manufacturers."

In light of the sudden re-impositon of tight money in June, Walter Gordon insisted that "we must not resort to a resumption of tight money and high interest rates whenever the authorities in Ottawa get panicky or our creditors abroad put on the pressure."

> A tight money policy in Canada is ruinous for small businessmen, for farmers, for municipal governments, and for the poorer provinces. It is much less onerous for the larger corporations, the great majority of which are owned or controlled by non-residents of Canada and are usually well financed. Because of this, a tight money policy tends to accelerate the trend under which so much of Canadian industry has been acquired by foreigners.[11]

In contrast to "the dead hand of this benighted policy," Gordon urged the expansion of national credit through a municipal development fund, and consistency and moderation rather than abrupt changes in interest rate policy.

This important speech established the themes for Liberal discussion of economic policy in the months ahead. It left the impression of growing confidence and restraint among the leaders of the Liberal party. The emphasis was on precision and financial responsibility rather than on the exuberant promises of benefits to all which had sometimes dominated the election campaign of the previous spring. The lessons of that campaign and the financial crisis had made Walter Gordon more cautious and specific in his economic prescriptions. His general diagnosis had not changed, but the evidence of a critical electorate and the real likelihood of approaching power pointed to a measured withdrawal from the exposed positions of June. A few weeks later Gordon acknowledged in another speech that, in the June campaign,

> We were criticized and rightly so because the program was not pinpointed on relatively few items and wasn't explained. . . . We did not tell the people how we would pay for the program.[12]

The major themes now to be emphasized were those long advocated by Walter Gordon for the creation of an autonomous national economic community whose goals and priorities could be set within the country under the leadership and stimulus of the federal government.

Parliament at last reassembled on September 27. Walter Gordon was puzzled that Lester Pearson made no formal move to name him financial critic for the official Opposition; but with the encouragement of his colleagues Gordon gradually assumed that role in practice. He noticed also that there was muted conflict or misunderstanding among the leaders of the party about the appropriate parliamentary tactics to be used against the demoralized government. Gordon and some of the newly elected members wished to maintain the initiative by challenging the government as often as possible in the House, in the hope of an early defeat and another general election. Gerald Waring reported in September that Walter Gordon had never ceased campaigning since June 18, "in line with Liberal strategy of seeking to overturn the Diefenbaker government in the Commons with (hopefully) a Pearson government as a Christmas present for the nation."[13] But Gordon's aggressiveness was tempered by the somewhat greater caution of Pearson's veteran associates on the front bench, Paul Martin and J. W. Pickersgill. They were wary about the public response to an unrelenting Liberal offensive and the prospect of an early election.

The outcome was a Pearsonian compromise: while Gordon and Pearson were outspoken in their attacks on the government, the Liberal party was reluctant to seek voting alliances with the other Opposition parties which threatened to defeat the government. They were assisted in this by the greater reluctance of the New Democratic and Social Credit parties to face an early dissolution. On one non-confidence amendment on November 5, the Liberal party did support Social Credit in a determined effort to outvote the government. (While Gordon and Paul Martin favoured this step unhesitatingly, Lester Pearson agreed only reluctantly, out of his embarrassment at voting for a Social Credit monetary resolution.)[14] The closeness of the vote (121-113) revealed the government's precarious hold on office; but on the main vote that followed Social Credit sustained the government against the combined Liberal-NDP opposition. For the remainder of the autumn session, the Opposition parties avoided putting the life of the government in danger. The result of this disinclination to force the government to the wall, in the opinion of one partisan observer, was that the Liberal parliamentary party did not coalesce as an effective alternative government during the first session of the new Parliament.[15]

The relatively passive stance of the Opposition left the Diefenbaker government to disintegrate according to its own rules of chaos. Donald

Fleming had been replaced as Minister of Finance by George Nowlan, and Wallace McCutcheon had entered the Cabinet as Minister without portfolio in August;[16] but such cosmetic attempts to bolster the government's reputation had not resulted in any greater initiative or signs of self-confidence in the Cabinet. (Nowlan and McCutcheon were soon, in fact, leading members of the conspiracy to replace the Prime Minister, which gained momentum behind the scenes during the autumn.) The speech from the throne offered no inspiration to the Conservative party or the nation.[17] Walter Gordon commented drily:

> It was expected that the throne speech would contain an outline of a long-term constructive program for dealing with our country's basic problems. It did not do so. Instead we were treated to a rag bag collection of odds and ends, including a few items plucked at random from the Liberal Party program and two proposals made nearly six years ago by a royal commission of which I had the honour to be chairman. With these exceptions, the throne speech was a barren document.[18]

For two months the House of Commons, meeting in an atmosphere of increasing irascibility and frustration, received little government legislation to deal with. On December 8, 1962 the *Globe and Mail* noted that while "the Liberals have certainly wasted a great deal of time with their frantic efforts to harass and defeat the government, the government cannot claim that its plans have been frustrated because it has given no evidence of having any real plans. . . . It is becoming increasingly difficult to escape the impression that the government is deliberately holding back on important and controversial legislation for fear of suffering defeat in the Commons."[19] In December the House again granted interim supply, which now covered ten months of the fiscal year out of twelve, in default of adoption of the Estimates. The immobility which had characterized the government since the year began had now hardened into a state of desperate inactivity. Walter Gordon commented on December 14:

> Because of the lack of a long-term program, the absence of a budget, the obvious uncertainty about the length of time the government will be able to survive and the lack of leadership by the Prime Minister, members of all parties are feeling frustrated and, at times, irritated and annoyed.
> We're wasting our time.[20]

The divisions within the Cabinet grew deeper and more public; it was evident that a point of collapse was approaching. By the end of the fall session, the situation clearly called for an aggressive response by the Liberal Opposition on the brink of achieving power. As Walter Gordon had believed all through the autumn, the moment had to be seized. There was little doubt now that the moment was imminent. Precisely how it would be seized remained the prerogative, above all, of the leader of the Opposition.

Lester Pearson's self-assurance in the face of the government's weakness was manifest throughout the session. It was revealed most positively in his speech on French Canada in the House on December 17. Walter Gordon believed that in this speech Pearson revealed himself to be "the first English-speaking politician to have some understanding of what was going on in the Province of Quebec."[21] In it Pearson suggested that English Canada and French Canada had never viewed Confederation in the same way. While French Canadians considered that the union had created "a bilingual and bicultural nation" involving partnership rather than domination, most English Canadians assumed it meant "that, for all practical purposes, there would be an English-speaking Canada with a bilingual Quebec. What is called the "French fact" was to be provincial only."[22] Now that French Canadians were actively asserting their conception of the union, its successful maintenance depended upon the generosity and liberal spirit of the English-speaking majority. "Are we prepared," he asked, "not only to accept those long-term objectives of partnership but, perhaps more important and more difficult for us, to take immediate and concrete steps to achieve them?"[23] In January Prime Minister Diefenbaker had rejected the proposal of André Laurendeau, the editor of Le Devoir, for a major royal commission on French-English relations in Canada; now Pearson concluded his speech by endorsing that recommendation. The speech was greeted with enthusiasm on all sides in Quebec. Laurendeau responded that he could recall no English Canadian statesman in the twentieth century who had spoken so explicitly and firmly on the subject.[24] Mr. Pearson had chosen an occasion of mounting nationalist sentiment in Quebec to display his awareness of French Canada's evolution and his sympathy for her aspirations. By doing so he challenged John Diefenbaker's apparent indifference to the situation, and shrewdly reinforced the Liberal party's claim to Quebec's allegiance in the next campaign. The speech reflected the strong influence of Pearson's closest French-speaking adviser, Maurice Lamontagne. It established an optimistic and simple framework for the party's approach to the emerging crisis of French

Canada. If English Canadians would demonstrate their largeness of spirit, Mr. Pearson seemed to promise, French Canadians would respond by committing themselves wholeheartedly to the Canadian partnership. In the short term, at least, the statement was likely to pay dividends to the party in the areas most sympathetic to the Liberal message. It revealed sensitivity and a desire for action, and it was demonstrably the product of goodwill. The element of wishful thinking which it contained was consistent with the liberal view of history, and aroused no comment.[25]

Early in January, 1963 Walter Gordon visited Saskatoon and Winnipeg for campaign meetings with party organizers. He was buoyed up by the most recent Gallup poll results, which showed a ten percent gain in Liberal support since June 18, 1962 (from thirty-seven percent to forty-seven percent), a five percent loss in Progressive Conservative support (from thirty-seven percent to thirty-two percent) and a four percent loss in the popularity of the New Democratic Party (from fourteen percent to ten percent). "It seemed clear from this poll," wrote Gordon, "not only that the Tories would lose, if an election were held at this time, but that the Liberals should be able to win an over-all majority."[26] Gordon believed that the government was boxed in and vulnerable, and wondered aloud whether Mr. Diefenbaker would wish to meet Parliament again. He suggested that the Prime Minister might request a dissolution in the coming week, and made clear that the Liberal party was now eager to confront the government wherever Mr. Diefenbaker might choose, in the House or on the hustings.[27]

The last crisis of the administration had finally matured. Its seeds were planted in 1959 and 1960, when the government had undertaken to equip Canadian forces at home and in Europe with four weapons designed to carry nuclear warheads.[28] By late spring in 1963 this whole range of weapons would be in the hands of Canadian troops; but the government had not yet concluded formal control agreements with the United States to arm them. It had, on the contrary, temporized over the ultimate decision as long as some of the weapons were not actually in its hands; and as long, it appeared, as public division in Canada, and American tolerance, permitted it to hesitate.[29] During 1962 the Prime Minister seemed to take a position on the question which was militarily perverse, but politically understandable. Peyton Lyon commented:

Almost everyone agreed that to fight a nuclear war would be the ultimate disaster – that nuclear weapons existed to deter not only aggression but their own use. Mr. Diefenbaker, however, refused to contemplate nuclear arms in Canadian hands when they might

115

serve to deter, and he expected his countrymen to be comforted by the assurance that, after deterrence had failed, their soldiers would take possession of nuclear weapons in time to join in the fray.[30]

As delivery of the remaining weapons approached, the pressures for a clear-cut decision by the Cabinet – from its own members, the press, the Opposition, and privately from NATO, the American administration and the Canadian armed forces – intensified.

The Prime Minister's role of less than complete support for the United States during the Cuban crisis the previous November had catapulted the defence question to the forefront of political discussion in Canada. Until then, the Liberal position on nuclear arms had been that defined by the 1961 party rally: no nuclear weapons for Canadian forces in NORAD, and "the possibility of nuclear arms for the Canadians in Europe if requested by the NATO Council; if they were solely for "defensive, tactical use" against forces similarly armed; and if they were subject to NATO rather than national control."[31] This position was slightly amended in the direction of greater obscurity during the 1962 campaign, when the question of nuclear weapons did not feature as a matter of prominent debate. (*La Presse* referred to the Liberal position in 1962 as "not necessarily nuclear arms but nuclear arms if necessary.")[32] Mr. Pearson's immediate reaction to the Cuban crisis was to urge a re-examination of NATO nuclear strategy, possibly leading to a nuclear-free zone in central Europe; and then to argue that Canada should end its indecision either by negotiating itself out of its nuclear commitments in NORAD or by accepting them without ambiguity. He had not yet taken a firm position on the problem, but was giving it renewed attention and believed that a decision of some kind was necessary and opportune. In November, the party's defence critic, Paul Hellyer, attended the meetings of the NATO parliamentary association in Paris, and carried out his own review of Canadian weapons policy at Canadian bases in Europe and in a private interview with the NATO commander, General Lauris Norstad.[33] On his return, Hellyer presented a memorandum to Lester Pearson arguing for a clear Liberal commitment to accept nuclear arms for Canada's NATO and NORAD forces.[34] Publicly, he stated that "Canada should sign a bilateral agreement with the United States which will permit the supply of atomic weapons to Canadian forces as required."[35] Pearson indicated that for the time being Hellyer had gone beyond party policy, which was stated in the House of Commons by Charles Drury on December 14: "we must either forthwith and now honour these undertakings; or ... in the fullest consultation with our partners, initiate alternatives which are satisfactory not only to us but to them."[36]

While the Prime Minister discovered further justifications for indecision in the Nassau conference with President Kennedy and Prime Minister Macmillan just before Christmas, Lester Pearson continued to ponder his own position over the holiday. The dissatisfaction of the NATO military command with the Canadian posture, which had been conveyed privately to Paul Hellyer in November, was exhibited publicly on January 3, 1963. General Norstad, on his retiring visit to Ottawa, declared under persistent questioning at a press conference that in his view Canada had indeed neglected her NATO commitment to accept tactical nuclear weapons.[37] This intervention by an American serving officer brought the controversy close to the point of explosion. While the debate raged, Lester Pearson departed for a private visit to New York City, taking with him Hellyer's memorandum and the transcript of Norstad's press conference.[38] He returned from New York to address the York-Scarborough Liberal Association at the Canadiana Motor Hotel in Toronto on January 12, 1963.[39]

Lester Pearson made his own decisive contribution to the arms controversy without informing his closest colleagues in the Liberal party what he intended to say. On the day after Walter Gordon told a Liberal audience in Saskatoon that "the most important thing for Canada now with regard to her defence policy ... particularly as it concerned recent statements by retired NATO commander General Lauris Norstad on Canada's commitments to NATO, was to find out exactly what those commitments were,"[40] Pearson announced his firm personal conclusions about those commitments:

> ... both in NATO and in continental defence, the Canadian government has accepted commitments for Canada in continental and collective defence which can only be carried out by Canadian forces if nuclear warheads are available. Since then, however, the government has refused to make the decision, either to alter the commitments or accept the warheads. Those are the facts about our nuclear defence situation today. If there were any doubt about those facts, that doubt was removed the other day by a man who should know, General Norstad, the man who for many years was supreme NATO commander.
>
> As a Canadian, I am ashamed if we accept commitments and then refuse to discharge them. In acting thus, we deceive ourselves, we let our armed forces down, and betray our allies. As I understand international affairs, and I think it is the understanding of all Canadians, when you make, and continue to accept commitments, you carry them out. If we had not done so in the past, Canada would not have achieved a position of respect and influence in the world.

... What should the Canadian government do in these circumstances? It should end at once its evasion of responsibility, and put itself in a position to discharge the commitments it has already accepted for Canada. It can only do this by accepting nuclear warheads for those defensive tactical weapons which cannot effectively be used without them, but which we have agreed to use. An agreement with the United States for this purpose would have to be negotiated. This would be similar to those already signed by the U.S. government with the United Kingdom and other NATO countries to provide for joint control of the use of the weapons, if and when they are accepted. In such an agreement, a U.S. finger would be on the trigger; but a Canadian finger would be on the safety catch.[41]

Mr. Pearson sought to strengthen his case with three complementary recommendations: Canada should "support any move for genuine collective control of all NATO tactical nuclear weapons"; she should "not contribute to the strategic, nuclear deterrent" and should "oppose any additional independent national nuclear forces"; and perhaps most important (because it appeared to promise eventual release from the commitment):

The government should re-examine at once the whole basis of Canadian defence policy. In particular, it should discuss with the United States and with NATO a role for Canada in continental and collective defence which would be more realistic and effective for Canada than the present one. This examination would be concerned, among other things, with the necessity of building up NATO's conventional forces and the part Canada could play in this. However, until the present role is changed, a new Liberal government would put Canada's armed services in the position to discharge fully commitments undertaken for Canada by its predecessor.[42]

The speech did not go very far beyond the position already taken by the Liberal party. But its language was strong – even hyperbolic – and it was intended as a dramatic step away from ambiguity. In the atmosphere of uncertainty and tension created by the government's procrastination, the speech created a sensation. As he began, Mr. Pearson reaffirmed his hope that the parties would "try to take defence and foreign affairs out of the arena of party controversy." That was lip-service uttered by a politician who was now, almost for the first time, performing with a confident and professional partisan instinct.

He was attacking the Prime Minister at his most vulnerable point, fully expecting to increase the government's disarray. For that substantial gain, he judged that a certain loss could be borne. Pearson "knew that he had become identified with the opponents of acquisition by Canada, and that a change in his position would provoke bitter recrimination. On the other hand, as the leader of a political party, he was naturally interested in the report of the Gallup poll that fifty-four percent of the Canadian population favoured nuclear weapons for their armed forces, while only thirty-two percent were opposed."[43] His statement, he knew, would reassure Canada's NATO partners; it would probably, on balance, please the electorate; and it would help to precipitate the final eruptions within the Conservative Cabinet and caucus. It was a perfect issue for exploitation in the House of Commons. Mr. Pearson seized the opportunity. "That," he said, "was when I really became a politician."[44]

For his colleagues who had not been warned of the speech in advance, some quick footwork was necessary. In Winnipeg, where Walter Gordon had gone that day to address the annual meeting of the Manitoba Liberal Association, the Young Liberals "had just passed a resolution opposing the acceptance of nuclear arms; this had to be revised and lamely resubmitted later in the day."[45] In the evening, Gordon departed from his prepared text before a banquet audience of more than 500 persons to defend Mr. Pearson's initiative with some notable qualifications. He began by noting that Pearson had urged that "Canada's defence policy should be based on the industrial structure of our economy and that it was time we started spending our defence dollars wisely," and added "that it should not be allowed to become either fixed or frozen ... if Canada had commitments to its allies – commitments our allies counted on – then we must honour these commitments. It would be shameful to do otherwise." But this "does not mean that we are committed to any one course indefinitely."[46]

Gordon's hedging reflected his "considerable dejection" at both the change in Pearson's position and the manner of accomplishing it. He doubted the validity of a distinction between tactical and strategic nuclear weapons, and therefore stood by the position of the 1961 Liberal rally which had, he believed, "come out strongly against the use of nuclear weapons":

> ... it seemed to me at the time, and still does, that Canada should give an example by refusing to manufacture, control, or use nuclear weapons of any kind. If that means qualifying our position under the NATO or NORAD treaties, we should do so.[47]

The leader's independent action was equally unsettling. "Some of us," wrote Gordon, "did not believe the leader of the party had the right, or should have the right, to reverse this policy unilaterally."[48]

> ... I was seriously disturbed to think that he would make a decision of this magnitude without consulting his closest friends and colleagues in the party. When I spoke to him about this, he told me he had been struggling with the problem for some time and had only made up his mind about it a few days before the Scarborough speech while on a visit to New York. He seemed to be genuinely sorry he had not spoken to some of us beforehand, and stressed his intention to have a thorough review made of Canada's defence policy if a Liberal government was elected, the clear implication being that we would forego the use of nuclear weapons at that time. In the meantime, he felt we had made definite commitments and should live up to them.[49]

For Walter Gordon the rationale for coming to terms with the decision was the prospect of a defence review and a reversal of policy. For others no accommodation was acceptable. Jean Marchand and Pierre Elliott Trudeau, who were being wooed by the Quebec wing of the Liberal party as potential federal candidates, denounced Mr. Pearson and refused to consider nomination in 1963. A representative of the nuclear disarmament movement accused Mr. Pearson of a "tragic betrayal" of his reputation, and others urged that his Nobel peace prize should be revoked.

Politically these criticisms were embarrassing; but Lester Pearson was not troubled, as some of his critics were, by any naive judgment of the moral situation. Canada had long before accepted the American nuclear deterrent as the cornerstone of its defence policy, and supplied uranium for the making of American nuclear bombs.

> To say ... that, on moral grounds, we will not accept any nuclear weapons in any circumstances is dishonest and hypocritical unless we are at the same time willing to withdraw from NATO and refuse to export, to anyone, uranium for military defence purposes.
> The fact is that the argument for or against nuclear weapons for Canada is a political not a moral one.[50]

The speech placed the Liberal party firmly in opposition to the Prime Minister's indecision on nuclear weapons. But the pledge to re-examine Canada's obligations was a concession to those in the party, like Walter Gordon, who believed that the more sensible international role for Canada was a non-nuclear one. Five days later, in another speech, Pearson gave greater emphasis to this side of his policy. The effect, however, seemed to be to obscure the apparent clarity of his Scarborough statement.

> The party managers reported that the valuable new image of a decisive Pearson was already being blurred. After trying for a while to explain the time considerations involved in his approach, Mr. Pearson was persuaded to take the easier course of simply demanding that Canada accept its nuclear obligations – period.[51]

The party's long-term policy was thus put into doubt. For Walter Gordon the pledge to reassess the nuclear commitment remained because it had been made; for Paul Hellyer and Lester Pearson, the pledge retained decreasing force as it gradually disappeared from their speeches. The Toronto *Star* commented that "Mr. Pearson and his colleagues ... are shifting the party's position on the issue to what appears to be a clear-cut policy in favour of nuclear arms. Whatever one may think about the party's pro-nuclear stand ... it is clearer than the position Mr. Pearson enunciated last month."[52]

Anything the Opposition could do to undermine public confidence in the government brought the Cabinet nearer to open division and the prospect of defeat in the House. The issues in the nuclear weapons debate were relatively complex, and therefore lent themselves to dramatic oversimplification. Mr. Pearson's initiative had focussed on the logical conclusion of the government's weapons policy; the Cabinet rebels who shared Mr. Pearson's logic were nudged closer to an attempted coup, and Social Credit found the justification of its voting support for a disintegrating government more difficult. Over the next three weeks the momentum of the crisis built up, through the annual meeting of the Progressive Conservative Association and the reopening of Parliament. Before the House of Commons on January 25, the Prime Minister once more avoided clarifying his position, in what Peyton Lyon described as "one of the most baffling and controversial speeches to be found in the parliamentary record."[53] Mr. Diefenbaker's case for delay was that the Canadian decision on nuclear arms should await the policy review to be undertaken at the NATO Council meeting in May. His speech prompted clarifications from the Minister of National Defence and the United States Department of State, and these, in turn, led to emotional scenes in Cabinet over the weekend.

A Liberal motion of non-confidence in the government's defence policy was introduced by Lester Pearson on February 4, setting the stage for two more days of debate which would culminate in a vote on the evening of February 5. When it was unable to secure the guarantees of good conduct it sought from Mr. Diefenbaker, the Social Credit party determined to vote with the Liberal and New Democratic parties to defeat the government. The Prime Minister's speech was full of passionate intensity, but his pride and confusion prevented the concessions of policy that might, if made in time, have saved his administration. Shortly before 9:00 P.M. on the evening of February 5, 1963 the government was defeated by 142 votes to 111 on two motions of non-confidence. "Across the country," wrote John Saywell, "there was almost universal relief that, after agonizing death throes, a paralyzed Parliament and a paralyzed government had been put out of its [sic] misery."[54]

This was not, as the commentators recognized, Lester Pearson's triumph so much as John Diefenbaker's disaster. But Pearson had accurately judged the situation, and contributed what he could to the debacle. He had chosen the issue and the occasion for the challenge, and the challenge had succeeded. Here was the immediate political justification for the Scarborough speech. The government and his own party were unexpectedly in the presence of a resourceful politician.

While the Cabinet indulged its taste for melodrama in a constantly surprising series of attempted coups, resignations and reconciliations ("Best caucus we've ever had ... we're hitting the road and we'll lick hell out of the Grits," said George Hees, arm-in-arm with John Diefenbaker on the day of parliamentary dissolution, three days before his resignation from the Cabinet.),[55] the Liberal party intensified its campaign preparations. Walter Gordon had remained chairman of the National Campaign Committee, and with Keith Davey he had organized the party's timetable "on the assumption that the next election would be held at the end of March, 1963."[56] Once again fortune and the Prime Minister obliged: polling day was announced for April 8.

> Liberals everywhere were cheerful and optimistic, and this was particularly true in Ontario. The National Campaign Committee was working well, and the whole organization under Keith Davey was in good shape and becoming more competent and professional all the time. Everyone was confident that, after the next round, the Liberals under Mike Pearson would be called upon to form the government.[57]

Gordon was encouraged by the nomination of more promising Liberal candidates, among them Guy Favreau, René Tremblay and Jean-Luc Pepin in Quebec, J. J. Greene in Ontario, Sidney Buckwold in Saskatchewan, Harry Hays in Alberta, and Tom Kent in British Columbia. Favreau, especially, was counted on to refresh the party in Quebec. He was, in Gordon's view,

> . . . a lovable, warm-hearted, gregarious man with an excellent legal mind. Unfortunately, he was not familiar with politics or with the key political personalities in Quebec. However, Pearson thought he would soon overcome any handicaps of this nature and obviously had him in mind as a replacement for Lionel Chevrier as Quebec leader, and perhaps eventually as his own successor.[58]

Tom Kent had been chosen as the Liberal candidate in Burnaby Coquitlam, against the sitting member and leader of the New Democratic Party, T. C. Douglas. He therefore left Pearson's office shortly after the campaign began, and succeeded in pinning Douglas down in his own constituency for much of the campaign.

The general election campaign of February, March and April, 1963 was an extension of the 1962 campaign, both simplified and complicated by the addition of the nuclear arms controversy. For the Prime Minister the parliamentary defeat, the divisions in his Cabinet, the interventions of General Norstad and the State Department, and the commitment of Lester Pearson to accept nuclear arms for Canada, all contributed to his self-image as the harassed victim of conspiracy. The Chief did what he could to turn his accumulating misfortunes to advantage on the hustings; the prominence and apparent simplicity of the nuclear issue made it possible for him to escape discussion of economic questions, which could not be so easily simplified. "No Prime Minister," said Murray Beck, "has ever discussed the issues less meaningfully than Diefenbaker did in 1963."[59] The financial interests of Bay Street, the Canadian press, the Prime Minister's old enemies in the Conservative party, the American government and periodical press, and the Liberal party could be thrown together indiscriminately into a nefarious alliance, described as "them," which was out to deprive John Diefenbaker of power and ordinary Canadians of their independence and dignity.

But the Prime Minister was also constrained by the contradictions of his outlook. While observers and critics watched carefully for and condemned the signs of anti-Americanism in his campaign, the Prime Minister never fully justified their expectations. Because he remained a faithful advocate of the western alliance and American leadership, he could not carry his analysis to the point of reassessing Canada's intimate relationship with the United States. For him there could never be any question of Canadian withdrawal from NATO, NORAD or the Defence Production Sharing Agreements. His point of challenge thus remained essentially trivial: he objected not to the substance of arrangements with the United States but to the rudeness and imperiousness of the intrusions into Canadian policy-making by General Norstad, the State Department, and *Newsweek* magazine, and to the implied links that these instances revealed between the policies of Lester Pearson and President Kennedy. John Diefenbaker would not, or could not, debate the deeper implications of the crisis, and so left his own case inconclusive. The Liberal party, as a result, did not have to elaborate its stance, which remained almost as obscure and self-contradictory as that of the Prime Minister.

Lou Harris's surveys told Keith Davey and Walter Gordon that defence policy was not the main issue in the contest.[60] The party had carefully planned its campaign as a sequel to 1962, and this involved continuing concentration on the program for economic revival.

> The issues concerning the public were much the same in the April, 1963 election as they had been in June, 1962. Unemployment and the need to do something about it was the number one question, according to our surveys of public opinion. As usual, people were complaining about high prices. They wanted more to be done for older people in terms of pensions. There was more concern about foreign policy and the question of nuclear arms than there had been in 1962, but it was not nearly as important to the voters as questions of domestic policy.[61]

Walter Gordon underplayed the issue of nuclear arms and attempted to make the best of it as an example of Mr. Pearson's decisiveness. "Walter Gordon: Liberal Chief Has Courage to Take Stand," read the *Globe and Mail's* headline reporting a speech by the campaign chairman in Chatham, Ontario on February 28.

> Walter Gordon, former member of Parliament for Davenport, said last night that Canadians should have a feeling of relief that there is one leader in public life capable of making decisions regardless of their political consequences.[62]

Five days later, under the headline " 'Boost in Economy is The Thing, A-Arms Overblown' – Key Liberal," the Montreal *Gazette* introduced its account of Gordon's visit to Montreal.

The much-publicized issue of nuclear weapons – to have or not to have – does not really stir much interest in the minds of Canadian citizens, a Liberal shadow cabinet member theorized yesterday.

"The defence issue is not one an ordinary citizen worries too much about," said economist Walter Gordon at a press conference yesterday morning. "It's the job of the Prime Minister to make decisions about defence."

"With the assistance of his Cabinet ministers," he hastily added.

As for the Liberal party defence policies, he felt Mr. Pearson has received "a tremendous vote of confidence on the line he has taken."

At the half-hour conference, he ranged over a variety of election issues, with an emphasis on this country's economic problems and his party's solutions.[63]

There was a subtly defensive tone in these statements, which implied a fear that Mr. Diefenbaker had the edge in public discussion of this sensitive issue. The inspired initiative that had precipitated the government's defeat in the House did not promise such obvious benefits to the Liberal party on the hustings. Walter Gordon noted that:

> ... while according to our surveys early in the election campaign approximately three out of five people in Ontario and Quebec thought the Diefenbaker policy on nuclear arms was wrong, opinion at the end was about equally divided.[64]

This slide away from Mr. Pearson's position on nuclear arms was assisted by the NDP which, on most other issues, tended to reinforce rather than undermine the Liberal critique of Mr. Diefenbaker's government. The party emphasized its unambiguous opposition to Canada's acceptance of nuclear arms. Mr. Douglas held that "the election is, first of all, a referendum of the Canadian people on the question of nuclear warheads."[65] The NDP leader pressed the logic of the Liberal position to indelicate lengths.

At Saskatoon (March 10) he charged Mr. Pearson with converting the Liberal party into an American satellite: "If Mr. Pearson wishes to challenge this proposition, I suggest that he show his good faith by revealing to the Canadian public the magnitude of the contributions to the Liberal war chest in this election by American-owned mines, American-owned pulp and paper companies and other American-owned corporations." And to 8,500 applauding supporters in Vancouver on April 3 he stated bluntly that Liberal policies were "made in the United States" and that when one country has a heavy stake in another "it must begin to make sure that it is going to get a government elected that is friendly so that it can go on collecting its pound of flesh."[66]

In Quebec, where the Liberal party counted above all on securing its majority, the nuclear controversy had peculiarly embarrassing consequences. Both *La Presse* and *Le Devoir* supported the New Democratic Party, and there was bitter denunciation of Mr. Pearson from union leaders and intellectuals. The invective reached its peak in the April issue of *Cité Libre*. Pierre Elliott Trudeau explained cynically, in terms close to those used by Mr. Diefenbaker, that John Kennedy's clique was determined to see Diefenbaker out and Pearson in.

> You think I dramatize? But how do you think politics work? Do you think that General Norstad, the former supreme commander of allied forces in Europe, came to Ottawa as a tourist on January 3 to call publicly on the Canadian government to respect its commitments? Do you think it was by chance that Mr. Pearson, in his speech of January 12, was able to quote the authority of General Norstad? Do you think it was inadvertent that, on January 30, the State Department gave a statement to journalists reinforcing Mr. Pearson's claims and crudely accusing Mr. Diefenbaker of lying? You think it was by chance that this press release provided the leader of the Opposition with the arguments he used abundantly in his parliamentary speech on January 31? You believe that it was coincidence that this series of events ended with the fall of the government on February 5?
> But why do you think that the United States should treat Canada differently from Guatemala, when reason of state requires it and circumstances permit? . . . [67]

The dismay in Montreal at Pearson's speech on nuclear weapons seemed to temper Jean Lesage's enthusiasm for the federal party. He did not enter wholeheartedly into the campaign until mid-March, and Walter Gordon considered that this hesitation may have been fatal.

It is tempting to speculate that if he had come out for Pearson earlier, it might have made the difference of the four additional seats needed for an over-all majority.[68]

The complications created for the party by its nuclear weapons policy were electoral, and possibly also moral and financial. They were bound to be particularly awkward for Walter Gordon, the nationalist, whose chief object in politics was to avoid the entanglements with American policy which opponents now accused the Liberal party of embracing. The circumstantial evidence offered some support to the Conservative and NDP case that there was a coordinated campaign from abroad to force a policy and a government upon Canada – whatever the truth might be behind the surface of events.

The decision to support the acquisition of nuclear arms was – apart from maintaining the existing position of uncertainty – the easiest and most natural among the alternatives facing Mr. Pearson. If he had renounced nuclear weapons and urged negotiations to relieve Canada of her obligations, he would have offended the internationalists in his party and the American administration. There might have been a time, shortly after John Kennedy assumed office in 1961, when Canada could have retreated from a nuclear role without American disfavour. But in January, 1963 Pearson knew that impatience in Washington had gone too far for that. His experience and predisposition led him, in that circumstance, to seek reconciliation rather than conflict with the United States. Because this choice also promised a parliamentary advantage, Pearson was inclined to underestimate the broader political effects. If he had made the opposite decision, or made none at all, he might not have provoked the government's defeat in the House on February 5; but it would probably have fallen soon after on some other issue. He would have avoided the electoral difficulties which his pro-nuclear stance created for the Liberal party. If he had done nothing, he would have lost the considerable advantage of appearing to be decisive; if he had rejected nuclear arms, on the other hand, he would have gained as much admiration for decisiveness as he did by accepting them.

An outright rejection of nuclear arms would have been a striking declaration of the Liberal party's independence. It would have demonstrated in the most tangible way that on a central matter of Canadian-American relations, Lester Pearson could challenge American expectations. It would have offended President Kennedy and diminished the prospect for an easy return to good relations with the U.S. administration. It would have defied the pressures of major American subsidiary companies in Canada for the acceptance of nuclear weapons, and might thus have had some effect on the party's fund-raising efforts. It would have shaken the complacent assumption, which still dominated the party's thoughts, that the normal condition of Canadian-American relations was one of amity and virtually automatic recognition of common interest. Lester Pearson had long before warned that this assumption was unwarranted; but he had never faced so hard a challenge.

Mr. Pearson was not inclined to confront the situation in this way. All suggestion of conspiracy or collusion aside, the leader's choice did not augur well for Walter Gordon's nationalist program. It created expectations in Canada and the United States that a Pearson government would not pursue an independent policy to the point of major disagreement. It strengthened the confidence of those in the party who could not imagine an independent Canadian policy. It was the kind of international commitment which carried with it a whole complex of unspoken implications, and made future inconsistency more difficult. The tremors of doubt and anxiety which Walter Gordon felt after the Scarborough speech were prophetic. On the surface the party's adherence to his nationalist program was unchanged; but whatever might now be said in reassurance, beneath the surface Mr. Pearson's speech had shaken the forces in the Liberal party into a new balance which weighed heavily against nationalism. It is perhaps understandable that, rather than allowing these ominous considerations to become explicit, Lester Pearson preferred to keep his own counsel in reaching his decision. The bitterest irony of the situation was that he may have lost the prospect of a parliamentary majority by making the choice he did without consultation.[69]

The Liberal election campaign had begun in optimism, with the focus in Quebec on the party's promise to admit French Canadians to full partnership in the union, and in the whole of Canada to restore prosperity, growth and a sense of direction to the economy. The party program and the speeches of the party leaders reflected greater concentration than in 1962 upon the discontents of Quebec and the Atlantic provinces, the two regions where a Liberal majority might be made up. And in counterpoint to the charges about Liberal subservience to American direction on nuclear weapons, Walter Gordon wrote and spoke more prominently in the 1963 campaign than he had in 1962 about his proposals for Canadian economic independence from the United States.[70]

Once more, John Diefenbaker's energy and rhetoric set the tone of the campaign. While his exuberant whistle-stopping progress rejuvenated the Prime Minister, the distasteful effort of electioneering drained Lester Pearson as it had in previous campaigns. The chemistry of the situation was soon demonstrated in the public opinion polls. National support for the Conservative party held steady at thirty-two percent from January to April, NDP support grew from ten percent to fourteen percent, but Liberal allegiance fell from forty-seven percent in January to forty-one percent in March and April.

Earlier in the campaign, out of the party's impatience with John Diefenbaker's casual attitude to fact, Walter Gordon and Lester Pearson had accepted Keith Davey's light-hearted recommendation for a 'Truth Squad' which would trail the Prime Minister and issue balancing statements to counter his distortions and exaggerations. This bit of flummery expired almost at birth and in full public display under the Prime Minister's withering ridicule. Other minor pieces of stage whimsy proved similarly imprudent; but the Liberal managers nevertheless maintained their belief in the electoral value of such mass advertising techniques. When the Liberal campaign began to flounder, they looked more seriously at the kind of device which might restore the party's initiative.

> Quite frankly, we were worried. Something drastic was needed to sharpen up the Liberals' campaign during the last two weeks before election day or we would lose the great opportunity we had been hoping and working for during the previous five years.
>
> In mid-March, Keith Davey, Royce Frith, and Dan Lang met in my office in Toronto to discuss what could be done. . . . And we felt we must convince the public that we knew what had to be done and how we planned to go about it if we were elected to form the government on April 8. To be successful, this had to be presented in simple terms and with conviction. We decided – it was Keith's suggestion – to recommend that in the last two weeks Pearson should stress in specific and unqualified language what a Liberal government would plan to do about domestic issues in its first one hundred days in office. We listed ten topics to be dealt with in ten short, separate speeches during the last two weeks of the campaign, all encompassed in the theme of "one hundred days of decision."[71]

Gordon arranged to meet Pearson in Halifax on March 21. He found both Lester and Maryon Pearson "tired and dispirited" in their suite at the Nova Scotian Hotel.

> Mike was fed up with campaigning, and I had some difficulty in persuading him that a new approach was imperative for the next and last two weeks if he was not to be defeated. I said that even if the present trend were checked and then reversed, he could no longer hope for a clear majority. This was a bitter blow to him after

working so hard for five years on the reorganization of the Liberal party, and I doubt if he believed me. He had been so sure the election was in the bag.[72]

Eventually Gordon interested the leader in the principle of a new initiative; but Pearson objected to the slogan "one hundred days of decision" – because it might recall Napoleon's hundred days before his defeat at Waterloo. Gordon countered that the allusion was little known in Canada, and that the promise might instead bring to mind the hundred days of action following Franklin D. Roosevelt's inauguration as president in 1933. "Pearson, however, as an old history professor, was adamant." He was also reluctant to devote his last speeches to domestic affairs. In response Gordon "showed him the latest opinion surveys which indicated that unemployment and the need to do something about it was the issue that the public was most concerned about. Foreign policy and the question of nuclear arms were far down the list of issues in terms of the public's interest."[73]

Pearson finally acceded to the persuasion of his campaign chairman, but insisted that the promise of "one hundred days of decision" had to be altered.

He called me after I had returned to Toronto to say he had decided to make it "sixty days of decision," a major reduction in the time in which we were committing ourselves to act on a variety of issues. We were all to regret this when soon afterwards Pearson was called upon to form a Liberal government.[74]

Gordon believed, however, that the leader's spirits had revived, although he was uncertain how long this might last.

He was very tired and beginning to show his age. And the uncertainty about the outcome of the election . . . was making him irritable and nervous.[75]

Pearson entered the last two weeks of the campaign in "an all-out quest for striking national headlines and the crucial urban vote"[76] at Hamilton on Monday, March 25. As he had agreed, he promised that

. . . in the first sixty days . . . his government would do more to clean up "the existing mess in Canada" than any administration since Confederation.[77]

The next night he was in Kingston, then Regina, then Edmonton, then Victoria, repeating the pledge and calling for stable government, portable old age pensions, a national health scheme, and renewed economic expansion. Gordon and Davey were pleased by the favourable public response.

> He did depart from the theme once or twice and he was less specific in his policy statements than we could have wished, but on the whole he was much more effective during the last two weeks of the campaign than he had been earlier.[78]

Following the Victoria speech on March 29, the Pearsons went into retreat for the weekend at Eaglecrest Lodge on Vancouver Island.

> Keith and I decided I should visit him again mainly to give him encouragement, but also to stress the importance of sticking to the theme we had agreed upon. I flew to Vancouver and then by helicopter to the house on Vancouver Island where the Pearsons were staying. Again, I found an atmosphere of depression, but for a different reason. Pearson was ill with a heavy cold and laryngitis, and was running a high fever. It seemed unlikely that he would be able to continue the campaign. He was in bed with nurses in attendance who had strict orders from the doctor that no one was to see him. However, when he heard I was in the house, he insisted on talking to me. I reported that in the previous week he had managed to put new life in the campaign with the "sixty days of decision" theme. I urged him to continue with this theme if he were able to campaign at all during the final week. I told him I felt better about the prospects than I had done in Halifax the week before, but urged him not to count upon an over-all majority. I said I thought we would win between 125 and 135 seats, but that my own guess was it would be closer to the lower than to the higher number. Pearson said that while he was very tired and was feeling awful, he would go through with his program for the last week if it killed him.[79]

He did so, addressing mass rallies in Vancouver on Monday, Winnipeg on Tuesday, Montreal on Wednesday, and Toronto on Friday, holding closely to the approach agreed upon. In Winnipeg, before a partisan audience of 9,000, he made clear the central role that his Minister of Finance would have to play in the decisive first weeks of a new Liberal administration:

... Pearson promised that within a month he would introduce a budget that included a long-term program for economic expansion, the elimination of unemployment, the reduction of the balance of payments deficits, and a reversal of the trend towards absentee ownership of resources and industries. The four-point program for full employment involved the establishment of a department of industry, a municipal loan fund, a national development corporation, and the expansion of foreign trade.[80]

Meanwhile, after the weekend rendezvous with Lester Pearson at Qualicum, Walter Gordon met the press in Vancouver to discuss his party's electoral prospects. The prediction he offered publicly was no different from that he had given privately; but it was phrased more positively for the sake of the headlines. "We are on the verge of winning an overall majority," he reported.[81] The party expected gains in the Maritimes, Quebec and Ontario which should give it the necessary 133 seats. But no one among the Liberal leadership was now certain of victory. It would have to be squeezed out along the margins of existing party support; there would be no landslide.

The accuracy of this assessment was revealed on the evening of April 8 as the results of the poll flowed in. With 129 seats, the Liberal party registered twenty-nine gains (six in the Maritimes, twelve in Quebec, eight in Ontario, three elsewhere) but remained disappointingly on the verge of a majority, as Gordon had predicted a week before. Progressive Conservative membership in the House fell to ninety-five, and six ministers lost their seats. There was no doubt who had been defeated, but once more the defeat was inconclusive. John Diefenbaker had revealed his tenacious ability to hang on to the core of his support in the prairies, the Maritimes, and rural Ontario. The NDP held steady, and Social Credit remained a barrier to Liberal recovery in rural Quebec.

For reassurance, Walter Gordon turned his comparisons on the debacle of 1958. He reflected later that:

This was a truly remarkable victory for Mike Pearson who, people were saying a short five years before, would never make a politician. He succeeded where most men would have given up because of his many talents, including his courage and determination, his inner strength and sense of humour, his intelligence and ability to keep cool in periods of crisis and because of his charm and persuasiveness in getting new men and women to help him. But not even this could have made success possible in such a short time if Mr.

Diefenbaker had not made so many blunders; he should be credited with an assist in the great Liberal win.[82]

Not everyone would have described the result on April 8 as "a great Liberal win"; but the battle had been long and wearing, and the satisfaction was deserved. A win it certainly was. The Prime Minister hesitated for a few days while the armed forces vote was counted and the Social Credit party burst asunder; and then on April 17 Mr. Diefenbaker offered his resignation to the Governor General. On April 22 Lester Bowles Pearson took office as Prime Minister of Canada.

7   Confidence

The anxieties of the previous weeks disappeared once power had been won. For Walter Gordon, the prospect of office meant the Ministry of Finance, and responsibility for applying the party's economic program. In outline, that program was clear. It remained to be elaborated in detail and applied with the despatch that the electorate had been promised. Gordon and Davey had inspired the commitment to the "days of decision" – one hundred rather than sixty, as it became – in order to emphasize the party's activism and sense of purpose. The determination reflected in that slogan was real, and Walter Gordon expected to begin the government's term with a display of efficient and purposeful activity which would indelibly mark the contrast with the Diefenbaker administration. The slogan sharpened the risks of, and set a limit to, the initial period of challenge. What had always been intended as an active beginning was now bound to become hyperactive.

There was just one moment of doubt about Walter Gordon's role, which he recalled later in a personal memorandum:

> Before the April, 1963 election, Mike asked me – with Maryon present – if I would take the Department of Industry (I'm sure he had C. D. Howe in the back of his mind) with Sharp at Finance. I said no; that if we were to make the kind of changes we said we had in mind I should be in Finance. (Maryon suggested I should take whatever portfolio the "PM" wanted me to take!) This was not raised after the election. I was appointed to Finance without further question. (I would not have joined the Cabinet otherwise.)[1]

Gordon was surprised by this incident, because he had assumed since 1959 that he would take Finance. The suggestion (made "rather casually") that Gordon should lead the new department instead "raised a small doubt in my mind respecting his views about his new government, and the extent of his personal commitment to the policies we had fought for."[2]

But the conversation was forgotten for the moment. The leader's work of Cabinet-making proceeded, and on April 22 the swearing-in ceremony for Prime Minister Pearson and twenty-six ministers took place in the Governor General's bedroom at Rideau Hall, where General Vanier was confined because of a recent heart attack. Among the Prime Minister's veteran colleagues on the Opposition front bench, Paul Martin became Secretary of State for External Affairs, Lionel Chevrier became Minister of Justice, Paul Hellyer took the Ministry of National Defence, J. W. Pickersgill became Secretary of State and Leader of the House of Commons, and George McIlraith became Minister of Transport. The new wave was represented by Gordon in Finance, Guy Favreau in Citizenship and Immigration, Charles M. Drury in Defence Production (and, once the department came into existence in July, Industry), Allan MacEachen in Labour, Judy LaMarsh in National Health and Welfare, Mitchell Sharp in Trade and Commerce, Maurice Lamontagne as President of the Privy Council, and Harry Hays as Minister of Agriculture.[3]

The press congratulated the new Prime Minister for the Cabinet's conventional balance of regions, interests and political views rather than for any surprising appointments, and noted what it saw as an auspicious level of talent in the new administration. "Mr. Pearson looked for a Cabinet of all the talents and no doubt stepped into yesterday's sunshine feeling he had done well," said the Ottawa *Journal*.[4] "Mr. Pearson seems to have chosen well," said the Winnipeg *Free Press*.[5] "Prime Minister Pearson has chosen experience over youth and service over promise. . . . Wherever Mr. Pearson had a choice, he appointed the men he knew and trusted rather than the glamorous rookies," commented the Ottawa *Citizen*.[6] In the Toronto *Star*, John T. McLeod described the ministry unreservedly as "the most impressive array of brains ever assembled in a Canadian Cabinet,"[7] and John Meisel wrote in the *Canadian Forum* that "It is made up of persons of outstanding talent, and whatever other characteristics they display in the next few years, there is every expectation that they will provide an efficient and incisive administration."[8]

But several commentators also noticed a characteristic of the Cabinet which was of special significance for Walter Gordon. John Meisel added:

... the members of the new Cabinet are not only gifted and strong personalities; they have in the past displayed a wide diversity of views. If they are to function smoothly as a team for any length of time, they will have to work out a coherent social and economic philosophy or, if this term is thought unduly to inflate the language, at least a reasonably homogeneous social and political outlook.[9]

The *Free Press* warned that "It will be surprising if there is not criticism of the new Cabinet on the ground that it contains too many of the 'old guard' and too little new blood,"[10] and the Montreal *Star* fulfilled the prediction.

If we are to have the promised "sixty days," if we are to "get the economy moving again," nobody will believe that the old guard will do it. These faithful, loyal time-servers will provide competent administration. Goodness knows they have the experience for that. But for the new, imaginative approach, the breaking of new ground, it will be the new members of the Cabinet who will provide it, or nobody will. It will be Mr. Pearson's task to hold up their hands and – above all – to give them a lead.[11]

Walter Gordon shared the *Star*'s judgment:

... the over-all impression of the first Pearson government was that the "old guard," who were not wholeheartedly in sympathy with the party's new policies, many of whom had not contributed very much to the electoral victory, were to predominate. In a way, it was a triumph for seniority over the new spirit which had been created in the Liberal party.[12]

If the Prime Minister had shown more caution in his appointments than Gordon, Kent and Davey would have preferred, he had by no means crushed their expectations. On the contrary, he had encouraged them. Walter Gordon had the senior portfolio, and was given a free hand to produce the first Liberal budget; and Tom Kent came into the Prime Minister's office as Pearson's "coordinator of programs."[13] All the public indications were that Prime Minister Pearson leaned heavily on Walter Gordon as his chief lieutenant and source of initiative.[14]

Gordon acted vigorously on this assumption. At Rideau Hall after the swearing-in, he told reporters that the sixty days of decision had commenced, and that he would introduce a budget within that period. He had already begun to orchestrate the budget process in appreciation that there was very little time to achieve his objective. The deadline was the kind that he liked to set for himself. He knew that the budget was bound to be regarded as the culminating point of the first sixty days, and that it provided the occasion for him to entrench his political reputation and his central influence in the administration. As a self-confident man and a relative political novice, he faced the risks of his boldness with equanimity.

There were immediate difficulties which Gordon recognized. From his experience of Ottawa and the civil service, he knew that the Department of Finance was no longer the energetic and purposeful institution that it had been under Clifford Clark. Gordon believed that the Department would need a new Deputy Minister to restore its vitality, and he had chosen his man. R. B. Bryce, whom Gordon had known and admired since his wartime service in Ottawa, held the senior position among Ottawa civil servants as clerk of the Privy Council and secretary to the Cabinet. Shortly after the election Gordon proposed to Pearson that Bryce should move at once to Finance to replace Taylor as Deputy Minister. The Prime Minister-elect agreed.[15] On the morning the government took office, Gordon met Bryce by chance, and told him of his advice to Pearson that Bryce should join him in Finance. Bryce replied warmly "that he would be delighted to do so if the Prime Minister so requested."[16]

After the ceremony at Rideau Hall, Gordon made his first visit to the Minister's office in the Confederation Building, where George Nowlan, the retiring Minister, welcomed him and introduced him formally to the senior staff.[17] When the reporters had departed, Gordon faced his first unpleasant task as Minister.

> I thought it would be unfair to Kenneth Taylor, the Deputy Minister, to start on a false note, especially as he is a man whom I had known and liked for over thirty years. Accordingly, I told him frankly of the decision to make changes at the department and to appoint Bryce as Deputy Minister. Taylor was polite about this, but naturally was unhappy and upset.[18]

The Minister then met the senior Assistant Deputy Minister, A. F. W. Plumptre (another old acquaintance).

> He volunteered the information that the Department was in a mess; that the assistant deputies went their separate ways, and that there was no coordination or direction of activities. He implied that he assumed a new Deputy Minister would be appointed and that he

naturally hoped he would be considered for the post. I told him immediately that Bryce was to be appointed. Plumptre replied that Bryce was the most respected member of the civil service and that in his view this was a wise and proper choice. He readily accepted the decision in a most generous way.[19]

Gordon's conviction that "the Department badly needed to be pulled together" was strengthened by his conversations with the other three Assistant Deputy Ministers, Claude Isbister, Simon Reisman, and G. G. E. Steele.

A major embarrassment and potential source of malaise arose almost at once when

> ... the Prime Minister told me that, while we had promised a budget within sixty days, he thought it would be impossible to release Bryce from the Privy Council office until some time in July and that, therefore, I would have to get along as best I could without him. I said this would be very awkward, particularly as I had informed Ken Taylor of the decision to replace him, but Pearson was firm about not being able to get along without Bryce for at least two months.
>
> Budget making in these circumstances became extremely difficult. A budget had not been presented for two years. Ken Taylor's nose was a bit out of joint about the plan to appoint Bryce as Deputy Minister, and the rest of the staff, while willing enough, needed new direction. It was understandable, also, that the sense of urgency which I felt, having just finished a successful election campaign and before that a highly critical session in the House of Commons, was not shared by all the civil servants in the Department.[20]

Great diplomatic skill would be necessary to minimize the Department's confusion and demoralization. The patient exercise of such diplomacy, however, would probably threaten the integrity of a reforming budget. Instead, out of his optimism and penchant for action, Gordon chose to put his program ahead of appeasement of the Department. Whatever its condition, he was determined that it should produce the materials for a distinctive budget reflecting his own sense of purpose. The Minister thus inevitably challenged the Department's self-esteem and goodwill. For senior officials, and for some politicians and observers, the normal relationship between civil servants and politicians in Ottawa was the comfortable harmony of the Howe-St.

Laurent period. After April 8, the prospect of Liberal rule brought with it a general assumption that the old order – so rudely interrupted by the Diefenbaker interlude – would return.[21] But Tom Kent had already shaken the complacency of a group of the government's senior advisers when he briefed them secretly on the party's sixty day program before April 22;[22] and now Walter Gordon, the other influential reformer in the party leadership, demonstrated the same indelicate preoccupation with the primacy of his own, political authority. Without the pressure of a sixty day timetable, the Department might have readjusted gradually to the new circumstances. But the pace was being forced.

As another means of avoiding the potential reluctance or disorganization of the Department, and providing himself with the materials for a budget within eight weeks of the general election, Gordon decided shortly after April 8 to recruit a few temporary personal advisers from outside the civil service. He was familiar with this practice from his own experience in conditions of wartime emergency in Ottawa; and he approached his first budget with the same sense of urgency. David Stanley (an economist with Wood, Gundy and Company in Toronto who had written speeches for Lester Pearson during the 1963 campaign) was his first choice. Gordon was in touch with him a few days after the election.[23] When the government took office on April 22, Gordon had taken on Stanley, Geoffrey Conway (then a Ph.D. student in economics at Harvard University and a former employee of Clarkson, Gordon & Co.), Martin O'Connell of the Toronto investment firm of Harris and Partners, and Rod Anderson of Clarkson, Gordon & Co.[24] They occupied desks in his ministry office in the Confederation Building.[25] As the controversial process of constructing the budget proceeded, their presence and activity grated more and more on the sensitivities of permanent officials in the Department. The abrasion arose above all from disagreement over policy; but this conflict provoked resentment over the prominence of the special advisers' role, and disgruntled comment about the personalities of the intruders.[26] Gordon himself was probably unaware of the strength of feeling generated by their presence.[27] There was nothing devious or secret about the appointment of these advisers, and on May 18 Clive Baxter reported unsensationally on their work in the *Financial Post*.

While the preliminaries of budget-making had begun, Gordon was still engaged in recruiting his personal staff. At the end of April Edgar Benson, MP for Kingston, joined him as parliamentary secretary. On May 10 Brian Land, an assistant librarian at the University of Toronto who had worked for Donald Fleming in Eglinton constituency during the 1962 campaign, became Gordon's executive assistant.[28] A few days later Nancy Burpee returned from work in Nigeria to become Gordon's private secretary.[29] Muriel Mersey, who had been a member of George Nowlan's staff in Finance, remained with the new Minister to take special responsibility for constituency matters. Later Barbara Hunter became associate private secretary.[30] This group coalesced in loyal and good humoured support for the Minister.

> It was a small staff compared with those of other ministers, but most effective. Of equal importance everyone was always cheerful no matter what the circumstances. This made a good impression, as did our firm rule that all incoming letters must be answered without delay. I am convinced I had the ablest and most effective personal staff of any Minister during my time in Ottawa.[31]

Walter Gordon's insouciance and independence were nicely illustrated in his ministerial office arrangements. His own office contained an antique desk rather than one of standard issue. For Miss Burpee, he ordered a red IBM electric typewriter. The order produced a long memorandum from the Treasury Board explaining that government typewriters were grey. Gordon persisted and acquired the typewriter.

> There it sat, right outside his office, and every passing civil servant glared at the saucy typewriter, as if enough dirty looks aimed at it could somehow repress the highly developed sense of the irregular that possessed this strange new Minister.[32]

In the first few weeks after April 22 the Cabinet met in almost daily session to plan the government's legislative program for the first session. The Prime Minister chose the beginning of May, before the opening of Parliament, for symbolic fence-mending visits to Prime Minister Macmillan of Britain and President Kennedy of the United States. At the president's home in Hyannis Port, Massachusetts, during a congenial day, Pearson and Kennedy agreed to conclude an agreement on nuclear warheads, to reopen discussions on the Columbia River treaty, and to reconstitute two inactive joint Cabinet committees. The Prime Minister was flattered when the president hauled down the presidential flag from its sea-front standard and presented it as a memento of Canadian-American reconciliation.[33] Walter Gordon's nationalism, in the view of Donald Creighton, "contrasted very oddly" with the "sweeping continentalism" the Prime Minister demonstrated in this day of agreement.[34] But the situation was more ironic than that. Lester Pearson did not believe that his continentalism contradicted his nationalism; the one could only exist for him, in fact, under the umbrella of the other. When the Prime Minister returned from Hyannis Port, he told Gordon "that it seemed as good a time as any to go ahead with the Canadianization measures the Finance Minister was planning for his first budget, on the theory that relations with the United States were at such a friendly pitch they could stand the minor disruption of a few nationalistic laws."[35] What was necessary and acceptable, in Lester Pearson's view, was a moderate readjustment in the economic relationship with a tolerant and benevolent neighbour. This was what he believed Walter Gordon, too, had planned; and it was a fair general estimate of Gordon's intention.

*

On May 16 Parliament opened, and the government presented its program in a concise speech from the throne. The introductory paragraphs reflected the overriding concerns of the Prime Minister to assure that "the basic partnership of English-speaking and French-speaking people" should be "truly equal"; that "the spirit of cooperative federalism" should govern relations between Ottawa and the provinces; and that "the armed forces of Canada should have available the modern weapons necessary to perform effectively the defensive tasks which Canada has undertaken in the alliance." The rest of the speech was pure Gordon. "This was undoubtedly the first time in Canadian history," wrote John R. Walker of Southam News Services, "when the major part of a new government's program was lifted straight out of a book on economic problems," Gordon's *Troubled Canada*.[36]

The pledges of four years were to be redeemed. Trade expansion negotiations would be pursued; special assistance for technical training would be extended; a department of industry, an economic council, a municipal development and loan board, a Canada development corporation, would be established; capital assistance for Atlantic development would be provided; a national contributory pension scheme would be adopted. The Montreal *Star* judged that "probably no peacetime Parliament in the country's history has opened with so full and specific a load of work set out for it in such brief words."[37] Moving the address in reply the next day, the new Liberal MP, Pauline Jewett, noted that "I think we should make it clear that these measures are not simply a sort of potpourri of the kinds of things we thought might be meaningful to a particular group of voters here or a particular group of voters there. These measures are part of an integrated whole, designed to restore and promote our society's economic health and social well-being."[38]

The careful balancing of conservative and reformist members in Mr. Pearson's Cabinet appointments a month earlier had not yet, it was clear, fixed the character of the administration. The speech from the throne indicated that behind a façade which scrupulously respected old political claims, the Prime Minister was giving the first move to his reformers. This was what Walter Gordon had expected ever since his decision to enter politics. The significance of the speech for the balance of forces in the Cabinet and party was not widely noted, although Douglas Fisher, the rough and ready philosopher and NDP member of the House for Port Arthur, analyzed it perceptively in a speech in the House on May 29. He believed that "as a politician the Prime Minister is almost completely eclectic, that he has an open mind and no set position, and that he takes things, or ideas as they come."[39] Fisher, whose interest was to promote "radical and progressive ideas, ideas which show an increasing urgency on the part of the government to give leadership and accept responsibility in economic matters," said that he wished to "watch very closely and distinguish the influence of the various pressure groups" on the malleable Prime Minister.[40] He could see three tendencies in the Cabinet.

> ... I have marked up what I might call the three positions, the Gordon position, the Sharp position and the Pickersgill position. If I might use United States personalities, I would compare the Pickersgill position to that of Senator Harry Byrd, the Gordon position to that of Hubert Humphrey and the Sharp position to that of Mr. McNamara, the United States secretary of defence. . . . If we look at the Byrd position, or the Pickersgill position, this is really the attitude that the Liberal party can handle things very well by divine right. In their minds they have the ability to straighten out the country and keep it going. This I mention first because it is the aspect of the Liberal party about which we have the least hope, because I think this ability is questionable. We will be watching very closely for the emergence in domination in the party of the divine right concept. We have very little hope for that and we think it could tend to merge into what we call the Sharp position, or, in paradox terms, the McNamara position, that is, the administrator of some genius and moderation.[41]

Fisher hoped, instead, that the influence of Gordon, Maurice Lamontagne and Tom Kent would predominate.

The Ottawa correspondent of the Montreal *Star*, W. A. Wilson, saw that possibility foreshadowed in the speech.

Assuming that this group does not lose its force and energy – and it is this more than anything else that distinguished the Liberal party of 1963 from the aging formation of 1957 when Mr. St. Laurent left office – passages in the throne speech which today can be viewed as pleasant enough rhetoric will reasonably be seen later as the clear warnings of great change.[42]

Wilson believed that the willingness of the progressive group in the Cabinet to undertake "government intervention in the economy on a massive scale" owed its inspiration to the experience of postwar European planning rather than to socialism. He recognized that this willingness would precipitate a divisive, though potentially creative, national debate.

The debate which the action-minded wing of the Liberal party is bound to produce in this country . . . will not permit much of the road-straddling of Canadian politics, since many of the courses that will produce the debate will be hateful to part of the population and the beckoning road to the future for other parts.[43]

That debate could not be compressed into the first sixty days. It could hardly even begin, because the looseness of the parliamentary timetable retarded the legislation promised for discussion in the throne speech. The question period stretched out without limit day after day. The general debate on the speech lasted for eight days; an interim supply motion required four days' discussion before passage; and a resolution to establish a special committee on defence prompted four days' further repetition of the controversy over nuclear arms. By mid-June formal discussion had begun on the economic council, the department of industry, and the minicipal loan fund; but not a single piece of legislation had passed the House. The Opposition was aggressive and the government was on edge. "It was soon apparent," Walter Gordon recalled, "that the bitterness, the irritations, and the irascibilities of the previous Parliament had been carried forward to the new one, with Diefenbaker and Pickersgill and sometimes Pearson contributing as much as anyone to the sharp exchanges."[44] The lack of legislative progress in these first weeks meant that the budget, which was now promised for Thursday, June 13, drew increasing attention as the theatrical climax of the sixty days – the anticipated source of redemption for the government, and the major target of attack for the Opposition. The Minister of Finance, whose political reputation had been inflated by three years of uncritical attention in the press, was cast as conqueror – or, according to one's perspective, as sacrificial victim – in the impending drama.

At the close of the election campaign, Walter Gordon had promised that his first budget would contain three leading elements:

1. A long-term program for economic expansion and the elimination of unemployment.
2. A program for reduction of our balance of payments deficit.
3. A program for reducing the present trend towards absentee ownership of Canadian resources and Canadian companies.[45]

W. A. Wilson reported on May 4 that the first priority of the Pearson government was the restoration of international and domestic confidence in Canada, and that the absence of confidence was "to a very great extent" an economic problem falling to the Minister of Finance for solution. Wilson perceived that Gordon would have to perform a delicate balancing act in his budget address.

> He should on the one hand, contribute to the restoration of confidence which his Prime Minister is seeking. In the international economic community, this can be regarded as giving some acceptable indication that the nation's long series of budget deficits will gradually be brought to an end. On the other hand, he must be extremely careful to do nothing that would slow down the period of economic growth now under way in Canada after a long era of semi-stagnation. And he must do his utmost, so far as he can influence the problem through budgetting ... to reduce the still-high level of unemployment.[46]

The budget would have to be both restrained and expansionist. Wilson concluded that the Minister might choose to develop his program in stages, with a preliminary display of conventionality and restraint.

> There have been indications that, because of the limited time he has had at his disposal, that [sic] Mr. Gordon will bring down a fairly routine budget in June, including a taste but not much more, of the incentives the government favours. If this proves to be the case, it is likely that he would then present a considerably more radical supplementary budget sometime in the autumn, bringing a far wider range of economic weapons into play against the nation's plaguing ills.[47]

But Walter Gordon's instinct was for more decisive action than this. He was determined to encompass all his chief purposes in that first crucial statement to the House of Commons.

The work of preparation proceeded at hectic pace throughout May. The discontents in the Department of Finance were temporarily contained by the pressure to produce the budget; but beneath the surface resentments festered, manifesting themselves in obscure and only half-conscious ways.[48] The Minister himself, because of his self-confidence, his briskness, his public reputation, and his unorthodoxy, was regarded with a certain reserve. The senior civil servants, Taylor, Plumptre, Isbister, Reisman, and Steele, undoubtedly sought to suppress this reaction in faithful service to the Minister, but it found release at other levels in the Department; and as the budget process continued, even they were alienated.

At a plenary meeting on May 25 of the government's senior economic advisers, the three special advisers and the Minister, Gordon reviewed the objectives he hoped the budget would achieve. In economic terms alone, he conceded, these "might appear to be contradictory."[49]

First and foremost, it should include measures to stimulate the economy and provide more jobs. I thought it especially important to do things which would promote activity in the depressed areas of the country. This did not provoke any disagreement in principle.

Second, the budget should raise more revenues so that the government's finances would be brought under reasonable control within twenty-four months. I argued that it was much better to do this in the first year in which the government was elected than to try to do it later. All of the officials were in favour of raising additional revenues and I asked them for suggestions. They recommended, among other things, that the exemption of the sales tax from building materials and from production materials should be rescinded. I had some reservations about rescinding the exemption, insofar as production materials were concerned, but the officials pressed me hard to face up to this. . . .

Third, I believed the budget should include measures to encourage Canadian subsidiaries of foreign concerns to sell more of their shares to Canadians. Most of the officials were opposed to this. . . .

Fourth and finally, I insisted that there should be amendments designed to block some of the existing loopholes in the tax laws. I stated that, as a professional accountant who was fully aware of these loopholes, I could not bring in a budget that did not make some attempt to stop current abuses. As I recall, there was a mixed reaction to this on the part of the officials.[50]

In the discussion which followed, the views of the permanent officials were frequently contradicted by Gordon's temporary advisers. Gordon described the disagreements mildly as "a bit of conflict."[51] According to Peter Newman, however, R. B. Bryce, Louis Rasminsky, Simon Reisman, and Claude Isbister agreed after the meeting "that this budget had every prospect of becoming the least articulate statement of the country's financial position ever produced but no one seemed quite sure what, if anything, could be done about it."[52] The problem for them was the incompatible mixture of objectives sought by the Minister: on the one hand, the expansion of revenues and the demonstration of financial respectability necessary to impress the international financial community; on the other hand, the measure of economic stimulation likely to offset additions to revenue, and especially the proposals for limiting the extent of foreign control in the economy. The most serious dispute was over the measures to deal with foreign economic influence. The purely domestic measures, after all, were bound to depend upon varying assessments of the economic situation, and would always reflect a compromise among these assessments. The economy was on the upturn, but there were uncertainties and regional variations in the recovery; a careful selection of devices seemed appropriate in the circumstances. And the Minister had agreed, at the urging of his officials, to adopt the building and production materials tax as the major revenue producing measure: that was a substantial concession to restraint and economic orthodoxy which might compensate for his proposals for selective seasonal and regional stimulation. But the two major suggestions for restraining foreign investment – an alteration in the withholding tax on investment income to discriminate against foreign investors, and a takeover tax on the sale of controlling interests in Canadian businesses to foreign purchasers – profoundly challenged the liberal assumptions of the government's senior economic advisers. They were orthodox disciples of the postwar school of international economics, favouring internationalism, the free flow of investment capital and the reconciliation of conflicting economic interests by quiet diplomacy. Walter Gordon's proposals were seen from that perspective as an offence to decency, economic sense and American interests; and they would overshadow, in controversy, all the contructive elements of the budget. But how could a determined Minister in a hurry be opposed?

Gordon's strategy and specific proposals on foreign investment

146

originated outside the permanent staff in the Department of Finance; and even though they had heard Gordon preaching his cause for several years, they were unprepared to assist that cause with any conviction. Gordon favoured the adoption of a legislative package designed to promote Canadian participation in equity ownership. The package would consist of some limited restrictive measures designed to discourage the growth of foreign ownership, and other positive incentives aimed at attracting new Canadian capital investment. In principle, Gordon wished to avoid a program that would seriously antagonize the American government or create "an unfavourable climate for foreign investment."[53] Thus the attraction for him of a single package enacted quickly: the presence of exhortations and incentives to Canadian investors would demonstrate that the primary purpose was positive and expansionist rather than discriminatory; and a complete program adopted at once would give evidence of the firmness, moderation and stable purpose of the Canadian government.

From the moment of the election victory, Walter Gordon was thus determined to act quickly and comprehensively on his foreign investment program. The details of that program were largely supplied to him by Geoff Conway, and worked out in consultation among Gordon, Conway and David Stanley. Conway's letter to Gordon of April 13, 1963 was a prolific source of inspiration. In it, the takeover tax had taken form.

> The first requirement is to prevent future sell-outs. You were interested in a special tax on further sales of Canadian companies to non-residents. An income (i.e. capital gains) tax on only this type of transaction would be impractical. We cannot tax the buyer because of the question of jurisdiction. Therefore a transfer tax (or excise tax if question of provincial jurisdiction) would appear to be the best available tax. All sales of equity and debenture stocks in private and public companies could be taxable, but an exemption would be given to sales to residents or for transfers to non-residents if purchaser and associates own less than say five percent of outstanding shares. A substantial rate of say ten to fifteen percent would be quite a deterrent and the tax would be easy to administer. However, not only might the tax not be enough to stop some sales but it would be unpopular with many small shareholders receiving a takeover offer.[54]

Gordon wrote in the margin next to this paragraph: "Stanley says apply this tax on *all* equity sales to non-residents without exception."[55]

Conway coupled the prevention of takeovers with "the question of regaining equity interest already held by non-residents." Within Gordon's framework of "a statement of general government policy in this area ... and then the provision of incentives and/or penalties in tax legislation to encourage the fulfilling of such goals," Conway suggested special depreciation and depletion allowances, tax holidays and rebates for companies meeting the government's definition of Canadian ownership. He made the proposal for an increase in the withholding tax for foreign-owned companies, and suggested that one of the functions of the new national development corporation would be to purchase shares as they were offered for sale by non-residents, and to finance private Canadian purchases through long-term loans. The whole bundle of measures (most of which eventually found their way into the budget) gave neat expression to Walter Gordon's long-term purpose, the repatriation of control in the Canadian economy under the firm guidance of the federal government. The objective was both nationalist and *dirigiste*, and it raised complex questions of administration and sustained political will. It obviously needed the most thorough study and preparation among those who would have to carry it through. In sum, it was probably more radical and comprehensive than most of Walter Gordon's political colleagues had realized. For the senior civil servants who met Gordon and his consultants on May 25, it was far beyond what was acceptable. There could hardly be any easy reconciliation if the Minister remained committed to his nationalist purpose and to the interloping technicians who abetted it.

The conflict was patched up temporarily that day in agreement that the permanent officials, under A. F. W. Plumptre's supervision, should produce a draft budget speech. This was done within two days, and for a short interlude the senior officials were reassured that the Minister had restored what was, for them, the proper balance of influence in the Department.[56] But they were now engaged in a rearguard action whose object was essentially to keep measures out of the budget, and they soon learned that this attempt would not succeed. Gordon commented later on the Plumptre draft:

> He writes very well and I was grateful to him for this. However, the draft that I received did not reflect all the points of view I wished to make, and with Stanley's help we produced an alternative which, after much editing and polishing, I felt portrayed my understanding of the Liberal government's philosophy and policy.[57]

The Department's version was discarded, and a chasm opened between

Gordon and his personal staff on one side and the permanent civil servants on the other.

The Deputy Minister, Kenneth Taylor, remained passive throughout this period of turbulence, and his inactivity tended to inhibit the assistant deputy ministers from asserting their own positions firmly. Isbister and Reisman did, nevertheless, prepare memoranda which criticized the proposals for a development corporation and a takeover tax "as premature and not well enough thought out."[58] There were further face-to-face encounters in which Gordon was told bluntly that the takeover tax was unworkable. The Minister patiently resisted this advice.[59]

For Walter Gordon, the crucial test of his proposals would be the response of Prime Minister Pearson. Gordon warned Pearson that the governor of the Bank of Canada, Louis Rasminsky, "was opposed to parts of the budget for fear they would annoy the Americans. He did not wish us to do this because of his experiences the previous year over the exchange devaluation. I said I felt that the Prime Minister should hear these reservations from Rasminsky himself rather than have them retailed through me."[60]

On May 31 the Prime Minister joined the Minister of Finance for lunch with the governor at the Bank, when Rasminsky "voiced his strong objections to the proposals designed to encourage foreign-owned subsidiaries in Canada to sell some of their shares to Canadians. He was particularly critical of the proposed differential in the withholding tax."[61] After the meeting Gordon and Pearson walked back to Parliament Hill from the Bank, while discussing Rasminsky's comments.

> ... Pearson said he did not take them seriously and that I should not give way on the withholding tax differential. I asked him whether it would not be wise to discuss the budget proposals with a committee of the Cabinet, including Lamontagne and Sharp in particular, in view of the fact that it introduced so many new features. Pearson replied that if we brought in a group of Cabinet ministers, they would all want to make changes and he did not think this was desirable.[62]

This discussion was followed by a number of meetings in which Gordon and Pearson reviewed the draft text of the budget speech. "He expressed great delight with it and said he felt it would put the Liberal party on the map. The budget was my responsibility of course but it was reassuring to know the Prime Minister was so pleased with it."[63]

Gordon's desire for reassurance was more than a sign of his anxiety as a novice Minister of Finance about to present his first budget; it was a reflection, above all, of the resistance his measures had provoked in the Department of Finance and the Bank of Canada. Now, having failed to gain the Prime Minister's approval for discussion of the budget by a Cabinet committee, Gordon requésted authority to review his proposals with the Prime Minister's policy adviser, Tom Kent. Pearson also vetoed this suggestion.[64]

The Prime Minister had clung firmly and with complete propriety to the conventions of budget secrecy. Gordon recalls this with some regret.

> Therefore, the budget proposals were not discussed in Cabinet until either on the morning of their presentation to the House or perhaps the day before. No one voiced any serious reservations about any of the proposals, although quite obviously they had no real chance to study them.[65]

This limited opportunity for discussion of the budget with his political colleagues later seemed inadequate to the Minister,[66] but at the time, with very slight unease, he accepted the approval of the Prime Minister as sufficient authority to proceed with the budget without substantial amendment. Gordon put the warnings and protests of the officials behind him.

The "sixty days" reached their climax on Thursday evening, June 13, when the Minister of Finance rose in the House to deliver his budget address. His opening words had a normal partisan edge to them which aggravated members across the floor:

> ... in delivering tonight the first budget of this new government I am aware that it is my duty to present the facts as we found them on taking office. It is also my duty to ask honourable members and the Canadian public to face up to these facts and, having done this, it is my further duty to indicate the kind of measures which are needed to put our national affairs in order once again. ...
>
> We on this side of the House take the budget very seriously. We look upon it as an annual occasion of great national importance. It is an occasion when the government is expected to give to Parliament and to the people a clear appraisal of the nation's financial and economic condition. It is an occasion when the government must outline the short- and long-term economic and financial policies it proposes to pursue to overcome the problems and to

convert the prospects into realities. Above all, it is an occasion initiating a grand scrutiny by Parliament of the financial affairs of the nation. It is an occasion which should not and must not be avoided or delayed.

It is now almost exactly two years since there was a budget debate in this House. . . . [67]

The Minister said that he would "speak in human terms tonight, and about the human tragedies that inevitably result when economic conditions are unsatisfactory and our national affairs mismanaged."[68] Throughout a long and detailed speech, Gordon returned in chorus to this theme: the new government would "begin to put our national house in order"; it would "deal with . . . any other skeletons that may still remain to be uncovered in our national financial closet"; the country's improved economic circumstances were "due in part, as I have said, to an increase in confidence as a result of the election and to the prospect of decisive and far-sighted government in Canada once again."

For Walter Gordon himself, accustomed to three years of political argument phrased in similar or stronger terms, the speech did not appear unduly partisan; nor was it, by the standards of the House. He had deleted some passages "which I felt to be more critical than might be called for in a budget speech," and believed, as the Prime Minister had told him, that the text was "very mild."[69] But Gordon had come to office with a substantial reputation for objectivity and wisdom above the battle which his budget speech, perhaps unrealistically, was expected to sustain. His combative flourishes disappointed some of the government's own followers in the House while they irritated the official Opposition. The cheers of the more thoughtlessly partisan Liberal backbenchers — which accompanied every barb — did not help to sweeten the atmosphere.

In the body of the speech Gordon noted the economic recovery which had followed the financial crisis of 1962 and predicted its continuance in 1963, but emphasized the persistent high level of unemployment, the chronic imbalance in Canada's balance of payments, the record of apparently uncontrolled budget deficits, and the continuing trend toward non-resident ownership and control of Canadian industry. These concerns were all familiar ones that Gordon had expressed repeatedly during the party's years in Opposition. As the commentators had predicted, the problems he pointed to were varied, and their solutions, too, would have to be. The need to restore confidence in Canada's economic management, and to dampen any inflationary pressures, seemed to require a major increase in tax revenues which would give promise of an eventually balanced budget. The need to stimulate employment, exports and Canadian participation, on the contrary, required positive incentives to capital spending through tax benefits or subsidies; and the marked regional variations in employment suggested some selectivity in the application of these incentives. An entirely cautious and orthodox budget would probably have given first priority to the restoration of confidence, with some secondary attention to the stimulation of employment in the most depressed areas; but even the most conventional Finance Minister would have faced hard dilemmas of balance and equity in trying to achieve these objectives.[70] It was becoming clear in Canada as elsewhere that there was no simple trade-off between unemployment and inflationary expansion, and that the traditional instruments of postwar fiscal and monetary policy were inadequate means of maintaining full employment, price stability and economic growth at the same time. Walter Gordon had inherited a complex task, added to it his special concern for the repatriation of control in the economy, and approached with a humane bias which markedly influenced his scale of priorities.

The Minister placed the relief of unemployment first among his objectives. This meant that the government was committed to a number of programs of regional grants, winter works, tax concessions, employment bonuses, and industrial retraining which added to the spending estimates.[71] These schemes were balanced by a number of measures aimed at increasing tax revenues and demonstrating the government's ability to assert its control over public spending. A series of tax reforms were introduced to plug loopholes in business taxation,[72] and provision was made for the earlier payment of corporate income tax.[73] Walter Gordon's disinclination to seek additional revenue from the income tax, and the growing favour of indirect taxes, led him to recommend extension of the eleven percent manufacturers' sales tax to building materials and production machinery, as his officials had suggested.[74] This was the chief proposal in the budget for increasing revenue: it promised an estimated $170 million in the fiscal year 1963 – 1964, and $360 million in 1964 – 1965. But it had the disadvantages of its strongly deflationary effect (which Gordon sought to offset for consumers by easing the burdens of National Housing Act mortgage loans) and its unpopularity with the construction and manufacturing industries.

The accumulated reduction in the deficit represented by all these programs amounted to an estimated $155 million, from a calculated deficit of $720 million before the tax changes to $565 million afterwards. Gordon noted that this represented a reduction of almost $200 million in the deficit as compared to the previous year.

> I am sure that honourable members will agree that this is a substantial move in the right direction. To do more this year would not be wise having regard to the state of the economy. To do less would be irresponsible.[75]

In fulfillment of his promise to confront the problem of increasing foreign control of the economy, Gordon announced the two measures which had been the objects of contention during preparation of the budget. The first involved revision of the fifteen percent withholding tax on dividends paid to non-residents. A reduced rate of ten percent would apply to dividends of companies "beneficially owned by Canadian residents to the extent of twenty-five percent or more," and an increased rate of twenty percent would apply to other companies, "including those which are wholly-owned subsidiaries of foreign parents."[76] Gordon hoped that this differentiation would promote the government's policy of "growing partnership between Canadian investors and investors abroad."[77]

The second measure was more bold.

> As I indicated earlier, it is the policy of this government to encourage direct foreign investment in new enterprises in this country on the basis of partnership with Canadian residents. While this type of investment is of great value to Canada, it is our view that non-resident takeovers of established Canadian companies rarely confer any benefit on the Canadian economy. We shall therefore propose a measure of taxation of certain sales which might contribute to such takeovers. We shall propose that effective tonight a thirty percent tax be levied on certain sales by Canadian residents to non-residents and non-resident controlled companies, of shares in Canadian companies listed on Canadian stock exchanges. There is to be no liability for the tax when such sales are made on the floor of a Canadian exchange in the normal trading manner and do not form part of sales exceeding $50,000 per day by any single seller. Effective tonight also, we are proposing a similar thirty percent sales tax on the sale by a listed Canadian corporation of the whole or substantially the whole of its property to a non-resident or a non-resident controlled company.[78]

Gordon's determination to make the takeover tax an effective deterrent was evident from its severity. (In the course of planning, the tax had grown from Conway's suggested rate of ten percent or fifteen percent to thirty percent.) This initiative, like the alteration in the sales tax and the withholding tax, was predictably offensive to strong elements in the business and financial community – including both potential Canadian sellers and potential foreign buyers.

Walter Gordon felt satisfaction, as he ended his address to the House, that he had made a forthright and courageous start on the Liberal party's program of economic reform. He had not tried to avoid political difficulty, but fully expected it. He was confident that he could triumph over it because the electorate had granted a mandate to the party to carry through its proclaimed economic commitments, and because he had, apparently, the wholehearted support of Prime Minister Pearson, the Cabinet and the parliamentary caucus. Although there might be some rough days of debate ahead, the Minister of Finance could look forward to nothing but vindication.[79]

The Conservative financial critic and former minister, George Nowlan, followed Walter Gordon with a preliminary reply the same evening that reflected Nowlan's offence at "the most miserable, petty, picayune, party address that has ever been given in Parliament."[80] Nowlan's remarks had a tone of sarcasm and resentment about them which was unusual in this genial man; the Minister's speech had thrown him off balance. He did not attempt to respond at once to Gordon's substantive proposals, which were, he said, "of a nature that one would not want to speak casually or quickly about them."[81]

The preliminary reaction of the editorial writers the next day was cautious but sympathetic. "There should be no quarrel with the objectives that Mr. Gordon declared in his budget speech," commented the *Globe and Mail*;[82] the Toronto *Star* reflected that " . . . the long-term impact on the nation's economy should be substantial. . . . In all, the budget won't have Canadians dancing in the streets. But it does provide assurance that purpose and direction have been restored in the handling of the nation's economic affairs."[83] The Winnipeg *Free Press* said admiringly that "Mr. Walter Gordon's first budget sets at least one Canadian precedent. Never before in our history has the Finance Minister of a minority government so resolutely set aside considerations of immediate popularity in order to administer strong medicine to an ailing economy."[84]

8   Checkmate

The implications of the budget could not be absorbed overnight, but required careful reflection. The next morning, Douglas Fisher rose in the question period to enquire about the circumstances of its preparation:

> Mr. Speaker, I should like to ask the Minister of Finance a question regarding the preparation and provenance of last night's budget speech. Can the Minister assure us that he and his government officials alone prepared the budget speech without the assistance of outside consultants or ghost writers from Toronto?[1]

Following an admonition from the Speaker that "that is not the type of question which we enjoy in this House," Fisher reworded his enquiry:

> . . . I think a simple "no" answer is important because of the tradition that budget information should be privy to the Minister and his officials until the very last minute. All I am asking, and asking seriously, is for a simple assurance that this was the fact and that outside consultants were not involved.[2]

The Minister did not wish to deceive the House, but neither did he wish to embarrass his advisers and the permanent members of his Department. He sensed danger and yet, in his parliamentary inexperience, sought to sidestep it.

Mr. Speaker, as Minister of Finance I take full and sole responsibility for everything which was contained in the budget.[3]

The old fox, John Diefenbaker, was on his feet at once to respond that
"I think the acceptance of responsibility is no answer to a question of
very serious importance indeed."[4] Douglas Fisher added that "When
reports are existent that the Minister has brought down people from
Toronto to help him in the preparation of his budget who may be
outside the government service, I think I deserve a denial or an explanation of this matter."[5] Gordon Churchill asked the Minister whether
"the outside consultants who conferred with him with regard to the
budget" had taken the oath of secrecy, to which Gordon replied that
"everyone who assisted me with the preparation of the budget" had
taken the oath.[6] For several minutes more the Minister was harried
with further questions about his assistants, which he refused to answer
directly. J. W. Pickersgill, the Secretary of State, came to Gordon's aid
to insist that

> . . . all the authorities are agreed that any Minister of the crown is
> entitled to seek advice from any source he chooses, as long as he
> assumes full and exclusive responsibility for the action which has
> been taken. . . . It seems to me the only point which has arisen is
> whether everyone who assisted my honourable friend took the oath
> of secrecy, and he has assured the House that this was done.[7]

The Speaker terminated the exchange by pointing out that a Minister
could not be forced to answer questions; but that was hardly a satisfactory end to the matter. Gordon's reticence had left the Opposition
holding the advantage. Either he was concealing information which was
politically important or, more likely, he could be embarrassed by being
made to appear to do so. The House was not going to let go of the issue.
    Gordon soon realized that the skirmish had created rather than
calmed suspicions, and later in the day, following consultation with the
Prime Minister, he made a further statement to the House.

> This morning some honourable members raised questions in the
> House concerning personnel participating in the preparation of the
> budget. Officials of the Department of Finance and several other
> departments, including Justice, National Revenue, Labour and the
> Bank of Canada have participated actively both in the discussion
> of proposals and in the drafting. In addition I had the assistance
> of three special consultants who joined the Department of Finance

on a temporary basis shortly after the government took office, because of the very heavy volume of work involved in preparing legislation and in minimizing delay in presenting the budget.[8]

Gordon identified O'Connell, Conway and Stanley, and reported that they had taken the oath of allegiance and the oath of office and secrecy. Their appointments had been authorized by the Treasury Board. The Minister concluded:

> I regret my hesitancy this morning to reveal the names of the three individuals I have mentioned. This hesitation stemmed from my feeling that the budget is the product of the work of a great number of departmental officials and I did not think it fair to single out individuals for certain attention. . . .
> Since these three gentlemen had all taken the necessary oaths, it did not seem to me that there could be any special question about their status. However, it now seems desirable that their names should be made public and certainly I have no reason to make any mystery of them.[9]

Mr. Diefenbaker accepted the Minister's statement in good faith with the admonition that "I hope his experience today will be a salutary lesson to him and to other ministers like-minded, that when Parliament asks for information, the information should be provided, rather than a series of evasive statements which result in an accumulation of suspicion which had to be answered frankly this afternoon by the Minister."[10] T. C. Douglas, however, continued probing. He suggested that "this is a much more serious thing" than the indiscretion of Hugh Dalton, the postwar British Chancellor of the Exchequer, in revealing budget information to a reporter on his way into the House – a lapse which cost the Chancellor his position.[11] Douglas followed this careless and damaging parallel with a series of further questions.

> Did these men continue their association with the investment companies with which they were connected? Have their services with the government now terminated? Have they gone back to work for these companies? Was there any way in which these persons could personally gain as a result of the knowledge which they secured during their preparation of this budget?[12]

Douglas Fisher lengthened the list by asking whether they were still being paid by their firms, whether they were carrying out work for their firms, and what precedents the Minister could cite for this kind of relationship. Gordon asserted in reply that "any suggestion that they would do anything improper is something that is hardly fair to the three people in question," and added frankly:

> I will be glad to answer those questions, Mr. Speaker. The two gentlemen referred to were given leave of absence by their firms. They were paid by their firms. They have not been back to their firms but have been working full time for the Department of Finance. As to precedents, I cannot give many because I have not looked the matter up, but I can cite one precedent which occurred in connection with the 1941 budget, I think it was, when I served the then Minister of Finance in exactly the same way and on exactly the same terms that these three gentlemen have just been serving me. With regard to the question as to what is their status now, they are in the same position as they were on May 1; they are still serving the Department of Finance and I hope they will continue to do so for at least some weeks to come, perhaps longer than that.[13]

The sudden and burgeoning dispute now involved three distinct issues: the conventions of budget-making in the parliamentary system, the effect of temporary appointments on the status of permanent civil servants, and the relationship of special ministerial advisers to their regular employers. John Diefenbaker was aroused once more by the exchanges, and offered his interpretation of the parliamentary convention to the House.

> Is it not a fact that the essence of budgetary secrecy under the British system is that in the United Kingdom no one knows of the particular contents of a budget excepting the Chancellor of the Exchequer and those within the civil service who operate with him and the Prime Minister? No one else has that information; so far as the Cabinet is concerned it just receives a general outline. In the particular circumstances relating to the preparation of budget matters of financial importance in respect of which illicit profits could be made, is it not necessary that under no circumstances should individuals be called in from outside, who, no matter how honest and whatever their integrity may be, are placed in an impossible situation?[14]

There was material for solid constitutional discussion on these questions: was the British convention, when interpreted strictly, perhaps unnecessarily rigid for the needs of modern budget-making? Was the historic practice in Canada as pure as Mr. Diefenbaker implied? But the House was too partisan a forum to examine these questions with care. What the Opposition wished to reveal was the existence or appearance of impropriety, not the nature or efficiency of conventional practices. Walter Gordon was confident that there had been no impropriety, but the House continued to worry the issue.

Stanley Knowles touched a sensitive nerve by enquiring whether

> ... these three gentlemen ... took precedence over the Deputy Minister of Finance and other top civil servants in the preparation of the budget. ... I should like to ask whether these people were given a position of precedence over those in the Department who would normally do this work, and is there any relationship between this and the request of the Deputy Minister of Finance to be moved to another position?[15]

The questions were mischievous; Stanley Knowles knew that a responsible Minister could not properly reply to questions seeking to penetrate the façade of unity and anonymity of a department. Gordon replied with the appropriate discretion.

> These three gentlemen did not have precedence over the officials in the Department. Each of them has specialized and useful knowledge in a particular field which was made available to the officials, and most certainly this has nothing to do with the change in position of Dr. Kenneth Taylor, for whom I have the very greatest regard, respect and admiration.[16]

T. C. Douglas commented harshly on the question of conflict of interest.

> If the government needs to bring in advisers from time to time, surely they ought to be hired by the government, paid by the government, and wholly under the control of the government during the time they are employed. To ask any man to serve two masters, to be working for the government but receiving pay from his own company, is putting a strain on that individual to which no person ought to be subjected. ... Obviously, from time to time people will be brought in to advise on legislation, but that is a totally different thing from helping to prepare the budget. While we may take strenuous objection to the budget being inclined

toward Bay Street, we take even stronger exception to Bay Street itself drafting the budget.[17]

The discussion concluded without resolution.

There had not yet been any formal debate on the budget in the House, but the controversy over the three consultants had gained its own momentum and threatened to cast the budget measures themselves into the shadows. On the weekend the executive of the Ontario Young Progressive Conservative Association passed a resolution (by the narrow margin of 15-13) calling for Walter Gordon's resignation on the ground that his use of "ghost writers" for the budget was "a breach of confidence and principle."[18] By Monday morning the Opposition was ready to seek an emergency debate on what was being described as "the Gordon Affair." Gordon Dewar reported in the Ottawa *Journal* that some Liberal members would welcome the chance to clear the air of the subject in one day rather than seeing it drag through five days of regular budget debate.[19]

When the House met that day, Douglas Harkness (the Conservative member for Calgary North) rose on a question of privilege to raise further doubts about the secrecy of the budget process. A Calgary law office, he said, had received a twenty-five page summary of the budget prepared by Clarkson, Gordon & Company in Toronto by the first morning mail on Friday, June 14. He reviewed airline and postal schedules to cast doubt on the possibility that the memorandum could have been prepared after the budget on Thursday evening. Gordon replied:

> I am hardly in a position to speak on this matter without looking into it, mainly because I am no longer a member of Clarkson, Gordon & Company. I do know that for many, many years that firm, as well as many other firms in all parts of Canada, including all banks and various other institutions, have received copies of the budget speech after it has been delivered in this House from the offices of the Bank of Canada in their area. I know that this particular firm, Clarkson, Gordon & Company, have in the past made a point of summarizing the main points in the budget that night and issuing them that night or the following morning at an early hour. Apart from that, I am not in a position to say anything about this matter until I make inquiries.[20]

Gordon realized that the implication of the question was ominous. He immediately telephoned J. R. M. Wilson, the senior partner of the company, to establish the facts, and later in the question period Gordon read to the House Wilson's telegram in reply. The message explained the company's procedure in preparing the summary after 9:45 P.M. on budget night and assuring delivery across Canada by air the following morning. Wilson confirmed that the practice had been the same as that followed in previous years.[21]

The same afternoon John Diefenbaker asked leave to move the adjournment of the House under standing order 26, to discuss "a definite matter of urgent public importance," which he described as

> ... facts relating to the preparation of the budget, which facts constitute a flagrant departure from constitutional budgetary practice, imperil the traditional and essential secrecy of the budget, and which have had an unsettling effect on this House and on the country.[22]

The language of attack was becoming inflated. The Speaker ruled against the request, on the ground that the regular budget debate would provide sufficient opportunity to discuss all matters relating to the budget. On appeal to the House this ruling was upheld.[23]

The mood of the House was now tense and unpleasant, and the storm was still mounting. The question of the consultants continued to plague the Minister repetitively each day. The single serious issue of constitutional prudence that appeared to be involved was that the salaries of O'Connell and Stanley were being paid by their firms while they were in temporary government service; but the whole range of accusations remained in the air. The *Globe and Mail* commented on June 17 that "The important thing ... is not who is privy to government secrets, but to insure that the secret information is not put to any improper use. In the case of Mr. Gordon's advisers, there is no suggestion of impropriety and the criticism is irresponsible."[24] The Montreal *Star* made an increasingly obvious point the next day.

> It is sadly true to form for the House of Commons to get far more excited about the Finance Minister getting expert outside help in the preparation of the budget than in the budget itself. That document is full of tough meat and will need long chewing and digestion. The House shrinks from such hard work. It prefers the much easier task of denouncing Mr. Gordon for getting studies and analyses made by three bright young men with training for the job.[25]

It is conceivable that if the budget had not been rushed, if the consultants had played a more discreet and cautious role within the Department of Finance, and if, as a result, the Department's annoyances had not been multiplied and broadcast in the parliamentary corridors, the reckless curiosity of the House might not have been aroused. But the role of the consultants was a reflection of Walter Gordon's approach to policy-making, and could not be separated from the substance of the budget measures. Gordon had brought in his special advisers because he was determined to present the kind of budget he did. The House's assault on the advisers was the reflex action of an Opposition choosing the most vulnerable point of attack; but it was also tentative warning of a probable assault on the proposals themselves. The House sniffed controversy and prodded mischievously for three days while the reactions of interested parties to the budget measures were crystallizing. Even after criticism of the budget itself had gained some focus, harassment of the Minister on this secondary issue continued. The House was intent upon inquisition, and displayed its persistent capacity for vindictiveness and triviality as the exchanges continued.[26]

Meanwhile the protests against parts of the budget gathered force outside the House. The construction industry complained against the imposition of the sales tax on building materials in a flood of telegrams, letters and urgent requests for interviews with the Minister. The executives of the Montreal, Toronto and Vancouver stock exchanges and the Investment Dealers' Association of Canada sought clarification of the takeover tax, and delegations from the Toronto and Montreal exchanges met Gordon on June 17 and June 18.[27] The president of the Toronto exchange, General Howard Graham, had made a preliminary statement of restrained support for the takeover tax, and following his meeting with the Minister of Finance he told Gordon that while the Toronto exchange was not happy about the measure, it believed that the technical difficulties of administering the tax could be solved satisfactorily.[28] When the House met on June 18 Gordon said that he would be meeting the president of the Montreal Stock Exchange, Eric Kierans, at 5:30 P.M. that afternoon, and that "as far as the government is concerned, we propose to go ahead" with the takeover tax.[29]

The meeting with Kierans was turbulent.

He arrived to see me . . . with eight or nine members of his committee, all of whom were prominent members of Montreal Stock Exchange houses. Kierans handed me a letter criticizing the budget and particularly the proposed takeover tax couched in highly intemperate language. He then proceeded to harangue me in my own office and practically incited the stock brokers present to sell the market short when it opened the following morning. He admitted that his letter to me had been given to the press before he came to Ottawa, so the fat was in the fire.[30]

The takeover tax was unacceptable to Eric Kierans. His letter to Gordon began in hyperbole.

> The financial capitals of the world have just about had enough from Canada. Last Friday, the initial reaction to the budget was one of bewilderment and dismay. Yesterday, it was anger and scorn. Today, our friends in the western world fully realize that we don't want them or their money and that Canadians who deal with them in even modest amounts will suffer a thirty percent expropriation of the assets involved. And their reaction? If that is what Canadians want, let them have it.[31]

Kierans objected to the foreign ownership measures on every conceivable ground. He denied that non-resident takeovers offered no benefit to the Canadian economy; he argued that a twenty-five percent equity shareholding by Canadians would not result in the degree of control the Minister considered adequate, that Canadians were disinclined to invest in Canadian subsidiaries, that the takeover tax was an unjust capital levy which would seriously depress the securities market, that it was an invasion of property and civil rights and therefore within provincial rather than federal jurisdiction, that the tax would create two markets and two prices for Canadian securities – "one in Canada where the tax is applicable and liquidity reduced and the other in New York where transactions can take place among non-residents free of tax" – and that the tax would encourage Canadians as well as foreigners to avoid the Canadian securities market. Kierans had not come to Ottawa seeking compromise. His object was to force the government's surrender on the application of the takeover tax through the use of all the influence his position commanded. Walter Gordon understood the bluntness of the challenge.

> It seemed clear that if nothing were done there would be a very serious break in the stock market despite the fact the officials of the Toronto Stock Exchange had by this time let me know that they could work out the technical difficulties. I thought this over during the evening and the following morning informed the Prime Minister that I felt there was no alternative but to withdraw the proposed tax "because of administrative difficulties."[32]

Increased selling on the exchanges on Wednesday morning confirmed Gordon's fears. He still believed that the real administrative difficulties of the tax could be overcome; but the crucial factor now was the defiance of the Montreal Stock Exchange and its immediate effect on the market. Gordon and Pearson agreed that the government would have to capitulate. At noon the Cabinet met to hear and approve the Minister's recommendation for retreat.[33]

Shortly after 2:30 P.M., at the opening of the House, Gordon announced the temporary withdrawal of the proposed tax. He conceded that "it may take a little time" to work out the detailed regulations required to administer the tax, and said that in the interim the government did not wish to inhibit "new financing now under way for the expansion of existing business." He reviewed briefly his consultations with representatives of the securities business, and added that:

> Most of the people I have talked with have pointed out the administrative difficulties I have referred to, but are anxious to find a solution that will be consistent with the government's statement of disapproval of takeovers of Canadian concerns by non-residents.[34]

Eric Kierans was an exception, and Gordon singled him out for special comment.

> ... This attitude is not shared by the president of the Montreal Stock Exchange. In a letter to me dated June 18 he states that "a non-resident takeover confers great benefits on the Canadian economy." Either before or just after an interview with me yesterday, and without informing me of his intention to take such action, the president of the Montreal Stock Exchange handed copies of his letter to members of the press. The letter is intemperate and irresponsible in tone and content.
> *Some hon. Members*: Oh, oh.
> *Mr. Gordon*: It is a strange communication coming as it does from a man who holds the position of president of an important Canadian stock exchange. I want to make it clear that this government disagrees completely with the interpretation of the national interest expressed by the president of the Montreal Stock Exchange. Our attitude to the desirability of maintaining and increasing Canadian ownership of Canadian assets was clearly set out in the budget speech. It remains unchanged.[35]

This rebuke did not quite say that Kierans had been responsible for the government's change of policy; but it came as close as self-respect permitted. At the Montreal Stock Exchange the evidence seemed clear; when the news of Gordon's statement reached the exchange, traders carried Kierans around the floor on their shoulders in triumph.[36]

Trading picked up sharply in the closing minutes of the stock exchange day following the announcement. It was soon evident in the House that the Minister of Finance had committed a major blunder, open to dangerous misinterpretation, by making his announcement before the close of the market, in violation of the normal parliamentary practice. Later in the afternoon George Nowlan asked: "Why withdraw the provision twenty minutes before the stock markets in Toronto closed today? Why withdraw it at that time and have the markets boiling again? It was a rather injudicious act and due notice should be taken of it."[37]

Nowlan's question foretold a new cascade of criticism. Every sentence, now, that Gordon uttered in the House was subjected to ruthless scrutiny by the government's opponents; every hint of ambiguity was searched for evidence of deceit, arrogance or incompetence. A central measure of his budget had been suspended even before the beginning of the regular budget debate; a government that had promised efficiency and order was in sudden disarray; and the man praised as the inspiration and wonder-worker of the Liberal party's recovery was the source of its humiliation. The fall from grace was precipitous, and Walter Gordon left the House on Wednesday evening feeling bruised, depressed and isolated. On Thursday morning the *Globe and Mail* called for his resignation, and by the time he read the editorial Gordon himself knew that the imbroglio had forced that question upon him.[38] He cancelled his early morning appointments in order to see the Prime Minister, and told Pearson that he would go if the Prime Minister wished him to do so. A subtle exchange followed.[39] Pearson took a middle position between requesting his Minister's resignation and affirming his confidence in Gordon. He asked Gordon whether he had the confidence himself to carry on. From the Prime Minister's point of view, this may have been an understandable expression of neutrality which reflected both his personal affection for Gordon and his political reserve at the embarrassments Gordon had brought upon the government. But it was not quite what Gordon needed from his superior: a declaration of total confidence. Walter Gordon's uncertainty had been over his continued usefulness to the Prime Minister and the party, not over his own estimate of himself. He had no difficulty telling Pearson that he still possessed his self-confidence. Pearson allowed that affirmation to settle the question, and

Gordon remained in the Cabinet as Minister of Finance.[40]

By throwing the choice back to Gordon, Pearson had signalled a new restraint in the relationship between the two men which was reflected in the House of Commons and remarked upon by a few perceptive reporters. Reviewing events in the House a few days later, I. Norman Smith of the Ottawa *Journal* noticed that the Prime Minister's assistance to his besieged colleague was limited to occasional "bristling" interjections.

> Mr. Pearson was in a dilemma. Party solidarity and his natural instinct to stand by a friend prompted him to defend Mr. Gordon. But one felt that as an experienced civil servant his heart wasn't in it, nor did he want too exuberantly to champion Mr. Gordon's methods before the country's gaze.
>
> Mr. Knowles and Mr. Diefenbaker harried the Prime Minister but he took little part in the exchanges except intermittently to rise and say in effect "he's my man." One missed in him the parliamentary experience that would have enabled Mr. King, say, to speak so often, so long and so disarmingly that the Chamber would lose sight of the main offence and, perhaps so too the press and the country.[41]

Walter Gordon was alone in his political distress, without the full-spirited support that a Minister normally expects from his Prime Minister and Cabinet colleagues. Among them, only Mitchell Sharp came vigorously to his defence on June 24, and that defence was limited to justifying Gordon's use of temporary advisers.[42] On the substance of the budget, he was left to fend for himself with the aid of two parliamentary secretaries, Edgar Benson and Jack Davies.[43] This was a quite extraordinary failure, and a source of disappointment for Walter Gordon. Soon afterwards Gordon expressed some of his feelings in a letter to a friend:

> The going has been pretty rough but I suppose I was vulnerable. I am not at all sure how things will work out but will continue to get along as best I can in a strange and somewhat discouraging atmosphere.[44]

The storm had to be endured. The question periods on June 20 and 21 involved prolonged baiting of the Finance Minister which was joined by some of the mildest members of the Opposition. The possibility of the Minister's resignation, which had already been denied outside the House by the Prime Minister, was denied again inside.[45] (Speculation was kept alive by the knowledge that Richard O'Hagan, the Prime Minister's press secretary, had conducted an informal poll of members of the press gallery asking whether the Minister of Finance should resign. This indiscretion, which followed Pearson's and Gordon's agreement that he should remain in the Cabinet, was an unexpected further blow to Gordon's morale. The Prime Minister denied knowledge of his press secretary's action.)[46] Under pressure to explain whether the announcement suspending the takeover tax was made before the close of the market "by deliberate decision or through inadvertence," Gordon sought the protection of collective Cabinet responsibility. "It was the view of the government," he replied, "that as soon as a decision was reached it should be announced."[47] As long as he remained in the Cabinet, this sharing of responsibility was the proper formula for his defence on the issue. Yet neither the Prime Minister nor any other Minister came to his support.

The six-day formal debate on the budget began on Wednesday, June 19 and ended a week later on June 26. Twenty-six MPs participated, in addition to the Minister, but there was scarcely any coherent analysis of the budget measures. Few Opposition members even attempted to consider the budget carefully as a whole and on its merits; the suspicion must arise that the House was almost universally deficient in economic understanding. Only Colin Cameron and T. C. Douglas for the NDP made articulate efforts to examine the weaknesses of the budget. Their case was that the economy remained stagnant, and that the budget failed to provide the necessary expansionist stimulation. Colin Cameron compared the speech to "a patchwork quilt made out of a lot of scraps of pre-Keynesian economics, tattered attempts at modern economics, and in the end producing a bed cover that is not going to keep us very warm in the forthcoming cold weather."[48] He was puzzled by the Minister's inconsistency.

> Our Finance Minister made ... a very slight bow in the direction of acknowledging the role that deficit financing has in periods of economic stagnation and high unemployment. I was relieved to hear him say that, but then astounded a few minutes later to hear him produce a complete non sequitur and to proceed to chase a "will o' the wisp" of a balanced budget when he told us that we must begin now to move towards balancing the budget under conditions of high employment. ... This move in the direction of a balanced budget is, of course, well calculated by every respectable economic opinion in the country, and indeed in the world, to prove

a complete obstacle to attaining that period of high employment and economic activity towards which the Minister is looking.[49]

The major elements in the budget, Cameron held, were hold-the-line or regressive. Tommy Douglas concurred.

> The Minister began his speech by making a good Keynesian case for deficit financing and then, having made his proper genuflections to the mecca of Keynesian economics, he took off across the arid sands of orthodox financing that lead to the land of unemployment and economic stagnation.[50]

While the NDP sympathized with the Minister's desire to meet the challenge of foreign ownership, its spokesmen were sceptical that this could be accomplished by exhortation or adjustment "within the framework of our traditional economic and social relationships."[51] Cameron asserted that only massive public investment in the resource industries, undertaken in cooperation with the provinces, would begin to meet the problem.

The irresistible target of condemnation for Opposition members, of course, was what they described as the Minister's incompetence in proposing the takeover tax without foreseeing its difficulties, and then withdrawing it in confusion. This easy criticism did not require any analysis or judgment of the tax, and what was not required was not volunteered. In a second contribution to the debate on June 24, Walter Gordon told the House that the tax, "while highly desirable in its objective," was "not practicable for this budget" and would therefore not be reintroduced.[52] The subject had become so sensitive and so obscured by political complications that it was impossible to consider with any calm and rationality. Edgar Benson, in his defence of the Minister, made only passing reference to the takeover tax as one "which formed only a minor part of this program and which has since been withdrawn."[53] Jack Davis, who was the only member to devote his speech to the question of foreign ownership, did not mention the takeover tax as one of the budget measures until he was questioned. But then he came to its support:

> . . . there are undoubtedly many measures which are required and they will have to dovetail together in order to ensure a substantial measure of Canadian ownership and control. I believe that the thirty percent tax or something of that type, is one of the essential ingredients necessary in order to arrest at least the substantial swing to foreign ownership and control.[54]

These brief words from a young parliamentary secretary were the only support offered for the takeover tax during the entire debate by any member other than the Minister of Finance.

The government was never in danger of defeat on the budget resolution. In two votes on June 24 and June 26 it survived by 113 to 73 and 119 to 74, sustained by Social Credit and the abstentions of the NDP. But in spirit it had been badly shaken, and the end of the budget debate did not promise great relief. Intensive lobbying on behalf of the housebuilding industry against the sales tax continued. The Cabinet felt vulnerable under such pressure after one retreat, and for a few days at the end of June and beginning of July it was left without direction when Prime Minister Pearson entered hospital for surgery to remove a cyst in his neck.[55]

On June 24 the Minister of National Revenue, J. R. Garland, made a statement of clarification to the House enumerating various exemptions from the tax on building materials. Still the pressure for further exemptions, or for cancellation of the tax, mounted. It was clear that there were serious problems in administering the tax, that considerations of equity weighed in favour of wider exemptions, and that imposition of the tax might seriously depress the level of new investment in construction. Criticism of the tax measures designed to encourage Canadian ownership also persisted. By the end of the month officials in National Revenue and Finance were at work on a series of amended budget resolutions in the expectation that the Minister would shortly make another budget statement; but the substance of these resolutions awaited the approval of the Minister and Cabinet.

On July 1, Garland proposed to an informal meeting of ministers that the sales tax on building materials should be altered to apply in stages, according to a recommendation made the previous week by the National House Builders' Association. Walter Gordon's inclination to refuse any more major concessions on the budget was supported by Mitchell Sharp and Maurice Lamontagne.[56] On July 5 the Cabinet met at the Prime Minister's summer residence on Harrington Lake (where Pearson was recuperating) to review the situation, and Gordon again argued for a policy of firmness on the sales tax. But the "Pearson Team" was disintegrating in the absence of strong guidance from the Prime Minister.

By this time only Harry Hays, Judy LaMarsh and Maurice Lamontagne backed me up. I felt I had the choice of resigning or agreeing to amend the original resolution. . . .

As I had no intention of resigning, I decided to succumb to this pressure from the Cabinet and to bring in new resolutions to the Income Tax Act and the Excise Tax Act.[57]

Judy LaMarsh recalled how Gordon's position was abandoned, and how easily it might have been sustained that day at Harrington Lake:

> And so, item by item, we backtracked from the proposals in the budget speech and left it in shreds around Walter. Some were reluctant to say what they thought should be done. Others of us simply didn't know; we were too green. Had Sharp at that point stood solidly behind Walter, the team would have been unimpaired and the government strengthened, not weakened. And Pearson's standing by his most important Minister would have impressed us all deeply, as we were impressed by his failure to do so.[58]

The House had already agreed to set aside time on the evening of Monday, July 8 for the Minister of Finance's statement, which was mockingly referred to by Conservative members as "the baby budget" and by the NDP's Stanley Knowles as "the anticipated modification of the budget."[59] Charles Lynch commented that "Finance Minister Walter Gordon is going through his fourth straight weekend of crisis since he brought in his budget," and predicted that "what he says and does in the House of Commons on Monday night at eight o'clock will have a decisive effect on his own personal future, and perhaps on the future of the Liberal party."[60] He described the Minister's forthcoming statement as "The Great Rescue Operation," which would have to remove all the remaining doubts about the application of taxes imposed in the budget. Lynch believed that there had to be "a clear limitation on the changes that he will announce Monday night – he could not bring in major revisions and remain Finance Minister."

> If the Monday night statement is a flap [sic], then Mr. Gordon could be out in a hurry, of his own volition. His intimates doubt if one of so proud a nature can take much more in the way of all-out criticism, and by the same token they say he would never agree to move to a lesser portfolio in the Cabinet.
>
> One mystery that awaits clarification Monday night is why, if he merely intends to clarify the tax measures, Mr. Gordon did not do it in some less spectacular way than by a formal statement in the House of Commons, in circumstances that exactly parallel the making of a budget speech.[61]

The reason was that Gordon had already decided to concede further substantial changes in the budget – and to hold on as Finance Minister in spite of the resulting humiliation.

When Gordon made his painful statement to the House on Monday evening, he had already suffered so much punishment from Parliament in the previous weeks that his grit and integrity now attracted palpable sympathy from his antagonists.[62] Nevertheless the speech was a humbling performance of great courage, delivered to an audience that could not restrain its urge to jeer and laugh. "No government and no Minister of Finance," Gordon began, "should be reluctant to reconsider and revise proposals if public discussion shows it to be desirable."[63] He systematically reviewed a dozen changes and clarifications in the budget resolutions. Most important, he announced that the sales tax on building materials would be applied progressively in three stages over a period of eighteen months, and that the definitions of Canadian ownership required for the application of the reduced withholding tax and increased capital depreciation allowances would be substantially eased.[64] The Minister conceded that the alteration of the sales tax would reduce anticipated revenues by $115 million in the current fiscal year and $125 million in the succeeding year (thus largely wiping out the predicted reduction in the budget deficit which Gordon had emphasized in his speech of June 13). But Gordon believed that

> . . . on balance the changes now proposed will be helpful. They do not alter the objectives of the budget. They will improve its imme- diate economic effect and stimulate expansion and employment.[65]

In his response on behalf of the NDP, Colin Cameron needled the Minister.

> The budget is to be improved, and it has been improved undoubt- edly, by taking the exact reverse position from that which the Minister took less than a month ago. It seems to me that if these retreats do as the Minister suggests tonight, stimulate expansion and employment, then the budget as a whole, as I said earlier in the House, is not calculated to stimulate employment or expan- sion.[66]

The press, predictably, showed no more kindness to Walter Gordon and the government for their display of uncertainty and irresolution.[67] In the course of his disorderly retreat, the Minister of Finance had

effectively put into limbo two of his professed objectives: the movement toward a balanced budget and the repatriation of control in the
Canadian economy. Whether or not one accepted the legitimacy and
importance of these goals, the spectacle of withdrawal had been disenchanting.

The ordeal was not yet over. Gordon had still to endure nine days
of detailed discussion of his measures, and the revelation of more
unforeseen complications, in House committee. But the worst embarrassments passed on July 8. Gordon himself led the committee of ways
and means through the details of the revised budget resolutions, and
there were a few welcome days when other government measures
occupied the House. In the meantime, however, the government faced
another unexpected crisis.

*

On the morning of Thursday, July 18, the counsellor for economic
affairs at the American embassy, Francis Linville, telephoned Gordon
to request that the Minister meet at noon with Merlyn Trued, a deputy
assistant secretary of the U.S. Treasury, who had flown to Ottawa with
an important message for the Minister.[68] Gordon had previously
agreed to meet James S. Rockefeller of the National City Bank of New
York at the same time, and did not wish to postpone this engagement.
He thus arranged for the senior Assistant Deputy Minister, Wynne
Plumptre, to take Trued to the Rideau Club for a drink before Gordon
joined them for lunch.[69] When Gordon met them shortly before one
o'clock, Trued gave him a letter from Douglas Dillon, the United States
secretary of the Treasury, and suggested that Gordon should read it
at once. Gordon did so with growing alarm. Dillon's letter informed
him that President Kennedy was proposing to Congress that day a
special tax on American purchases of foreign securities which was
designed to overcome the serious American balance of payments deficit. The tax was to be generally applicable, with specific exemptions
for developing nations such as Israel and Mexico, but no exemption
for Canada. Its effect would be to increase the cost of selling Canadian
securities in New York by the equivalent of more than one percent in
interest for Canadian provinces, municipalities, and private borrowers,
driving them back into the domestic market for their funds. The
sudden expectation of losing this major source of capital was bound
to cause panic on the Canadian stock exchanges, a run on the dollar,
and probably another forced devaluation. "This," Gordon was
convinced, "would mean a financial crisis of major proportions. It
would be a long time before faith and confidence in the Canadian

dollar could be re-established."[70] (The Minister of Finance had reason to be sensitive to the jittery state of the Canadian market after the response to his own takeover tax one month before.)

Gordon excused himself immediately and returned to his office to prepare a statement for the opening of the House at 2:30 P.M. When the House met, he reviewed the details of the president's tax proposal, and reflected cautiously that if Congress approved the program, the repercussions "may well have an important effect upon Canada's balance of payments and upon the Canadian economy as a whole."[71] The crisis, however, was immediate; and Gordon's statement was intended as reassuring notice that the government was alert to the situation and would act expeditiously to relieve it. Gordon concluded that "It would be unwise for me to say more than this, however, until there has been time to give careful study and consideration to all the implications of the president's proposals."

Panic selling had already begun on the Toronto and Montreal exchanges, and on Thursday and Friday there was what the Minister of Finance described as "a fast walk" on the Canadian dollar. Canadian reserves of U.S. dollars fell by $110 million as investors sought to protect themselves against the possibility of devaluation; by Monday, if expectations had not changed over the weekend, a major devaluation would be inevitable. Following his short statement to the House, Gordon and his officials acted decisively.

> I called Douglas Dillon on the telephone and gave him some indication of our concern. I asked him if he would be able to receive someone from Canada to discuss the matter some time on the Saturday afternoon or evening. Dillon agreed to this and Louis Rasminsky, Wynne Plumptre and Ed Ritchie, of the Department of External Affairs . . . left for Washington. I did not go myself because I thought this would attract too much attention to the seriousness we attached to the president's message.[72]

That evening the Secretary of State for External Affairs, Paul Martin, met with the American ambassador, Walton Butterworth, and Merlyn Trued to inform them that Canada would seek exemption from the interest equalization tax. The degree of Canada's alarm, and the developing chaos in the Canadian stock market, came as surprises to the Americans.[73] Trued returned to the United States on Friday to brief his colleagues in the Treasury Department, and Gordon talked again to Dillon on the telephone.[74] "By Friday evening," wrote Gerald Wright, "Dillon had been in touch with President Kennedy and the way was being cleared for some kind of Canadian exemption."[75] This was not known to the Canadians, however, until Sunday afternoon, and in the interval the delegation to Washington had to make its case in person to the secretary of the Treasury. On Saturday they met Dillon, under secretaries Robert Roosa and George Ball, and the assistant secretary of the Treasury for tax policy, Stanley Surrey.[76] Rasminsky argued that the inflow of American capital contributed essentially to financing American exports to Canada, and that any interference with this capital flow would seriously affect the scale of Canada's imports from the United States – thus harming the American balance of payments, the ailing patient which the American measures were intended to cure. Perhaps this argument influenced the Americans; more probably, it appears, they "were moved to grant the exemption less by the substance of the Canadian argument than by the financial panic spreading in Toronto and Montreal which posed the present threat of a Canadian devaluation with harmful consequences for both countries."[77] In return for a partial exemption, they demanded, and received, a *quid pro quo* from Canada which suggests that they were not convinced by the claim that their own interest would inevitably be damaged by applying the tax to Canadian securities.[78] The Canadians were in a weak bargaining position, and by Sunday afternoon they had agreed to a joint communiqué which would halt the financial panic in Canada, but at a price. At 6:00 P.M. on Sunday evening the two governments made simultaneous announcements in Washington and Ottawa of their agreement.

For many years the capital markets of the two countries have been closely interconnected, and United States exports of capital to Canada have financed a substantial portion of the Canadian current account deficit with the U.S. This need continues. A portion of these flows must be supplied through the sale of new issues of Canadian securities in American markets. U.S. officials had considered that ample flows for these needs would continue under the proposed interest equalization tax. However, Canadian representatives stated that this would require a very substantial rise in the entire Canadian interest rate structure. It was recognized by both governments that such a development would be undesirable in present economic circumstances.

In the light of this situation U.S. officials agreed that the draft legislation to be submitted to congress would include a provision authorizing a procedure under which the president could modify the application of the tax by the establishment from time to time of exemptions, which he could make either unlimited or limited in amount. The president would thus have the flexibility to permit tax free purchases of new issues needed to maintain the unimpeded flow of trade and payments between the two countries, and to take care of exceptional situations that might arise in the case of other countries.[79]

The next paragraph outlined the Canadian concession.

> The Canadian authorities stated that it would not be the desire or intention of Canada to increase her foreign exchange reserves through the proceeds of borrowings in the United States, and it is the hope and expectation of both governments that by maintaining close consultation it will prove possible in practice to have an unlimited exemption for Canada without adverse effect on the United States.[80]

The agreement left the Minister of Finance with mixed feelings of satisfaction and anxiety. The emergency had been overcome promptly, and this owed something to the alertness of Gordon and his associates in the Department of Finance and the Bank of Canada. But in the end the resolution rested on the good grace of the American government. A lack of disposition to cooperate, on the part of Dillon or President Kennedy, would have been disastrous for the Canadian economy. The voluntary limitation on Canadian exchange reserves, it soon appeared, would be interpreted strictly by the American administration, and would therefore be a significant inhibition on Canada's freedom to conduct an independent monetary policy. When Prime Minister Pearson reported to the House on the agreement the next day, the leader of the Opposition warned that the settlement "still leaves, as I see it, a veto with the president of the United States with regard to the expansion of Canada's economy, which is something that is not in keeping with the sovereignty of this nation."[81] Walter Gordon did not need to be told.

It was ironic that this crisis followed so closely on the Minister of Finance's unsuccessful attempt to extricate Canada from its dependence upon the American capital market (and indirectly, as the affair illustrated, upon the policies of the American administration); that the American tax was designed to achieve a similar end; and that it had the same unsettling effects on the Canadian market. Inevitably, some Canadian observers wondered whether the application of the interest equalization tax to Canada was an act of retaliation for the foreign ownership measures of the budget, a brutal reminder that Canada could not safely enter on the path of independence without incurring the giant's wrath.[82] (Had the American action, perhaps, been prefigured a month before in Eric Kierans' warning to Gordon that the international reaction to his budget was "If that is what Canadians want, let them have it"?)

The Prime Minister would not admit this hypothesis, and took pains to insist that relations between the two countries were still governed by the spirit of the Hyannis Port communiqué, which had said that discussion of joint problems of trade and payments should always occur "in a positive and cooperative manner."[83] The dominant view, too, among senior officials in Ottawa has been that the crisis was not "intended to put a bumptious Canada in her place."[84] But this conclusion requires the implausible assumption that the American Treasury was both technically incompetent and politically guileless in applying the tax to Canada.[85] The economist A. E. Safarian has offered this judgment of the case:

> You must remember that the Americans had had a balance of payments problem for years before the July, 1963 Interest Equalization Tax was announced. . . . You must also remember that the American authorities had been talking in general terms about the possibility of restraining capital outflows for at least two years prior to that. One must ask why they decided to use this particular time, July, 1963, knowing full well what the implications for Canada would be . . . no great amount of expertise was required to anticipate what the immediate effects would be. It may have been colossal thoughtlessness or incompetence and not outright retaliation, but it was done in a context in which we had set a precedent by interfering with the flow of capital through Mr. Gordon's June, 1963 budget. The Americans may well have felt this freed them to experiment with controls on the flow of capital too.[86]

Gerald Wright offers evidence for a similar but more complex explanation. The Treasury considered but rejected an exemption for Canada prior to the president's announcement. Treasury officials had previously sought Canada's agreement to convert Canadian holdings of U.S. dollars into a form other than U.S. Treasury bills, which would not be recorded as a liability in American balance of payments statistics, but agreement had failed at the technical level.[87] When the new Liberal government sought also to limit the flow of American capital into Canada, the U.S. Treasury concluded that Canada's clear intention was to withdraw from any special economic relationship.

176

Henceforth, it appeared, the most mutually satisfactory method of treating Canadian-American economic issues was to include these in the purview of policy towards other western nations rather than accord the country any special dispensations. Such dispensations, with their attendant costs for Canadians in terms of national self-esteem, were likely only to create acrimony between the two governments.[88]

What is more, the annoyance caused in Congress by the Canadian budget made it difficult to offer Canada an exemption in the original announcement of the interest equalization tax. Circumstances required that the diplomatic game should be played out, the Canadian purpose tested, and the price of cooperation exacted from the Canadian government, if it wished to cooperate.[89] In the result, Washington gained an influence over the management of Canada's international reserves which was more substantial than the bookkeeping advantage it had previously sought from the Diefenbaker government. The crisis illustrated Canada's complicated entanglement in the American economic system. But it passed so quickly that the implications were only slowly absorbed into the discussion of Canada's economic relationship with the United States.

*

When the wearying month of July was over and the House adjourned for the summer on August 2, the Minister of Finance's measures had not entirely cleared the House, but the budget controversy had faded and the Minister had survived – preserving his outward calm, but bruised and disappointed, in a certain way more human than the public figure of June 13. In retrospect he could admit the folly of the "sixty days" and the unrealizable expectations the slogan had aroused (among the Cabinet and party as much as the public); he could see that others might fairly consider the government's self-confidence unjustified; he could even, in his detachment, see justice in some of the rebukes that had ended the "sixty days." Colin Cameron described the train of events soon after budget night in the imagery of Greek tragedy – with some exaggeration perhaps, but not too much:

> . . . I cannot help thinking that the unfortunate Minister of Finance is a victim of what the old Greeks called the sin of hubris, overweening pride, which invites the furies, and the inevitable punishment.[90]

Walter Gordon's pride was part of the collective pride of a complacent and over-confident Cabinet. But when the crisis came, most of its members, including the Prime Minister, neglected to share the Minister of Finance's humiliations. They may not have been particularly wedded to his policies, they may have expected him to resign, they may simply have been startled and confused by the quick succession of embarrassments. But beyond the budget's inadequacies, the prolonged failure of the Cabinet to defend the Minister was unedifying and revealing. The Prime Minister's decision not to ask for his Minister's resignation was an indication of Pearson's respect for and loyalty to a friend which other prime ministers might not have demonstrated in the circumstances. But once that choice had been made, Gordon was left to defend himself. He kept his dignity through it all; and because his colleagues did not share his defence, neither did the government gain collective credit for his steadiness and honesty. His immediate policies were in shambles, his reputation for administrative competence was undermined. He had lost his place of dominant influence with the Prime Minister and Cabinet and could only hope to recover it by cautious and patient advance, if at all. His cause and the government's reputation had suffered; but in the turbulence he had also revealed to the party and the public his quality as a man. That was something which found its reward more and more in the affection of his close colleagues in Cabinet and the Liberal caucus. As the pressures of the political relationship complicated his friendship with the Prime Minister, the bonds of friendship and mutual loyalty with other political colleagues were reinforced. These new bonds reflected, perhaps, his very lack of power. They were compensation for the political life nonetheless, and Gordon accepted them with gratitude and lightness of spirit. Not long after the misfortunes of June and July, his sparkle and self-deprecating wit had returned.

The budget debacle inevitably strengthened the element in the Cabinet which had no commitment to Gordon's program of repatriating control of the economy. In combination with the crisis over the American tax, it had also illustrated the complexity of the task: and this Walter Gordon himself had not entirely foreseen. His campaign to commit the Canadian government to his views through the persuasion of Lester Pearson and the Liberal rally, followed by an electoral victory, had evidently been inadequate preparation. It was not just that the rush to produce a budget had left insufficient time to elaborate the details and assess the possible effects of his policy; it was also, more significantly, that when the policy was shown to be imperfect it suddenly had no defenders. The Cabinet, the party, the parliamentary Opposition, the government's advisers, the press, and the public did not comprehend and were not committed to Walter Gordon's nationalist policies. None of them, when their support was needed, could carry that support beyond the most vague approval in principle. Walter Gordon had underestimated the strength of the financial community's reactions, or overestimated his power as Minister of Finance to control those reactions. (Perhaps that miscalculation could be narrowed down to the failure to anticipate Eric Kierans' actions – because without his intervention the difficulties of the budget might possibly have been managed without fundamental damage to Gordon's policies.)

The general failure of understanding was not the responsibility of Walter Gordon. He, after all, had begun the nationalist campaign and persisted in it virtually alone since 1957. In that campaign he had conspicuously lacked the help of economists or publicists (aside from the notable assistance of Beland Honderich and the Toronto *Star*) to deepen his case or propagate it vigorously. He had been arguing against some of the dominant assumptions of the postwar world, and within a party which had given its faith to those assumptions. His failure to make much progress by 1963 is not surprising. What seems rash in retrospect was his assumption before June 13 that he had laid adequate foundations of support for his radical program. That assumption followed, above all, from his trust in Lester Pearson, his belief that Pearson fully shared his commitment, and his optimism that the leader of the Liberal party could act as a free agent in power. When the crisis came, Gordon discovered that the market could defeat his objects, and that Mike Pearson was no nationalist ideologue.

Pulling Apart or Pulling Together
            1963 – 1964

Despite the chastening experience of the budget
crisis, the government came out of the summer session of Parliament
with considerable credit. One parliamentary reporter assessed the
record as "adequate but not inspiring,"[1] another called it good, and
a third judged that "the government probably got more legislation of
a substantially reforming nature on the books in two and a half months
than any new government has before." The veteran commentator
Bruce Hutchison summarized the government's achievements in a
mood of tolerance which was common.

> The successes of the Pearson government are substantial and
> would be clearer to the public if they had not been obscured by
> certain failures.
> In the first place, it is remarkable that a minority government not
> only has survived at all but seems sure of survival for some time
> to come. In the second, it has restored normal relations with our
> friends abroad and ended years of barren quarrel. In the third, some
> hopeful policies have been launched and some unsuspected talent
> discovered. Above all, the public sees that the government wants
> to get things done and this in itself is a refreshing change.[2]

The new government's initial fund of goodwill had not yet been
exhausted.
Before the adjournment, four major pieces of economic legislation – all of which had been dominant in the Liberal party's electoral
program – had passed through Parliament into law. The Department
of Industry, the Economic Council of Canada, and the Municipal Loan

Fund had been created, and the Atlantic Development Board had been transformed from an advisory to an executive agency with a capital fund of $100 million to assist industrial growth in the four eastern provinces. A parliamentary committee on defence had been appointed under the chairmanship of Maurice Sauvé, the Royal Commission on Bilingualism and Biculturalism had been established, salaries and allowances for MPs had been raised from $10,000 to $18,000 a year, and a private member's Bill had been passed ridding the House of Commons of its anomalous duty to legislate for all divorce cases in Quebec and Newfoundland. These were all, of course, achievements in potential, whose substance would only gradually emerge as the new agencies and committees began to do their work.

The members of the ministry were beginning to establish their relative weight and influence in Cabinet, and to convey this balance to the House of Commons and the public. While Walter Gordon's status was now uncertain (although he was still close to the Prime Minister), that of J. W. Pickersgill and Paul Martin had been reinforced. The Prime Minister tended to lean more on their advice after the budget crisis.[3] Among the new ministers Mitchell Sharp had shown the most obvious ability to assert his influence, and Guy Favreau, Allan MacEachen and Bud Drury had made strong impressions.[4] The outlines of the reformist-conservative division in the Cabinet were faintly emerging, although John Bird (writing in June) could not see any "present signs of an open tug of war, though this may develop later."[5] (It seemed to be presaged fairly quickly thereafter in the crucial Cabinet meeting at Harrington Lake on July 5.) Bird had no doubt that Mitchell Sharp was "the ablest, most articulate 'right-winger' of the Cabinet," and grouped Pickersgill, Chevrier and McIlraith clearly with him. Walter Gordon and Allan MacEachen were obviously "well to the left" of Sharp, and Drury stood somewhere between. Walter Gordon felt himself closest at this time to Pearson, Maurice Lamontagne, Harry Hays, Judy LaMarsh, Allan MacEachen, and Guy Favreau.[6] Gordon's supporters in the Cabinet took for granted his leadership of the reformist group, and increasingly saw Gordon's position not just as the leader of a faction but as the only source of articulate direction in the Cabinet. As Judy LaMarsh wrote:

Walter Gordon was the only member of the Cabinet to have an overall view of where we were intending to go – the rest just saw their own narrow area of activity. I am far from sure that Pearson himself had a good view of what he intended to accomplish. If there was one, it was Walter Gordon's.[7]

Through 1963 and 1964 Gordon believed that the Prime Minister still allowed his progressive instincts to dominate; and this meant that the relatively cohesive group of Gordon and his closest associates, who normally shared views on policy, "consequently ... had considerable influence in Cabinet. As a rule, the Prime Minister ... agreed with us – or we agreed with him, whichever way one likes to put it."[8] These were early days. Spirits were not yet exhausted by the excessive acrimony of the parliamentary conflict; the lines of division within the government had not yet hardened; and the wit and good humour of Pearson, Gordon, Pickersgill, Martin, and Judy LaMarsh helped to sustain the Cabinet's morale and smooth the rough edges of disagreement.[9]

During the parliamentary recess – which offered the Minister of Finance the chance for only eight days' holiday – Gordon made two trips to Washington. The first was intended as an occasion to meet Douglas Dillon, the U.S. secretary of the Treasury. Gordon took the opportunity on August 2 to press for a blanket exemption for Canadian securities (old as well as new) from the interest equalization tax. Gordon found Dillon to be "a pleasant, straightforward man with a considerable understanding of and sympathy for the Canadian position";[10] but Dillon refused the exemption. This diplomatic venture did not help Gordon's faltering public reputation, and Gerald Waring (who assumed that the purpose of the visit was limited to discussion of the interest equalization tax) reflected toughly that the mission had been "foolhardy and deserved to fail."

> In the diplomatic business you don't expose your throat for the friendly caress of your opponent's knife. Before Gordon went to Washington he should have obtained private assurances from the Americans that his visit would not be fruitless. His record just couldn't afford failure.
>
> In his own mind, attuned to the ways of the business world, his mission no doubt seemed a worthwhile gamble – nothing to lose and much to gain. The worst Dillon could do was say no.
>
> But Mr. Gordon is not in business; he's in politics, where values are markedly different. And so what is left of his election prestige took another severe blow. . . .
>
> Nowhere in the course that Gordon followed is there any indication that Martin or Pearson dutch-uncled the Finance Minister on these fine points.
>
> Pearson believes in letting his ministers run their own shows. Gordon does not welcome advice from other Cabinet ministers.

Martin was one of those on whose faces smug satisfaction was seen when Gordon was mired in his budget woes.

What it all adds up to is a glaring lack of teamwork, of backstopping, of base coaching.[11]

After his meeting with Dillon, Gordon and the Canadian ambassador, Charles Ritchie, met the under secretary of state, George Ball.

> Ball and I were on a first name basis and I was, therefore, somewhat startled when, almost immediately after Ritchie and I arrived in his office, he began a tirade in which he criticized Canada and the Canadian government in general and me and my June 13 budget in particular. His tone was heated, his choice of language gaudy, and his facts inaccurate. But this did not seem to trouble him in the least. By the time he first stopped to draw breath, some twenty minutes later, I had decided to reply in the same vein. I made it clear that he had no right to speak to a member of the Canadian government in the way he had done, and pointed out, moreover, that he did not seem to know what he was talking about.[12]

Gordon reviewed Canada's case for seeking exemption from the interest equalization tax, and emphasized that the country's concern over non-resident control of industry stemmed from the unusual magnitude of this control, which rested mostly in American hands. "George agreed at once that he had not understood the problem and thanked me for explaining the situation to him. When we left his office we were on good terms again."[13] That evening, following dinner at Douglas Dillon's, Gordon recalls that Ball

> . . . made a short speech in which he said he had come to the dinner to thank me for the way in which I had explained the Canadian situation to him that morning. He said he had learned more from me about Canada in half an hour than he had ever known before. Ritchie remarked to me afterwards that he felt this was quite a triumph and he hoped I would come to Washington more frequently.[14]

To teach George Ball would certainly require regular visits. By the time he published his memoir, *The Discipline of Power*, in 1968, he had Canada neatly placed within his expansionist perspective. Gordon may have sharpened, but did not alter, that perspective. A few condescending paragraphs contained Ball's definitive response to Gordon.

Canada, I have long believed, is fighting a rearguard action against the inevitable. Living next to our nation, with a population ten times as large as theirs and a gross national product fourteen times as great, the Canadians recognize their need for United States capital; but at the same time they are determined to maintain their economic and political independence. Their position is understandable, and the desire to maintain their national integrity is a worthy objective. But the Canadians pay heavily for it and, over the years, I do not believe they will succeed in reconciling the intrinsic contradiction of their position. I wonder, for example, if the Canadian people will be prepared indefinitely to accept, for the psychic satisfaction of maintaining a separate national and political identity, a per capita income less than three-fourths of ours. The struggle is bound to be a difficult one – and I suspect, over the years, a losing one. Meanwhile there is danger that the efforts of successive Canadian governments to prevent United States economic domination will drive them toward increasingly restrictive nationalistic measures that are good neither for Canada nor for the health of the whole trading world.

Thus, while I can understand the motivating assumptions of the Canadian position, I cannot predict a long life expectancy for her present policies. ... Sooner or later, commercial imperatives will bring about free movement of all goods back and forth across our long border; and when that occurs, or even before it does, it will become unmistakably clear that countries with economies so inextricably intertwined must also have free movement of the other vital factors of production – capital, services and labour. The result will inevitably be substantial economic integration, which will require for its full realization a progressively expanding area of common political decision.[15]

Seven weeks after Gordon's first ministerial visit to Washington, the eighth meeting of the joint Canadian-American cabinet committee on trade and economic affairs (the first since the formation of the Pearson government) was held in Washington from September 19 to 21, 1963. It was attended for Canada by Gordon, Martin, Sharp, Drury, Hays, Rasminsky, and Charles Ritchie, and was the occasion for a Canadian reprise on the balance of payments and the interest equalization tax.[16] At the opening reception, Gordon encountered George Ball in heated discussion with Louis Rasminsky on the balance of payments, and was surprised that Ball "evidently had forgotten all about my conversation with him in August, [and] was saying that

Canada was being anything but helpful in these matters."[17] Twice, in the two days of meetings that followed, Gordon lectured the Americans "carefully and in some detail" on the Canadian case that her imports of American capital helped to finance American exports to Canada and therefore deserved protection from the American legislation. He explained the Canadian government's anxiety over the scale of direct U.S. investment, but stressed the assistance which Canada was giving to the American payments position. At the end, Gordon "did feel that the Canadian position was more clearly understood by our American opposite numbers."[18] When the interest equalization tax legislation finally made its way through Congress later in the year, a number of amendments which improved the prospects for Canadian treatment had been incorporated in it as the result of various pressures. But the repeated Canadian request for total exemption was never granted.

Two of the new Liberal government's programs had provoked severe criticism from the provinces during the opening session of Parliament. These were the Municipal Development and Loan Fund and the proposed national pension plan, both of them positive federal initiatives to promote public welfare in fields of jurisdiction where the provinces expect to exercise priority. Both challenged the autonomist sentiments of the Quebec government, and the interest of all the provinces in increasing their shares of the collective tax dollar. In introducing the Municipal Loan Fund Bill to the House on June 11, Walter Gordon insisted that loans would only be made with the approval of provincial authorities and in forms "which fully observe both the spirit and letter of the constitution."[19] Nevertheless the fund was to be federally administered, and the legislation had been prepared without consulting the provinces. The Opposition pointed to the paradox this action represented for a government pledging itself to the restoration of federal-provincial harmony. On June 26 the Quebec legislature, under pressure from the Union Nationale Opposition, unanimously adopted a resolution of censure on Ottawa describing the Bill as "a serious infringement upon the exclusive jurisdiction and the autonomy of the Province of Quebec." Two weeks later Premier Lesage wrote to Prime Minister Pearson accusing him of "a breach of your promise fully to respect provincial rights," and on July 12 Pearson met the complaint by calling a federal-provincial conference for July 26-27. Premier Robarts of Ontario joined the public chorus of protest on July 19.

The conference of July 26-27 was marked by Lester Pearson's flexibility. "There was no doubt," wrote John Saywell, "that the Prime Minister displayed his considerable diplomatic talents in setting the right tone and keeping discussions amicable."[20] The loan fund was salvaged and the provinces were appeased by conceding that loans should be provincially administered and divided among the provinces according to population. The provincial premiers and most newspapers regarded the outcome as a triumph for the new spirit of cooperative federalism. Few recalled that the conference had been precipitated by Ottawa's original failure to consult, or noted that the loan fund's professed object of channelling capital to areas of high unemployment had been defeated by the agreement to distribute funds by population. Walter Gordon judged that

> ... the division of the fund according to provincial population made something of a mockery of this important legislation to relieve unemployment. It seemed pointless to allot about five percent of the fund to Saskatchewan, for example, where there was little unemployment, and only four percent to Nova Scotia where unemployment was very high.[21]

The pension plan, too, fell victim to the government's haste and impatience. After April 22, as the Minister of National Health and Welfare, Judy LaMarsh, her officials and Tom Kent began to work through the immense complications of a contributory pension scheme, they realized that a Bill could not possibly be prepared for the summer session of Parliament as the Cabinet had intended.[22] Among other difficulties, a rushed timetable would not permit adequate consultation with the provinces; yet this was indispensable. Ottawa's constitutional jurisdiction over a new scheme was in doubt, and full provincial cooperation seemed necessary if the plan were to proceed. By early summer there were strong hints of caution from Quebec and Ontario, and Prime Minister Pearson agreed to place the subject on the agenda of the July federal-provincial conference. At that meeting the federal government sketched out its preliminary proposals. Premier Lesage responded that Quebec intended to create its own pension plan, and Premier Robarts of Ontario (who was preparing for a provincial election in September) reserved judgment until more details were available. Further discussion was postponed until a joint meeting of Health ministers on September 9 and 10.

Quebec's intransigence and the fact of delay both posed embarrassments for the Pearson government. Pensioners under the existing non-contributory security plan had been promised an immediate increase, to be financed from the contributory fund, in the Liberal electoral program. Now that the legislation had been set back, pressure mounted for a separate act to raise pensions at once. This, however, would involve a substantial addition to the government's spending estimates, which Walter Gordon had been struggling to control. Judy LaMarsh wrote that "It was with a big gulp of apprehension that I recommended that the old age increase be split off from the plan and paid as soon as Walter Gordon . . . thought it could be done."[23] Early in August, before she had made this recommendation, Gordon was reluctant to consider the prospect. He pointed out to the Prime Minister on August 8 that a $10 increase in the old age pension would add $120 million to the deficit. "Whether you personally and some of the rest of us could accept this after all we've said is debatable."[24]

But the survival of the new pension plan seemed to be threatened by the reluctance of Quebec and Ontario to cooperate, and political considerations thus took precedence. Could this reluctance be dissipated? Ottawa's first problem was how to respond to Premier Robarts in the coming provincial election. Should John Wintermeyer, the provincial Liberal leader, concentrate his attack on Robarts on the issue of support for the national pension plan? Should the federal Cabinet publicly throw its assistance to Wintermeyer in the hope of a provincial Liberal victory on the issue? In that case, would a Robarts victory humiliate Ottawa and kill the federal plan?[25] Gordon took a stark view of the alternatives.

> We might be able to get off the hook by making it clear ahead of time that we would have to drop our pension scheme entirely if Robarts wins the election and if he and Lesage continue to oppose it. This would be our justification for helping Wintermeyer. If by chance he won, we would then be in a position to go ahead with our plan as fast as possible with some provisions for leaving out Quebec.
> The alternative, of course, is to sit on the sidelines during the Ontario election and assume that Robarts will win it. If this proves to be correct, we would then quietly drop our pension scheme although we should not delude ourselves into thinking that the pressures to increase the present amount of the old age security payments will be reduced.[26]

The situation soon revealed itself as more complicated than this. The federal party decided to support Wintermeyer, and Wintermeyer chose to make the pension plan his central theme in the campaign. But Robarts undercut him by agreeing in principle to a national pension plan. Interest thus shifted to the question of the existing pension. If the prospects were, as seemed likely, for a Robarts win and continued pressure for an increase in old age security, the politic act for Ottawa might be to concede to that pressure at once and take whatever political credit there was to be gained from the concession. If there were a chance of a Wintermeyer victory, on the other hand, the promise of a pension increase following a Liberal win might help Wintermeyer along. This tactic was the one decided upon by the federal Cabinet in August. (It had the hallmark of Jack Pickersgill's excessive subtlety.) The Cabinet agreed to increase the pension by $10 a month, to $75, "as soon as Parliament reassembled on the last day of September."[27] Then John Wintermeyer was told in confidence of the Cabinet's decision.

> This was done in order to help him in his speeches, so that he might call for such an increase during the election, and point to the benefits to be expected by his election as a government friendly to the new Pearson government.[28]

Wintermeyer's chief adviser, however, immediately leaked the plot to the *Globe and Mail*. Robarts made the next cryptic move by announcing on September 8 that he would attend the conference of Health ministers beginning in Ottawa the next day. Judy LaMarsh wrote:

> It was unheard of for a premier to attend a meeting of lowly ministers. As unexpected as it was, it was as unwelcome. Cabinet hurriedly convened, and a statement was prepared for me to read at the meeting, which Pearson would simultaneously give out to the press in his own name, belatedly announcing the increase, which had already so infuriatingly been leaked. Robarts, in what I can only still think of as grandstanding (and damned effective, too), appeared at the meeting, and read a bland statement. It could have meant absolutely anything about his province's intentions regarding the pension plan. Upon the conclusion of the meeting ... Ontario's provincial treasurer ... told me privately that Ontario would be in, without any doubt.[29]

Score so far: a draw, with gains for the pensioners and the public amusement. From this point on Ottawa's persistence seemed perplexing. At the press conference concluding the meetings, Judy LaMarsh lashed out vigorously at Lesage and Robarts for opposing the federal pension plan, and followed this by throwing herself noisily into the Ontario campaign. When the Robarts government emerged, predictably triumphant, on September 25, the political reputation of Miss LaMarsh and the Pearson government were further battered. But planning for the pension plan could at last proceed for a few months out of the limelight.

Walter Gordon, fortunately, sat in the background for this performance, suffering no more than the $120 million drain on his bleeding deficit. In the early stages, however, he did fear that the Cabinet might abandon the contributory pension plan; and in his memorandum of August 8 to the Prime Minister he expressed an anxiety that could not be suppressed after his experience of the Cabinet's first months:

> What troubles me is what we do if we have to drop our present pension scheme without putting up a fight. I do not see how the government can be successful if it has no objectives or philosophy apart from sound administration. While the latter might be sufficient for the business community and the members of the party who are identified with that community, it will not be sufficient to retain the loyalties of many of the backbenchers from Ontario or of the people across Canada who helped to get us elected.[30]

This feeling that the government had to be seen "putting up a fight" may explain Judy LaMarsh's intervention in the Ontario campaign; but the battleground and the issue were ill-chosen in the circumstances.

The government's miscalculations appeared by this time to be the responsibility of two ministers, Walter Gordon and Judy LaMarsh. When the Liberal caucus met for three days just before the reassembly of Parliament on September 30, there was sustained criticism of the Cabinet for its performance, and above all for its failure to consult the provinces and the caucus during the formation of policy.[31] Not surprisingly, the criticism centred on Gordon and LaMarsh, and reports circulated that the Prime Minister was under pressure to shift them to other portfolios. On September 30, after a morning meeting of Cabinet, Mr. Pearson told reporters that the Cabinet had found the caucus "most useful and valuable," and remarked: "That doesn't look as if anybody's head is going to fall because of this meeting." When members of the press pointed out later that he had neither confirmed nor denied the existence of pressure from the caucus, the Prime Minister's office issued a second statement of clarification. "I have already denied," said the Prime Minister, "and I deny now categorically that there is any basis of fact in these reports."[32]

*

The autumn session of Parliament began in confusion and rancor when a splinter group of twelve Quebec Social Credit MPs under the leadership of Real Caouette requested recognition as a party in the House and precedence over the ten-member Social Credit rump. When a parliamentary committee rapidly recommended their recognition as a "group" but without precedence over Social Credit, there were allegations in the House that the government majority on the committee had accepted the compromise in return for assurances of Social Credit voting support for the government. This kind of exchange, given the government's precarious position, was quite understandable; but the more appropriate parliamentary arrangement for the reform wing of the party would be an understanding with the New Democratic Party. On October 10 the Toronto *Star* speculated editorially on the advantages of such cooperation:

> The obvious candidates for a progressive alliance would be the Liberals and the New Democrats. The NDP leaders have ruled out any organic union of the two parties, on grounds of principle, and there is no point in urging them to change their minds at this stage. But cooperation in a parliamentary alliance is a different matter. There would be no dishonour in the NDP agreeing to support the Liberals (or at least to abstain from voting) on confidence motions, in exchange for a government undertaking to proceed with important social reforms, such as national medical insurance.
>
> A limited alliance of this kind could offer Canada both progress and stability for the next three or four years, the normal life of this Parliament.[33]

With this speculation in the air, the Liberal leaders agreed to some preliminary soundings.

> It was in this connection during the fall of 1963 that Keith Davey came to see me to say that he and Douglas Fisher of the NDP, whom he had known since college days, had had an off-the-cuff talk to see if there would be any possibility of the Liberals and the NDP agreeing to some kind of formula for working together. He said Fisher seemed to be receptive and thought a few representatives of each party should meet to talk things over. I consulted Pearson about this; and while he did not expect anything would come of it, he thought we should explore the subject. It was agreed that we would meet quite informally in my apartment on a Sunday afternoon. Mike Pearson, Allan MacEachen, Keith Davey, and I were

to represent the Liberals, and Tommy Douglas, Douglas Fisher and David Lewis the NDP. It transpired that neither Pearson nor MacEachen were able to come at the last moment. Pearson called my apartment to explain his absence to Tommy Douglas and apologize for it. However, his failure to appear may have raised suspicions in the minds of the visiting NDPers. Tommy Douglas said very little, and David Lewis made it clear he would oppose any kind of working arrangement with the Liberals. Pearson, with his authority as Prime Minister and his talent for negotiation, just might have been able to produce a plan that would have appealed to them, but Davey and I were not able to make much progress. It was a friendly meeting, but nothing came of it.[34]

The government managed, in spite of this, to manoeuvre its way through the parliamentary votes of the autumn without disaster. But the Opposition harried, and the progress of the legislative program was exasperatingly slow. "The 26th Parliament," wrote W. A. Wilson early in the resumed session, " ... has long since become as sterile and hopeless a body as the 25th was."[35] In mid-October the House accepted the Prime Minister's proposal for a special committee on procedure which would seek to improve the House's operations, and at the end of the month the House agreed to a number of the Speaker's proposals to contain the question period. These limitations were only marginally helpful, and the government's legislative program continued to fall behind its timetable. The Minister of Finance's income tax amendments moved slowly through committee, but without further trials for Walter Gordon. His interventions in debate were infrequent and cautious. "His lesson learned, he knows that silence is golden," commented Marcel Gingras in La Presse.[36] When Gordon did speak, he impressed the House and the press gallery with his directness and lack of cant, and by the end of the year there were distinct indications that his parliamentary reputation was recovering.[37]

When the session ended in December, Parliament had increased the old age pension, imposed a system of public trusteeship on the maritime unions as recommended in the report of the Norris Royal Commission, completed its adoption of the budget measures, and approved the Estimates for all government spending in the current fiscal year. The Canada Pension Plan and the Canada Development Corporation, however, along with a long list of other government measures, had been held over to the next session.

The six week parliamentary holiday allowed the Pearson government time to draw breath and regroup. On December 27 the Prime

Minister announced his first Cabinet changes, when Lionel Chevrier and Azellus Denis retired; and this was followed by intensive – and probably inspired – public speculation about a major Cabinet reorganization which would precede the opening of Parliament in February. There were two major subjects of curiosity: who would be Mr. Pearson's choice as his Quebec lieutenant to succeed Chevrier, and how would the balance between reformers and conservatives be altered? There was little doubt that the Prime Minister's choice as his senior minister from Quebec would fall upon Guy Favreau, the Minister of Citizenship and Immigration. He was an ardent advocate of Lester Pearson's "cooperative federalism" and an enemy of Quebec separatism, and he had made an impressive personal reputation for generosity and liberalism in the sensitive portfolio of Immigration. But John Bird noted two sources of slight anxiety accompanying Favreau's rise to prominence: he had been lucky to avoid any political challenges of real difficulty; and he had "not yet had time to build up a great reputation in his own province as a federal voice of Quebec."[38]

The setbacks to the government represented by the budget and the pension plan seemed to have shifted the balance of influence in the Cabinet toward the cautious administrators. Now, Douglas Fisher believed, "Messrs. Sharp and Pickersgill look formidable blocks to one who wants to change the direction of the nation." He was impressed above all by the sudden dominance of Mitchell Sharp.

> Mr. Sharp has come on fast, perhaps too fast for a Prime Minister's comfort. Mitchell Sharp is the expert on everything. . . . He reminds me of a Sunday school superintendent of my boyhood: decent, capable, confident, always available and ready to help on anyone's problems, and so full of unavoidable rectitude. Mr. Sharp is a great asset, a real discovery. But if he gets much more weight and influence, one can foresee the fading away of the radical impetus of the government in favour of administrative competence and caution.[39]

The Prime Minister, Fisher thought, remained close to his reformers (chiefly Gordon, Lamontagne and MacEachen), and "would like to bring in left-wingers and radicals. . . . Therefore, Maurice Sauvé or Jean-Luc Pepin seem promising." But Guy Rouleau and Yvon Dupuis had greater seniority, and were being strongly promoted by party traditionalists in Quebec. Fisher predicted the promotions of Rouleau and Dupuis.

He had misjudged the Prime Minister's sense of balance. Guy

Favreau was appointed to the Ministry of Justice and the House leadership, Maurice Sauvé was named Minister of Forestry (and subsequently also of Rural Development), René Tremblay (who was also regarded as a progressive) became Minister of Citizenship and Immigration, and Maurice Lamontagne became Secretary of State with responsibility for the Economic Council, bilingualism in the public service, and cultural institutions. Offsetting these promotions were two more junior appointments for the Quebec conservatives: Yvon Dupuis became Minister without portfolio, and Guy Rouleau became parliamentary secretary to the Prime Minister.[40] Mr. Pearson's desire to hold the Cabinet to a moderate reforming course seemed evident.

The focus of Walter Gordon's concerns during the autumn and winter shifted away from the House of Commons, to the Cabinet and Treasury Board where the estimates and budget for 1964 were under preparation; to the federal-provincial conferences where crucial matters of social policy and finance were in negotiation; and to Washington and Paris for further international economic meetings.[41]

Once R. B. Bryce's transfer to the Department of Finance from the Privy Council office had occurred in mid-summer, the Department's malaise was rapidly overcome and Gordon set out, with Bryce's support, to establish the government's financial priorities for the coming year. He had no doubt that the major objectives should be to assert control over the spending program and to work toward the elimination of Canada's current account deficit in international payments. His first experience of budget-making had revealed the very limited range of manoeuvre open to the Minister of Finance, given the government's statutory spending commitments and the persistent ambitions of most Departments to enlarge their jurisdictions. Unless these commitments and ambitions could be strictly restrained, he knew that the Cabinet would be reluctant to honour its expensive pledges to improve the welfare system (in particular, by adopting the pension plan and the medical care scheme). He believed, too, that the chronic deficit in Canada's balance of payments was a brake on Canada's prosperity and one of the sources of her increasing reliance on foreign capital investment. Reasonable growth, welfare and national autonomy remained the ultimate goals of his orderly program. He was determined, as well, to re-establish his own reputation for that "administrative competence and caution" which Douglas Fisher attributed to the Cabinet's right wing.

The check delivered to Gordon's foreign ownership strategy meant that his legislative preoccupation shifted for the present to the Liberal party's domestic welfare program. When Louis Rasminsky questioned whether the country could afford the Canada Pension Plan, Gordon responded in a letter to the Prime Minister that "the Pension Plan is being undertaken as a matter of social priority to which the government, Parliament and large sections of the public all attribute great importance notwithstanding some inevitable costs."[42]

But the argument of an obligation to be fulfilled had to be reinforced by a display of budget management. Here Gordon's emphasis was placed on a systematic review of all spending programs (including especially defence expenditures and all subsidy programs),[43] and reconsideration of the system of supervising spending. An intensive review of programs occurred under the Minister of Finance's direction from August to December, 1963.[44] In November Gordon reiterated to the Prime Minister that he wished to cut out unnecessary government programs, improve the efficiency of government operations, and move "faster on revising our defence policy – and in particular cutting defence spending abroad."[45]

The process of review made more evident the great difficulty of achieving any significant economies in domestic programs, and when the draft White Paper on Defence reached the Minister of Finance in February, 1964, he elaborated to the Prime Minister his belief that defence expenditures offered the best opportunity for diverting spending to programs of greater social utility.

> ... Canada's relative position in the western world has changed very considerably from what it was in the immediate postwar years and in the early fifties. In the ten years following the end of the war, the countries of Western Europe were tired and beaten, while Canada was enjoying a great period of development and prosperity. We were, therefore, in a position to give leadership in the Western Alliance and to exert a greater influence among our allies than would normally have been expected for a country of our size. These conditions no longer prevail. Europe has made a remarkable recovery, while in the last seven or eight years Canada's performance has been less than distinguished. I believe Canadians sense the fact that as a nation we are not as important in the scheme of things as we once thought we were. I, for one, have thought for some time that the Europeans should assume a greater responsibility for the defence of Western Europe and that Canada's commitments there should be substantially reduced.[46]

Gordon added that the provinces, "and particularly Quebec," had to have more money to spend according to their own priorities if the country were to hold together; and that defence spending abroad contributed substantially to the balance of payments deficit. He therefore concluded with a radical proposal:

I suggest this government could make no greater contribution to the fortune of this country than by diverting several hundred million dollars per annum from defence to the provinces, to be spent primarily on education.[47]

But the Minister of Finance could make little progress against the weight of conventional support for NATO in the Cabinet; what he did achieve was a low ceiling on increases in defence spending over the next two years.[48]

The Glassco Commission on government organization had recommended the removal of supervision over government spending from the Ministry of Finance to a new minister in the Privy Council office. Gordon commented to Pearson in the summer of 1963 that:

If you can find the right man, there is a lot to be said for having a separate Minister responsible for expenditures, although I am not convinced that he should be established in the Privy Council office. In the last three months, I have probably spent half my time investigating or approving expenditure items. This is too much in view of the many other things a Minister of Finance is responsible for.[49]

In January Gordon repeated his support for some reallocation of responsibility for the Treasury Board,[50] and this led to the appointment, on January 20, of George McIlraith as president of the Treasury Board under the general supervision of the Minister of Finance.

The discouraging process of financial review led Walter Gordon to consider the role played by the Cabinet in encouraging uncontrolled spending. As a result, his memorandum to the Prime Minister of January 2, 1964 concluded with a suggestion for rationalizing Cabinet operations.

The trouble is that when we discuss new programs in Cabinet, they are considered on their individual merits and not in the context of our overall commitments. This will always be the case in any group of twenty-six people. Your original intention as I recall was to have an informal executive committee which would meet regularly and which, among other things, would pre-examine all proposals before they went to Cabinet. (You may have intended the

Economic Policy Committee to fill this role but it has proved too unwieldy for that purpose.) As part of your proposed reorganization of the Cabinet, I do hope you will consider reviewing the idea of an informal executive committee which could meet with you not less than once a week. Without some such machinery as this, I think we shall fail to keep expenditures in check. And I feel sure this will be interpreted as a sign of weakness on our part.[51]

Three weeks later, in revealing his Cabinet changes, Prime Minister Pearson announced the creation of nine Cabinet committees charged with the preliminary review and coordination of policy.[52] The Prime Minister himself was to chair external affairs and defence and federal-provincial relations, and Tom Kent was to take responsibility for coordination. The chairmen of the seven other committees – Favreau, Gordon, Sharp, Pickersgill, MacEachen, Hays, and Lamontagne – "were soon billed as an inner council of the Cabinet,"[53] but apparently never worked together in that capacity as Gordon had hoped.

Parliament opened on February 18 with a throne speech "as grey as the February skies," which seemed to promise a safe and unexciting session.[54] Walter Gordon's Canada Development Corporation was not mentioned in the speech, nor in Mr. Pearson's opening address to the House on February 20.[55] For the Minister of Finance, the highlight of the session was bound to be the presentation of his second budget, an occasion billed by the press as "the threshold of full rehabilitation," "Gordon's second chance," and "a double trial as he attempts to wipe out memories of the calamities that befell his first budget last June."[56] There was general feeling among Ontario Liberals sympathetic to Gordon that the restoration of his influence in the party depended above all on "a good, safe budget without serious political targets at which the Opposition can take aim."[57]

A good, safe budget it was, delivered to the House of Commons on the evening of March 16.[58] The Minister's subdued words matched the content, and the Calgary *Herald* could find nothing more stirring to conclude its editorial comment than to say that "Scotch whisky is to be imported in twenty-five ounce bottles instead of twenty-six and two-thirds, to standardize containers with the U.S. market. This could mean a slight reduction in price but, since the provincial liquor boards retail the product, and their approach to matters of this kind is well-known, consumers would be ill-advised to indulge in hopeful speculation."[59] The Minister of Finance reviewed the year's improvements in production, employment and the balance of payments, and made optimistic predictions for the future, while noting the continuing problems of regional and structural unemployment which required specialized rather than general responses. The only notable features of the budget were an extension of family allowances to sixteen- and seventeen-year-olds still attending school, and an adjustment downwards of the 1963 proposal for the withholding tax on dividends of foreign controlled companies from twenty percent to fifteen percent. Gordon justified this reduction by arguing that the net effect of the fifteen percent tax would be "about the same" for American corporations as the twenty percent tax, given recent changes in U.S. corporate tax rates. But the claim was unconvincing, and observers pointed out that in fact the retreat "was a result of national and international pressure; there is no doubt of this."[60] That was indeed the case:

> ... at the Prime Minister's request I had had to agree. ... This removed one of the incentives for Canadian subsidiary companies to make shares available to Canadians, and in my opinion it was a mistake. But Pearson wished to meet the complaints of the U.S. State Department and of some sections of the Canadian business community.[61]

The effect of yet another concession, made in the context of an unassertive budget, was not to strengthen the Minister of Finance's position. The retreat from boldness was too complete. "The least we can say about the budget speech," said Le Soleil, "is that it was the speech of a prudent man."[62] That was not the phrase Walter Gordon would most desire for his political epitaph. His potential allies were vaguely disheartened, and Gordon later recognized that his position had been weakened.[63]

One of the objects of Gordon's early and non-controversial budget was to clear the decks for concentration on the federal-provincial conference to be held in Quebec City from March 31 to April 2. Here, after months of detailed preparation on both sides, the federal government and Quebec would confront one another over their plans for universal contributory pensions. The Canada Pension Plan was now first among Ottawa's major legislative priorities; but it was entangled in the web of conflicts over Quebec's autonomy and financial integrity. Prime Minister Pearson wished both to appease Quebec and to gain agreement on pensions. That promised difficulty.

In his budget speech, the Minister of Finance reiterated Ottawa's willingness, previously expressed by the Prime Minister at the November federal-provincial conference, to transfer responsibility and tax resources to the provinces for some shared-cost programs which fell within provincial jurisdiction. This display of flexibility was followed on March 17 by Judy LaMarsh's presentation to the House of Commons of the Cabinet's resolution on the pension plan – a tactic which risked embarrassment if Ottawa's plan were rejected at Quebec City.

The federal delegation went to Quebec City in apprehension, which was soon justified.

The federal government proposals, put forward by the Prime Minister, were received almost with contempt by Premier Lesage and his associates, who seemed to feel the federal authorities had no real understanding of what was going on in Quebec, or of the determination of Quebeckers, their government included, to be "maîtres chez nous." There was a serious disagreement over the proposed Canada Pension Plan, which was to be a "pay as you go" plan and not a funded plan. The Quebec government stated its intention to proceed with its own plan which would be fully funded. This meant collecting far more in pension contributions in the first decade or so than the amounts that would be paid out in pension benefits. The difference would provide the provincial government with badly needed capital funds for investment purposes. There were disagreements over the federal government's proposals to pay family allowances to young people of sixteen and seventeen who remained in school and to provide guaranteed bank loans for university students. And apart from everything else, there was an angry demand that the federal government should make more tax revenues available to the provinces.[64]

Pearson and his colleagues returned to Ottawa "thoroughly discouraged and feeling that Canada might well be on the point of splitting up."[65] But over the next three days Tom Kent produced a new federal proposal for integrating the two pension plans on terms close to the Quebec plan. With the Prime Minister's approval, Kent and Maurice Sauvé returned to Quebec City to negotiate a settlement; they reviewed the terms with Pearson, Gordon, Favreau, Lamontagne, and MacEachen at the Prime Minister's house on April 8; and carried through detailed drafting with the aid of Dr. Joe Willard of the Health and Welfare Department in the week that followed. On April 16 Pearson informed the provincial premiers of the agreement, and on April 20 he outlined it to the House.[66] The package also contained increased equalization and transfer payments to the provinces.

The provincial governments were pleased, while the federal parties and the press welcomed the fact of federal-provincial reconciliation. The Pearson government had shown its skill once more in the diplomacy of crisis. But there were evident costs. The Cabinet had again occupied an exposed public position, retreated in apparent disarray, and struggled desperately to re-establish a policy that would finally be tolerable to its antagonists. The Prime Minister, in assuming direction of the redeployment, had taken the conduct of policy out of the hands of the Minister directly concerned (Judy LaMarsh), and had — incredibly — managed the settlement without her participation and largely without her knowledge. "If Pearson had taken the trouble to explain things to her fully," wrote Walter Gordon, "and then asked her to back him up in the changes he believed to be necessary, I am sure she would have done so with the utmost loyalty. As it was, she felt ignored and hurt and reacted accordingly."[67] The public impression of irresolution and confusion in the Cabinet, and the private disillusionment of ministers who believed themselves to have been let down by the Prime Minister, were increasing burdens on the unity, morale and energy of the Cabinet. And there on the Opposition benches sat the troublesome Mr. Diefenbaker, ready to seize and magnify every evidence of the government's disorder.

The ambiguous quality of the Prime Minister's leadership showed itself anew in his campaign for a new Canadian flag. In 1963 the Liberal party had promised to introduce a distinctive flag to replace the red ensign within two years of taking office, and Mr. Pearson had intermittently repeated that pledge. When he gave notice in May, 1964 that his government would proceed at once to fulfill the pledge, he acted in a way intended to reassert his personal authority and demonstrate the firmness of his convictions. Members of the caucus were initially reassured that Mr. Pearson could offer the "hard, decisive leadership"[68] they wanted when he introduced the flag, to be based on the maple leaf, to a hostile Canadian Legion audience in Winnipeg on May 17. Ten days later the government's resolution on the flag was presented to the House of Commons. Its unexpected twinning of the new flag with the union jack as Canada's continuing symbol of membership in the Commonwealth and allegiance to the crown was entirely true to Mr. Pearson's sentiments.[69] He wanted both flags – one as a sign of historic association, the other as a unifying symbol for the future. As on nuclear arms, he made his choice alone. The Cabinet was not informed of the Winnipeg speech in advance. But two days after the speech the Prime Minister told the House that the Cabinet had discussed the matter that morning, and the resolution of May 27 had the Cabinet's support.[70]

Few ministers regarded the flag as a matter of high priority; they were happy to defer to the Prime Minister on the issue, in the expectation that the choice would be quickly confirmed by the House of Commons and that the leader's reputation for decisiveness would be strengthened as a result. But they had underestimated English Canada's sensitivities – and the capacity for compromise of the Prime Minister. The vigour of the public reaction to Mr. Pearson's Winnipeg speech immediately suggested that the flag would be grist for Mr. Diefenbaker's mill; the inclusion of the union jack in the resolution confused some of the Prime Minister's supporters and gave the mistaken impression that he had already backtracked under pressure from Premier Smallwood of Newfoundland; and the Prime Minister's lack of clarity about whether there would be a free vote on the resolution was the source of more confusion. Soon the Cabinet looked ahead in gloom to a disrupted parliamentary timetable dominated by a Conservative filibuster on the flag. The Prime Minister's determination to see the resolution through before a summer recess, expressed to the House on June 30, was just the sort of challenge relished by John Diefenbaker and a sizeable element of his caucus. The House moved unproductively through June and July in a spirit of bitter and often petty rancor.

The Prime Minister's brave attempt to reassert his authority had failed, and Cabinet and caucus were in a mood of deep depression. The prospect of defeat in the House had revived; and the Prime Minister's efforts of February to reorganize the work of the Cabinet had long since lost their momentum. Walter Gordon, however, was now receiving a good press and his supporters in caucus had gained assurance.[71] Early in July, Tom Kent, in exasperation at the Prime Minister's methods, had written to Pearson to offer his resignation as the Prime Minister's policy assistant. Pearson called on Gordon to use his good offices with Kent to sort out the dispute. Gordon accepted the commission, and took the occasion to write to Pearson on July 16, 1964 to examine "some of the reasons for the government's current malaise."[72] He opened his six-page memorandum, which he described as "a frank review of past mistakes and future action," with an attempt to place the government's troubles in balanced perspective. There were two facts, he believed, which deserved recognition above all.

> The continual harrying, the clever disruptions of the work of the House and the unforgivable personal attacks have made many of us wonder why we stay here at all. As a result all of us have been tired, discouraged, frustrated, over-wrought and overly critical of everyone, ourselves included.

Through all this your own position has remained unchanged. The party is all for you and there is genuine affection for you in the caucus. There is no other leader in sight either for the party or for the nation. In other words, your personal position is very strong.[73]

Gordon was concerned that the Prime Minister had not sufficiently mined that resource.

But if you want to make the most of it, we shall have to stop changing our minds and qualifying our decisions.

I seem to have been saying this to you off and on for the last four or five years and you are entitled to be irritated by the repetition. Nevertheless, this in my opinion is your and our Achilles' heel. It makes the government look weak and indecisive at a time when the country is calling for strong leadership.

The public applauded when you stood up to the angry Legion audience in Winnipeg. But this support can be nullified – and I suspect it has been to some extent – by subsequent backtrackings and qualifications. Naturally, Diefenbaker exploits this to the full. If we are to avoid mistakes in the future and temptations to adjust and qualify in the interests of perfection, or because of a penchant for tinkering depending upon the point of view, there will have to be constant and continuous consultation and communication between yourself and whomever you consider to be your key supporters and advisers.[74]

The problem, as the Minister of Finance saw it, was both personal and organizational:

In recent months you became increasingly dependent on Tom Kent because of his brilliance, his resourcefulness, his imagination and the fact that he was always there. But in the process, the regular lines of communication between you and the principal Ministers and their Departments became blurred and responsibilities became uncertain. This has been bad for morale and has led to mistakes that could have been avoided if the full resources of Cabinet Ministers and of the civil service had been engaged in the normal way.

If you accept the foregoing, then you should not try to replace Tom by someone in your own office who is free to cross departmental lines and assume on occasion the prerogatives of a sort of Deputy Prime Minister. If you want someone in the latter role, he should be appointed from the Cabinet. The alternative may be to appoint a first-class man from within the civil service to take charge of your office, including responsibility for dealing with the daily crises that arise but not for developing policy on issues of major importance.[75]

Gordon admitted that "it is difficult to advise anyone else on how he should best organize his personal affairs, including his personal office staff and I shall not presume to do so." But he did suggest firmly that Pearson was seeing too many of his own staff and too many visitors, and trying to do too many things himself, with the result that

> ... because there are limits to what any one man can do, you have had, very naturally, to rely too much on Tom. As a result of all this you have not had enough time for your key Ministers, except, perhaps, Paul Martin. I believe this, more than anything else, has led to many of our troubles. . . . [76]

Gordon warned that "unless a fair proportion" of Pearson's time was spent with his chief Ministers, "you cannot expect them to feel they are important members of your team. This lack of a team spirit or the team approach has led and could continue to lead to trouble."

The Minister of Finance proposed "regular but short meetings" with a small group of Ministers.

> If the inner Cabinet idea can be resolved, then this might be a meeting with six or eight Ministers (perhaps the chairmen of the Cabinet committees), say, twice a week. Alternatively, you might think it possible to meet with a small number (say, two or three or four) on a daily basis.[77]

He added that Pearson should direct more questions in the House of Commons from himself to Ministers for reply, that Guy Favreau should be relieved of his overburdening load as House leader, and that someone should take from the Prime Minister his party political chores because "from what I hear – to be blunt about it – decisions are not being made, and we would be in bad shape if suddenly we were faced with an election."

Gordon went on to consider the appropriate timing for the next election, suggesting that "the logical election date from our point of view would be next spring or autumn." Before the election, he urged above all that the House should adopt the flag, the Canada Pension

Plan, and the Canada Development Fund. For Tom Kent, he suggested a special assignment to produce "a lengthy paper" on "the study of economic interrelationships of the different sections of the country" that the Prime Minister had already committed himself to. Gordon had reviewed the project with Kent.

> As he and I have discussed it, this document would argue the imperative necessity of a united Canada and what the aims and objectives of a united Canada should be. Obviously if well done, it would make good campaign material. And clearly if it were well received, Tom would want to be a candidate in the next election.[78]

The long memorandum concluded with a last refrain: " . . . above all else, I think you can gain a great deal by pulling the Cabinet together. And I suspect everyone would be receptive to such an effort on your part."

But Gordon's suggestions had no discernible effect.

> Tom Kent . . . continued in his old position in the Prime Minister's office. Relationships between Pearson and the members of his Cabinet were not changed. Guy Favreau was not relieved of his responsibilities as House leader, as I had urged, for another four or five months. And the flag debate which had begun in June went on and on.[79]

On August 31 Gordon gave the Prime Minister another memorandum on the flag issue. He wrote in longhand that:

> 1. We simply cannot allow the present deadlock to go beyond say the third week of September, for several reasons, viz.
> a. Parliament is being made to look ridiculous – and many people blame the government for this.
> b. In any event the government is being shown up as weak and helpless.
> c. There is a lot of highly important legislation we should be getting on with.
> d. Many people will be offended if the present rather sordid squabble is allowed to go on while the Queen is in Canada.
> e. We shall need Interim Supply again before so very long.
> etcetera[80]

He admitted that the government had underestimated John Diefenbaker who, despite the divisions in his party, "seems to have things pretty much under his own control again." Gordon believed that "Diefenbaker & Co. may be able to keep the debate going for a long time yet, possibly until the middle of October." Faced with that prospect, the Minister of Finance saw five possible courses for the government: reference of the flag to a parliamentary committee, for report after the Queen's visit; the application of closure; dissolution and a general election, "asking for a clear majority in order to permit the government to get ahead with the business of the country – and with specific changes in the rules made one of the issues"; postponement of the flag debate until the next session; or dropping the flag "altogether or at least for the time being." Gordon ruled out the last two alternatives as unthinkable, and preferred that Pearson should appeal to the House to resolve the impasse through reference to a committee, with some time limit on its proceedings and the subsequent debate on the floor of the House. (This device was favoured by the NDP and many other members of the House.) But he did not rule out the possibility that a continuing blockade by the Conservatives would force the government, within "the very near future," to choose between closure and a dissolution of Parliament. Ten days later Pearson told the House that the parties had agreed to refer the question to a special committee. It reported back on November 30 with a different design, and the flag resolution was eventually adopted under closure on December 15, 1964.

The Minister of Finance, meanwhile, was quietly pressing on with his program of reform. In July, the House adopted his Canada Student Loan Bill, which provided for federally financed loans to university students to a maximum value of $40 million in its first year of operation; throughout the autumn he was engaged in preparation of the opting-out legislation promised to the provinces in the budget speech and negotiated with Quebec during May and June; and on September 22 he introduced legislation to require Canadian ownership of federally incorporated life insurance and trust companies and to encourage their purchases of Canadian equities. At the beginning of September, as relief from these months of hectic and generally frustrating activity, Walter and Liz Gordon enjoyed a ten-day visit to Tokyo for joint ministerial meetings and the annual meetings of the International Monetary Fund and the World Bank. On September 18 and 19 Gordon was home in Toronto to assist Andrew Thompson in his campaign for the leadership of the Ontario Liberal party, which Gordon had been actively supporting since the spring. Thompson's victory at the convention gave satisfaction and reassurance to Gordon. It allowed him

204

to repay some of his obligations to Thompson for electoral support in Davenport, and to express confidence in his associate; and it was another sign of the Minister's solid influence and reviving support in Ontario.[81]

While diversion of the flag debate to committee offered some relief to government and House in September — allowing passage of a number of Bills and the renewal of supply — the storms soon burst on the government again. First Guy Favreau faced the onslaught, then his Quebec colleagues René Tremblay, Maurice Lamontagne, and Yvon Dupuis. The Prime Minister's acts and judgment were at issue in every case.

But it was Guy Favreau who bore the brunt of the attack. Because of his parliamentary inexperience, his heavy workload, his casual approach to administration, and his lack of guile, the House leader had proved to be an easy target for the Opposition's poisoned barbs. For months he had wished to withdraw from the House leadership, but this was not arranged by Prime Minister Pearson until October 30, when George McIlraith succeeded him. As Minister of Justice, Favreau faced attack during the autumn for the apparent mishandling of the Hal Banks case. On November 23, the Rivard case, which was ultimately to shatter his career and break his spirit, was brought sensationally to the floor of the House by the Conservative member for the Yukon, Erik Nielsen.[82]

When Favreau presented the Justice Department estimates for debate, Nielsen told the House in detail of an RCMP report implicating members of the government service, "one in the Minister's office and one in the office of the Minister of Citizenship and Immigration," in attempts to bribe legal counsel in a major narcotics case. Favreau replied that, while there had been no prosecutions, the executive assistant to the Minister of Citizenship and Immigration, Raymond Denis, had been dismissed following a review of the case. But he had not referred the case to the Justice Department's legal officers for an opinion on whether charges should be laid. Favreau assured the House that while he may have acted naively in not seeking an independent opinion on the evidence, he had never "attempted to hide the truth to protect someone from justice."[83] He was willing to see a judicial enquiry into the circumstances of the case, to be carried on *in camera*. When Nielsen and T. C. Douglas asked whether anyone "higher up in the government" was involved, the Minister of Justice replied in uncertainty: "My recollection is not, but I would not care to make that as a firm statement."[84]

Overnight Tom Kent had tracked down the name of the person

"higher up in the government" referred to by implication: it was the Prime Minister's parliamentary secretary, Guy Rouleau.[85] After confirming Rouleau's involvement, Pearson met him at once and asked for his resignation.[86] When the House opened on November 24 Rouleau rose to announce his resignation as parliamentary secretary because he had "made representations in the case of one M. Rivard."[87] The Minister of Justice then told the House that the Cabinet had accepted the suggestion of the NDP leader that there should be a public judicial enquiry to examine the evidence placed before the Minister of Justice by the RCMP and any further evidence, and to report whether "it was a reasonable decision on the part of the Minister that there was not sufficient evidence to support a successful prosecution."[88] The Opposition charged that the proposed terms of reference were too narrow; Mr. Douglas insisted that what should be examined was "the whole procedure which was followed by the Minister and the government in dealing with this matter."[89] In particular, he wished to know the circumstances in which the Minister of Citizenship and Immigration had dismissed his executive assistant; whether the Minister of Justice had informed the Prime Minister of the involvement of Mr. Pearson's executive assistant in the affair; and if so, why Mr. Rouleau had resigned only that day. Favreau responded that "the Prime Minister was not apprised until yesterday,"[90] and Pearson added later that he was first informed of the affair by the Minister of Justice "on the day before his estimates were brought before the House."[91]

Walter Gordon noted the effects of these statements:

These replies placed Favreau clearly on the spot. After what Pearson had said, Favreau could not very well claim that he had told the Prime Minister something about the case some months before. He had not done this in a formal way but rather in the course of a more or less casual conversation on an airplane. . . . In these circumstances it was not unnatural that Pearson should have forgotten about it. But as Pearson did not correct the impression he had given in answering Harkness' question, he left himself open to the accusation that he had misled the House. And he left Favreau to defend himself against charges that not only had he failed to bring proceedings against government officials who were alleged to have offered bribes and to have brought influence to bear on behalf of an accused dope smuggler, but, moreover, that he had failed to inform the Prime Minister of any of the circumstances.[92]

Later that day Prime Minister Pearson left Ottawa for a political tour of the prairies while the Cabinet, under the chairmanship of Paul Martin, sought to navigate the storm. On Wednesday, November 25, Martin presented the formal terms of reference of the proposed investigation to the House. The Opposition acrimoniously demanded that they should be extended. For more than a day the Cabinet resisted, only to capitulate on Friday morning by amending the Order-in-Council to provide for specific study of the propriety of the acts of the RCMP, the Department of Justice, and the Minister of Justice himself in handling the case. The Cabinet's lack of resolution was doubly demonstrated by the absence of the Prime Minister and the now familiar concessions to parliamentary pressure: first an enquiry *in camera*, then a public enquiry, then an expanded enquiry to include judgment upon the Minister's use of his discretionary authority. Guy Favreau's isolation in distress was emphasized above all by the Cabinet's decision to allow his political judgment to be reviewed by a judicial enquiry. Ironically, this final concession was made on Favreau's own suggestion to the divided Cabinet, as a means of assuring NDP support in the non-confidence vote, whose withdrawal appeared, without such a concession, to threaten the life of the government.[93]

The political situation created by Erik Nielsen's revelations had a terrible familiarity. The Cabinet was exposed as confused, divided, demoralized, and leaderless; and two Ministers – both French-speaking Canadians – were left to the careless ravages of a not altogether scrupulous Opposition. Throughout the week Guy Favreau showed a hapless inability to defuse the crisis. Walter Gordon frequently reassured him in private, and on Thursday, November 26 he decided to go to the aid of his friend in public.

> I was influenced in this decision both by the need to refute the suggestion that the Ontario members were critical of two Quebec ministers, Favreau and Tremblay, and by my friendship for Guy Favreau, a wonderful, overworked man who was taking a bad beating in the House day after day.[94]

After a long address by John Diefenbaker, Gordon spoke in what he hoped would be, by contrast, "a quiet fashion and without any insinuations or innuendos."[95] In the face of constant interruptions from the Opposition benches, he calmly persisted in his case that no one "should take it upon themselves to judge the guilt or innocence . . . of individuals on the basis of rumour, and unsupported and loosely worded allegations." He asked the House "to respect the traditions of justice that we have inherited," and ended in controlled anger with a personal defence of his two colleagues.

In conclusion, Mr. Chairman, I wish to say a word about the way this matter has been used, deliberately or otherwise, in Parliament and in some sections of the press to undermine the unity of this country. . . .

We should not pay too much attention to speculative articles, but some members will have seen one this morning suggesting that the Prime Minister may be asked by a group of Ontario members to discipline two principal members in this government, not because they are guilty but in the interests of political expediency. Now, most of us who have known the Prime Minister of this country for many years know – and I say this categorically – that he is not the kind of man who would consider that kind of action for one moment. As a member of Parliament from Ontario I consider it a privilege and an honour to have as colleagues two Ministers like the Minister of Justice and the Minister of Citizenship and Immigration. We need more men like them in public life. I have no doubt about their complete honesty, integrity and courage. I have no doubt that they are here, like some other honourable members, not because they prefer this kind of life to something else but because they think it is their duty to do what they can in the interests of their country. . . .

They have the complete support, Mr. Chairman, of all of us who know them, particularly – and I want to emphasize this – of all the members from Ontario. There is no foundation for the kind of speculative articles to which I have referred. I can only say, Mr. Chairman, that if a man like my friend the Minister of Justice were ever forced to resign for the kind of political reasons suggested, I for one would not be happy to remain in this House.[96]

The speech was an assertion of leadership, collective loyalty and common decency which did something to fill a moral vacuum in the House. It was a rare example of generosity in a week of relentless inquisition when few men were prepared to come to the aid of Guy Favreau. It revealed the priority which Walter Gordon gave to personal loyalty over political prudence and constitutional propriety: for there was probably sufficient reason for the Prime Minister to request the resignation of the Minister of Justice while an enquiry into his conduct took place. Instead, Lester Pearson had neither defended nor sacrificed Favreau; he had opted out of the hard decisions by leaving Ottawa for his political visit to western Canada. As Richard Gwyn noted, Walter Gordon "spoke less to the Opposition than to his own government."[97] Gordon was not only expressing solidarity with his friend, but also –

though less obviously – disgust that the government could not unite in common defence when under attack.

The appointment of Chief Justice Frederic Dorion of the Quebec Superior Court to conduct the Rivard enquiry relieved the government temporarily of embarrassment. Guy Favreau was confident that the investigation would exonerate him fully. The unexpected blossoming of the Rivard crisis, however, and the revelation of the government's inability to meet the onslaught, spurred on the government's opponents and the sceptical press to other sensitive enquiries. They were, ironically, assisted in their vigilance by the Prime Minister, who wrote to his ministers on November 30 reminding them of the high standards of conduct required of members of the government and their staffs. The letter, which was soon in the hands of the press, left the impression that it had come too late and should not need saying; and it gave critics the Prime Minister's own words to throw back at him in the crises that followed.

Almost immediately there was fresh embarrassment, when Maurice Lamontagne and René Tremblay were implicated by the press and Opposition in the bankruptcy of a Montreal furniture store. Lamontagne and Tremblay had obtained furniture on unusual credit terms, and thus appeared to have violated the primary rule of conduct stated in the Prime Minister's letter, not to "place themselves in a position where they are under obligation to any person who might benefit from special consideration or favour on their part. . . . [98] On December 18, 1964 both ministers explained their transactions and repayment arrangements in detail to the House of Commons. There seemed, clearly, to have been imprudence but no impropriety in either case, and both ministers spoke bitterly of the unfair insinuations they had faced. In the general atmosphere of Liberal confusion and despair, the Prime Minister remained under pressure for months to remove the two from the Cabinet; and at last, following the election of November, 1965 Lamontagne and Tremblay resigned. Both, in Judy LaMarsh's view, had been "hounded out of office."[99]

The Prime Minister had to face one more unpleasant piece of business before the end of the year – again involving a Quebec Cabinet minister. Since the appointment of Yvon Dupuis as Minister without portfolio in February, Dupuis had brought no credit and some embarrassment to the government. In the autumn he was despatched abroad on a long protocol mission which kept him out of the limelight. The Prime Minister had been informed by Premier Lesage shortly after appointing Dupuis that he was under suspicion of accepting a $10,000 bribe in 1961 to assist in obtaining a race track franchise. By December,

Lesage feared that public accusations and criminal charges were imminent, and that another crisis might result in the defeat of the Pearson government before passage of the opting-out legislation he considered so crucial. He urged Pearson to remove Dupuis at once. After an RCMP investigation early in January the Prime Minister asked for the Minister's resignation. Five days later, following a period of intensive threats and persuasion by other Quebec ministers, Dupuis resigned under protest. The experience was squalid and unnecessary, and threw more doubt on the Prime Minister's judgment and ability to manage his task.

The year 1964 ended without solace for the harassed members of the government. The parliamentary situation seemed almost intolerable, and ministers wondered how long they could carry on without another general election. No one looked forward to meeting the House after the Christmas recess. For Walter Gordon there was only the personal consolation of a note from his friend Guy Favreau, written on December 30:

> I would not want to let the last day of this year pass, without sending you at least a brief note of gratitude and appreciation.
>
> I shall never forget your friendly words of comfort and your constant encouragement during the trying days of the end of November. I shall never forget either how you dared rise in the House in my defence, at the very moment when so many were speechless and I myself was performing so badly.
>
> You know how I feel about true friends at moments like these. I shall not elaborate except to say most sincerely "thank you!"[100]

10   Slow Movement

The Prime Minister's genial talent for relieving tension came to his aid at a year-end press conference on December 31. After wishing his audience "a happy, serene and restful New Year" he added wryly that "It seems to be infinitely desirable, if unobtainable."[1] But the Cabinet now had six weeks' relief from parliamentary pressures, and Mike Pearson sought a few days' rest in the Florida sun while his Minister of Finance holidayed in Portugal.[2] It was essential to turn away from the memory of a poisonous and debilitating session, and to escape briefly from the blighting presence of John Diefenbaker.

Before his departure, Walter Gordon had one political duty. His appointment as chairman of the National Campaign Committee of the party had lapsed after the 1963 election, and Keith Davey had carried on the work of organization in direct, though intermittent, liaison with the Prime Minister. The party's electoral organization could not be effectively maintained in this way, and throughout 1964 Davey, Gordon, Tom Kent and others periodically urged Pearson to name a campaign chairman and allow preparations for an election to begin.[3] Finally, in October, Pearson spoke to Gordon about the question. By this time Gordon's disenchantment with politics was running deep.

> I told him I had not been planning to run again. He asked if I would take another portfolio & I made it quite clear I would not even consider running again – and taking on the job of campaign chairman – unless it was understood I kept Finance for another two years at least. He agreed to this and pressed me to stay on and run the

campaign again. I agreed on the understanding there would be no more suggestions about my giving up Finance at least until I felt the job I had set out to do there was done.[4]

With this bargain renewed, Gordon again turned his attention to electoral strategy. On January 5, 1965 he met with the National Campaign Committee in Ottawa. The meeting was important as a stimulus to provincial organizers, as a means of shoring up the confidence of the Prime Minister and Cabinet with evidence of support in the country, and as a first and tentative effort on the part of Gordon and Davey to promote a June general election. Walter Gordon told the Committee that it should establish an election date "as a target for planning purposes only," and suggested that this should be "around June."[5] At the conclusion of the meeting he took "an informal roll call on a June election,"[6] and reported afterwards to the Prime Minister that "While there were a few dissenters, a large majority would favour a June election. . . . "[7]

The Committee reviewed electoral prospects across the country, and Gordon judged that "the provincial chairmen were being much more realistic than they were at any previous meeting I have attended." He concluded from their estimates that an immediate election might produce gains of from twenty to thirty seats for the Liberal party. These predictions, he told Pearson, probably erred on the cautious side.

> If the Dorion Report turns out well, if there are no more difficulties of that nature, if there is an impressive reshuffling of the Cabinet and if we get the pension plan and possibly one or two other things through, we might do appreciably better.[8]

Members of the Committee believed that "The Rivard case-cum-furniture episodes should blow over and will not do us much harm politically (provided, of course, there are no new developments which might keep the situation alive for some time)" and that John Diefenbaker was now "a big asset" to the Liberals.[9]

On Keith Davey's advice, Walter Gordon emphasized to the Committee that the party should make special efforts to add seats in western Ontario and western Canada, so that "after the next election, the party and the government could honestly say they were representative of all parts of Canada."[10] And he warned against the use of electoral "gimmicks," in the light of public reactions during the 1963 campaign.[11]

At the conclusion of the meeting, the Committee agreed to express its appreciation to Mr. Pearson "for his leadership in a very difficult situation."[12] Walter Gordon conveyed the message expansively to the Prime Minister.

We have just concluded a successful meeting of the National Campaign Committee and I was asked to pass on to you the feeling of the members that you have done and are doing a magnificent job as the leader of our party. The Committee was particularly enthusiastic about your skilful handling of the flag issue which none of your predecessors had the courage to deal with or the ability to bring to a conclusion. I was also asked to tell you by the provincial campaign chairmen that your stock is very high with all the members of the party.[13]

In spite of Gordon's efforts to play down public speculation about the meeting, the press and members of the Opposition regarded it as evidence of preparation for a June election.

That prospect was not welcome to many members of the Progressive Conservative caucus. The self-inflicted wounds of 1963 had never healed; the parliamentary party remained in the grip of a personality cult, its strategy limited to opportunist assaults on the integrity and good faith of the Pearson administration. The flag debate and the excesses of the autumn session had finally driven Quebec members of the caucus to the brink of revolt, and this was only averted by the diplomacy of the party president, Dalton Camp, in arranging a meeting of the national executive committee for February 5 and 6, 1965 to face the question of John Diefenbaker's leadership. Mr. Diefenbaker responded to the criticism from within the party by a familiar diversion. "The Liberal propaganda machine," he said, "is active and it is aimed at me, to take the public eye off their ill-handling of government."[14] The Liberal party, on the contrary, was only too relieved to let the Conservative party fight its own civil war. The Conservative executive meeting in February refused by a narrow margin to express its confidence or lack of confidence in the leader, and rejected a resolution calling for a leadership convention. John Diefenbaker had not vindicated himself, but had postponed any reconciliation of the party's bitter divisions. On February 18 Remi Paul left the party to sit as an independent member of the House, and he was joined in April by Leon Balcer.[15] A dozen members of the caucus now defiantly opposed the party leader, and were less than delighted by the prospect of another election fought under his command. The opinion polls showed a decisive shift of public support toward the Liberal party.[16] This knowledge helped to restore the Cabinet's confidence that it could control the political situation, and encouraged the activists to press on with their program of reforms.

For Walter Gordon, the most important measures to be dealt with in 1965 were the Canada Pension Plan (which passed the House on March 29), the opting-out legislation (passed the next day, on March 30), the Automotive Trade Agreement or Auto Pact, providing for free trade in automobiles and parts between the United States and Canada (signed by Prime Minister Pearson and President Johnson on January 16, and endorsed by the House on May 6), and the Minister of Finance's own new measures: the budget, legislation to maintain Canadian ownership of magazines and newspapers, the decennial revision of the Bank Act, and the long-gestating Canada Development Corporation. The bottlenecks and frustrations of the previous two years seemed suddenly to diminish, and for the first time the government saw real prospects of achieving its legislative program without constant setbacks in the House.

Parliament reassembled on February 16, 1965 to conclude the second session of the twenty-sixth Parliament, and on April 5, without an interval, a speech from the throne introduced the third session. In February, the Liberal party momentarily feared new explosions of scandal from John Diefenbaker, but his party's ominous motion for a debate on "the allegations and disclosures of widespread corruption, marked by the intrusion of undesirable influences into several federal government offices, including that of the Prime Minister, ... the conduct and public morality of those in authority,"[17] proved to be empty bombast. Two more minor cases of corruption and influence-peddling touched the government's fringes in the spring, but the greatest source of embarrassment was relieved by its absurdity. On March 2, while the Dorion enquiry was in the midst of its hearings, Lucien Rivard, the notorious central figure of the investigation, climbed the wall of Bordeaux jail in Montreal, commandeered a car, and disappeared. For a few days the escape gave John Diefenbaker the occasion for renewed and brutal attacks on the Minister of Justice, Guy Favreau. Here was the "new development which might keep the situation alive for some time" that Walter Gordon had cautioned against in January. Although Rivard had been held in a provincial prison, the leader of the Opposition threw responsibility for his escape on the federal government in a speech that was full of innuendo. "Is it not a strange thing," Diefenbaker asked, "an amazing commentary on the Minister of Justice and on other ministers in the government, that one man, one thug, on the basis of what is generally known and now proven last evening, should receive such comfort from a government. . . . Never before has a Canadian government shown such large solicitude for an ordinary thug – no, not an ordinary one, an extraordinary one; an international one."[18] The implication that the Minister of Justice had virtually boosted Rivard over the wall was too much for Guy Favreau; and twice, on March 3 and 10, he engaged in embittered dialogue with the member for Prince Albert which revealed not a guilty man but an outraged and imprudent one.[19]

These vicious interludes did not dominate the House in 1965, and after March 10 members drew back in distaste from the consequences of such alley fighting. On the government side, there was a new mood of urgency and firmness in the Prime Minister's leadership. On January 27 he wrote to his ministers that "the next few months will be important, and may be decisive, ones for the government."[20] He asked them to limit their commitments away from Ottawa to "the irreducible minimum" so that they could attend to their parliamentary duties without distraction. On the same day he wrote again requesting advice on legislation to be mentioned in the forthcoming speech from the throne. He noted that a number of measures the government had hoped to carry in 1964 were still to be implemented, and that "the scope for new proposals is therefore limited."[21] He insisted on realism in the Cabinet's planning.

> To make the right impression our program must be simple, clear-cut, realistic. We have to put a high premium on measures which are unlikely to take much parliamentary time.[22]

But the Prime Minister sought also to reassert the government's sense of direction with "an attractive and constructive program" which would be "striking enough to help shift the focus of political attention away from Opposition attempts to harry us on other matters, which may be smaller in substance but larger in politics." He therefore asked for

> . . . at least one imaginative measure which will be clearly seen as an important contribution to economic expansion. . . . As yet, we have not been given adequate political credit for the very real economic improvement that has accompanied our being in office.[23]

Other new proposals, he suggested, should contribute directly to the general welfare:

By the start of the new session, we expect to have implemented two out of the three main "social" measures in our election platform: extended family allowances, and the pension plan. The third was medicare. I do not think we can plan to take that on, at least in any comprehensive way, in 1965. But we do need to make some plans for dealing with the greatest needs in this area. We should also consider carefully the pension needs of people who are already retired, and therefore not covered by the contributory plan.

It occurs to me that these problems, and others, might best be approached by developing a Canadian version of "the war on poverty," though it might better be thought of as a campaign to improve the opportunities of all Canadians to participate in economic progress. An approach of this kind would have great advantages of flexibility. It is a heading under which one or two attractive and practical programs could be launched, possibly without much in the way of legislative requirements, and a shelf of further programs could be prepared, for introduction as circumstances make them appropriate.[24]

This was an exercise in image-building designed to erase the unfortunate memories of the first two years in office. But it was more than that too, for it invited the reformers in the Cabinet to reassert their influence against the missionaries of the *status quo*.

Walter Gordon replied on February 1 with a priority list of eight "essential measures" and seven further pieces of "desirable legislation." Among the essential measures was the legislation to create the Canada Development Corporation and to inhibit foreign ownership of Canadian newspapers and magazines. Gordon suggested that both measures should be mentioned in the throne speech. In addition, while he agreed that medicare could not be enacted in 1965 "given the other complications we are going to have with the provincial governments as well as with the budget in this next year or two," he urged that the speech should contain "some mention or reference to medicare" to remind the public of the government's commitment. Gordon added that

. . . we should make it clear that in addition to what we have done and are doing in the field of old age pensions, we hope to have important legislation to generalize our unemployment assistance act into a public assistance act that will further develop a humane and flexible approach to help those who are in need. . . . [25]

The speech from the throne took shape in February and March, in the course of continuous consultation among ministers. It soon had the appearance of an ambitious manifesto rather than a "simple, clear-cut, realistic" outline of parliamentary business for the session. There was a fine balance to be drawn between the inspirational and the prosaic, especially if the speech were to serve, potentially, as an electoral program. The Prime Minister's letter had not been clear about whether that was intended, but it left the option open, though unspoken. Walter Gordon, at least, had an election in mind, but he hesitated at the prospect of too many new commitments. In March he commented on the Prime Minister's first draft of the speech.

> As I mentioned to you after Cabinet, I think that in general the speech is too specific about too many new proposals, having in mind the timing of possible future decisions and plans. You suggested that some of the material could be incorporated in your own speech which would be better. Alternatively, it might be better to hold up some of the proposals until after an election has been called.[26]

On the other hand, Gordon was still battling the Cabinet's inertia on the Canada Development Corporation, which had not been mentioned in the draft speech.

> At a Cabinet meeting on February 18, it was agreed that the government's intention to establish a Canada Development Corporation would be stated in the throne speech and elaborated in the budget. It has been in the last two throne [speeches] and its omission would be commented upon. I would therefore ask that some reference be made to it.[27]

The Prime Minister acceded to the request and an appropriate sentence went into the manuscript.

On Monday, April 5 members of the House and Senate assembled in the Senate chamber for the traditional reading of the Governor General's speech. It was a solidly packed document, concentrating its focus on "a program for the full utilization of our human resources and the elimination of poverty among our people," but promising also the ratification of the Auto Pact; measures of parliamentary reform; the adoption of a formula for amending the B.N.A. Act in Canada; federal-provincial discussions on health insurance; revision of the

Immigration Act; legislation to promote Canadian publications, broadcasting and the film industry; the creation of a Science Council; a parliamentary vote on capital punishment; a measure to limit and provide for the public payment of election expenses; revisions of the Bank Act; and the creation of the Canada Development Corporation.

The speech contained substantial, mostly borrowed, window-dressing (the war on poverty was President Johnson's, and its essence amounted to the creation of a special secretariat to coordinate poverty programs in the Prime Minister's office; the Company of Young Canadians was a second-hand domestic Peace Corps); but it also forecast a real program of progressive reform in many fields, economic, social and cultural. The press approved, and the friendly Toronto *Star* called it "the largest, boldest and most sweeping program ever submitted to a Canadian parliament."[28] The political scientist Hugh Whalen pointed to the speech as an example of the "antagonistic symbiosis" that typified the relationship of the centre and the left in Canadian politics. "For in less than two years," he suggested, "the Liberals have again pre-empted much of the economic and social policy ground staked out originally by the New Democratic Party."[29]

Lester Pearson elaborated his underlying attitudes in his contribution to the throne speech debate on April 6. The Prime Minister offered his rationale for the government's social and economic policies in words that might have been those of his Minister of Finance:

> The economic foundations of whole communities can be knocked away almost overnight by new industrial processes, by automation, by what we call progress. Wide areas of farmland can become derelict and decaying; urban slum islands can develop in the richest of cities. The affluent society has given a new meaning and a new dimension to poverty; because as technology advances and business and the economy become more complex, the individual finds it harder to get a second chance. . . .
>
> It is here that the state must move in more vigorously than we have done in the past few years, in the name of both social justice and economic progress; because economic progress must include the fullest possible utilization of human resources.[30]

The successful application of these principles of what might be called "ameliorative capitalism," Mr. Pearson recognized, would be a complex matter. The coordinating secretariat had thus been established to help in creating the necessary new machinery. When it was proclaimed in

1965, the Canadian war on poverty was a humane declaration of hope rather than a coherent program; and so it was to remain.

The Prime Minister's second and parallel preoccupation was with the adaptation of the federal union to the stresses of mid-century. Here, too, what was essential in the Prime Minister's mind to begin with was the proper attitude of concern. For him, this required a generous recognition of French-Canadian nationality and constant sensitivity to the provincial, as well as the federal, interest in all parts of the country. Federal and provincial responsibilities could no longer be separated neatly according to constitutional compartments:

> A healthy federalism, a cooperative federalism is one in which the two levels of government both fulfill their own responsibilities; and respect each other's, but they do so taking into account their mutual concerns. Where they are responsible for parallel action it should be concerted action and therefore must be built on consultation and cooperation, I believe, Mr. Speaker, to a greater extent than previously, and that is the policy of this government. That is what we mean by cooperative federalism.[31]

This too was an open and flexible stance rather than a program, a diplomatic framework for responding to the pressures from the provinces – and chief among them, Quebec. It was a product of the Prime Minister's own judgment, not initially shared by Walter Gordon, whose original instincts were centralist. But after two years of difficult negotiation with Quebec, the Minister of Finance completely endorsed the Prime Minister's views, and deferred to him in his approach to the constitutional problem.

*

The notable feature of Walter Gordon's third budget, which was intended to mark the successful assertion of control over federal spending and the general health of the economy, was to be an income tax cut.[32] Gordon and Pearson had agreed upon this late in 1964, and the Minister of Finance repeated his intention in a letter to the Prime Minister on February 9, 1965. "This means," Gordon wrote, "that any important expenditure programs which may be presented to Cabinet for discussion would have to be resisted. I hope you will assist in this resistance. . . . [33] Gordon added his reasons.

> As you know, I feel strongly that this is the right course for us

to follow. First of all, I believe we must show that, as a government, we are able to say no from time to time and to resist some of the more obvious pressures. But apart from this, we have allowed public expectation of a tax cut to increase in recent weeks and months without throwing cold water on the general idea as I did a year ago.[34]

During the winter, Gordon hoped that the budget could be presented in the month of March. He told the Prime Minister:

When this is not done, the business community tends to defer the implementation of their plans with consequent effects upon economic activity generally.

It is especially important this year to bring down the budget as soon as possible because it will contain proposals which are designed to stimulate business activity. If these are not made known soon, their effect on the economy, insofar as this year is concerned, will be proportionately reduced.[35]

The last days of the second session dragged on into April, however, and following the conclusion of the throne speech debate, the House adjourned for a two week Easter recess. Finally, on April 26 (the first day of the renewed session), Walter Gordon was able to present his budget.

He regarded the evening with satisfaction as "a wonderful occasion for a Minister of Finance, especially one who had been criticized as severely as I had been less than two years before. Our policies had been proved successful, the Canadian economy was in excellent shape, and the prospects for the future were encouraging."[36] Gordon reported to the House that half a million new jobs had been created in two years, that unemployment rested at 3.9%, that the gross national product had grown by almost 16% in two years, and that the budget deficit had fallen from $692 million in 1962 – 1963 to only $82 million in 1964 – 1965.[37] Yet against these advances had to be set the need to absorb annual increases of 2.7% in the labour force from 1963 to 1970, a need which would require a prolonged period of "robust expansion." Gordon noted that Canada had "the most rapidly growing labour force in the industrialized world and it is better trained than ever before."[38] The Minister of Finance made the normal *tour d'horizon*, and ended by announcing a ten percent reduction in personal income tax, to a maximum of $600 per year. This was the most dramatic and popular item in a budget that the *Canadian Annual Review* described as "in most respects ... dull,"[39] but for Walter Gordon there were two other equally significant passages in the budget speech: his exposition of the Canada Development Corporation and his proposed amendments to the Income Tax Act disallowing tax deductions for advertising placed in non-Canadian periodicals and newspapers. While these proposals were anything but dull, Gordon had diplomatically cushioned them round with the soothing words of the remainder of his speech. The debate was uneventful, and on May 5 the budget resolution passed the House by a comfortable vote of 132 to 86.

*

Walter Gordon's Canada Development Corporation had its public origin in 1961 in a paragraph of his book *Troubled Canada*. The project was offered in the most tentative form as one possible instrument for promoting economic expansion.

> It might be desirable ... to create a National Development Corporation to sponsor and invest in large economic undertakings that may not be expected to pay returns for a considerable period. Large pools of private capital in such countries as the United States, the United Kingdom and France can be called on for such purposes providing the proposed projects are sound and can be expected to be profitable in the long term. There are not the same private sources of capital available in Canada, and as a result many of our more imaginative undertakings in the past have had to be promoted and financed by foreigners. In the future, there may be a place for some new kind of organization for such purposes possibly financed in part by the savings of a great many individual Canadians and indirectly on their behalf by life insurance companies and pension funds, and in part by government loans or with bonds and debentures guaranteed by the government.[40]

When the Minister of Finance spoke of the Canada Development Corporation in the 1965 budget speech, he discussed both its practical and its symbolic inspiration. On the one hand,

> It would be the function of this Corporation to share in financing the initial development, or expansion of large scale industrial projects in Canada, and to provide financing, including refinancing, for large Canadian enterprises which might otherwise be led to seek funds outside Canada, with a consequent loss of ownership and control to non-residents. The Corporation would be expected to

invest in projects and enterprises which are likely to contribute to the sound economic development of Canada and to be profitable in the long run.[41]

The Corporation would take the form of a public mutual fund, to which the government would normally subscribe no more than ten percent of the authorized share capital of one billion dollars. Voting rights would be restricted to Canadian shareholders, and the fund would seek to attract capital both from individuals and "from a wide variety of Canadian institutions, including insurance companies, banks, trust companies, pension funds, estates and trusts, credit unions, charitable foundations and, I may add, provincial governments and their agencies."[42] For Walter Gordon, the Corporation was intended to fill a crucial gap in the Canadian money market, by channelling the funds of Canadian investors to the service of Canadian economic development, and thus reducing the demand for imported equity capital with its accompanying packages of imported management, technology and economic priorities. It was a positive complement to his still incomplete structure of nationalist tax incentives and discriminations, and one part of his original program to stimulate private and public investment in Canada (which also included the Municipal Development and Loan Fund, the Atlantic Development Fund, and an extended Industrial Development Bank).[43] The CDC was intended as the instrument of economic nationalism most likely to draw wide popular approval and participation. Gordon told the House:

> We are convinced that thousands of Canadians will welcome an opportunity to share in the future growth and development of our country; that they will take pride in owning even a small interest in expanding Canadian industries. Participation in the Canada Development Corporation will provide this opportunity.[44]

But if there was a populist bloodstream to be tapped, Gordon was having some difficulty making the connection. This difficulty was illustrated by the two-year delay in bringing forward the measure after its first formal introduction in the speech from the throne and budget of 1963. The reasons for the delay were various. When Gordon offered the proposal to the Cabinet in April, 1963 he noted that:

> This memorandum has not yet been fully discussed with officials of the departments concerned and is thus subject to further revision in the light of their views. However, because of the time pressure

under which we are working, I have been asked to submit the memorandum to the Cabinet and to the interested officials concurrently.[45]

This memorandum on the Corporation made a full and confident assertion of its nationalist purposes, and argued for its appropriateness in a mixed economy.[46] The Corporation was to combine the advantages of wide private ownership and "extensive government influence."

> The basic economic policy of the new government is to further the development in Canada of a mixed economy involving some government ownership of industry where this is clearly desirable, but based primarily on the diversified ownership of Canadian industry by the largest possible number of small Canadian investors. This is envisaged as a clearly preferable alternative to state socialism which is bureaucratic and stultifying of initiative. The proposed Corporation will enable the widest possible private and institutional ownership to be combined with high quality direction and management, and the combination to be supported with government credit. At the same time it reserves an adequate measure of influence and control to the government without stultifying initiative. There is no reason why the proposed Corporation should not enjoy widespread support from the public and the financial community, and this will be necessary if it is to do its job properly.[47]

Gordon rejected the alternative of an agency "wholly owned and controlled by the government" on the grounds that it would be

> . . . opposed by public opinion in general and strongly by the business community in particular. It would be regarded as the effective beginning of state socialism. It would thus be obstructed in its operation and unable to call on the commercial and financial talent of the community.[48]

The draft memorandum outlined the operating principles of the Corporation and the provisions of its proposed charter. The influence of the government was to be asserted through the appointment of five out of twenty-five directors, and through the Minister of Finance's direct involvement in the approval of funded debt issues, investments of more than $50 million in the securities of single companies, the appointment of officers, and the removal of officers and directors. The

Corporation's operating costs were to be met for the first eighteen months from public funds, and the Corporation was to raise its initial capital by a share issue to the public of 2,500,000 common shares at $10 par value.

The memorandum was discussed at a meeting of the Cabinet committee on economic policy, trade and employment on May 1, 1963 attended by Gordon and David Stanley. Here, questions were raised (among other things) about the legitimacy of government guarantees to private investors, and the degree and quality of government involvement in the management of the fund. The Minister agreed to revise the memorandum and to return later to the committee for further discussion.[49]

Within two weeks Walter Gordon had prepared a draft speech intended to accompany the introduction of the Canada Development Corporation Bill to the House of Commons.[50] There were, however, obstacles of detail and public consultation to overcome before legislation could be drafted, and the speech was never delivered. Shortly after budget day, 1963, the Cabinet received a short memorandum on the Corporation from the Minister, and approved the terms of a resolution to be placed before the House of Commons as the first step in the legislative process.[51] The House received notice of this resolution on June 20, 1963, but meanwhile the budget crisis had intervened, and any immediate progress with the Corporation became impossible. Gordon was distracted from detailed consideration of the measure, and the resolution was not debated.

For several months Gordon treated the Corporation with caution. In November he received a further memorandum emphasizing the apparent difficulties which it faced, and suggesting certain major changes in the concept.[52] The memorandum expressed doubt that the Corporation was politically feasible, because the lay public seemed indifferent to the problem and the business community possessed too large a stake in the existing financial structure to regard the proposal with any favour. It speculated that antagonism could only be expected to disappear if more spectacular takeovers of Canadian companies like Canadian Oil awakened "the average voter" to the danger of growing foreign control in the economy, and if Canadian business and financial leaders came to recognize in this trend a direct threat to their own interests.[53]

The memorandum added that the Corporation's entry into the New York market for debt capital would require "some form of prior consent by the U.S. authorities," and wondered whether the American reaction to the Corporation might not be "jaundiced." For technical

224

Harry Duncan Lockhart Gordon

Above: Walter Gordon with members of
the Royal Commission on Canada's
Economic Prospects, 1955. Left to right:
A.E. Grauer, Omer Lussier, D.V. LePan,
Gordon, Raymond Gushue, Andrew
Stewart.

Right: At Keno Hill, Yukon, with the Royal
Commission.

Above opposite: At the Davenport
nominating convention, January 23, 1962:
L.B. Pearson, Walter Gordon, John
Wintermeyer.

Opposite right: 1962 campaign
photograph.

On the hustings with Mike, 1963.

The Pearson government, July, 1963.

The new Minister of Finance takes over:
Gordon and the retiring Minister, George
Nowlan, April 22, 1963.

5

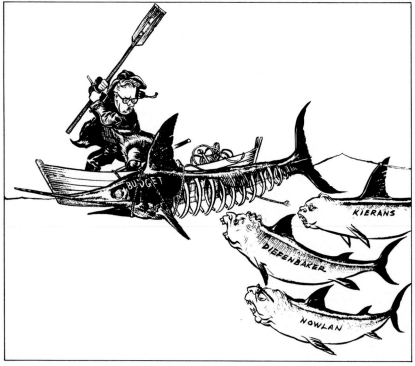

Preparing the budget: Gordon and Prime
Minister Pearson, spring, 1963.

Above: "Everything is go, Gordo.
Where you go, I go." June, 1963.

Opposite: Hammerheads. June, 1963.

Friends: Maurice Lamontagne, Walter Gordon and Guy Favreau, spring, 1963.

With Andrew Thompson, provincial leader of the Liberal party in Ontario.

Gordon announces his resignation, November 11, 1965.

Opposite: Publication of *A Choice for Canada*, May, 1966.

Meet the Author. May, 1966.

The Money-changers. January, 1967.

Return to Cabinet, January 4, 1967: "I am very happy to have the benefit of Mr. Gordon's energy, imagination, experience and strong Canadian viewpoint. We find ourselves in very close accord."

Above opposite: "We agree on a great many things. . . ." March, 1967.

Below opposite: "Hi!" March, 1967.

Above: May, 1967.

Before the Vietnam speech, May 13, 1967.

With the Queen and Prince Philip, July 1, 1967.

A little wounded but not slain. May, 1969.

reasons, the author doubted whether the Corporation could ever offer a high or stable yield for the individual investor, and recommended that its shares should not be offered to private investors "for a considerable period of time."[54] (This would reduce still further the Corporation's populist appeal.)

Nothing seemed to encourage haste in promoting this unexpectedly complex venture. Walter Gordon left the project in limbo over the winter. In March, 1964 he was ready to propose that the government should transfer three profitable crown corporations (the Polymer Corporation, Eldorado Mining and Refining Company Limited, and the Canadian Overseas Telecommunications Corporation) to the agency "to give it . . . something to build on"; but the result of further informal consultation outside the Department of Finance about the response of businessmen was still discouraging.

Spasmodic discussion of the project continued through 1964. By February, 1965 officials in the Department of Finance had prepared another memorandum to the Cabinet on the CDC. Revisions were made over the next two months, and in April the Minister of Finance sought the confidential advice of a number of leading business and financial persons. On April 23 Gordon presented his memorandum to the Cabinet seeking approval in principle for the creation of the Corporation; this was granted and the Minister made his statement in the budget speech three days later. On April 28, 1965, almost two years after the original and undebated resolution on the subject, Gordon presented another resolution to the House to authorize legislation establishing the agency. This resolution, like the first, was never debated. It was clear that the general support necessary to launch the Corporation remained uncertain; and its precise form remained undecided in a number of details. Gordon seemed to accept the views that the financial community would have to be reconciled to the project, and that the government would require the authority of a new parliamentary majority before attempting to launch the venture. These renewed references to the Corporation were therefore offered as trial balloons rather than firm notice of the government's intention to act. As Douglas Fullerton (a supporter of the project) wrote in the *Financial Times* on May 17, "This is not a precise blueprint that Mr. Gordon has drawn, and one suspects that he chose a rather vague form of wording in order to give Parliament and the public adequate scope for debate and discussion of the proposal before the Bill is introduced."

The Minister of Finance's private consultations and his cautious statement in the budget produced a large body of correspondence from the business and financial communities, much of it challenging the proposal on grounds already foreseen: that it fulfilled no pressing need and that it marked a dangerous intrusion of government into the operations of the capital market. Gordon remained convinced of the Corporation's potential value, but recognized that he was not yet in a strong enough political position to carry it through. He was working on several fronts to reinforce his position. Extensive consultation continued throughout the summer, in the expectation that legislation would be ready for adoption in the spring of 1966.[55] The technical problems of drafting the legislation in the light of criticism were being steadily overcome; and given a satisfactory general political situation, this timetable came to appear realistic. The greatest source of impetus was now the informed and enthusiastic advice of Maurice F. Strong, the president of the Power Corporation of Montreal, who was privately invited by the Prime Minister and the Minister of Finance to take the presidency of the Corporation on June 1.[56] Strong indicated his desire to accept the appointment, and worked closely with Gordon during the summer on the project.[57] Most of Gordon's friends in banking and finance remained reserved or hostile, but their scepticism in the face of what now appeared inevitable tended to take the form of detailed criticism designed to muffle the agency's impact on the market and to free it from political influence.[58] Gordon was prepared to reassure his critics, to make limited concessions, and to maintain his personal ties, but not to back away from the basic commitment. His confidence that the CDC would at last be born was reflected in a careful speech to the Canadian Institute of Actuaries on September 20, 1965.[59] But the general election and its consequences changed all that.

*

The subject of legislation to protect the Canadian magazine industry from domination by American publications had been a contentious one since the *Report* of the O'Leary Royal Commission on Publications in May, 1961; and no politician who took a position in the controversy remained unaware of the contending lobbies that were at work.[60] American magazines dominated the Canadian market, offered tempting appeals to Canadian advertisers, and thus appeared to be inexorably destroying the country's commercial periodical industry. Even the largest-circulation Canadian magazine, *Maclean's*, seemed threatened with extinction in the early 1960s. The Diefenbaker government had temporized, and for two years the Pearson administration worried the issue in an effort to work out a policy that would satisfactorily meet its own nationalist objectives and square the circle of conflicting opinions and interests. The government's first attempt to deal with the question was announced by Prime Minister Pearson in the throne speech debate on February 20, 1964. He noted that "the economic position of Canadian magazines has continued to deteriorate" since the publication of the O'Leary *Report*, and recognized that uncertainty about the government's intentions for the industry was a further source of difficulty which had to be dispelled.[61] His government, said Mr. Pearson, accepted the O'Leary Commission's view "that in order to survive – and I think the necessity for such survival is admitted, if it can possibly be brought about – Canadian publications must be assured of a reasonable share of the magazine advertising that is directed to Canadian readers." He therefore announced that "the Income Tax Act will be amended so as not to allow a taxpayer to deduct from his income, for tax purposes, expenditures after December 31, 1964, for advertising specifically directed at the Canadian market in non-Canadian periodicals." Split runs or regional editions of American magazines containing more than five percent of advertising space directed specifically at the Canadian market were to be prohibited entry into the country under amendments to the Customs Tariff. But there were to be two conspicuous exceptions to the rules, and these were the real source of political difficulty.

> Non-Canadian periodicals will be defined so as to include any future special Canadian editions of foreign periodicals not in existence today. Canadian advertisers in Canadian editions which already exist, for example *Time* and *Reader's Digest*, will continue to be allowed to deduct their expenditures for advertising in those periodicals. In making this exception we are taking into account the fact that these special editions have been established in Canada for some years and have made a place for themselves with Canadian readers.[62]

The Prime Minister admitted that the measures were imperfect.

> We must avoid any measures which would interfere with the free flow of information and opinion. That principle sets strict limits to the possible action in this field. At the same time we cannot permit our Canadian periodical press to disappear if we can prevent that disappearance. I believe that the action the government will propose is a proper balancing of these two essential considerations, and I hope it will be recognized as such.[63]

But the critics at once pointed out the irony that while the action inhibited new special editions aimed at the Canadian market, it would do nothing to prevent the growth of the two foreign publications chiefly responsible for the squeeze on advertising revenues in Canadian periodicals.[64] The Trojan horses could continue their voracious feeding; the remedy might be no cure at all. The lobbying on behalf of the two periodicals was known to be intense.[65] By proposing a weak palliative which conceded to this lobby, the Prime Minister had stumbled into another damaging political controversy. The instinctive reaction was to postpone the legislation and defer the embarrassment. While the necessary resolutions were drawn up for presentation with Walter Gordon's budget of 1964,[66] Gordon made no mention of the subject in his speech.

A memorandum of April, 1964 reviewed the government's dilemmas.

1. There is opposition in all political parties to the proposed exemption for *Time* and *Reader's Digest*.

2. The position of Canadian magazines in relation to these two special editions continues to deteriorate: in the first quarter of 1964 *Time* and *Reader's Digest* captured fifty-two percent of the advertising placed in all consumer magazines printed in Canada, compared with forty-seven percent in 1963.

3. The major cost advantage these magazines have over Canadian magazines is the fact that most of their editorial content is a by-product of their American editions.

4. A measure having the immediate effect of driving these two magazines out of business would be unfair to their publishers and their Canadian employees, and would have a serious effect on relations between the Canadian and United States governments.[67]

The memorandum advised against proceeding with the government's measures as they stood, on the grounds that the Cabinet might be defeated on the issue, and that there was diminishing reason to consider the measures "sufficient to preserve Canadian magazines." (The trend in advertising revenues indicated that.) As a practical addition to the legislation, it suggested offering free postal privileges to Canadian magazines only; and it proposed a transitional period for *Time* and *Reader's Digest* in which they would be required to meet a quota of minimum Canadian content and to establish a certain degree of local ownership in their Canadian operations.

The Minister of Finance had been consulting since the previous autumn about the ownership of Canadian newspapers as well; and by the spring of 1964 the possibility of major foreign takeovers of some newspapers seemed real.[68] In May Tom Kent prepared a new memorandum for the Prime Minister which linked the problems of the magazines and newspapers and offered a new approach to the delicate subject. He argued that removing the exemptions for *Time* and *Reader's Digest* would unduly antagonize the American government, offend against the acquired "squatter's rights" of the two periodicals, and annoy many Canadian readers of the magazines; finally, it would once again open the government to the charge of reversing itself and not knowing its own mind.

> Therefore the best solution is one that neither tries to force through the existing measure nor deletes the *Time-Digest* exemptions, but instead does something else to satisfy the people who are opposed to *Time* and *Digest*.[69]

The leading critics, he noted, were also the advocates of a general Canadian ownership policy in all the media.

> The Prime Minister has said several times, going back for some months, that the government is looking into such a policy. It would therefore be very easy to say that, while the original proposal was made only for magazines because of the urgency arising from prolonged uncertainty, the government has taken what advantage it could from the slowness of business in Parliament. Having meantime completed its consideration of the communication problem, it is now ready to absorb the magazine proposal into a comprehensive measure.
> This measure would be symmetrical with the magazine proposals. That is, it would disallow, as a business expense for tax purposes, advertising placed with any non-Canadian media of communication (magazine, newspaper, radio, TV). It would contain the same exemption for existing foreign-owned media established in Canada. That is, in addition to *Time* and the *Digest*, a few small newspapers (notably the Red Deer paper) would get "squatter's rights."[70]

This was the genesis – in May, 1964 – of the foreign ownership policy for magazines and newspapers which emerged into legislation in 1965.

Kent went on to mention a possible Canadian content rule of fifty-five percent with a three-year period of grace to meet it for *Time* and *Reader's Digest*, but added:

> The difference would be that, because we would be taking action

over a broader field, there would be far more satisfaction to nationalism and therefore it would be easier to get away with not requiring Canadianization of *Time* and *Reader's Digest* in ownership and control. I agree with Gordon that such a requirement would be a messy operation, difficult to make effective, and a cause of considerable friction with the U.S.[71]

Gordon concurred, and wrote in the margin of his copy that "I would be inclined to leave this out – not practicable for *Time* and *Reader's Digest.*"[72]

Kent concluded that while the measure would be approved by "the greater part" of the newspaper industry,

> The one real weakness of this solution is that it uses the advertising-taxation instrument, and some people would be uneasy about that as the thin end of a wedge. We would have to make it very clear that the last thing in the world we wanted was actually to disallow any advertising expenditures; the purpose is simply and solely to steer communication-supporting advertising to Canadian media of communication. It therefore might be desirable to accompany the tax measure by declaratory legislation prohibiting foreign ownership (unless already established) in the communications field. But the constitutionality of such legislation is open to question.[73]

After further conversations, Kent wrote a short memo to Gordon on May 24, 1964 indicating that the matter was still unresolved. Kent said that he understood that Gordon had "now come to the view that the existing provision for the exemption of *Time* and *Digest* should stand. You would be content simply with the extension of the general policy to newspapers, radio and TV, in addition to magazines." But Kent now argued that "we have to do something more" to save the magazine industry, and returned to the proposals for minimum Canadian content or ownership. A content requirement would be more useful than an ownership percentage rule, he believed, but an ownership rule "would be better than nothing. Certainly it would, I think, make the whole package easier to get through Parliament than it would be if we were to stick to the straight exemption of *Time* and *Digest.*"[74]

The political delicacy of the problem, the persistence of the rival lobbies, the problems of jurisdiction and drafting, and the frustration of the government's parliamentary timetable in 1964 meant that there was no progress on the legislation by the end of the year. Early in 1965 the issue took on new urgency, but another complication was added to the situation. While the danger of foreign takeovers of some newspapers seemed more immediate, the *Time* lobby against any interference with its established position seemed to grow more intense. Walter Gordon gained the impression that Henry Luce was prepared to use his influence in Congress to delay passage of the Auto Pact if Canada acted against the interests of *Time* magazine.

I was quite aware of the power and influence of Mr. Luce and of the difficulties being encountered in getting the U.S. Congress to approve the automobile deal. I was aware also of rumours that *La Presse*, by far the largest French-language daily in the province of Quebec, might be sold to European interests sympathetic to the separatist cause, and of another rumour that the proprietor of the *Globe and Mail* was considering the sale of his newspaper to American interests. In these circumstances, I thought it wise to support the compromise proposal, even though it meant exempting *Time* and *Reader's Digest*.[75]

Gordon had not only to support the measure, but to carry it through the House as Minister of Finance.

While the proposal came from the Prime Minister, it was up to me to present it to Parliament, as it involved amendments to the Income Tax Act and, therefore, was a budget item. The proposal to exempt *Time* was attacked strenuously in the House, and the Liberal caucus in particular was highly critical of it. Fortunately, I had always made a practice of being frank with caucus about any legislation I was responsible for sponsoring. I followed the same course of taking members of caucus into my confidence on this occasion and explaining the whole situation to them. I said I did not like the *Time* exemption any more than they did, but this was the price we had to pay to get approval of the automotive agreement, and at the same time to make sure that the two important newspapers referred to would not be sold to foreigners. I asked caucus to support me in a thoroughly unpalatable task, and members agreed to do so.[76]

It seems evident that the Cabinet's reasons for exempting *Time* and *Reader's Digest* were more complex than this, and that the essential commitment, once it had been made publicly, in February, 1964, could only have been withdrawn with extreme political difficulty. But to carry it through was also difficult in light of the obvious gap it left in

231

the legislation. Gordon's explanation to caucus provided an immediate rationalization of the Cabinet's position which enabled it to gain the party's support for the legislation, inadequate as it was. It may also have reflected accurately the kind of pressure that Henry Luce was prepared to exert on *Time's* behalf at any time the measure might have been presented. In one sense, Gordon made adept use of Luce's rumoured intervention in order to dampen criticism of the government in caucus and in the House. (In the debate on second reading in the House on June 22, 1965, Gordon told members, without further elaboration: "Let me begin with periodicals. Here, the main criticism, one that some honourable members feel very keenly about, is that *Time* and *Reader's Digest* are here given resident status. Those who oppose this look upon it as a surrender to the power and influence of Mr. Henry Luce. I expect that this is the view of at least some of the honourable members in all parts of the House."[77]) But later, when Senator Keith Davey's Special Committee on Mass Media reported Gordon's assertion "that the exemptions were granted in the first place as a result of severe pressure from Washington" affecting the progress of the Auto Pact, Lester Pearson denied that this had been the case.[78] In the absence of absolutely firm evidence, it is fair to conclude that both Gordon's and Pearson's accounts contain elements of the truth. There is no doubt that Gordon made the case to caucus in these terms, and believed it to be correct. There is no doubt either, from the record, that the Cabinet was prepared to allow the exemptions months before negotiations on the Auto Pact had concluded or been announced. Mr. Pearson's denial that this particular pressure occasioned the exemptions thus also appears technically correct, even though it may have been hinted at in the later stages. What is indisputable is that the presence of *Time* and *Reader's Digest* in dominant positions in the Canadian periodical market created the most awkward dilemmas which no government felt capable of escaping with dignity. The special exemption to *Time* and *Reader's Digest* remained a matter of public contention, and in 1970 Senator Davey's Committee on Mass Media recommended its removal on the familiar ground that it subsidized the entrenched success of these magazines to the detriment of their domestic competitors.[79] By 1973 no action had been taken on the recommendation.

The provisions affecting the ownership of newspapers faced more vocal, but in the end less influential, opposition from "a majority of Canadian newspaper proprietors" represented by the Canadian Daily Newspapers Publishers' Association, who asked for withdrawal of the measure with the claim that:

Regardless of any question of newspaper ownership, it is our opinion that to employ in any degree of manner a tax restraint or incentive on advertising as a means of regulating the press of this country, or its ownership, is a fundamental violation of long established press freedom in Canada.[80]

Early in May a delegation from the Association met Pearson and Gordon to express their objections – which, they said, did not concern the government's ends but only its use of tax discrimination as a means. (The virulence of some editorial attacks, however, particularly in the *Globe and Mail* and the Winnipeg *Free Press*, suggested certain more basic opposition.)[81] Gordon replied with confidence that the legislation in no way restricted anyone's right to publish anything. "All it did was to restrict the market available to Canadian newspaper proprietors who might wish to dispose of their properties to the highest bidder irrespective of who might be the buyer."[82] The strength of the publishers' reaction, it appeared, owed something to a fear (which Tom Kent had predicted) that the measure was the first step toward a general tax on advertising as tentatively proposed four years earlier in Kent's paper to the Kingston Conference.[83] After the government's explanations and reassurances at the meeting, some of the editorial opposition abated.[84] But St. Clair Balfour of Southam Press advised Gordon that he could expect one more round of editorial opposition "as the publishers felt this might be useful background if, in the future, any government should consider imposing sanctions on the press through the medium of tax legislation."[85]

The government made clear that it would welcome practical alternative suggestions from the publishers for maintaining Canadian ownership, but that in default of alternatives it would proceed with the legislation. When the Minister of Finance presented the amendments to the House on June 22 he repeated the pledge.[86] Gordon was confident that this mixture of firmness and reason would command wide public support, and this judgment seemed to be accurate. After passage of the legislation, the issue never again became a matter of public controversy.[87]

But the friction of passage left scars. While the legislation was the joint product of the offices of the Prime Minister and the Minister of Finance, criticism had focussed on Gordon, as sponsor of the measures, rather than Pearson. Gordon's belief was that the nagging reactions to the legislation left the Prime Minister with a residuum of irritation against his Finance Minister.[88] The concessions to *Time* and *Reader's Digest* had undermined the principle of the policy; both Pearson and Gordon knew it and were uneasy. The publishers' protests against the newspaper legislation were abrasive. The situation invited ragged nerves and misunderstanding, even between friends.

*

In Walter Gordon's judgment, the Automotive Trade Agreement, which was the product of more than a year's negotiation at the senior administrative levels between the Canadian and American governments (under the general supervision on the Canadian side of the Minister of Industry, C. M. Drury) was "a tremendously important achievement for the Pearson government."[89] It provided for free trade in automobiles and auto parts between the two countries which, when combined with agreements concluded between the Canadian government and the auto manufacturing companies, promised substantial increases in production beyond the normal rate of growth in the Canadian industry; maintenance of the existing proportion of Canadian content in the Canadian product; and an opportunity for rationalization of the North American industry which might lead to a major increase in the Canadian share of the American market.[90] The negotiation developed out of American dislike of, and potential retaliation against, an export incentive scheme for the Canadian auto industry introduced in the summer of 1963 by the Minister of Industry. The Auto Pact was attractive to the Canadian Cabinet because it offered the prospect both of increased production and employment and of a significant reduction in the trade deficit with the United States.[91] These were objectives which the Pearson government placed high on its list of priorities when it came to power in 1963, and when the agreement emerged, the potential advantages seemed easily to outweigh the disadvantages. Walter Gordon wrote:

> It meant a considerable capital investment in Canada to facilitate the greater volume of production that was called for. It meant the creation of thousands of new jobs and it relieved our balance of payments difficulties. It is true that it accepted rationalization of the automobile industry on a continental basis. I did not like this in principle, but as three companies dominated the industry on both sides of the border, this acceptance merely acknowledged the existing fact. It is not a pattern that should be adopted for other industries.
>
> As a result of the agreement, the long term trend in the United

States for the disappearance of independently owned parts manufacturers, or their acquisition by the Big Three automobile manufacturers, was speeded up in Canada. This was most regrettable, but
in the long run it seemed inevitable in any event.[92]

Gordon believed that the agreement made the most of Canada's
opportunities in the situation, given that more radical policies were
politically unacceptable.

> Short of expropriating the Big Three automobile manufacturers in
> Canada, or some form of detailed direction of their operations by
> the federal government, neither of which alternative was thought
> to be practical, there was no way of achieving the government's
> objectives except, of course, increasing the "Canadian content"
> requirement which would have been considered protectionist in its
> application.[93]

The results of the agreement in its first years of operation were even
more favourable for Canada than the Cabinet had foreseen in 1965.[94]
The paradox was that this undoubted economic gain tied Canada more
intimately than ever to the American economy and further reduced her
bargaining power.

*

The Cabinet had deferred its decennial legislation to revise the
Bank Act pending the publication of the *Report* of the Porter Royal
Commission on Banking and Finance early in 1964. In May, 1965
Walter Gordon was finally able to introduce the revised Bank Act in
the House of Commons following extensive review of the *Report* and
consultation with the chartered banks. Gordon, however, had been
unable to reach agreement with the banks on a number of aspects of
his legislation, and found himself engaged once again in public conflict
with the financial community. The major points of dispute were
Gordon's refusal to accept the Porter Commission's recommendations
to remove the statutory six percent ceiling on bank interest rate
charges, or to extend the banking legislation to cover "near banks"
such as trust and loan companies; and the provisions of the Bill limiting
foreign ownership of Canadian chartered banks.

The Minister did not accept the argument of the Royal Commission
and the banks that removal of the interest rate ceiling would stimulate
competition and force down interest rates in some parts of the market;
he feared instead that the oligopoly position of the banks would allow

them to raise their lending rates if the ceiling were lifted.[95] (In this he was supported by all parties in the House of Commons.) He therefore favoured a continuing measure of government control over banking operations, including interest rates, and the encouragement of increased competition.

> I believed the trust companies were the most practical source to look to insofar as competition with the Canadian chartered banks was concerned. Their business had been growing at a relatively faster rate, although from a much smaller base, than had the business of the banks in recent years. This was pointed out by the bankers, naturally enough, who claimed it was quite unfair that they should be restricted on the rates of interest they could charge while such restrictions did not apply to the trust companies. The trust companies at the end of 1964 still had only ten percent of the total deposits compared with seventy percent in the case of the banks. It seemed to me their relative advantage in respect to the rates of interest they could charge might well be continued at least for the next ten years.[96]

Gordon promised the House that the government would be prepared to reconsider the interest rate ceiling if "at some future time there should be a general rise in world interest rates which would make these proposals unworkable."[97] This assurance did not appease the bankers, who carried on a dogged campaign of opposition to the restriction for the next six months.

Gordon's decision not to include the "near banks" within the jurisdiction of the Bank Act coincided with his wish to stimulate the competitive strength of these institutions rather than to limit it; but the choice was primarily the outcome of his desire to avoid a constitutional battle over the issue.

> ... the Royal Commission on Banking and Finance recommended that ... the "near banks" should be embraced under federal legislation and thus become subject to federal supervision. Nothing was said in the Commission's report, however, as to how such action could be justified under the Constitution. Under the British North America Act, "banking" is designated as coming within the federal authority. There is no definition of the word "banking," however, and I could find no support either from the law officers of the Crown – that is, the Department of Justice, or from outside counsel whom I consulted privately – which would have justified the federal

government assuming the proposed powers of supervision over the so-called "near banks." Moreover, the government concluded that any attempt to arbitrarily usurp such powers would automatically provoke a major controversy with the provinces which was the last thing we wished for at that time.[98]

Constitutional niceties and political calculation were of less concern to the banks, and the government's choice was another source of displeasure to add to their growing list of grievances.

Walter Gordon's intention to limit foreign participation in Canadian banking had been known since 1963; and when he introduced legislation to maintain Canadian ownership of insurance, trust and loan companies in September, 1964, he had affirmed that "similar provisions would be included in the Bank Act and made retroactive to that date."[99] The new Act proposed in May, 1965 provided that "not more than twenty-five percent of the shares of any Canadian bank could be held by non-residents, and that no single person or associated group, resident or non-resident, could hold more than ten percent of the shares of any bank."[100] In addition the legislation forbade the creation of agencies of foreign banks in Canada. The case of the Mercantile Bank of Canada (the only foreign-owned bank in Canada) required further specification. It had been purchased by the First National City Bank of New York from its Dutch owners in 1964 in spite of Walter Gordon's private warnings to Citibank officers before the purchase that Mercantile could not claim exemption from the forthcoming legislation.[101] Rather than denying renewal of the Mercantile charter under the strict terms of the revised Act, the Cabinet agreed to renew the bank's charter but to restrict its growth severely as long as Citibank retained an interest in it greater than ten percent. Gordon's announcement of the limitation provoked intensive lobbying on behalf of Citibank to remove this discriminatory feature of the Act. Citibank officers themselves, American government officials, and the presidents of several Canadian banks expressed their opposition to the Minister of Finance, and this was echoed by some of the Liberal press.[102]

The soundness of Gordon's instinct about the urgency of this legislation had been confirmed for him the previous autumn, when David Rockefeller, a vice-president of the Chase Manhattan Bank, had visited him in Ottawa before dinner with Prime Minister Pearson.

Rockefeller reminded me that the Chase and the First National City Bank of New York were rivals; . . . and that, if Citibank were coming into Canada, then it was important to him that the Chase should also be represented here. Rockefeller said that he had decided the best way for the Chase to accomplish this objective would be for it to acquire effective control of the Toronto-Dominion Bank, the fifth largest of the Canadian chartered banks, which of course had offices all across the country. I pointed out that, under the proposed legislation, his bank would be entitled to acquire a ten percent interest in the Toronto-Dominion Bank. He replied that this was not enough for his purposes; that he had concluded that anything less than a twenty percent interest would not give the Chase effective control over the management of the Toronto-Dominion Bank. He asked, therefore, if the Canadian government would not reconsider its decision in order that the Chase Manhattan might proceed with its objective.

I explained to Mr. Rockefeller that this was the very thing the proposed legislation was intended to prevent. This did not seem to satisfy him, however, as he raised the matter again that evening with Pearson. The Prime Minister spoke to me about this the next day, or shortly afterwards. When I explained the situation, Pearson agreed with me that we would be in difficulties if we allowed the Chase Manhattan to acquire control of the Toronto-Dominion Bank. If that occurred, it would be almost inevitable that the other large banking institutions in the United States would follow suit . . . it would not be long before Canada would lose control over the banking institutions in this country.[103]

But if this was reason for preventive action, it was also another source of complication for an embattled Prime Minister. Gordon's nationalist arguments might be overwhelming in the end; but as in the case of the newspaper legislation, Gordon believed that "despite some rationalizing about this matter, Mike did not like the controversy & criticism & was inclined to blame me for them."[104]

The whole affair was deferred after the Bank Act amendments received second reading on June 14, 1965, in the expectation that parliamentary committee hearings would take place when the House reassembled in September. Public notice had been given of the government's intention to act, and this would safely forestall any foreign takeovers in the interval; but as long as the revised Act had not become law, those who challenged the legislation could see hope for its withdrawal. While the breathing space was welcome to the Cabinet, the strength of the interested opposition seemed to Walter Gordon to be one more good reason for seeking a decisive mandate from the voters in a new general election.

In July, 1965, the Canadian and American governments released simultaneously a joint report on *Canada and the United States: Principles for Partnership*, the product of a two-man working group consisting of A. D. P. Heeney for Canada and Livingston T. Merchant for the United States, which had been created sixteen months earlier by Prime Minister Pearson and President Johnson. The report rather complacently emphasized the intricate relationship of interdependence between the two countries, and in two paragraphs which soon dominated public comment on the document, argued that "It is in the abiding interest of both countries that, wherever possible, divergent views between the two governments should be expressed and if possible resolved in private, through diplomatic channels."[105] This preference for "quiet diplomacy" was widely interpreted in Canada to mean that the Canadian government should muffle and restrain legitimate Canadian objection to American policy, and that the Canadian participant in the study, Arnold Heeney, wholeheartedly accepted a subordinate status for Canada. This oversimplified (though not entirely inaccurate) summary of the report's message offered evidence to sensitive nationalists of an alarming spirit of colonial dependency among the Ottawa mandarinate. Without the authors intending it, the report thus gained a symbolic place in the record of Canadian dependency. Walter Gordon made no public comment, but privately he was convinced that its spirit and substance were damaging to Canadian independence.[106] He made his views known courteously to his friend Arnold Heeney.[107]

*

The new session of Parliament had not begun to meet the timetable laid out earlier in the year by members of the Cabinet. Peter Newman reported that the House, "still exhausted by the emotional splurge of the flag debate, stumbled listlessly through a few procedural reforms, then adjourned on the last day of June, its schedule of legislative priorities virtually untouched."[108] Two days before, at the lag end of the session when Prime Minister Pearson returned to Ottawa from a Commonwealth Prime Ministers' Conference on June 28, the *Report* of the Dorion enquiry was delivered to him. It did not, as Guy Favreau and his colleagues had confidently expected, vindicate Favreau for his handling of the Rivard affair. Walter Gordon wrote:

As soon as we heard the findings – that, in the opinion of the chief justice, there was a *prima facie* case against Denis, that Favreau should have submitted the case to the legal advisers in the Department, that Rouleau had tried to use his influence to secure bail for

Rivard, etc. – it was clear that Guy would have to resign as Minister of Justice and that his political career was probably finished.[109]

Favreau in fact gave his letter of resignation to the Prime Minister at 10 A.M. on June 29, in a painful meeting before Cabinet assembled to consider the consequences of the *Report*.

The state of public anticipation made any delay in the Cabinet's response impossible, and ministers knew when they met at 11 A.M. that the Prime Minister would have to make a statement to the House that day. In his apparent surprise and consternation, Prime Minister Pearson did not (as is normal in the case of ministerial resignations) make a private decision in the exercise of his undoubted prerogative. Instead he threw the anguished problem to the Cabinet. Pearson's first, generous response to Favreau's offer of resignation was to ask him to take time to think, but Favreau insisted that he must go. During the morning, however, Favreau's close friend Jack Pickersgill came to the conclusion that "the worst of the storm could be avoided if Favreau were to resign from the Justice portfolio but remain in the Cabinet in a different post."[110] Members of the Cabinet were soon determined to persuade Favreau to take this middle course, and before the House met at 2:30 P.M. they had done so in a series of interviews with him. Favreau was naturally reassured by the warmth of his colleagues' feelings in his distress. The Prime Minister made a point of walking into the Commons chamber with his beleaguered friend, and later in the day Pearson told the House that Favreau, "a man and a Minister of unimpeachable integrity," had resigned as Minister of Justice but would take a new portfolio.[111]

During the day, Walter Gordon had been one of the first to offer his sympathy to Guy Favreau.

> I left Cabinet to go and see him. . . . He was in Jack Pickersgill's office away from prying newsmen. He was upset but courageous as always. I stayed with him for about half an hour, and it was only as I was leaving that he told me of Jack's suggestion. . . . I had some private reservations about this but it did not seem the proper time to voice them. My personal opinion was that he might be better off to get out of politics – he was not likely to recover in any complete way from this disaster – and return to the practice of law. Perhaps I should have said so.[112]

Instead, the Cabinet had found a momentarily comforting device which evaded the necessity for hard choice and stretched the constitutional conventions governing membership in the Cabinet. Walter Gordon's unvoiced reservation was politically and constitutionally more sound, and probably also kinder to Guy Favreau.

This was a sad and unexpected ending to the parliamentary session, made sour by the effrontery and carelessness of the commissioner in his judgment of the evidence.[113] The next day – predictably – there was more unpleasantness, when Gordon Churchill raised the question of Mr. Pearson's failure to inform the House that he had, in fact, been told by Favreau of the Rivard affair in the previous September. (Pearson had written to Chief Justice Dorion on December 14, 1964, to correct the record, but had never made a statement to the House.) Churchill added vaguely that there must be action to deal with what he described as "findings that international crime has infiltrated into high circles of the government."

> The man who can take action is the Prime Minister, but he is not a man of action. He will just shift and sway and, as I have said on more than one occasion, make statements in the House on which I am not able to place complete reliance.[114]

The revival of political recrimination of this kind marked a distasteful return to the atmosphere of the previous winter, and the summer adjournment of the House that day offered welcome release. But Walter Gordon feared renewed attacks on the Prime Minister if Parliament met again, as Lester Pearson had just announced that it would, in September.

11   An Election of Convenience

For more than six months Walter Gordon had urged a general election on the Prime Minister, in the belief that the electorate would at last return a majority Liberal government. The confidence and authority which that victory would confer on the Cabinet, he hoped, would restore its energy and sense of purpose, and destroy the pernicious influence of John Diefenbaker. The newly mandated government could then proceed undistracted to complete its reforming program.

Gordon first made the case for an election in a memorandum to Mike Pearson delivered on December 31, 1964. It began:

1.   The first thing to be decided (tentatively) in our present situation is whether or not it is in our interests to have an election this year (i.e.1965). As I see it the pros and cons (in reverse order) are as follows:

Cons
- The public doesn't want an election.
- There would be some objection to an election before redistribution becomes effective.
- It would be very difficult to raise the money. (This will be true for all parties.)
- I'm sure another national campaign is the last thing in the world you personally would wish to contemplate.

Pros
- We could not survive another year like 1964.

- We could win an election now (according to the December pre-scandal survey). The alleged scandals should not make too much difference if handled firmly.
- We need Diefenbaker this time – and he may not be around indefinitely.
- We should strike while economic conditions are favourable.
- It will be most difficult if not impossible to deal successfully with a host of major issues as a minority government e.g.:

The Carter Commission report on taxation. This will pose some awkward & controversial questions.

Our tax arrangements with the provinces.

Banking legislation

Transportation

Unemployment insurance

etcetera

It seems to me these various considerations lead to the clear conclusion there should be an election in 1965 (provided a new survey in say February indicates we can win it). If you agree the next question is whether it should be in June or September. I would be inclined to the earlier date for the following reasons:
- Having decided on an election (if you do) we should get on with it. Otherwise we will lose our drive. And we will be hurt if the House bogs down again.
- The economy is in good shape now.
- Diefenbaker
- I would prefer to go before not after the Carter Commission report is published.[1]

This advice was reiterated the following week when Gordon reported to Pearson on the January 5 meeting of the National Campaign Committee. But the Prime Minister made no decision, partly because he believed it unwise to enter a campaign before receiving the report of the Dorion enquiry and judging its repercussions. Through February and March there was continuous speculation in the press about a June election, and almost universal editorial opposition to the suggestion. (This speculation was fed by the obvious preparations being made across the country by the party organization since the Campaign Committee meeting in January, and by the relatively uninhibited talk of some ministers and their aides in Ottawa.) On March 10, the Prime Minister met Gordon, Martin, Favreau, Pickersgill, and MacEachen at 24 Sussex Drive "to discuss general political strategy and the possibility of an election."[2] W. A. Wilson put the ministry's dilemmas crisply in the Montreal *Star*:

To go while Mr. Diefenbaker is still there? To risk facing a new Conservative leader? To wait out the aftermath of the Dorion enquiry? To gamble that the enquiry will turn out well for the Cabinet? To take time to build a new image in Quebec? To assign what man to what task? To wait for the advantages – and fairness – of redistribution? To continue to face a hopeless Parliament? Indeed, to go or not to go?[3]

By the end of March the Prime Minister had assured the House of Commons that an election was not imminent. Peter Newman reported in his column on March 30 that the decision had been taken on the ground that the voters did not desire a campaign; that the Dorion report might be damaging; that NDP strength was growing; that no early replacement of Mr. Diefenbaker need be feared; and that an immediate election, in the prevailing atmosphere of French-English tension, would be exploited in dangerous ways by the Conservative party.[4] Beyond all these specifics lay the Prime Minister's emotional distaste for the business of campaigning, which he did not hide from his closest associates.

But the situation was uncertain; Walter Gordon, at least, believed that the question remained open. On March 31 the Minister of Finance reviewed electoral prospects in another letter to the Prime Minister, and urged that polling should take place in late June or July.

These are my reasons:

(a) Our organization is enthusiastic and as ready as it will ever be. It will be hard to get people in the same mood again after a two-month summer let-down.

(b) Economic and employment conditions are excellent. One cannot be certain this will continue to be the case in the fall.

(c) The situation in Quebec is relatively quiet at the moment but again there can be no certainty that this will continue to be the case.

(d) The polls of individual ridings all show we could win.

(e) This minority government has gone on long enough. As the throne speech made clear, there is a great deal of work to be done – but it will take new elections and a majority government to do most of it.

(f) Finally, and this is the really telling point, if Diefenbaker should announce his intention of retiring in June (as many Conservatives think he is planning to do) with a Conservative convention called for December or January, our hands would be tied until the new leader was chosen. And it would be difficult to have an election in 1966 until after redistribution.[5]

Gordon reported that Oliver Quayle, the successor to Louis Harris as the party's opinion pollster, was conducting another national survey whose results would be known about May 10, "to make absolutely sure . . . or as sure as one can ever be about a horse race" that the Liberal party could win a parliamentary majority. Gordon recognized that the result of this poll and the Dorion report would come too late to allow the calling of a June 28 election after their receipt, and thus argued "strongly for a July election with dissolution in mid-May, provided the results of the survey are encouraging. . . . As I see it," he concluded, "there are no good reasons for waiting until the fall – and many serious risks in doing so."

Under Keith Davey's and Walter Gordon's supervision, the campaign organization continued to build up its momentum during the spring, while the Prime Minister left the key decision in abeyance. The party's electoral machinery was put in order: campaign appointments were completed, nominations were promoted, funds were tentatively budgetted, a series of campaign colleges was scheduled, the framework of a party platform was constructed.[6] In a concise statement to "Key Liberals Across Canada" in May, signed by John Nichol, Walter Gordon and Keith Davey,[7] members of the party were "encouraged to talk about the following subjects to the exclusion of all others": the Canada Pension Plan, the "dramatic improvement" in economic conditions (the slogan "Liberal times are good times; Tory times are hard times" was resurrected), the tax cut, and the new flag. ("Mr. Pearson's tremendous personal contribution has been the unification of Canada. We can truly say he is a greater leader for all of Canada, one who has the affection, the loyalty and the respect of all Liberals. The new flag is a symbol of which all Canadians can be proud.") Liberals were advised, as they had been before, to "avoid personalities; above all, the leaders of the Opposition parties."[8] This was undisguised election propaganda, and it would not retain its freshness for many months.

The results of the April survey by Oliver Quayle were doubtful, and Quayle himself concluded that an election would be risky.[9] This advice was sufficient to close the Prime Minister's mind to an election before the publication of the Dorion report, which was now expected late in June. Walter Gordon accepted the postponement of a decision with reluctance.[10]

The National Campaign Committee met again on June 24, and the next day Gordon reported to Pearson on its major political conclusions. "There were no reservations or qualifications about these points," wrote Gordon, "which is unusual to say the least."[11] The Committee had agreed that there should be an election before the end of October, that it should occur before redistribution, that there should be "firm and fast action ... following publication of the Dorion report," and that special emphasis should be given to a program particularly attractive to the western provinces.[12] Gordon estimated once again that the party could win between 155 and 180 seats.

On June 30 (the day after Guy Favreau's resignation as Minister of Justice) Gordon renewed his pressure with another personal letter to Mike Pearson "Re: An Election this Fall." The arguments were by now familiar, but Gordon somewhat varied his emphasis. He reported on the weight of influence in favour of an election:

> At the end of last week, the Federal Executive, the organization (i.e., the National Executive Committee) and almost every member of the Cabinet (except Drury and MacNaught) were in favour of an early election and a big majority of the caucus were in agreement.[13]

The Minister of Finance speculated on the alternative of waiting for the completion of redistribution:

> If we do not have an election soon, we will become the captives of the Opposition because of redistribution. Theoretically, the redistribution scheme could be passed by Parliament by March, 1966. However, most people seem to think there will be delays and that the new system will not be in operation before the end of 1966. No one will want an election in the first half of 1967. Most people reason from this that if we do not have an election now, we will not have one (failing a defeat in Parliament) for over two years. Once the Opposition parties realize this, they will be able to make our lives extremely difficult.[14]

Gordon conceded that "the main argument against an early election is that now that most of the redistribution maps have been published, we should wait until redistribution is in effect before going to the country. Some people feel quite strongly about this although I suspect they have not thought through the implications of waiting as long as two years."

Gordon judged that there were "two compelling reasons" for an autumn election.

The first is the need for vindication of the action you take on the Dorion report. The second is a request for a mandate to implement the program outlined in the speech from the throne. A combination of these two subjects should justify any government in asking for a renewal of public confidence – or if you like, make it desirable to do so.[15]

He proposed an election "at the earliest possible date," and suggested September 27 or October 4 as possibilities. While the letter was long and courteous, there was an undertone of sharpness about it which reflected the gradual decline of good feelings between the two men. If Gordon was impatient with Pearson for his indecision, Pearson might equally have been irritated by Gordon's persistence.[16] The inconclusive discussion dragged on interminably.

The Prime Minister had certainly not ruled out an autumn election; and in July his public acts seemed to point less obscurely in that direction. Early in the month Pearson announced that Yvon Dupuis would not again be a Liberal candidate; the perennially anticipated Prince Edward Island causeway was promised once more on July 8; and on July 19 the Prime Minister introduced Ottawa's medicare plan to a federal-provincial conference. In August the government gained the windfall advantage of a large grain sale to the Soviet Union. The drift toward an election was gaining strength. But all these warning signs prompted the opponents of a campaign to make even stronger demands that the Prime Minister should resist the temptation to dissolve Parliament. On July 27 the *Globe and Mail* commented cynically:

> The role of most Liberals in this elaborate charade is clear; they want an election by any means. But Mr. Pearson's role is more difficult to decipher. Is he honestly resisting the pressure of party opportunists to call an election and honestly intending to wait, as he should, until redistribution can give Canadians more equitable representation? Or is he pretending his reluctance to hold an election, posing as the statesman who puts the needs of the elector- ate first and planning all the while to yield to the opportunists in the end, claiming that the Opposition or that something has forced him to call an election? . . .
>
> The truth is that there is no reason, except the convenience of the Liberal party, why an election should be called before redis- tribution; and the best of reasons why it should not. Such an election would rob most Canadians of the full power of their ballots. . . .

Only a Prime Minister who had deserted statesmanship for opportunism could consider an election in such circumstances.[17]

This put the case far too simply and unsympathetically. Shortly afterwards Prime Minister Pearson received a long and more persuasive memorandum opposing a general election from a party colleague in Montreal, John de B. Payne.[18] Payne argued that the party had no major issue on which to campaign, and that it had accomplished too much in a minority Parliament to make a convincing claim that it required a parliamentary majority in order to carry on governing. "The simple request for a majority so that we could govern more effectively," he wrote, "has no political sex appeal."[19]

Payne held that there had been no notable change in the mood of public uncertainty. "The public opinion polls do not show any significant change from those of 1962 and 1963 which would suggest that the composition of the House would be different than it is or that a majority government would emerge. The NDP is the only party at which the public is not mad."[20] He feared that the Liberal party would come out of a campaign without national representation, rooted more exclusively than ever in French-speaking Quebec.

> This equation results from the prospects of heavy gains in Quebec, minor gains in the Atlantic provinces and a status quo or slight loss in Ontario and western Canada. This could mean the end of the party as a dominant political force in the country.[21]

Payne believed that "redistribution is the hard core of the government's decision." The Liberal party had emphasized its concern for equitable representation; it had criticized the Tories for their inaction in power, and for their obstruction during passage of the Act. Was the party now to take responsibility for extending the inequities of the old system for the life of another Parliament? The question was a moral one, which Payne saw in the same light as the editors of the *Globe and Mail*:

> The moral posture of a government seeking to ease the parliamentary role of its ministers, through the calling of an election the reasons for which, beyond those of self-interest, would be difficult to state, would be offensive to many Canadians and many of our partisans. It would be a sorry historical commentary if a party, which has always placed public interest above those of privileged groups and always above its own, should call an election which would be self-seeking.[22]

The absence of clear justifications for a dissolution, and the issue of redistribution, obviously made an impression on the reluctant Prime Minister. On July 5 the acting chief electoral officer prepared a memorandum for the Secretary of State, Maurice Lamontagne, which concluded (with a certain indirectness) that a general election held under the new redistribution scheme would be possible by late November, 1966.[23] On August 10 the Prime Minister's office obtained a legal opinion from the Department of Justice which confirmed this view.[24] There was thus sound reason for the Prime Minister to believe that a decision not to call a general election in the autumn of 1965 would tie his hands for no more than a year.

This question, among others, was the subject of discussion between Mike Pearson and Walter Gordon at lunch on August 13; but Pearson did not inform Gordon of the opinions of the chief electoral officer and the Justice Department.[25] After their conversation, Gordon wrote to Pearson to reiterate his views on the "moral argument." That case, Gordon claimed, was "completely phony or, at best, ill-informed."

The facts of the matter are that if you do not call an election this fall, the government will be "locked in" for eighteen months to two years until redistribution can become effective (I suspect this is not fully appreciated by some of your correspondents). . . .

If you call an election and win it with a good overall majority and a better representation from western Canada (and I believe both these objectives would be achieved), both you, the Cabinet and the caucus would get a tremendous psychological lift. We would regain our collective confidence and in that case we could be a much better government than we are. It would be the end of Diefenbaker and this in itself would be a great thing for Canada. Quite apart from everything else, we would be able to deal with the Quebec situation fairly and reasonably but from a position of strength rather than weakness.

If there is a moral issue in all this – and I suspect there is – it is your responsibility to see that Canada is not left without an effective government for eighteen months to two years. I do not see how in good conscience this could be condoned.[26]

The persistent advocate was stretching his claims to offset the reservations of the Prime Minister. Against the potential psychological advantages of a majority victory, Gordon did not contrast the equally demoralizing effects of failure.

But he believed that the Prime Minister had finally accepted the case for a general election. "You left me today with the distinct impression," he wrote to Pearson, "that for all practical purposes, you have made up your mind."[27] (Gordon had not yet gauged the full convolutions of that process.) A week later Pearson departed for a political tour of western Canada which took the form of a preliminary campaign, replete with parades, banquets and largesse dispensed from the federal pork barrel. In Vancouver the Prime Minister told Bruce Hutchison "that an election would be called provided a private party survey being taken proved to be favourable, and that he would resign if his government didn't win a majority mandate."[28] Publicly, the Prime Minister said that he would announce his decision within two weeks, and that there would be an election either in November, 1965 or the autumn of 1967: the redistribution, he said, would hold up an election on the new boundaries until 1967, and "the end of 1967 would be a better time than the beginning, in view of the nature of the [Centennial] year."[29] This was precisely Walter Gordon's case. But John Nichol, the president of the National Liberal Federation, also met Pearson in Vancouver to caution him against the electoral enthusiasm of Walter Gordon and Keith Davey.[30]

Pearson returned to Ottawa on August 29, tired and depressed by his journey.[31] The next day Gordon, Tom Kent and Keith Davey met him to review the latest Quayle report on public opinion. It showed a slight improvement in Liberal support, and a slight loss in Conservative favour, as compared with the previous party survey of April, 1965.[32] But Quayle was exceedingly cautious about what this meant. He believed the party could win a majority of seats, "but it will certainly not be easy"; his estimate was "that at the present time there will be a total pickup of eleven to fifteen seats, to make it 140-45."[33] The report concluded that "the present margin seems slim. And we will remain frightened until the day of the election, and hope everyone runs scared."[34] The advice was not encouraging, and Paul Martin interpreted it the same day as too uncertain to justify an election.[35] This was a plausible reading of the evidence; the thirteen-point gap in popular support between the Liberals and Conservatives could be misleading because Liberal support was heavily overbalanced in Quebec and because twenty-two percent of the electorate was undecided. Walter Gordon summarized his own conclusions from the Quayle report in restrained but more optimistic terms.

> As of now we should win an additional ten to twenty seats, say fifteen, mostly in Quebec. These will be at the expense of the Creditistes and the Tories. The Tories should lose seats to the Socreds in the West.[36]

Gordon advised the Prime Minister, as he had before, to fight a campaign that would avoid discussion of the Quebec problem ("not because we do not consider it the No.1 domestic issue but because people in English-speaking Canada do not like being reminded of it"), ignore Mr. Diefenbaker, and concentrate on the government's achievements and the need for a strong mandate. Given that kind of campaign, he repeated his belief (which went beyond what could be read into the opinion survey) that "we should make nearly as many gains in English-speaking Canada as in Quebec – for a total of, say, 150-155 seats."[37] The strategic advice was repetitive, and in the face of Quayle's judgment, Gordon's estimate of Liberal gains was questionable. It depended on the assumption of a vigorous and convincing Liberal campaign that would win voters to the party as it progressed; but that assumption ignored the Prime Minister's weariness and hesitation, the absence of a fresh party program, the resilience of John Diefenbaker, and the hard experience of two previous campaigns in which the Liberal party had lost ground, not gained it, as polling day approached. The strongest arguments for dissolution, it now appeared, were simply the momentum and expectations that had been generated in the party organization during the months of preparation.

Gordon's memorandum to Pearson on the Quayle report added rather bleakly that "a different campaign stressing the Quebec issue would result in a loss of seats in English-speaking Canada. How many it would be hard to say. We might lose as many as we can expect to pick up in Quebec and then end up about where we are at present but with a different geographical distribution."[38]

Gordon and Pearson both sensed their unhappy position when they met for an hour and half on the morning of Tuesday, August 31.[39] Gordon wrote afterwards:

> Mike said he would announce his decision Thursday after getting the Cabinet's views tomorrow. He made it clear he is against an election – mainly I felt because he does not want to face up to campaigning. However he made it clear he wished to hear the Cabinet's views. I asked him if he wished me to express my opinion at Cabinet and he said he thought I should do so. (He, of course, knows I am for an election.)[40]

The conversation widened into a general discussion of Cabinet reorganization, Gordon's position, and the strained relations between the two men.

> In the course of our conversation I reminded Mike that while we

had been friends for years, I was quite aware of the fact that I had been irritating him of late – and by the same token that he often irritated me. I said this seemed to be inevitable, given our respective jobs and responsibilities and the pressures we have been working under. I said I accepted the situation as just that – but added that as I had told him before I would be more than happy to drop out altogether if he would like me to (in order to placate big business). I said I was aware this would not be a good political move in wider circles but nevertheless. . . . [41]

The Prime Minister preferred compromise.

Mike said he did not wish me to drop out but asked if I would consider External Affairs, say next spring, if he can get Paul Martin to drop out.

I said I would only consider External if I wanted to be P.M. someday. I said I didn't want this; that my object was to get out. (Mike made it clear – and I believed him – that he would get out today if he could and in any event would do so before long). . . . I merely said that if I went to External people would assume I had ambitions which I had not. I added that in fact as Minister of Finance I was No.2 in the govt. and I could not take a demotion. I said however I might be more than willing to leave the govt. to become chairman of the Can. Dev. Corp. sometime next year. We did not pursue this thought. [42]

(In his revised memorandum of September 12, Gordon added to this that "Mike seemed interested – there is no doubt he would like to improve relations with big business and can't see how to do this with me in Finance.")[43] For Walter Gordon, this exchange ended by confirming his hold on Finance; for Lester Pearson the conclusion must have been less definite.

Before the meeting ended, Gordon mentioned one consequence of a decision to carry on into 1966 without a general election.

At some point . . . I said if he did not call an election I would have to speak to him about my giving up the chairmanship of the Campaign Committee – and my plans for getting out of the govt. in the not too distant future – say next spring. [44]

The Prime Minister's indecision had by this time produced intense confusion and distress among his ministers and staff.

Late Tuesday afternoon, Paul Martin called me in an agitated state to see if he could see me. We had dinner together and he told me he had seen Mike that afternoon and that Mike had changed his mind and was not going to call an election. He said we would be beaten if we went ahead. Paul seemed to think this reversal would be very hard to explain![45]

Gordon called the Prime Minister and arranged to see him at 9 A.M. the next morning before Cabinet.

When I got to Mike's office the next morning his staff (Kent, et al) were in a state of gloom – the election was off, they said.

I told Mike of my conversation with Paul Martin; that I thought it would be a fatal mistake to reverse himself at this late stage after encouraging the country – and the party – to expect an election. I said he would be accused of further vacillation and indecision and that such charges would be valid.

I went on to say I understood his mood – that he found himself exhausted by his western trip; that the thought of another campaign was repugnant to him, especially against Diefenbaker; that he was worried by the editorials and personal letters urging no election – and so he was looking for an out.

I said that if he ducked out now, I would expect all of us including him to take a terrible beating in the House over the next twelve to eighteen months. I said we couldn't stand it and that he [would] be destroyed in the process. I said that for him it would be far better to be beaten in an election and get it over with.

I also said the campaign we planned would take him out of Ottawa for only two or three days a week and there was no real reason why it should be too strenuous.

I told him Martin had got the wrong impression from him about our chances. I reviewed them with him – we are thirteen percentage points ahead of the Tories according to the Quayle poll. We should win an overall majority. I predicted that we would do so. He said he would resign if we did not and that I would have to go with him. I said I would do so. But assured him that if we do not mismanage the campaign (or if he doesn't) we should win.

I asked him in putting the question to the Cabinet not to give a wrong impression about the latest poll as he must have done to Paul. He agreed.

When I left he was in a quite different frame of mind. I felt the election would go forward.[46]

The Cabinet met soon afterwards to offer its collective advice to the Prime Minister.

Mike was cheerful and seemed confident. He put the question of the election to the ministers quite fairly – if anything he gave the impression he wanted to go ahead. He asked everyone's opinion, starting with Paul Martin. Paul asked if he could speak last (so did Jack P.) to which Mike agreed.

Mike said of those absent Harry Hays was all for an election and that Laing had called to say he had changed his mind and was now for it. My recollection is that all the other ministers were present. All said they favoured an immediate election except:

MacNaught – who was strongly opposed.

Sauvé – who was opposed except if certain new and able people from Quebec were willing to stand now but not later (i.e., Marchand, Pelletier and Trudeau). If we lose, Sauvé will have been proved right!

Hellyer – who said he did not have all the facts we did but that in Toronto in his opinion we would not do as well as before (I think he is right).

and Paul Martin – who despite some pressing refused to give an opinion and this after asking to come last. It was typical Martin indecision.

Mike said he would make his decision by the following Tuesday (after Labour Day) but it was clear – or reasonably clear – he would go along with the views expressed by the great majority of the Cabinet.[47]

At the same time Gordon privately reaffirmed his own decision to resign if the election did not produce a clear victory for the party.

Note: I am more responsible than anyone for the decision – one Mike did not want to make. If we do not get a majority I will have to offer my resignation from the government – whether Mike does so or not. I would have no influence left anyway.

If we win the election with a reasonably good majority – say 150 or more – I should be in a reasonably strong position (for a while!).[48]

But the preliminaries were not quite played out. The same day Pearson wrote to the acting chief electoral officer to request "a statement . . . indicating the date by which you expect redistribution to be completed and giving your estimate of the earliest date thereafter on which a general election could be held?"[49] Nelson Castonguay replied the next day that he had "nothing to add or delete" from his previous report of July 5 to the Secretary of State (which had indicated the possibility of an election by late November, 1966). On September 3 the Prime Minister again asked for Castonguay's advice, in the light of the Justice Department's opinion that preparations could, in fact, be made under the new redistribution by late October, 1966 rather than November. Castonguay replied on September 7 that the Justice Department's estimate was, indeed, reasonable. The case for an inevitable delay of eighteen months or two years under the new Act was thus effectively destroyed; but by this time the impression had established itself in the party and other factors had taken precedence.[50]

On September 3 the Prime Minister met informally at Harrington Lake with Gordon, Kent, Davey and the members of his staff to confirm the choice of November 8 as election day.[51] Four days later Governor General Vanier granted the dissolution, and the Prime Minister announced his decision to the nation on television that evening. Even this anticlimactic release from suspense, however, was mishandled. The networks had arranged for instant responses to the Prime Minister's announcement from the four Opposition party leaders.

Pearson was unaware of all this until he arrived at the CBC's studios to give his broadcast. Just before going on the air he was told that his seven-minute message would be followed by twenty-three minutes of criticism from the other party leaders. This so unnerved him that he botched his performance, making it sound as though he were still unsuccessfully trying to convince himself that a general election really was justified.[52]

Any satisfaction that the decision brought to a confused nation was dispelled by the Liberal party's inability to explain the reasons for its choice. The Prime Minister's vague rationalization was that there were "major problems" which could best be faced by a majority government.[53] A few days later he told a reporter delphically that "I have my reasons. And my reasons are very good."[54] The reasons were those offered to the Prime Minister in the previous eight months by Walter Gordon and Keith Davey; and they had been critically assessed by John de B. Payne in his paper for the Prime Minister.

The public is not concerned with our difficulties and discomfitures in Parliament. Their disgust with Parliament has not been dissipated. The Tories may be the villains, but our image – and we must be frank with ourselves – has been tarnished too. The scandals have hurt. But our real problem is the damage to our reputation as "the Great Administrators" by a series of incidents during the past two years.[55]

The manner of taking the electoral decision did nothing to enhance that reputation. Who could describe the Liberal government of Prime Minister Lester B. Pearson, in the autumn of 1965, as self-confident, purposeful, energetic, or efficient? The Cabinet's very substantial accomplishments since 1963 were themselves obscured by the claim that the government could not act effectively without a parliamentary majority.

On September 10 the party received an encouraging boost in the province of Quebec with the announcement that Jean Marchand, Gérard Pelletier and Pierre Elliott Trudeau would enter the campaign as Liberal candidates.[56] Walter Gordon welcomed the announcement. "I was delighted, as this new blood was needed from Quebec and, in addition, it indicated that the strength of the more progressive elements in the party would be enhanced after the election."[57]

But Gordon's pleasure was immediately clouded by a piece of fresh news from the Prime Minister:

> . . . just when I was thinking what a coup this was for Mike, he telephoned to say that Robert Winters was considering going after the nomination in York West, the seat previously held by Red Kelly. I protested that Bob, much as I liked him personally, with his conservative outlook and his association with "big business" would not help us in the Toronto area where our main opposition would come from the NDP. I said it would be assumed that Bob would be in the Cabinet, which would mean four Cabinet ministers from Toronto. Apart from everything else, this would retard the opportunities for men like Donald Macdonald, David Hahn, and other excellent MPs from the Metro area. Moreover, I suggested that coming after Marchand, Pelletier and Trudeau, Bob's addition to the Liberal team would be confusing to the public who were uncertain enough as it was about what the party stood for.
>
> After thinking the matter over, I called Mike back again to say I thought it was unfair to Bob to encourage him to return to politics. I assumed he would be doing so only if he and his friends believed he was the man to succeed Pearson as leader when the time came.

But I pointed out the Liberal party was now very different from the one when Bob had been C. D. Howe's protégé in Ottawa. I suspected that he did not fully appreciate this, and that if he were elected he would be an unhappy man with little chance of realizing his ambitions. Mike replied that it was all settled, that Bob was going to run.[58]

Gordon was not troubled by any implied challenge to his own position which the return of Robert Winters might have represented. But some others wondered whether Winters was a prospective Minister of Finance.[59]

His candidacy was in fact the clearest indication of Gordon's eclipse, although the Minister of Finance was unaware of the full story. Winters was invited to run by Prime Minister Pearson at an interview in Toronto on September 13. This followed representations from bankers and businessmen who suggested the return of Winters and the replacement of Walter Gordon in Finance as the price of financial support for the party.[60] Robert Winters and his advocates believed that the invitation implied the removal of Gordon, and no one denied this implication in the early weeks of the campaign. The understanding may have been imprecise or unspoken, but it was sufficiently strong to be retailed as fact by some supporters of the party in the business and financial communities. The Prime Minister was engaged in a delicate task of fencemending, believing perhaps that he had Walter Gordon's own tacit acknowledgement of the exercise. That belief could not be sustained after their most recent conversations; but by then the approach to Winters had been made and accepted, and the ambiguous situation offered temporary advantages to the party – as long as no one pressed too hard for a clear explanation of the situation. The potential muddle would somehow have to be sorted out after November 8. It promised more serious misunderstandings than Pearson realized.

*

Gordon, Davey and Kent had agreed that the Prime Minister should not conduct a hectic and continuous campaign, but should emphasize his position above the political battle as the incumbent Prime Minister preoccupied with affairs of state. He would not rush into a tiring national tour, but instead would make occasional flying visits from Ottawa to the regions, concentrating his activity in the last three weeks before election day. Whatever the provocations, he would not enter into personal combat with John Diefenbaker. His major visits would be to the larger cities where the party hoped to maintain its strength, and to other, smaller centres in southern Ontario and the prairies where the gains necessary for a strong majority were required. In the first weeks Mitchell Sharp, Paul Hellyer and especially Walter Gordon led the Liberal campaign in public appearances across the country.

It was clear to Walter Gordon almost at once that the campaign was going wrong.

> The campaign got off to a bad start, thanks to Jean Lesage who insisted on proceeding with a prearranged speaking tour of western Canada despite the federal election. I urged Pearson to persuade Lesage to defer his trip in everybody's interests, his own included. Pearson told me later that he had tried to do this but that Lesage would not hear of it. He proceeded out West, ostensibly to explain and get support for the aspirations of Quebec and the objectives of his government. But his trip was a disaster. He gave the impression of being arrogant, he refused to answer questions, and he engaged in controversies with the press and with members of his audiences. The headlines were very damaging. The result was to foster the anti-Quebec feelings which had been stirred up by the activities of the separatists and accentuated by the Rivard and furniture affairs. Not only did Lesage's trip spoil our chances of picking up a few seats on the prairies, but it hurt us badly in some parts of Ontario and other sections of English-speaking Canada.[61]

To these parts of English-speaking Canada John Diefenbaker made his resourceful appeal. The memory of the winter scandals, the unsubstantiated hints of fresh ones, and the uninspired lethargy of Mr. Pearson's campaign provided the leader of the Opposition with the destructive ammunition for his renewed assaults. The divisions in the Conservative party were temporarily hidden as the party's leading professionals rallied to the cause.[62] Sixteen daily newspapers that had supported the Liberal party in 1963 transferred their allegiance to the Conservatives. (Chief among them was the *Globe and Mail*, which returned reluctantly to John Diefenbaker on October 30.) In the constituencies, party support seemed to settle roughly into the established patterns of 1963, and thus to deprive either party of the prospect of a substantial majority.

In mid-October Walter Gordon conveyed the discouraging results of the latest Quayle survey to the Prime Minister.[63] It revealed drops in Liberal support in Quebec and the Maritimes, and an overall spread between the two major parties about the same as in the 1963 general election. (A regional distribution somewhat different from that of 1963 offered no encouragement to the Liberal party.) Gordon reported that the prospects were for a small Liberal majority broken down as follows:

- We will lose some seats in the Maritimes;
- We should win a lot of seats in Quebec;
- We should hold our own or pick up three or four seats in Ontario;
- We should not count on anything in the prairies;
- We should hold our own or do a little better in B.C.[64]

The position could be improved, Gordon argued, "if we campaign all out on *our* issues in the last three weeks." He commented laconically on the meaning of this advice:

(a) On no account should you talk about Diefenbaker or the scandals. You should never mention either subject in any derogatory sense.

(b) We should talk and talk and talk about:

(i) Prosperity and the fact that people must have jobs.

(ii) Canada and Canada's position in the world. You do this with authority and feeling. The more emotion you get into it, the better.

(iii) The need for a strong majority government in Ottawa (this idea is getting across).

You should have one speech with a few variations . . . , and keep on repeating it.[65]

The advice was wearily familiar and probably unconvincing. It was offered without supporting argument, and in contrast there was the hard evidence of declining Liberal support. An ominous ritual of appeal and response was being re-enacted; Mike Pearson remained as ineffectual as ever on the hustings. Now, in addition, he was tired and without a novel program. Murray Beck wrote that "Pearson's real failure . . . was not in his arguments but in the manner of presenting them. Why his strategists believed he could enact the exacting role they had assigned to him in 1965, after his disappointing performances of 1962 and 1963, is somewhat mystifying."[66]

Meanwhile Gordon's place in the Pearson government was becoming an increasingly contentious subject of rumour and debate. Early in the campaign Senator Wallace McCutcheon, the Minister's Bay Street friend and political opponent, described Gordon as "the most dangerous socialist in Canada today," and urged that "Gordon must go . . .

or the consequences would be black for the Canadian economy and the country's relations with the United States."[67] McCutcheon objected particularly to Gordon's "anti-American bias" in his banking and foreign investment policies – policies, he warned, that were bound to provoke American retaliation. Gordon took up McCutcheon's challenge by suggesting facetiously that "if Wally McCutcheon really had such strong feelings, he should give up his Senate seat and run against me in Davenport. . . . The next day, McCutcheon replied: 'If all the people who disagree with Walter Gordon were to run against him in Davenport, there would be more candidates than voters.' There is no doubt he scored on the exchange."[68]

This banter hinted at the manoeuvring in the Liberal party over Walter Gordon's future. There were inconclusive editorial glosses on the struggle in the *Globe and Mail*, the Toronto *Star* and the Montreal *Gazette*. The *Globe* defined the problem as a conflict of approach over foreign investment policy between the Minister of Finance and the Minister of Trade and Commerce, Mitchell Sharp.

> At least one item of Liberal policy – the matter of foreign involvement in the Canadian economy – is all so blurred around the edges that it will be necessary to hold a preliminary bout (something in the nature of a nominating convention perhaps) in order to select the principal contenders.
>
> A good, hard-hitting public debate between the two ministers would do much to help clear the air – if they can be persuaded to talk to each other.[69]

The *Globe* shared Mr. Sharp's view that a restrictive attitude to the flow of foreign capital "could only weaken our economic structure and increase the temptation to join the United States" but wondered wryly what the party line really was.

The Toronto *Star* recognized the same uncertainty, but took Walter Gordon's part against the other prominent representative of the open door, Robert Winters. Did Winters agree or disagree with Gordon's nationalist approach to foreign investment? Did he share the distaste of many business leaders for any restrictions on the flow of capital into Canada? The *Star* called on Winters to reply because "if he is elected, and the Liberals are returned, he will presumably receive a high post in the new Cabinet."[70]

No clarification was forthcoming, and ten days later the Montreal *Gazette* challenged the Prime Minister, rather than Robert Winters, to resolve the central question:

... what is to be the future of the Hon. Walter Gordon in Prime Minister Pearson's government? If Mr. Pearson is returned as Prime Minister, is the country to continue to have its economic policies influenced by Mr. Gordon's peculiar theories and practices? ... The adhesiveness of Mr. Pearson to old friends has, until now, given poor hopes for change, even where the national interest requires it. Is it then to be assumed that Mr. Pearson is asking for support on the basis of policies that so much of responsible economic opinion in Canada emphatically rejects?[71]

These editorial comments reflected the now persistent rumour that the Prime Minister had somehow indicated his intention to remove Walter Gordon from the Ministry of Finance after the general election.[72] Gordon had seen Pearson only infrequently during the campaign, but on October 26 he shared the platform with the Prime Minister on a campaign tour through southwestern Ontario that ended with a rally in Wallaceburg. In the course of his speech that evening, after Gordon had received an enthusiastic welcome from the audience, Pearson remarked pointedly that Walter Gordon would continue as Minister of Finance in his new government.[73] This unusual commitment to a controversial colleague effectively scotched the rumour.

It also confused the Prime Minister's relations with Robert Winters. Winters had not expected this public endorsement of Gordon.

Winters called on Pearson the next day at the Constellation Hotel near Malton where Mike was staying. They had an angry altercation about my role in the next government. Apparently, Pearson had promised to appoint Bob Minister of Trade and Commerce which to Bob might have meant that he could become a second C. D. Howe. Bob might have assumed that Mitchell Sharp would move from Trade and Commerce to become Minister of Finance. All I know is that Mike and Bob ended up shouting at each other, forgetting perhaps that there are Liberals everywhere, including employees in hotels. It was a matter of hours before I heard all about the argument.[74]

The Prime Minister told a reporter after the meeting that "I can expect to resume the relationship with [Mr. Winters]. We were both in Cabinet together. ... I'm glad to have a talk with my friend Bob Winters."[75] But:

Mr. Winters was noncommittal. He said he was running as a

private candidate and would discuss his future with Mr. Pearson after the election.[76]

Robert Winters had received a public rebuff. The Toronto *Telegram* put the implication more strongly in an article titled "Was Winters double-crossed on Cabinet?" which concluded:

Whether he was promised the Finance portfolio, only the Prime Minister and Mr. Winters know. If he was, then he has been double-crossed.

If he wasn't, then Canada's business community has been double-crossed. For it was generally believed when he decided to return to public life that a man with his background would be the logical choice for this important post.[77]

Walter Gordon did not allow these speculations to trouble him. He had taken for granted from the beginning of the campaign that he would remain in Finance, and the Wallaceburg speech merely confirmed his assumption. Yet the reports and rumours were inevitably disquieting, and gave warning of potential difficulties after election day. If the party were to win its majority these might not amount to anything. Gordon was committed to that faith and had no misgivings.

The campaign, however, was still not going well. Walter Gordon recalled:

Pearson was determined to fight this election on his own, and he discouraged his colleagues from participating on any important scale. He seemed anxious to disprove the public's assessment of him as a vacillating politician, as reported objectively, but unhappily, by all the opinion surveys. He was not successful. He could not bring himself to be specific about future policies and gave the impression of being indecisive. The public was confused.[78]

Without the appropriate touch of political genius that matches a campaign to the public mood, the Liberal party stumbled through the last days toward November 8. At the Prime Minister's rally in Toronto on October 27 the public address system failed; in Vancouver he was constantly interrupted by hecklers; in Montreal he did not complete his speech when faced with a noisy separatist demonstration.[79] Mr. Pearson's two undoubted triumphs were his final rally in Hamilton, and his television broadcast on October 21 when he ignored the injunction against responding directly to Mr. Diefenbaker.

Pearson did show that Davey and I were wrong on at least one point. We had urged him not to reply to what Diefenbaker was saying about the Rivard and furniture affairs. But Pearson insisted upon doing so . . . on a national television program. He appeared on the program looking angry and indignant; it was his best TV performance in the campaign, and quite effective.[80]

In Walter Gordon's own constituency of Toronto Davenport there were never any signs that the Minister of Finance was in difficulty. His organization conducted an inexpensive campaign which cost less than half that of 1962.[81] Gordon's Conservative opponent, Dan Iannuzzi, made no perceptible ground with the complaint that Gordon was conducting an absentee campaign because he feared to face his own electors. It was ill-judged and insensitive to accuse Walter Gordon of lack of courage. Gordon replied calmly that while it was true that he had spent less time in the constituency than in previous campaigns, "I'm meeting the people. I'm standing on street corners, at bus stops, rapping on doors and visiting supermarkets." A *Telegram* reporter added that "The electors still like Mr. Gordon, if a casual survey is any indication. He has become a more personable, less remote campaigner."[82] Gordon was Goliath, and Iannuzzi was no David.

*

November 8 came.

I believed right up to the end of the campaign that we would win by a small margin and that at long last Pearson would become Prime Minister with a majority behind him. We had started the campaign with 129 seats, which meant we only needed to add another four for an over-all majority. But we failed to do this, principally I think because of: Lesage's western trip which was very damaging from our standpoint; Diefenbaker's skilful anti-French-Canadian campaign; and Pearson's inability to be specific about policies. More than anything else, we failed to keep to our own issues. Instead, a great deal of attention was paid to the question of Quebec and the difficulties of some of the government's French-speaking ministers. This was fatal for the Liberals.[83]

The Liberal party returned 131 members – two short of a majority – concentrated more heavily, as Gordon in his more pessimistic calculations had predicted, in Quebec. The new Liberal caucus would have less balanced representation than before dissolution; and the party had lost almost two percent of its popular support as compared with 1963. The Opposition parties had only marginally improved their standing, but their failure offered no consolation.

> I called Mike on election night . . . and reminded him of my undertaking to resign if we did not get an over-all majority. He sounded tired, dispirited, and thoroughly exasperated by the fact we had failed to win our majority. He said it would be he and not I who would be doing the resigning, and that he intended to do this right away. I said I would talk to him about this when I arrived in Ottawa the next day or on Wednesday. I did not see him on the Tuesday. Pearson met with members of the Cabinet on Wednesday. While he said something about resigning, everyone urged him to stay on which, quite properly, he immediately agreed to do.
>
> In the course of the discussion, I said I had advocated the election more strongly than anyone else and felt I should bear a large share of the responsibility. Someone remarked that, with only two or three exceptions, we had all been in favour of the election. Someone else said we could have won it if it had been held in June or July or in September, that we had put it off too long. And, of course, while the results were disappointing, we were in a much stronger position after the election than we would have been if it had not been held.[84]

Walter Gordon had committed himself to resign if the government failed to win a majority (as had the Prime Minister), and Gordon was determined to submit his resignation to Mike Pearson as he had promised. But after Pearson's own decision to stay on, and the Cabinet's assumption of collective responsibility for the defeat, the potential meaning of this action seemed, for Gordon, to have changed. It was a point of honour to be fulfilled. But the possibility was that Gordon would now accept mild persuasion to remain as Minister of Finance.[85] Given his characteristic self-restraint, this inclination could not be conveyed explicitly to Mike Pearson. The message would have to get through by hint and indirection. It probably did get through, but the Prime Minister chose not to respond.[86]

> I had lunch with Pearson the next day at Sussex Drive. I found him flushed and irritable. He started right in to say there would have to be some major changes in the Cabinet. From the way he spoke, I interpreted this to mean he wished to raise the question of the Finance portfolio once again, despite what had been said

264

about this both before the campaign began and publicly in the course of it. I replied that he did not need to worry about me. I had said I would resign if we did not get an over-all majority and was prepared to go through with my undertaking. I had my letter of resignation with me. I handed it to him and he put it in his pocket with a nervous gesture without reading it. I said I would like him to read it so he pulled it out and did so.

Pearson appeared to be unhappy about the ending of our political partnership but did not seem to realize that as well it would mean the culmination of our long personal friendship. He asked me in a casual kind of way – because he knew what my reply would be – if I would accept another portfolio. He then asked if I would like to go to Washington as ambassador. I reminded him that he had offered me the Washington post on two occasions before I had entered politics. I said I still had no interest in such an appointment. He then told me that Keith Davey would have to go immediately and that he wanted to get rid of Tom Kent as soon as possible. In addition, he said that Lamontagne and Tremblay would have to leave the Cabinet. I was left to wonder how he would get along without these men – Lamontagne, Kent and Davey – who had helped him so loyally through numerous crises and vicissitudes.[87]

While "It was a pleasant, friendly conversation and a bit emotional – more for Mike than for me," there were inevitable undercurrents. "I say this because Mike was taking advantage of my offer to resign if the election went against us in order to make a change at Finance – despite his promises to me privately and his public statement during the campaign to the contrary. We both knew this."[88]

The Prime Minister accepted Walter Gordon's resignation. The letter of resignation, dated November 9 but delivered on November 11, read:

Dear Mr. Prime Minister:

For many months as one of your senior ministers, I urged you to call an election on the grounds we needed a majority to govern the country well and to ensure the kind of stability I thought was needed.

As chairman of the Liberal party's National Campaign Committee I believed that if you conducted a good campaign we would obtain a comfortable majority. Your campaign was superb in every way. You could not have done any better or any more than you did.

The conclusion is quite clear. I gave you bad advice, both as a

265

minister and as campaign chairman. I accept full responsibility for this and therefore submit my resignation from the Cabinet.

If there is anything I can ever do for you at any time, you know all you have to do is let me know.

With very best wishes,

Yours sincerely,

W. L. Gordon[89]

*

The Prime Minister replied:

Dear Walter:

I have received your letter and I have also thought over the talk which, at my request, we had subsequently this afternoon.

I cannot accept your assumption of responsibility for the decision to hold the recent election which, while it confirmed our position as a government with considerably the largest support in the House of Commons, did not give us the majority of members we sought. You and others advised me to hold the election at this time, for reasons which seemed perfectly valid, but the decision was mine and the sole responsibility for the decision remains mine.

Nevertheless you have confirmed to me verbally the wish you expressed in your letter, to resign from the government. You know how much I regret this decision and my inability to persuade you to take another Cabinet post where the responsibilities would not be so heavy and continuous as they have been in Finance. In the circumstances, I have no choice but to accept your resignation. In regretfully doing so, I want to add this.

No single person has done more, indeed I do not know anyone who has done as much, to restore the fortunes of our party from the low point of 1958 to a position which resulted in our victory of 1963 and the defeat of the attempts of the Opposition parties to reverse that victory in 1965. I am in the best position to know what we owe you for your wholly dedicated, efficient and untiring work in the party organization.

I also want to express my deep appreciation for what you have accomplished as Minister of Finance in putting into effect fiscal policies which have done much to bring about and maintain the expansion and prosperity Canada at present enjoys; and for your effort to ensure that Canadians maintain the maximum control possible over their own economic and industrial development as essential to the development of the nation. You know that I share this objective with you.

Beyond adequate acknowledgement, is what I owe to you in friendship, encouragement and support. I know that your withdrawal from the government will not alter our personal relationship in any way, as something which has meant so much to me over so many years and which will continue.

Kindest personal regards,

Sincerely,

L. B. Pearson[90]

Walter Gordon's droll reference to the Prime Minister's "superb" campaign was a bit of diplomacy which was not intended seriously. Mike Pearson's reply was even less to be taken at face value. In rejecting Walter Gordon's responsibility for the decision to hold an election, the Prime Minister was also dismissing Gordon's reason for offering his resignation. And yet the resignation was accepted on the wholly separate ground that Gordon could not be persuaded to take another Cabinet post. (Gordon himself had no feeling that his duties in Finance had been too "heavy and continuous.") Walter Gordon – and others – could not help concluding that the Prime Minister had taken advantage of a convenient occasion to let Gordon go as the scapegoat for an unsuccessful campaign and a controversial administration.

Gordon departed at once for a holiday in Ireland. As he left Malton airport that evening he told Patrick Watson of the CBC: "I'm going to Ireland, mainly because I think it's going to rain in Ireland in November, so I won't have to go out. And I'll just have a rest."[91]

12   After the Fall

Soon after Walter Gordon returned to Canada in December, Lester Pearson announced a series of Cabinet changes arising out of the general election. According to prediction, Mitchell Sharp succeeded Gordon as Minister of Finance, and Robert Winters returned to the Cabinet as Minister of Trade and Commerce.[1] René Tremblay and Maurice Lamontagne resigned from the Cabinet at the Prime Minister's request. Keith Davey's forthcoming departure as national director of the Liberal party became known at the same time, and Tom Kent prepared to move from the Prime Minister's office to become Deputy Minister of the new Department of Manpower under Jean Marchand, the influential freshman member of the Cabinet from Quebec.

The Cabinet reorganization could not be interpreted on the surface as a blunt repudiation of the reformist wing of the Liberal party. A number of Gordon's close friends and supporters – including Judy LaMarsh, Edgar Benson, Guy Favreau, Allan MacEachen, and Larry Pennell – remained in Cabinet; MacEachen was promoted to Health and Welfare, and Jean Marchand came in identified as a leader of the reformers in Quebec. The readjustment involved the usual muddled compromise of political views and inclinations. But the departure of Gordon, Lamontagne, Kent, and Davey from the Prime Minister's inner councils reflected Mike Pearson's preference for a less venturesome and controversial second term of office: the reforming leadership was gone.

The leaders of the party's ginger group were now disarmed and dispersed. Mike Pearson had been harshly criticized for his excessive loyalty to faithful friends and associates; now he countered that criticism by separating himself from the closest of them in the aftermath of an unsuccessful campaign which they had advocated and managed. Because he had stuck by them – although passively – through the worst of their trials (as they had stuck by him), this belated purge left Gordon and his friends surprised and resentful. Gordon pressed Pearson, and the Prime Minister agreed, to grant Senate appointments to Lamontagne and Davey after their retirement.[2] Tom Kent was able to redirect his great energies to the problems of national employment policy. Of the four, Gordon found himself in what was probably the least satisfactory personal position. He had held the most senior office; he considered his task as Minister of Finance only half completed; and he had no interest in the role of an ordinary backbencher. But he could not consider immediate resignation from the House. His constituents had re-elected him by a large majority, and he felt an obligation to remain in the House "for a time at least"[3] as a mark of good faith toward them. He was not happy, and foresaw a period of relative inactivity in the House before his retirement from politics. He had suffered from severe pains in the cervical vertebrae of his neck since the beginning of the election campaign, and these continued under treatment after the end of the year.

As Gordon reflected on his resignation and learned more about the circumstances of Robert Winters' return to politics, he felt extreme disappointment over his treatment by Mike Pearson. On January 15, 1966 Gordon confronted Pearson with the charge that he had committed himself before the general election to move Gordon out of Finance soon after the election. Pearson admitted that he had promised Trade and Commerce to Robert Winters (with the implied understanding that Sharp would move to Finance), and that he had also assured three prominent businessmen that Gordon would not remain in Finance.

> I said that all this could easily be interpreted as a deal to get rid of me as Minister of Finance after the election following which the interest ceiling would be lifted. . . .
>
> This conversation was very much in low key: no raised voices, no strain as at our last meeting; all smiles and cosy.
>
> Mike didn't seem worried about the point I made . . . nor did he seem at all bothered by the fact he had told me one thing before and during the election about my remaining in Finance and had given the financial community an entirely opposite impression. Knowing Mike this must have been quite deliberate. . . .
>
> If I had not resigned after the election I wonder how Mike would have resolved the various claims of Winters, Sharp and myself?[4]

Gordon was determined not to reveal his outraged feelings publicly, or to encourage others to exploit the break in his association with Pearson.[5] This was a mark of Gordon's moral sense and his long affection for Pearson rather than of political calculation; on matters of policy he did not hesitate to express his differences from the Cabinet. He expected such differences to arise once he lost his own position of influence. While he was "discouraged by my inability to persuade the public, and especially the business community, of the need to safeguard Canada's independence,"[6] he retained the energy and will to carry on that campaign. He decided to write another book setting out his views, and to spend most of his time in the early months of 1966 at his farm near Schomberg doing so.

> This I proceeded to do . . . lying on my back to ease the pain in my neck and using a board to write on.[7]

Before that project began, Gordon entered into conflict with his successor Mitchell Sharp. In December Gordon telephoned Sharp to congratulate him on his appointment, and offered to meet Sharp to discuss, in particular, budget planning for 1966 and the outstanding revisions to the Bank Act. Sharp acknowledged the suggestion, but neglected to arrange a meeting. When Gordon heard rumours at the beginning of January that Sharp intended to make new concessions to the chartered banks in his presentation of the Bank Act amendments, Gordon wrote to Sharp to express his concern, and to correct an impression – which Sharp had left with the party caucus – that Gordon himself approved the changes.

> You mentioned in caucus that I had planned to propose some new amendments to the Bank Act. This is absolutely correct, but while the amendments are a bit lengthy they do not amount to much in substance. While Lou Rasminsky and Elderkin would have liked me to propose lifting the ceiling on interest rates, I told them I could not recommend this in view of the line taken by the government when the Act was introduced and the very favourable reaction from all sides of the House to this particular point.[8]

Gordon recalled that he had left a loophole in introducing the Bill, by agreeing to reconsider the question if there were a general international rise in interest rates. This had occurred, and before his resignation Gordon discussed with his officials in Finance the possibility of a formula tying the ceiling flexibly to changes in the bank rate. But he could not support outright removal of the ceiling.

Quite apart from everything else, such a move would be looked upon as a complete reversal of previous government policy. You may not have anything like this in mind, but just in case you have, I thought it worth while suggesting it might be useful for us to have a talk about it well in advance. . . . I am sure you will appreciate that my only purpose in writing to you . . . is to avoid the possibility of finding ourselves in a difficult position through a misunderstanding. For this reason I think I should mention the matter to Mike as well as to yourself.[9]

The same day Gordon wrote to the Prime Minister enclosing his letter to Sharp, and suggesting a talk on the subject.[10] On January 15, after Pearson's return from the Commonwealth Conference in Nigeria, the two met at Sussex Drive. Pearson agreed with Gordon that the issue should be raised in caucus before reintroduction of the Bill:[11] an undoubted indication that Sharp did wish to remove the ceiling. Mitchell Sharp did not reply to Gordon's letter.

The debate in caucus occurred on January 26, on a proposal by Jean Chretien (the parliamentary secretary to Mr. Sharp) to establish a caucus committee on financial legislation. The Minister of Finance was not present, and the government did not reveal its position on the interest rate ceiling; but Walter Gordon, Maurice Lamontagne and others argued the case against any change in policy.[12] Gordon framed his argument within a general review of the party's prospects and public reputation.[13]

He began by telling the caucus that he would not speak often, or ask difficult questions of his former colleagues. But he did wish to comment on the election results and their lessons – "if we want the Liberal party to continue as a major force in Canada." He warned that the party had been lucky to win two more seats in November in spite of a fall in its popular vote, and that it should not expect the same luck again. The party had three choices about its future: it could "drift into Conservative attitudes – as the Liberal party did in the fifties. From the outside it was not difficult to guess what was going to happen – in those days." It could "become a truly progressive party again with new policies and new ideas"; or it could "waffle in between."

I hate to be pessimistic but I'm very much afraid we may waffle for awhile and then gradually become more Conservative. That will be fatal.

I believe many people are watching us very closely – and that some of their first impressions of this government may be lasting.

Because of this I believe the government's decisions about the Bank Act will be of very great importance.[14]

Gordon said that "The kites that have been flying suggest the government is planning to lift the interest ceiling. Certainly the financial community thinks so. Bank stocks have been going up." A decision to remove the ceiling would be wrong on both economic and political grounds, because interest rates would rise to the detriment of persons the Liberal party should be serving.

My idea of the Liberal party is that we should represent and fight for the great mass of small and inarticulate people. We should be thinking about what is best for them.

It's not our job to worry about the bankers. Their profits are going up enough already.[15]

Gordon urged the Cabinet not to make a quick decision on the matter without considering the views of a caucus committee. "The long term future of the Liberal party," he concluded, "is far more important to Canada than the goodwill of the bankers."

These remarks were widely supported in caucus. Gordon's speech helped to reveal the substantial extent of his following in the parliamentary party on more issues than the Bank Act. James Walker, the former party whip and MP for Toronto York Centre, told a reporter a few days later that "There's no argument at all about who is left or right wing in the party at present. . . . It's a straight split between the nationalists and continentalists"; and Walter Gordon, he believed, was increasing his nationalist following.[16]

The debate in caucus retarded the Cabinet's timetable on the Bank Act, but did not divert Mitchell Sharp from his course. The caucus committee was not established. In May there were further discussions in caucus of a compromise proposal by the Minister of Finance to retain the ceiling only for bank loans under $25,000. The opposition was led by Maurice Lamontagne and Walter Gordon, and the suggestion was withdrawn in response to their warning that Liberal abstentions might lead to the government's defeat in the House. Finally, the Minister settled on another formula which effectively removed the ceiling but tied it to the interest rate on short-term bonds. Before Sharp achieved this, Jean Marchand told the Prime Minister he would resign from the Cabinet in protest. Mitchell Sharp reacted by threatening his own resignation if the Prime Minister gave way, and Marchand was eventually propitiated by the agreement of Sharp and Pearson to an

increase in the old age pension. On July 7, in the absence of Lamontagne and Gordon, the House adopted the resolution removing the
interest rate ceiling.[17] The whole affair generated more bad feeling
among the leading Liberal participants in the controversy.

*

Walter Gordon's perspective on the government after November
was not that of a complete outsider; the Prime Minister remained
accessible, and in the first six months of 1966 they met in Pearson's
home or office on at least half a dozen occasions.[18] The Prime Minister
seemed concerned to show that Gordon's resignation had not affected
their personal friendship; and as the winter passed Gordon sensed that
Pearson wished to make amends for the "misunderstanding" of the
previous autumn. The continuing subjects of discussion in these meetings were Mike Pearson's plans for retirement, the problem of the
succession, and the question of Walter Gordon's political future.
Gordon noted Pearson's political disenchantment. While the Prime
Minister publicly denied the persistent rumours that he was contemplating an early retirement ("I'm good for as many miles as the
youngest MP in the House," he told a meeting of Toronto Liberals on
February 2),[19] in confidence he did not hide from Gordon his intense
desire to return to private life. In mid-January he told Gordon that
there was nothing left for him to do in office, that he had no interest
in being Prime Minister during Centennial year, and that he wished
to retire in the autumn of 1966.[20] Gordon judged that Pearson had
grown weary, indifferent and careless about politics. "While I daresay
he will change his mind," Gordon wrote, "I think this morning he
really wanted to get out as soon as possible."[21]

Already there were five active candidates for the succession. Paul
Hellyer had told Pearson of his intention to seek the leadership, but
promised his complete loyalty as long as Pearson remained in office;[22]
Paul Martin, Mitchell Sharp, Robert Winters, and John Turner had
given public evidence of their ambitions. Jean Lesage was spoken of
as the only prominent Quebec Liberal who seemed capable for the
moment of succeeding to the national leadership. As the Prime Minister's political fatigue revealed itself to his ministers, and as speculation
about his retirement increased, self-interested calculation and
manoeuvre were bound to become more dominant features of the
government's life. The Cabinet's fragile unity disintegrated.

Lester Pearson's desires were emphatic; but when they would be
satisfied was unclear. The realistic prospect was that there would be
a long twilight while the mutual respect of ministers for one another,

for their Prime Minister, and vice-versa, would be worn away in uncertainty. For a few months Pearson considered resignation in the summer of 1966, in time to transform the National Liberal rally of October, 1966 into a leadership convention. But by the end of March he had told Walter Gordon that he intended to remain in office until the fall of 1967.[23] Some of the considerations affecting his choice were the absence of any obvious candidate who could command the Prime Minister's full confidence; the benign anticipation of playing host for the country's Centennial celebrations in 1967; and the provision for the Prime Minister's pension. (Under new legislation, former prime ministers qualified for a retirement pension equal to two-thirds of the prime ministerial salary if retirement came after their seventieth birthday or after four years in office. L. B. Pearson would become seventy one day after the fourth anniversary of his accession to power on April 22, 1967.)[24] Perhaps, too, there were other less rational influences: a reluctance to close a long public career by surrendering power, and a certain grim determination to outlast John Diefenbaker on the front benches.

Mike Pearson first raised the question of Walter Gordon's interest in the succession on January 26.

> He said I would have to make up my mind before the Liberal rally in October whether I should seek the leadership. I said I didn't want it – and as he knows I'm too impatient for it. He said these were not good enough reasons etc., etc. . . . [25]

On March 15, at a lunch with the Prime Minister which Gordon described as "very relaxed and friendly," Pearson again asked Gordon whether he would contest the leadership.

> In reply to his direct question I said I had not made up my mind as to whether I should seek the leadership. I said I could think of a lot of reasons why I wouldn't be a good choice. I added that if I was seriously after it I would not have written my book; that the latter would deal only with policy but on that subject I would go all out. Mike said he rather thought that was what was needed now. . . . He said if I was interested he would do what he could to help. (He did not specify.) He thought I should make up my mind by the time I come back from Europe.[26]

Two weeks later, during another luncheon conversation, Pearson and Gordon again discussed the succession at length. The Prime Minister frankly expressed his doubts about all the prominent candidates, and Gordon in turn reviewed his own uncertainties.

I said I hadn't made up my mind – or talked to Liz. I told him my neck seemed better & the reassuring reports from the doctors. I said I would think the matter through while we are away but that he (Mike) is in the best position to size everyone up and if I did not turn it down cold I would have to ask him – when I get back – who he honestly believes would be best suited for the job. We were both serious about this and he said he would think it over & give me his unbiassed opinion when I return in May. . . .

Mike said I shouldn't run unless I thought I could win. I said I quite agreed. I thought I could win but I had to make up my mind first and then get his honest and carefully considered views on who would be best.[27]

None of this implied the Prime Minister's endorsement; but neither did it discourage Walter Gordon. Nevertheless, for Gordon there was a puzzling element in the conversations. Only a few months before Mike Pearson had accepted his resignation, apparently as a means of freeing the Cabinet from Gordon's reputation in the business community for dangerous radicalism; was Pearson now seriously contemplating Gordon as his successor? Perhaps the speculation was idle and unreflected, as Gordon was inclined to believe. Perhaps also it was the Prime Minister's means of offering recompense for his treatment of Gordon the previous November. Perhaps it was only a polite way of opening up the subject of the Prime Minister's own frustrations and uncertainties. For Walter Gordon, the succession was an unlikely prospect in the spring of 1966, and he could not easily come to terms with the possibility. But it was not quite inconceivable.

Meanwhile the House of Commons had reassembled on January 18, and the government immediately found itself preoccupied with political difficulties reminiscent of the previous Parliament. The Opposition's most dogged questioning concerned the dismissal from the civil service without pension rights of a Vancouver postal employee, George Victor Spencer, on suspicion of espionage. The Minister of Justice, Lucien Cardin, revealed to the House that Spencer remained under police surveillance, but that no charges had been preferred. He rejected suggestions that Spencer had been improperly treated, and that there should be a judicial enquiry into the affair. The Prime Minister told the House on February 23, after himself examining the file, that he supported the opinion of the Minister of Justice "that an enquiry into this matter is not necessary and would not be useful."[28] The full measure of John Diefenbaker's withering scorn was now turned upon the government for its treatment of the case, and of security in general; in demanding a royal commission of enquiry into national security on March 4, the leader of the Opposition accused the administration broadly of negligence in the field of security, injustice in the case of Mr. Spencer, and deception of the House of Commons.[29] Mr. Diefenbaker was especially contemptuous of Lucien Cardin, and reflected back four years to the occasion when Cardin had "last . . . made a vicious attack" on him in the House.[30] The peppery Mr. Cardin was aroused, and replied that John Diefenbaker's real purpose was to take revenge for that attack of 1962: "the great executioner," Cardin judged, "is now after my political neck."

> The right honourable gentleman's performance would have been as good and his speech would have been as vicious if in fact I had prosecuted Spencer and if I had not had proper surveillance mounted in regard to him. The real issue is not Spencer. This is merely an excuse to put into effect the execution which the honourable member has wanted to carry out for quite some time.[31]

Spurred by the applause of his supporters (the Prime Minister among them), and by the renewed defiance of Mr. Diefenbaker, Cardin charged that "of all the members of the House of Commons he – I repeat, he – is the very last person in the House who can afford to give advice on the handling of security cases in Canada."[32] Cardin added that "I want the right honourable gentleman to tell the House about his participation in the Monseignor [sic] case when he was Prime Minister of this country."[33] Without the Prime Minister's fore-knowledge, the Minister of Justice had thrown back at John Diefenbaker the charge of negligence toward the country's security, and opened the case of Gerda Munsinger to fascinated public gossip. (This challenge, and the Minister's remarks at a subsequent press conference which was also arranged without the Prime Minister's knowledge, led inevitably to the creation of the Spence Royal Commission of Enquiry into "The case of one Gerda Munsinger.") But for the time being the tantalizing accusation hung in the air while the House continued its debate on the George Victor Spencer case.

Cardin, Jean Marchand and Lawrence Pennell spoke in defence of the Cabinet's refusal to authorize a judicial study of the case. Later in the afternoon, however, after David Lewis of the NDP had read a tele-gram to the House asserting that Spencer desired an enquiry into his dismissal, Prime Minister Pearson told the House that he would personally telephone Spencer, and establish a public enquiry if this was indeed Spencer's wish. Walter Gordon commented that this reversal "cut Cardin's legs from under him."[34]

On Monday, March 7 the Prime Minister placed before the House the terms of an Order-in-Council establishing an enquiry into the Spencer case. Not surprisingly, this confirmation of the government's turnabout produced a Cabinet crisis, and Walter Gordon became involved.

> Maurice Lamontagne came to see me the following day and said Cardin intended to resign; that Cardin was a hero to the members of the Quebec caucus who were delighted with the way he had stood up to Mr. Diefenbaker and brought the Munsinger case out in the open; and that Marchand and other French-Canadian ministers planned to resign with Cardin as they felt Pearson had let him down very badly. Maurice and I agreed that if Marchand and other French-Canadian ministers were sufficiently incensed, as they seemed to be, the only alternative if the government was not to be defeated, would be for Pearson to resign as Prime Minister in favour of someone else. Maurice said that Cardin was coming to see him and urged that Marchand and I join them and plead with Cardin to accept some compromise solution of the problem. I protested that, like Lamontagne, I was no longer a member of the Cabinet and that in any case this was something that should be settled by the French-Canadian members of the party. But Maurice persuaded me that, as Cardin and I had considerable respect for one another, I should join him and Marchand in trying to avert what appeared to be a calamity of major proportions for the Liberal party.
>
> We spent several hours with Lucien Cardin that evening. To begin with, he was quite determined. Pearson had let him down. He had done the same thing to Guy Favreau. Lucien was fed up with politics and intended to resign. Marchand made it clear that he would go with him and that meant that most of the French-speaking ministers from Quebec would do the same.
>
> Maurice and I argued that this simply could not be allowed to happen. Pearson could not possibly accept the resignations of Marchand and most of the French-speaking members of the Cabinet. Rather than this, he would have to resign himself, leaving no opportunity for any of us to consider who might be the best man to succeed him. After a great deal of discussion, Lucien said he could see the logic of our analysis. His only wish was to get out of politics, but he would agree not to resign immediately.[35]

The crisis passed. When Gordon lunched with Pearson a week later, while the Munsinger controversy still raged in the House, he thought the Prime Minister was "very relaxed" and "did not appear at all disturbed." Gordon associated this mood with the Prime Minister's belief that the Munsinger case would "be the end of Diefenbaker."[36] In the course of their conversation, Pearson acknowledged the indispensable role played by Lamontagne and Gordon in resolving the resignation crisis.

In the aftermath of the Munsinger affair, there was renewed speculation about the Prime Minister's retirement and the succession. On the last weekend in March, seven ministers, including four self-declared candidates for the succession (Martin, Sharp, Winters, and Hellyer), made conspicuous appearances at the annual convention of the federal Liberal party of Quebec. Peter Newman commented:

> The presence of the ministers is probably most significant in terms of what it indicates about Lester Pearson's hold on the Liberal party. Provincial association meetings are not usually considered important enough to warrant ministerial attention. . . . [the] situation . . . leaves very little doubt about the fact that Lester Pearson's term as leader of the Liberal party is running out. Following the Spencer-Munsinger mess it was generally agreed among Liberals in Ottawa that one more shoddy parliamentary performance would foreclose Mr. Pearson's stewardship.[37]

But Newman reported that there was no consensus in the party on a new leader: "It looks very much as though the picking of Mr. Pearson's successor will develop into a most un-Liberal power struggle." After reviewing the potential strength of the leading candidates, Newman said this of Walter Gordon:

> Although his post-election resignation was supposed to have killed the former Finance Minister's political career, a "Gordon-for-Leader" group has recently developed within the Liberal party. Surprisingly Mr. Gordon's supporters don't envisage this as an "ideological candidacy," designed to give Mr. Gordon a chance to exercise some left-wing leverage with the new leader, in return for giving up his delegates. Instead, it's a serious attempt by the Liberal left to recapture control of the party. Mr. Gordon's audacious candidacy could turn out to be an important factor in a race that remains wide open.[38]

John Bird suggested in the *Financial Post* that if Gordon were to run, he would be unlikely to win; but that his candidacy would "signal to the Gordon activists across the country that their guide, philosopher and friend was uneasy about the directions in which Hellyer might lead them." He was certain that "the key to the leadership race lies with the Gordon men, his activists who rebuilt the party under Pearson from the wreckage after 1958. The Gordonites still control the party organization and are its most exciting, active workers." Above all, Bird judged that the party wished for more time – "at least eighteen months" – during which it might look beyond the established candidates to test the performance of others like John Turner and Jean Marchand.[39]

By the beginning of May Walter Gordon was ready to emerge from six months of relative seclusion to reassert his position as goad and conscience to the party. Copies of his new book, *A Choice for Canada*, were distributed widely to journalists before publication. Gordon's ideas and political future were the subjects of fascinated speculation in the party and among members of the press, and his press conferences in Ottawa and Toronto on Thursday, May 5 to promote the book were anticipated with intense curiosity. To Gordon's surprise, he was upstaged by Mitchell Sharp, who chose an address to the Association of Canadian Advertisers in Toronto on May 4 to express his views on "Strengthening Canada's Independence." Charles Lynch reported that the speech "was prepared, obviously, after he had enjoyed a preview of the Gordon book."[40] In it the Minister of Finance staked out his position as an economic nationalist somewhat more moderate in approach than his predecessor. Sharp acknowledged that the scale of foreign investment was 'a serious matter of concern for Canada, and committed himself to continued support for a number of policies promoted by Walter Gordon: more adequate disclosure of the financial operations of foreign-controlled companies; creation of the Canada Development Corporation; and the maintenance of Canadian control in the fields of banking, insurance, trust companies, transportation, radio, television, and newspapers. But he rejected discriminatory tax legislation directed against foreign investors.[41]

The speech was variously interpreted as a "deeply committed" statement of belief in Canadian independence, a tactical bid for support in the leadership contest from Walter Gordon's wing of the Liberal party, and a declaration of war over policy between Sharp the moderate and Gordon the radical. Its timing and substance drew attention to the persistent strength and influence of Gordon's advocates in the party, and probably increased public interest in Walter Gordon and his book. (Many of the news stories announcing publication of *A Choice for Canada* linked it with Sharp's "economic manifesto.") Some Liberal MPs understood the complicated nuances of the byplay. The Toronto *Star* quoted one member anonymously:

"The goals are emotionally desirable to many Canadians," said one prominent Liberal. "I don't think Gordon could carry them out, however, whereas I think Sharp could. To carry out these policies requires the confidence of the business and financial community. Sharp has it. Gordon doesn't."

However, he asserted, if Gordon hadn't written the book, Sharp wouldn't have made his speech.

"I wish there were some way to combine the two," he said.[42]

The *Globe and Mail*'s impressionist survey indicated that "business leaders and economists came down predominantly on the side of the more moderate policies proposed by Mr. Sharp . . . ," but the reporter conceded that "the battle is not yet over."[43]

A Choice for Canada was slightly shorter than *Troubled Canada*, wider ranging in its consideration of foreign policy and the position of Quebec in the federation, but essentially a modest and often sketchy reassertion of Gordon's concerns over foreign investment and Canadian independence. While the text sometimes made reference to Gordon's experiences in office to support his familiar position, it did so only briefly and with discretion.[44] His case remained moderate and largely intuitive rather than analytical; his proposals, Gordon concluded, "are not, by any stretch of the imagination, revolutionary proposals. But I believe, if taken together, they would be effective."[45] His immediate objectives were to encourage Canadian equity shareholdings in foreign subsidiaries; to reduce the deficit in the current foreign trade account; to offset the effects of American balance-of-payment guidelines; and to transform capital inflows from equity to debt capital.

The evolution in Gordon's thought had to be sought out in the book's slight shift of tone as compared with *Troubled Canada*, and in a few statements which suggested both greater pessimism and greater determination in the cause. Gordon asserted his ultimate objective of buying back predominant control in the economy; committed himself afresh to the use of a takeover tax as one means of approaching this goal; warned of the political dangers of retreat on the Bank Act and the prohibition of foreign ownership in banking; and spoke more sharply than before of "colonial dependency" as the only alternative to a positive assertion of Canadian economic independence. He offered more concrete evidence from his experience as Minister of Finance of the inextricable relationship between economic and political dependency. In one paragraph he wrote of the complex failure of a sense of separate Canadian identity:

During the two and one-half years I held that office, the influence that financial and business interests in the U.S. had on Canadian policy and opinion was continually brought home to me. On occasion, this influence was reinforced by representations from the State Department and the American administration as a whole. It was pressed by those who direct American businesses in Canada, by their professional advisers, by Canadian financiers whose interests were identified directly or indirectly with American investment in Canada, by influential members of the Canadian civil service, by some representatives of the university community, and by some sections of the press.[46]

The range of Canadian independent action was diminishing as the momentum of the American economic takeover increased. The time for speeches, Gordon believed, was past; the time for specific action was at hand, and it was not unlimited. Gordon was convinced that Canadian self-assertion, while it might be troublesome to the United States, would be regarded with respect by Americans.

They are likeable, tough-minded, business-like, and go after what they want. At the same time, on the whole, they do not resent people who have the courage to stick up for their rights and aspirations. Canadians are much more likely to be respected in the U.S. if they fight for their interests and their independence, than if they give in silently and without protest every time Uncle Sam looks cross.[47]

Self-respecting nationalism, Gordon believed, was a natural and commonplace sentiment which did not require special justification.

In wanting to retain our independence, we are no different than the British, the French, the Swiss, the Japanese, or the people of other countries, including the United States. Some may call this nationalism, and so it is. It is a proper respect, loyalty, and enthusiasm for one's country, and a legitimate optimism and confidence about its future.[48]

A Choice for Canada was intended as a challenge to the Liberal party's drift into indifference and inaction; it was seen also, in potential, as Walter Gordon's leadership manifesto. For Gordon himself that implication was not yet certain; for many of his supporters it was already taken for granted.[49]

The book was the subject of widespread comment in the editorial and opinion columns, and it was at once a best-seller. (More than 12,000 copies were sold.) The commentators agreed that the impact of the book lay as much in the circumstances of its publication as in its content. Bruce Hutchison described it as "a literary anti-climax when the Ottawa pundits had expected some sort of explosion," but went on to examine Gordon's leftism in domestic policy and nationalism in foreign policy at length in two moderately critical articles.[50] Charles Lynch dismissed the book as "neither interesting nor enlightening," because it almost totally neglected the inside story of Gordon's controversial career.[51] Claude Ryan, in *Le Devoir*, wrote that "Mr. Gordon's book is not the powerful and decisive manifesto which certain commentators had led us to believe. It is, on the contrary, a modest work, not sufficiently backed up, very hesitant in many places, and very vague in many of its conclusions." But he praised Gordon for reminding Canadians of "the ineluctable link which . . . ties the political destiny of peoples to their economic situation."[52] Eric Kierans, Quebec's Minister of Revenue, noted in the Montreal *Star* that the book would have "a wide appeal not only to the voter but also to the young militants of the party."[53] The editorial writers lined up in regular ranks, alarmed, equivocal or grateful to Gordon according to predisposition.[54]

The harshest commentary on the book, avowedly bitter, came in Douglas Fisher's column in the Toronto *Telegram*. Fisher described *A Choice for Canada* as "a regurgitation, without any candor about the intervening months, of what we got in *Troubled Canada*," which would serve the bogus purpose of giving the Liberal party "an apparently radical and nationalistic face" before its October convention. It was all a familiar example of "the chameleon bent of the Grits." Fisher put bluntly his perplexity about Walter Gordon's career.

> A few will lament that their party should be the one for a man like Walter Gordon. They will be the ones who cannot appreciate that as much as Mr. Gordon wants to be radical and a nationalist, he couldn't face leaving the decent confines of a respectable party.
> With the Liberals he can be both bold and easy, a right-thinking pillar and a reformer, diffident gentleman and thoughtful radical, visionary and intra-party organizer.[55]

As long as Gordon remained in political life Fisher stood there behind him, bold and rude, commenting irreverently on his career, conscience to his conscience.

In a speech to the annual meeting of the Liberal party of Ontario on May 7, Gordon asserted anew his anxieties about the Liberal party. He repeated publicly the warning he had offered to the caucus in January: that the party would be defeated if it "waffled in between" the positions of caution and progressive reform, squeezed on one side by a rejuvenated Conservative party and on the other by an aggressive NDP. He called for the adoption of "a frankly progressive line with clearly defined policies on all the issues of the day," and said that he planned to express his own views "on a variety of subjects" in the coming months preceding the national party convention in October. That meeting, he hoped, "should open up a whole new perspective for us. It should give us a new lease on life."[56]

Within the Liberal party, Gordon's initiatives provoked the most vocal reactions from provincial leaders in western Canada. The counterattacks were led by Gordon's old antagonist Ross Thatcher, the premier of Saskatchewan. He told the Ottawa Rotary Club on May 30 that Gordon's prescriptions were "naive, misguided and obsolete," and that the federal Liberal party could never recover its strength in the west if it abandoned its commitment to free enterprise and "the middle of the road." Any attempt to restrict the free movement of capital into Canada would impoverish and divide the country. If the party wanted votes in the prairies, it would reject Gordon's socialism.[57] Gil Molgat, the Manitoba Liberal leader, Ray Perrault, the B.C. leader, and Adrian Berry, the Alberta leader, expressed their opposition in similar language. All of them saw Gordon's nationalism through western eyes as a protectionist device serving central Canadian interests. The western Liberal press echoed their sentiments.[58]

After this prolonged spell of public attention in May, Gordon's conversations with the Prime Minister were renewed. On June 9, 1966, at the Prime Minister's invitation, Gordon joined Pearson for lunch at Sussex Drive. The Prime Minister appeared "tired and nervous," and again suggested that he might resign in time to transform the October conference into a leadership convention.[59] The alternative, he said, was the fall of 1967 "at the latest"; Gordon responded "that in my opinion that should be the date. I said that in his own interests he should not stay longer. He agreed."

After lunch, Pearson suddenly came to what Gordon assumed in retrospect had been the point of the conversation. Would Gordon consider returning to the Cabinet, perhaps as Minister of Transport?

I said I was not interested in a slugging administrative job like Transport – but quite apart from that the thought of going back to the Cabinet in any capacity had much broader implications. I mentioned:

– that Liz would much prefer me to get out of politics altogether let alone going back into the government.

– that I had been badly hurt last November both at the way I was asked to get out and by what I had learned later. I said that while I was old enough not to become overly preoccupied by this, I naturally did not wish or intend to be hurt in the same way again.

– I told Mike that there were two major questions that he and I would have to think through and resolve.

The first was the whole question of policy. I reminded him that I have written a book. He said he agreed with my views – I reminded him he had agreed with them before I ever agreed to enter politics – but would always plump for a major international agreement of some kind if this were ever practicable. We talked about this for a few minutes. Neither of us thought (or said we thought) these policy issues should be too difficult to resolve. But I insisted they would have to be threshed out in detail before I could seriously consider returning to the Cabinet. . . .

I said the second major issue was the succession. I reminded Mike that two months or so ago he had asked me if I wanted the leadership because if so he could help me. I said I had not taken him up on this because (a) I did not think he had thought it through and (b) I did not know if I wanted it. . . .

I said it was sometimes harder to get out of politics than into it; and that I could not serve under any of the present contenders. Therefore if I was not interested in going on I would be much better advised not to go back into the government.

I asked Mike if he realized the implications of my going back. I said it would be interpreted to mean (a) that I would seek or accept the leadership on his retirement and (b) that he thought I was the best man for it. Mike had not thought about this – although he agreed I was quite right. In these circumstances I said both of us should do some heavy thinking following which we should meet again – with enough time to talk things through.

Mike started to wonder about the reaction in the Cabinet to my return – in the light of the above comments. I said that half of them would welcome it; the other half (the contenders or aspirants) would not. Mike agreed – and said he didn't care anyway.

I had a feeling that Mike in his usual way had opened up a can of worms – by his invitation to me – without thinking it out. Now he is confronted with a major decision. I said I wanted that decision made soon because I planned to make up my own mind about the leadership question in any event by the end of June.

We agreed to have dinner next Tuesday, June 14.[60]

In reflecting with the Prime Minister on his possible return to Cabinet, Gordon planted a germ of strategy. He told Mike Pearson that Pearson's last months in office should be devoted to "cementing relations with French Canada" and dealing with international issues. (Gordon had frequently mentioned his dissatisfaction with Paul Martin's caution and conformism in External Affairs.) Most domestic matters, Gordon proposed, should be left "to others to struggle with." The thought as he expressed it that day was tentative and undeveloped; and Gordon left it at that, to germinate or die.

On June 14, according to arrangement, Gordon dined with the Pearsons. He recorded that "the atmosphere was relaxed and pleasant," but that the Prime Minister was "very tired" following his speech the previous weekend in Springfield, Illinois on Vietnam, and his success-ful settlement of the Montreal longshoremen's strike early that morn-ing. Before dinner Pearson and Gordon talked alone for about an hour.

He said he had thought about the points I had raised last week. He agreed he had to make up his mind about his own plans before asking "his friends" to decide anything. He said he didn't know whether he would decide to leave this fall – or the fall of 1967 at the very latest. He said he thought he would have to decide this by the end of July or middle of August.

He said he knew that if I returned to the Cabinet in any capacity it would be interpreted as meaning he thought I was the man to take over. He said he would not say so publicly but nevertheless that would be the interpretation.[61]

Pearson was unenthusiastic about all the declared contenders for the leadership, but did not express any clear opinion about Gordon's position. Gordon pressed him gently, and Pearson temporized.

I said I had decided that if I returned to the Cabinet I would have a crack at the leadership job when Mike retired; and that I would not go back unless he knew this and was prepared to agree with this conclusion.

He said he would let me know by the end of July.

All very nice and cosy! But?[62]

This disbelief was soon confirmed. June and July passed without any further discussion of Walter Gordon's plans.

In the absence of the Prime Minister's explicit support, Gordon did not pursue his thoughts on the succession or reappointment to the Cabinet. Without Mike Pearson's endorsement to offset them, Gordon believed there were strong reasons why he should not contest the leadership.

My friends in the party insisted that if I wanted the leadership I should stop talking about such controversial subjects as the increasing foreign ownership of Canadian resources and Canadian business enterprises. I agreed that their advice was good but I was not prepared to accept it. I felt too keenly about the foreign ownership question to let it drop.

Moreover, I believed very seriously that in the best interests of the country, as well as of the Liberal party, the next leader should be a French-Canadian, if one could be found who was qualified and whose reputation had not been compromised in the public mind. I felt also that, if possible, the next leader should be in his forties or early fifties. I was sixty years of age, which is too old to take on the toughest job the nation has to offer. While I did not believe that any of the principal candidates being talked about – Martin, Hellyer, Winters, Sharp – were what was wanted, I kept hoping that someone else would turn up in time.[63]

By midsummer Gordon had decided that he would resign from the House of Commons and retire from political life. He planned to do so at the end of 1966; before that, he would "give voice to my opinions both in a series of speeches in September and at the Liberal convention in October."[64] He accepted speaking engagements in Saskatoon, Edmonton, Calgary, Port Arthur, Sudbury, Vancouver, and Toronto. Before he could begin, Ross Thatcher intervened.

Ross Thatcher, the premier of Saskatchewan, had decided to organize a meeting of more or less hand picked Liberals from the western provinces to decide on the line of policy the West should plump for at the National Liberal Conference in October. Thatcher . . . was bitterly opposed to the policies I had advocated in my book. . . . His meeting was held in Saskatoon on Friday and Saturday, August 12 and 13. It so happened that I had been invited to address the Saskatoon Rotary Club on Monday, August 15. . . . I thought if I arrived in Saskatoon on the Sunday afternoon, I would have an excellent opportunity to comment on the resolutions passed at the Thatcher conference.

But when Thatcher heard I was to speak to the Saskatoon Rotary Club, he gave instructions that the invitation should be withdrawn, and this was done. No contrary views were to be expressed in Saskatchewan while the reactionary-minded premier remained the boss there. Joey Smallwood had done exactly the same thing a few years before, when Donald Fleming turned up to address the Rotary Club in St. John's. Thatcher was smarter. He did not wait until the meeting was in progress, so there was no bad publicity to worry about.[65]

In Edmonton a month later, Gordon told his audience that the maintenance of Canadian independence and affluence required, not "narrow, ultra-nationalistic or protectionist" policies, but hard-headed calculation of the country's long-term interests. Canada should not sell her natural resources abroad "at what may seem like ridiculously low prices twenty years from now"; she should obtain foreign capital through borrowing rather than the sale of equity; she should process raw materials into finished products before export. He replied briefly to those who denied that foreign economic control necessarily influenced Canadian political independence:

> These people are sincere in their opinions. But, based on thirty years' experience in professional practice and in business and some experience in government, I am convinced that they are wrong.
>
> In my recent book I gave a number of examples in support of my conviction. But it is not the kind of question that can be proved empirically to everyone's satisfaction. I do not believe it needs to be. Most people realize what is going on. They can see the takeover of Canadian resources that is taking place. They can feel it and they can sense its implications. There would not be so much interest in this issue – and the mail I get and the space given to it in the press and the time devoted to it on the air attests to this great interest – unless a great many Canadians were seriously concerned about it.[66]

This impressionist sense pervaded the speech. Gordon confessed that "I am not wedded to any particular proposals. If there are better solutions than those I have put forward in my book, let us consider them by all means. All I say is that we have had enough of talking about this question and enough speech making. We shall need some action soon if this problem is to be resolved before it is too late."

Gordon mentioned the complicating factor of federal-provincial conflicts over foreign investment policy, but moved away from it with the general advice that "we must never allow regional interests and objectives to take precedence over those of Canada." His prophetic vision of Canada was simple and entirely benevolent:

Those of us who are proud of our country and are not ashamed to say so have our secret dreams of what Canada may become, say, in forty or fifty years from now.

My own dream is of a nation of 50 million people of many diverse backgrounds and cultures who have learned to live together without prejudice or hate. It will be an immensely rich country with a standard of living much higher than it is today. We will have opened up the North, developed our resources and reclaimed the slum areas in our cities. Our people will be better educated, both to equip them to work in a highly scientific industrial society and to enjoy their lengthened hours of leisure.

I see a Canada that will be respected by other nations as an influence in the world for good, a Canada whose contributions in terms of foreign aid and peace-keeping forces are accepted universally. There are no ulterior motives or territorial ambitions behind our efforts to help other people who are less fortunate than we are.[67]

The blandness of the "comfort, security and boredom of the affluent society" conveyed by this vision, Gordon suggested, would be dissolved by the infusion of nationalist will – "the will to stay Canadian." The speech proclaimed Gordon's intuitions and his emotional commitment to Canada; but it ended in a certain vagueness.

It was, after all, only the first of a series of talks which Gordon conceived as a whole. Before a critical audience of Young Liberals in Calgary the same evening, he discussed the future of the Liberal party, reiterating his desire for a progressive party that would offer no haven "for rightwingers and reactionaries." He called on the party to be "precise in what we approve of in October." In the field of trade, he warned against the "trigger-happy" adoption of an across-the-board policy of free trade with the United States. He asked for completion of the social security system through alterations to the unemployment insurance system, a guaranteed income for the elderly, insurance against technological unemployment, and the adoption of national medicare. He advocated complete federal withdrawal from established federal-provincial cost-sharing programs, and the provision of equivalent tax points to the provinces to finance these programs. He proposed that the Liberal party "should go on record as being ... in favour, in the future, of a substantial proportion of election expenditures being charged to the federal treasury."

Half the speech was devoted to the familiar theme of foreign ownership; and this time, Gordon gave substance to his arguments with a vivid example.

> What I am sure I do not need to enlarge upon is the position that Canadian professional and service people find themselves in when too much of our industry is controlled abroad. ... I am thinking of geologists and engineers, of advertising people and insurance agents and professional consultants of various kinds. Some foreign controlled companies in Canada go out of their way to employ Canadian professionals. But in many cases – perhaps in most cases – they retain the services of the professional firms they have worked with at home, or the affiliates or subsidiaries of these firms in Canada. This is understandable, of course, but can be discouraging to Canadians who, given a chance, are just as able as their confreres in any other country.[68]

For example, he said, the American subsidiary company which received the contract to construct the new medical building at the University of Toronto had "called in American architects and engineers" to do most of the design and supervision. For Gordon this example represented an unfortunate state of mind:

> ... if we Canadians allowed ourselves to get into the habit of thinking we must employ Americans to do everything for us – if we get into the habit of thinking we have no people in Canada who can do, or learn to do, anything that needs to be done as well as anybody else – if we get into the habit of thinking we must always look elsewhere for the capital and the know-how required for every new development – then we shall become second-class citizens in our own country. And we shall deserve nothing better than a kind of colonial status.[69]

This was not an example of political dependency, but of a colonial economic relationship and its mentality of subordination. The effects of that mentality in politics could easily be projected, and Gordon let the point stand by implication. He suggested that the Liberal party should accept as its goal "that foreign control of our important industries – or most of them – should be reduced to not more than one-third by the end of this century."[70]

In Port Arthur, Gordon discussed Mitchell Sharp's announcement of the previous week that the medicare legislation would be postponed as one contribution to the government's anti-inflationary program. The press accurately interpreted Gordon's remarks as an attack on government policy under the new Minister of Finance. Gordon held that the Cabinet could not honourably abandon its firm commitment to medicare.

The argument that medicare should be put off in order to combat inflation will not stand up upon reflection. On the other hand, the decision is being hailed as a great victory by those who are opposed to medicare in any form at any time. I believe Parliament should proceed with the medicare legislation this fall and be prepared to implement it as soon as it has been accepted by a number of provinces representing a majority of the population – or some alternative along these lines. If a majority of the provincial governments are not prepared to go ahead with medicare – perhaps because they feel their electors are not prepared to pay for it – quite obviously it cannot, and should not be forced on them. But after all that has been said about medicare in the last few years – including the clear intimation it would be proceeded with this fall – it seems to me the onus should be placed squarely on the provincial governments if it is to be deferred.[71]

In Vancouver and Toronto, before student audiences, Gordon returned to the theme of foreign investment, with sardonic emphasis on the contrast between safety and adventure in a man's life.

If you are content – as far too many of my generation seem to be content – to see us go on as we are, you should be able to live out your lives in some comfort, some security and considerable boredom.

You should be able to find jobs working for the absentee owners of Canadian businesses. Naturally, it will be they who will take the responsibility for making the important decisions. And, naturally, it will be they who will take most of the profits. As for you, it may not be a very interesting life, or a very exciting one, but you should be safe – or as safe as the subjects of any satellite or colonial state can ever be.

Of course, you will be subject to the whims and the changes in policy of your employers – employers who do not live in Canada. But if you keep your noses clean you should probably be reasonably secure.

To me – and I hope to most of you – this kind of prospect, this kind of life, would be detestable.[72]

The speeches added up to Gordon's most systematic attempt to influence the party program since 1960 and 1961. But now his opponents in the party held power while he did not, and no one benefited from the patronage of Lester Pearson. In 1961 the party had submerged its differences in the common pursuit of power; in 1966 Gordon's leading antagonists believed that their retention of power would rest largely on neutralizing his proposals. While some of Gordon's friends (Andrew Thompson, Maurice Lamontagne, and Donald Macdonald were chief among them) sought rather diffidently to organize support for his measures at the October conference, his opponents (under the active leadership of Ross Thatcher) were determined to overwhelm them. Gordon himself was no longer committed, as he had been in 1961, to seek personal power in order to apply his policies. The signs for October were all unfavourable. In his September speeches and press conferences, Gordon did not hesitate to sharpen and personify the conflict in the party, to challenge party members to make clear-cut choices, and thus also to reduce the prospects for compromise. The effect on reporters and headline writers, as much as on members of the party, was to arouse the expectation of a final and decisive battle. Once that expectation had been created, the press had an independent interest in seeing its prophesy fulfilled.[73]

The western Liberal conference in Saskatoon in August gave Gordon no encouragement. Two resolutions favouring the Canada Development Corporation failed to reach the convention floor, and resolutions were adopted supporting greater capital imports, a North American free trade area, and increased oil exports to the United States. The occasion was essentially a display of anti-Gordonism, and more than four hundred western delegates came to the October conference pledged to policies which he rejected.

Gordon's policy lobby at the October meeting was haphazardly organized, and one after another Gordon's causes were lost.[74] Mitchell Sharp's defence of the postponement of medicare led to the adoption of a compromise resolution regretting the decision but affirming the party's intention to apply the program not later than July 1, 1968. (This was only a partial victory for the Minister of Finance.) The western delegates gained majority support for their free trade resolution (although it was later repudiated by the Prime Minister). And Gordon's foreign investment policy was submerged in confusion. A workshop rejected the resolution of the Gordon group, and substituted for it the Saskatoon resolution welcoming foreign capital.

When the issue was raised in plenary session, Donald Macdonald, who was acting as a kind of floor manager on my behalf, ran into procedural difficulties. The issue provoked a heated debate which I, among others, felt could be damaging to the party. Accordingly, it was arranged that about thirty delegates representing both sides of the question should meet in the evening under the chairmanship of Maurice Lamontagne to work out a compromise.

The compromise suggested included nearly all the points that Macdonald and I had been putting forward. Sharp agreed to this and suggested that he move the compromise resolution with me as seconder. The object was to arrive at something that everyone could go along with and, since the resolution covered ninety percent of what I had been asking for, I thought this would be quite satisfactory. However, after Sharp had made his proposal, Mike McCabe, his executive assistant, shouted: "You should not move that resolution, Mr. Minister." Nevertheless, both Lamontagne and I were left with the clear impression that Mitchell agreed with the comprehensive resolution even though, on Mike McCabe's advice, he decided not to move it.

But once again there was a procedural debate, and the various points were put through in a piecemeal fashion, instead of in the form of a comprehensive resolution as had been agreed to. The Sharp forces managed to persuade the press that this was a great victory for Mitchell and a devastating defeat for me. And this was the way the press played it.[75]

As finally adopted, the foreign investment resolution called for Canada to continue "to welcome the inflow of international investment capital and, without penalty to other forms of investment, provide encouragement for a greater percentage of international investment funds in bonds and other fixed term securities, and that government policy encourage association of Canadian equity with international equity investment."[76] The statement was mild enough to satisfy Mitchell Sharp; and anything which could do that was sufficient to undermine the claims of the Gordon lobby. The propaganda battle to establish a precise nationalist and left-wing program for the party was lost.

Without the promise of Walter Gordon's continuing leadership, the nationalist campaign at the conference was anticlimactic and less than wholehearted. Its failure reinforced Gordon's decision to retire from politics, and late in October he told Mike Pearson of his intention.

He asked me about my plans. (There was no reference to our talks of last March when he offered to help me get the leadership if I wanted it or to our talks last June when he raised the subject of me returning to the Cabinet.) I said I could not put in another year like the last one and intended to resign my seat. He was not surprised but said he hoped I wouldn't do so until the House rises in December. I said I planned to do it during the Xmas recess. I added that I would be honest in giving my reasons – that I am not in sympathy with the party's present policy direction.

Mike asked me if I would like to be High Commissioner in London. (He asked me this once before as I recall.) While this was a genuine offer I was noncommittal and said I'd let him know.[77]

Gordon devoted one final address, on October 25, to free trade and Canadian economic independence. "The complete integration of the lives and working habits of two animals so different in size and character as an elephant and a mouse – or, if you will, a beaver –," he told the Toronto Advertising and Sales Club, "would not be likely to work out to the best advantage of the beaver."[78] Canadian secondary manufacturing industry, he warned, would suffer devastation in the continental rationalization that would follow free trade with the United States. Free trade in agricultural implements since 1949 had already resulted in expansion of the industry in the U.S. rather than Canada; the same thing would have happened in the auto industry without the special safeguards of the Auto Pact. In the electrical, appliance and metal industries too, free trade would mean dislocation for Canadian plants and unemployment for many thousands in Canada. Gordon asked his audience to "be sure that we know what we are in for, before we embark upon a policy from which there would be no turning back."

While free trade was not an immediate prospect, its advocates shared an indifference to Gordon's proposals for reducing foreign control in the economy. When he turned to that subject, Gordon reflected on the lessons of his recent experience in the Liberal party.

I do not see any prospect of the increasing absentee control of the Canadian economy being reversed by professions of hope or ringing phrases. Quite frankly, I doubt if attempts at compromise between diametrically conflicting points of view will do much good. It is unlikely that much action will be taken if those responsible are unconvinced of its importance.[79]

13   On the Brink

Walter Gordon's friends in the Liberal caucus were unwilling to accept his resignation from the House. That gesture, they believed, would be the final mark of the government's retreat into caution and inaction, the signal of failure for the reformers in the party. When his firm intention became known in October, a number of Gordon's colleagues set out to reverse it. Over the next nine weeks they campaigned to convince Gordon and the Prime Minister of Gordon's importance to the party, and to persuade them both that he should return to the Cabinet. Gordon and Pearson were both surprised by the strength of his support.[1]

The first open manifestation of its existence was a dinner for Walter Gordon offered by members of the Ontario caucus in the Parliament Buildings on November 9. More than thirty members attended, and the urgency and warmth of the speeches made clear that this was no polite farewell to a departing general. The Prime Minister and Minister of Finance were both present.

> Many very flattering speeches including Harry Harley (very eloquent) Herb Gray, Larry Pennell, LBP, Bob Stanbury, Mitchell Sharp (a difficult job for him), Keith Davey, Walter Foy, Walker, Andras, Munro. . . .
> The backbenchers made it clear they look to me for leadership and wanted me to stay around. . . . [2]

The occasion was high-spirited and emotional; some of the speakers were in tears. Keith Davey recalled:

After a lot of this tearfulness and affection, Walter got up, and said blandly, "I'm very moved by this demonstration," and he was, but he couldn't show it. So I yelled, "Well then, for Chrissake show it!" That broke the tension, and everyone laughed.[3]

In October, with regret but some relief, Mike Pearson had favoured Walter Gordon's decision to retire;[4] now it was becoming obvious that Gordon's departure could not be accomplished quietly and easily. Maurice Lamontagne had already urged the Prime Minister to invite Gordon, with Lamontagne's help, to prepare "policy themes" for the National Liberal Federation for the coming five years.[5] The Prime Minister knew that Gordon would not remain in the House as a backbencher without a leading role in the government; the precondition for keeping him there, it appeared, would have to be an arrangement for his return to the Cabinet. Given the mounting pressure on behalf of Gordon, that choice began to offer the path of least resistance to the Prime Minister. While Gordon's resignation would demoralize and embitter a substantial element of the caucus, and perhaps split the party (Gordon still promised to speak out on the reasons for his resignation), Pearson believed that his reappointment might bring the factions precariously together.[6]

There seemed to be only one possible means of sidestepping Gordon's supporters without damage to the party: that was to persuade Walter Gordon graciously to accept a kick upstairs. It had not worked before, and the Prime Minister was uncertain where "upstairs" might be for Gordon; it was certainly not the Senate. But Pearson was ready to try two other possibilities before falling back on the more obvious choice. On October 29 he offered the High Commission in London to his friend; and when Gordon turned this down on November 10, Pearson countered with the presidency of the CBC.[7] Gordon needed no decent interval of reflection to reject that invitation.[8]

Gordon's advocates persisted in their entreaties. On November 16 the Ontario caucus decided, "after considerable debate and some opposition,"[9] to send a delegation to the Prime Minister asking him to urge Gordon to remain in the House and, if possible, to bring him back into the Cabinet. After receiving this delegation, a perplexed and hesitant Prime Minister invited Gordon to discuss his situation once more at the end of the month. Reluctantly and against their better judgment, Pearson and Gordon were being forced into negotiation. Pearson made one vague concession.

He said he had promised to urge me to stay on and help choose his successor. .... I repeated I was not prepared to do nothing for another year. Mike did not press me on this.

He said that when we talked last spring he had hoped I would return to the Cabinet in the fall. However while he did not disagree with the speeches I made this fall, in view of the way they were played up in the press, he could not ask me to return to the Cabinet in which Sharp is a member! I emphasized I was not asking to go back to the Cabinet or for anything else. Mike agreed.

Before we separated I said I wished to be clear on what I was being asked to do i.e. merely to stay on with no specific responsibilities, etc. Mike replied he simply was not prepared to make changes in the Cabinet – to change its attitudes and the "image" of the party – when he intended to get out so soon. I said this meant he might be turning over the party to his successor in no better shape than it was in when he inherited it. I was blunt and he did not like it. However he made it quite clear he is not going to do anything.

Why the hell he asked me to come to Ottawa for this kind of conversation was not explained.[10]

If the interview was intended as a warning to Walter Gordon to call off his emissaries, it could not succeed. Gordon did not control them, and had no contact with them.

Two weeks later Maurice Lamontagne sent Gordon a long memorandum intended for the Prime Minister on "The Federal Liberal Party" in which he pointed out that, according to the opinion polls, "the position of the Liberal party has probably not been worse than it is now since the beginning of 1960, *in spite of the disintegration of the Conservative Party.* The Conservatives will go through a difficult period in 1967; however, early in 1968, they will have nowhere to go but up. Meanwhile, the main threat is represented by the NDP, especially in Ontario."[11]

Lamontagne wrote that Liberal backbenchers, particularly in Ontario, were worried that the party would suffer substantial losses at the next election unless it acted soon to recover its popularity.

The leadership race leaves them indifferent and confused. On the other hand, complacency and a business-as-usual attitude seem to characterize the more conservative members of the Cabinet who are, for the time being, the most influential. They do not appear to be interested in reform and they resent those who regard change as inevitable. The orientation of policy is left to the managerial group in the Cabinet, which uses its influence to paralyze and even to eliminate the more dynamic elements in the party.

Only the Prime Minister can inject a new spirit of reform into the party. Such an injection is essential and urgent in order to keep the party alive and in balance. If the Prime Minister decides to initiate this operation, he will get the enthusiastic support of the younger ministers and of a great number of members and active Liberals who are now becoming more and more disillusioned.[12]

Lamontagne called for a series of reforms in 1967: a thorough renovation of the rules of the House of Commons to restore its efficiency and public reputation; a radical reorganization of the structure of federal administration; the preparation of a new, "imaginative and responsible" party program for the 1970s; and renewal of the party organization. He urged the Prime Minister to ask Walter Gordon "to organize the preparation of the new platform and to set up the federal organization in Ontario," and warned that Gordon's departure from politics (if he were not given this kind of task) would create a dangerous vacuum in the party.

Walter Gordon responded in detail to this memorandum in telephone conversations on December 15 with Lamontagne and Edgar Benson. He told them that he could not believe the Prime Minister would invite him to take on such a job, in the light of the party's drift away from Gordon's beliefs and Mike Pearson's indifference. "Of course," Gordon added, "if there were a real change in attitudes, I would be willing to talk things over with the PM again if he would like me to do so – preferably with Benson, Marchand and MacEachen present. But, quite frankly, I doubt if Mr. Pearson appreciates what he is doing, in political terms, or if he does that he would be willing to do what is necessary to change things."[13]

Lamontagne interpreted this as an encouragement, and replied that he would urge Benson, Marchand and MacEachen to see Pearson at once; and Benson told Gordon he would indeed talk to the Prime Minister.

> Benson said he did not see any real difficulty in my returning to the Cabinet in any position; insofar as issues are concerned, there is not all that difference in the words that are being used. He said the real difference is that no one in the Cabinet was taking any action. I repeated that it was not my ambition to return to the Cabinet and certainly I was not asking for this or, in fact, for anything. I also repeated that it was my intention to resign between Christmas and New Year.[14]

Five days later, Benson telephoned to say that the Prime Minister had "liked the idea" of appointing Gordon as "Minister without portfolio responsible for organizing the work of the Cabinet."[15] He reported that Pearson had promised to call Gordon.

> I said I did not much like the proposed position & suggested I should be a Deputy PM. Benson did not respond to this and I did not push the idea with him. He said he would call me again on Thursday.
> Mike did not call.[16]

But the intermediaries were busy. During the evening Keith Davey telephoned from Malton airport that he was on his way to see Gordon. When they met, Davey said that the Prime Minister had called him in and asked him to meet Gordon on his behalf. "The proposition," Gordon recorded, "was much as Benson had suggested."[17] He replied to Davey that he "might be willing to do some kind of a supervision job over the business of the Cabinet" on certain conditions: that the Cabinet would "move on the foreign control issue" (as a minimum by creating the Canada Development Corporation and adopting legislation in financial disclosure); that his job could be clearly defined; and that he would hold a senior Cabinet post as Deputy Prime Minister or President of the Privy Council with an adequate administrative staff behind him.[18] Davey took Gordon's message back to the Prime Minister.[19]

With all the good offices of Gordon's friends, the negotiations were approaching some kind of climax. Just before Christmas, Pearson arranged to meet Gordon on December 29, and gained Gordon's assurance that he would not resign before they met. But after the telephone conversation Gordon concluded sceptically that "I'm afraid we are thinking on different wave lengths."[20]

The meeting on December 29 was not quite conclusive. Gordon wrote afterwards:

> He tried to outline what he had in mind; I was to help with organizing the work of the Cabinet – and with the business of the party. He talked for quite a while but did not make it very clear. In the end he said he knew exactly what he wanted to do and would dictate a memo on it and send it to me over the weekend.[21]

In reply Gordon repeated that if he accepted, the government would have to fulfill the expectations created by his return. There would have to be action on foreign investment, and acknowledgement of the views of the progressive wing of the party. Without those assurances, there would be no purpose in his return, and "the only proper course" for him would be to carry through his resignation.

> I reminded Mike that at one of our last meetings he had said he could not ask me to rejoin the Cabinet with Sharp there. He said he thought things had changed. (I presume he meant my position in the party is stronger than he thought.) I said everything would have to be ironed out with Sharp; that I was not prepared for any more conflict or dirty work. Mike said Sharp is not a conservative like Winters; that essentially he is a civil servant. . . . Mike said he would see Sharp but made it clear he expects no trouble from that source.[22]

The Prime Minister was now in a mood to settle the negotiation to Walter Gordon's satisfaction; and while Gordon remained cautious, he let his natural optimism express itself in his private record.

> Altogether it was an easy conversation. I think Mike realizes the importance of the foreign control issue (he had always been a nationalist at heart) and also my support in the party. The problem now is how to bring me back to the Cabinet and in what capacity.[23]

Gordon added a postscript:

> When I left I asked Mike if I was right in thinking that I would be returning to the Cabinet and that all the details, etc., could be worked out. He agreed completely.[24]

When he returned to his office after lunch with the Prime Minister, Gordon wrote to Pearson, carefully reviewing the points he had made during the meeting.[25] One of his suggestions had been that the government should produce a white paper on foreign control; and in response to a request from Pearson, Gordon enclosed a memorandum outlining his thoughts on the subject. It noted the recent evidence of surveys "that a considerable majority of Canadians are bothered about this issue and think the government should be doing more about it. . . . The question is, how can the Liberal party recapture this issue as its own?"[26] To do so, he argued that "we must demonstrate that we know what should be done and that we are prepared to take the necessary action." This should involve legislation on full disclosure of the financial operations of all companies over a certain size, creation of the Canada Development Corporation, and an expeditious study of further action.

I suggest that arrangements be made to publish a white paper dealing with this whole vexed question within, say, two months. I would hope that the task of preparing a preliminary draft could be entrusted to a very small committee which should be headed by a member of the Cabinet and which might include two members of the caucus. When completed, the draft should be carefully considered and revised by the Cabinet as a whole before publication. It should then be referred to the Committee on Finance, Trade and Economic Affairs for study and public discussion. The objective should be to introduce appropriate legislation some time next fall.[27]

Gordon had found the formula on which a dignified reconciliation might rest. The proposal for a committee and a white paper appealed to him as a means of acting quickly to prepare legislation on foreign ownership; it appealed to the Prime Minister as a conciliatory instrument which would give the appearance of action and the promise of mediation among differing members of the Cabinet. It was a convenient diplomatic means of postponing agreement on one of the central issues at stake. Given the Prime Minister's evident exhaustion in office, and the strength of the "managerial" group in the Cabinet, the chances for decisive action were perhaps not great; but neither Gordon nor Pearson was inclined for the moment to weigh the possibilities. Gordon did not wish to give up on the issue of foreign control, and was ready to make one more effort to convert the government to his views. The white paper was henceforth a central element in the package for both of them.[28]

Meanwhile Gordon kept his options open. The same day he drafted a letter to the president of his constituency association in Davenport riding, Lex Thomson, explaining formally the reasons why he had finally decided to resign his parliamentary seat. The letter was composed on the hypothetical assumption that Gordon's discussions with the Prime Minister had failed, and that there was "no assurance that the government would proceed with the kind of legislation on the foreign control issue which I believe is needed. In view of my strongly held convictions on this subject I could not become a member of the Cabinet under such conditions."[29] Gordon held the letter in reserve.[30]

He returned to Ottawa on Tuesday, January 3 after spending the weekend in Toronto.

. . . I found Mike's letter to me inviting me to return to the Cabinet but on completely unacceptable terms. It did not include any reference to the foreign control issue or to the proposed work in connection with the Cabinet. Moreover, it invited me to become Minister without portfolio with no suggestion that this would be changed in the future.[31]

Gordon met Edgar Benson and Larry Pennell as soon as he could do so that morning, and agreed that they should tell Pearson that, while the letter was acceptable as far as it went, it should also include references to foreign control, the organization of Cabinet business, and a regular portfolio ("although I volunteered that, if it would be difficult to arrange this immediately, I would be willing to serve as a Minister without portfolio for a few weeks"). Benson saw Pearson, and reported back that the changes were "quite satisfactory."[32]

With this assurance, Gordon drafted "the kind of letter I thought Mike should write to me."

I then had lunch with Mike who was at his very best – businesslike, down to earth and clear. I gave him back his original letter and also my draft which he said was quite satisfactory.[33]

Pearson and Gordon were both anxious to avoid any conflict with Mitchell Sharp, and therefore decided to meet later in the day with the Minister of Finance.

At 5 P.M. Mike, Sharp and I met again at Sussex Drive. Sharp said he was very much in favour of my returning to the Cabinet. I said the purpose of the meeting, as I understood it, was to make sure that if I did so, there would not be areas of conflict between Sharp and myself. In this connection I started off with the banking legislation and said that while I disagreed with Sharp's proposals respecting the interest rate, I felt this was a fait accompli and acknowledged this.

I said I assumed from what I had read that there would be no compromising on the subject of the Mercantile Bank. Mike and Sharp agreed. Mitchell added, however, that there was a loophole in the legislation at present in that the Mercantile could sell some of its shares to Canadians (who in effect would be their agents) who would agree not to vote their stock. In this way Mercantile would be assured of retaining control. Sharp said he was working on an appropriate amendment to deal with this. I then brought up the

301

question of agencies of foreign banks. Sharp said that he had announced in the House that he would be receptive to any recommendations to the Banking Committee in regard to this. I said I could not go along with this. Mike said that in effect this would mean a retreat and gave the impression he was completely sympathetic to my view.

I asked Sharp about developments in the field of security legislation and was satisfied with what he told me. I said I presumed there would be opportunities to discuss budget proposals, with which Sharp agreed. We then went on to discuss the importance of agreement between Mitchell and myself if I returned to the Cabinet and I said the way to ensure this was for Mitchell and me to talk things over in advance. Sharp acknowledged that if I came back to the Cabinet it would be necessary for him to say that he was in full agreement.[34]

By this time, on the afternoon of January 3, the negotiations had come to occupy virtually the whole attention of Pearson, Gordon, Sharp and the intermediaries, Benson and Pennell. Gordon appeared to have the strongest position, but the appearance was deceptive. The game had progressed to the point that both Pearson and Gordon were caught in it, and both were likely to be misled by their goodwill, optimism and desire for an accommodation. Gordon was able to seek firm guarantees before entry; but afterwards the advantage would be with the Prime Minister. Then Gordon would be subject to the disciplines of loyalty, secrecy and Cabinet unity: tattered as these conventions were under the Pearson administration, they had some force, and they were restraints applying to ministers rather than to the Prime Minister.

The precariousness of Walter Gordon's bargaining position could already be detected, and Gordon was wary. When he met the Prime Minister the next morning to conclude their compact, Pearson was not as explicit as Gordon desired him to be.

When we did meet ... he mentioned that Sharp had been to see him and that he was in a quandary as to the form and timing of any announcement: I said that I felt the earlier it was made the better, because there are all sorts of rumours flying around and speculative stories in the press. I asked him if he disagreed in any way with the draft letter I had handed to him yesterday and with which at that time he said he was in full agreement. He replied that he was in agreement with the letter although he might want to add something to it. He said, however, that he would not want to make it public. He said the public announcement should not give any indication that I was in disagreement with government policy up to date on the foreign control issue.[35]

The same afternoon, the Prime Minister discussed the announcement of Gordon's reappointment with Benson, Pennell and MacEachen. Very shortly before the hour, Gordon was invited to attend a press conference with the Prime Minister at 4:30 P.M.[36] He had not received Pearson's formal letter of invitation, but wrote at the top of the draft that he had given to the Prime Minister the previous day: "Before joining Mike in a press conference today Benson advised me that Mike had approved this draft and would send me a signed letter in these terms tomorrow."[37] The appointment, following weeks of cautious exchanges, was to be sealed not by a letter but by a hastily summoned press conference.

What the Prime Minister told the press that afternoon was genial but unusually vague.

I'm very happy indeed to be able to tell you that I have invited Mr. Walter Gordon, my old friend and colleague, to rejoin the government as a senior member of the government, and Mr. Gordon has agreed to accept the invitation. This gives me great pleasure, as I know it will give his colleagues in the government. For the time being Mr. Gordon will be Minister without portfolio. . . .
Question: Could you tell us what specific responsibilities Mr. Gordon will have?
The Prime Minister: Not at the moment. Mr. Gordon will be dealing with assignments that I will be giving him from time to time as long as he is a Minister without portfolio. . . . he'll be of general assistance to me and without, for the time being at least, any specific ministerial responsibilities, he will be available to do everything I ask him to do without having to worry about a department of government.
Question: After the temporary appointment, will there be anything?
The Prime Minister: Oh, there will be an opportunity, I'm sure, before long, to add to Mr. Gordon's responsibilities in a ministerial way. But I have nothing to say about that for the time being. . . .
I am quite sure we will be able to find ways and means of using Mr. Gordon's experience and services. . . . [38]

The Prime Minister said he would be writing to Mr. Gordon with "a long list" of assignments, but "I don't think it would be proper to give the public the special work he is supposed to be doing." This was reticence appropriate to the duties of a civil servant rather than a Minister. Gordon added hopefully that "I think it is fair to say that it is going to keep me busy."

In reply to persistent questions about the conflict between Walter Gordon and Mitchell Sharp, the Prime Minister replied that the three had met the previous evening, "and we find, as indeed we found ourselves when we previously worked in the government, in very close accord in regard to Canadian national policy." Pearson admitted that there would be "new measures" to achieve "maximum Canadian control of Canadian economic development and Canadian resources," but insisted that this involved no change in government policy.

The draft letter setting out the proposed terms of Gordon's return to Cabinet (which Gordon had prepared for the Prime Minister on January 3) was direct and specific in Gordon's manner. It listed seven duties which he should assume: 1. The chairmanship of a small committee to prepare a white paper dealing with corporate structure and the Canadian economy, to issue in "appropriate legislation"; 2. General supervision of Cabinet business; 3. Membership on a small Cabinet committee on governmental business; 4. "The planning and organization of political tactics, in particular putting into effect methods of improved communications and public relations"; 5. Liaison between Cabinet and caucus; 6. Liaison between Cabinet and the Liberal Federation, and "particular concern" for the party organization in Ontario; 7. Chairmanship of a party group "to plan the long term policies of the Liberal party."[39] It appeared to Walter Gordon, as to Benson, Pennell and MacEachen, that these responsibilities would make Gordon Deputy Prime Minister "in all but name."[40] Pearson himself had used that title casually in describing Gordon's proposed position to Keith Davey – although the phrase had apparently originated in Gordon's talks with Edgar Benson.[41]

When the Prime Minister wrote his letter to Gordon on January 5, Mitchell Sharp had already given the press fuel for controversy. After the press conference of January 4, Sharp told reporters, in contradiction to the Prime Minister's statement, that no new measures concerned with foreign investment were contemplated.[42] Mike Pearson began his letter to Gordon with a long paragraph insisting on the need to avoid such gifts to troublesome observers. And in contrast to the pointed listing of duties contained in the Gordon draft, the Prime Minister's outline of his new minister's duties was noticeably tentative in tone. This may have been no more than the reflection of two different temperaments and literary styles; but by now Gordon knew that these were precisely the sources – or the symbols – of complicated misunderstandings. Pearson's letter required careful reading. Gordon's responsibilities would be "for the time being"; they might be changed; they were not all-inclusive.[43] The Prime Minister's first request was that Gordon should assume a job he did not want and had not proposed: supervision of the Central Mortgage and Housing Corporation. The Cabinet committee on foreign ownership was offered according to Gordon's terms; the general supervision of Cabinet business was reduced to "collaboration" with the Prime Minister in this role; the liaison between Cabinet and caucus and Cabinet and Federation was hedged with the caution that "This does not mean, of course, that the chairman of the caucus and the president of the Federation would not continue to have direct access to me"; planning the party's long-term policies was diminished to beginning "the preparation of a program for the next election." At the end of the parliamentary session, Pearson promised Gordon the "assumption of a departmental post along the lines which we have already discussed."

There was nothing in the letter which specifically repudiated Gordon's understanding of the compact on which he had returned to the Cabinet; it was Pearson's very imprecision which was the source of unease. After four days' reflection, Gordon replied at length on January 9. His letter was cordial but blunt.

> . . . In the main I think your letter covers things very well. As I read it, it deals with the various matters set out in a draft dated January 3 which you told me and later told Benson you approved.
>
> I quite agree we must avoid any suggestion of controversy or division between members of the Cabinet, and especially between Mitchell and myself. I have refused to go on any of the principal radio or television programs since my appointment, or to give any press interviews for this reason. Moreover, both Mitchell and I went out of our way at the Ontario convention to soft-pedal any reports of differences between us.
>
> The fact remains, however, as I explained to you last October, that I was about to give up my seat in the House because I did not believe the government was moving on the foreign control issue. A good many people know of this including, apparently, some members of the press. I am rejoining the Cabinet at your invitation because you have convinced me the government will take action in this matter and because of the interest you expressed in the approach we discussed and which, at your request, I set down in

a very tentative and preliminary way in my memorandum of December 29, 1966.

Understandably, I was asked to reconcile the reasons for my intended resignation with my return to the government. It seemed to me that a vague reference to the proposed "new approaches" was about the least controversial thing for me to say in the circumstances. The press has not made very much of this, but I expect the sooner you inform the Cabinet of your intention to set up a small committee under my chairmanship to prepare a report on this matter preparatory to a white paper, the better it will be. May I suggest that you and I have a talk with Gordon Robertson as soon as possible so that the appropriate recommendations to Cabinet – including especially what you want me to do about the organization of Cabinet business and the expediting of decisions – may be drafted and I can be put to work.

Once Cabinet is informed of what is contemplated in the way of a white paper I should like this included in the list of matters to be initiated at the beginning of the new session. All that would be done at this time, of course, would be to refer the white paper to a House committee. The list of legislation for the second half of the session should include legislation arising out of the white paper and also the Canada Development Corporation which, in the present list, is put down for 1968. . . .

I am looking forward to doing anything I can to help you in any of the areas you have mentioned. When we have talked about them in more detail, we should agree on the specific terms of reference, including the question of authority as well as responsibility. You can put this preoccupation with precision down to my prejudices as a one-time management consultant. But I know from experience this is the way to avoid difficulty and misunderstanding.[44]

14   "The party is where it was; only Walter Gordon has lost his freedom."

Lester Pearson was aware of the antagonism Walter Gordon's attitudes provoked in some parts of the party; that had been demonstrated enough at the October conference. When Gordon returned to the Cabinet, there was no surprise in the comment of the Winnipeg *Free Press* that "It is almost beyond comprehension that Prime Minister Pearson could be so out of touch with Liberal thinking across the country as to have seen fit to reinstate Mr. Gordon. . . . "[1] That comment, from that source, could be brushed aside. What was perhaps more disconcerting was the general note of puzzlement in the press, the mischievous probing of reporters to draw out the latent conflicts between Gordon on one side and Sharp and Winters on the other, and above all the hostility within the Cabinet to Gordon's return.

The Montreal *Star*, in an editorial sympathetic to Mr. Gordon, suggested that the Prime Minister had bought temporary peace at no price by bringing Gordon in: "The party is where it was; only Walter Gordon has lost his freedom."[2] That judgment may have been unfair to the Prime Minister's good intentions, but it was not false to reality. When he talked to his friend, Mike Pearson perhaps genuinely hoped to satisfy Gordon's expectations. But this was wishful thinking. He no longer possessed the authority over his Cabinet or the staying power to see the commitments through. When his leading ministers balked, he had no means of commanding their allegiance or unity.

In his familiar way, the Prime Minister had taken the basic decision to invite Gordon back without consulting the Cabinet. The intermediaries – Benson, Pennell, MacEachen, and Marchand – knew of the negotiations; Mitchell Sharp was brought in at the end; but the remainder of the Cabinet learned formally of the appointment only on the morning of the press conference. Those who were absent for the New Year, including Robert Winters, read of it in the newspapers.[3] Winters publicly expressed his dismay that "there must have been a meeting of minds between Mr. Gordon and the Prime Minister" when he returned to Canada at the weekend, and sought clarification from Mr. Pearson in an interview a few days later.[4] "Informed sources" in the office of the Minister of Trade and Commerce then put it out that the Prime Minister had reassured him there would be no changes in foreign investment policy in spite of Walter Gordon's return.[5] George McIlraith and Senator John Connolly also "complained bitterly" about the appointment, and Gordon heard on the grapevine that Mitchell Sharp "was having second thoughts."[6] The Prime Minister seemed to have no stomach for more controversy, and his response "was simply to avoid implementing his undertakings. Perhaps he felt his own position was not strong enough to permit him to do so, but if this was the case he never mentioned it to me."[7] Pearson was reluctant to tell the Cabinet what Walter Gordon's duties would be, and this made it impossible for Gordon to begin his work.[8] After two weeks Gordon urged Pearson to discuss the foreign control issue with the Cabinet because some press reports had already mentioned the proposed study.

> I have a nasty feeling that any day now questions could be asked in the House or further speculative articles appear in the press – which would annoy members of the Cabinet if they had not been advised beforehand.[9]

Under this pressure Pearson met Gordon, Sharp and Winters on January 18 to discuss the foreign investment enquiry. One of the objects of the meeting, it appeared, was to test Walter Gordon's determination and if possible to divert him from the project.

> Winters joined us at 9 P.M. and we had a long (until 10:45) discussion of the proposed review of the foreign control issue. The following points were made:
> (a) Sharp suggested that in my own interest I should not be connected with the enquiry. (He obviously believes it will be a reflection on himself for not moving in this matter.)
> (b) Sharp made it clear he does not consider this a real major issue.
> (c) Mike asked if I really believe there is a danger that in ten to fifteen years if we do nothing it will be too late. I said I did.

(d)   Sharp & Winters argued I should accept some or several big administrative jobs. I said I was not interested. Mike brought up CMHC. The others agreed. I did not comment.

(e)   I repeated several times that I had not asked to come back to the Cabinet; that my plans were all set to retire; that I was not exactly fascinated by what goes on here; that Mike had come to me at the last possible minute presumably because he thought it wise to do so from a political point of view; that he asked me to do various things including the chairmanship of a Cabinet committee to look into the foreign control issue preparatory to the issue of a white paper; that because of my keen interest in this issue I agreed to come back into the govt., and that the understandings & agreement were confirmed in writing.

I mentioned that Sharp had been present during a discussion on policy which dealt with the above matter in some detail. Winters said he had not known about it. I pointed out it is the PM's prerogative to ask people to join the Cabinet and no one else's. No argument on this.

(f)   There was a lot of talk about the reaction of the business community. I told Winters that I had been a member of the business community in Toronto for thirty years and the only thing I was sure of is that one cannot generalize on what businessmen think; some feel one way on this issue – others think the opposite.

(g)   When it was clear I would not give in Sharp suggested Mike should head the enquiry instead of me. This would be ridiculous and contrary to the agreement but I did not say so.

(h)   There is no doubt that a. Sharp & especially Winters are strongly opposed to do anything (Sharp would go along with a whitewash approach); b. that Mike will renege if he can (perhaps I am being unfair); c. that nobody really gives a damn.[10]

After this purgative session, Pearson told Gordon the next morning that he was prepared to proceed.[11] The foreign ownership study would be carried out by a task force of professional economists, assisted by an interdepartmental committee of senior officials, and reporting to a ministerial committee under Gordon's chairmanship.[12] When it was informed of the proposal, the Cabinet disagreed over the composition of the task force, and finally accepted Gordon's concession that it should include "any competent economist whom any member of the Cabinet suggested."[13] The ministerial committee was made up of Gordon, Mitchell Sharp, Jean Marchand, John Turner, and Roger Teillet. (Robert Winters rejected an invitation to join the committee.)

On January 23 the Prime Minister revealed the study in a brief press release. The form of the announcement was a measure of the Prime Minister's sensitivity to further buffeting: a statement in the House was rejected by Pearson and Gordon because it "would provoke debate."[14] The announcement described the investigation as a study of "the structure of Canadian industry, with special reference to foreign ownership and control," which would "include the significance – both political and economic – of foreign investment in the development of our country, as well as ways to encourage greater Canadian ownership of our industrial resources while retaining a climate favourable to the inflow of foreign investment, as required, for Canada's optimum development."[15] Walter Gordon had been consulting his friend Abraham Rotstein at the University of Toronto about the composition of the task force, and a few days later its first members, under the chairmanship of Professor Melville Watkins of the University of Toronto, were announced.[16] The task force pursued its studies intensively in the months that followed, in liaison with Gordon. Since the major work was that of detailed research and analysis by the members and staff of the task force, the supervisory role of the Cabinet committee was not an onerous one during 1967.

The attempt to neutralize this enquiry had discouraged Gordon; and he was further disenchanted by the failure of Lester Pearson to reappoint Maurice Lamontagne to the Cabinet.[17] By the end of January the Prime Minister had still given no indication when (or whether) he expected Gordon to undertake the other duties outlined in their exchange of letters. The Cabinet was not informed. And the pious hope that Walter Gordon and Mitchell Sharp might avoid conflict through frequent consultation had evaporated; they were already engaged in a series of skirmishes over the revisions to the Bank Act. Walter Gordon was "thoroughly sorry I had agreed to return to the Cabinet. By that time I realized this had been a serious mistake."

I soon found that there was a very different atmosphere in the Cabinet I had rejoined in January, 1967 from the one I had resigned from fourteen months previously. The leadership contenders – especially Martin, Hellyer, Sharp, and Winters – were openly vying for position and were distrustful of one another. There was no air of camaraderie or team spirit. Cabinet meetings were disorganized. There was little or no discipline, and the leaks from ministerial offices, one in particular, were damaging to the government and sometimes to individual Cabinet colleagues. While Pearson continued to spend long hours in his office and was still as bright as ever when he addressed his mind to some particular issue, he was getting noticeably older, and his authority as a caretaker Prime Minister was often challenged.

I do not mean that discussions in Cabinet were always acrimonious. Frequently we had a good deal of fun together. But it was harder to arrive at a consensus. On many issues it would seem that Sharp, Winters, Hellyer, Pickersgill, Laing, McIlraith and Connolly would line up on one side, while Benson, Marchand, LaMarsh, Pennell, MacEachen, and I – and later, Trudeau, when he joined the Cabinet in April – would find ourselves together on the other. The probable position of the other members of the Cabinet, including that of the Prime Minister, was less certain. . . .

The trouble with the second Pearson government was that the Cabinet received no firm lead from the Prime Minister, while there were wide differences of opinion on policy matters and in political philosophy among the members of the Cabinet.[18]

*

Walter Gordon's Bill to revise the Bank Act had died on the order paper after second reading when the House of Commons was dissolved in September, 1965. In the first months of 1966 the government was subjected to pressure from the American government, some of the Canadian chartered banks, and the First National City Bank of New York (the owners of the Mercantile Bank of Canada) to amend Gordon's draft Bill in order to permit foreign-owned banks and bank agencies to operate without discrimination in Canada. The most significant protest came in a diplomatic note from the United States government on April 7, 1966 which declared that:

> The Embassy has been instructed to remind the government of Canada of the concern with which the United States government viewed certain aspects of the banking legislation introduced in Parliament last year but not enacted . . . , and express the hope that the banking legislation to be introduced this year will not contain provisions discriminating against American-owned banks.[19]

The Canadian government rejected the charge of discrimination on the ground that the legislation would apply equally to residents and non-residents, and explained the reasons for its approach in a diplomatic note of reply on June 29, 1966.[20] On July 7 Mitchell Sharp introduced his version of the revised Bank Act, which retained without change the provisions of the Gordon Bill defining the terms of bank ownership.[21]

Walter Gordon was pleased that his successor had maintained the established policy of the Canadian government.

The Bill received second reading in October and was referred for study to the House of Commons Standing Committee on Finance, Trade and Economic Affairs (under the chairmanship of Herb Gray, MP). American pressure intensified during the autumn; and on November 11 the Canadian ambassador in Washington, A. E. Ritchie, relayed a second American note to Ottawa. The note, which Ritchie described as "very rough," was handed to him by Nicholas Katzenbach, the under secretary of state. It threatened retaliation if Canada proceeded with "retroactive and discriminatory" legislation affecting the Mercantile Bank: "For its part, USA govt. continues to hold view that it is not rpt. not reasonable to expect that privileged position now enjoyed by Cdn. banks in USA would continue unimpaired if only USA-owned bank in Canada is subjected to retroactive and discriminatory treatment."[22] The existence and general terms of both American notes were reported in the press shortly afterwards, and under questioning in the House the Minister of Finance repeated the government's intention to stand firm against American pressure.[23]

This formal protest, and continued lobbying by Mercantile Bank directors (including a Canadian senator), the American ambassador Walton Butterworth and members of his staff, apparently inclined Mitchell Sharp and other members of the party (in spite of the Minister's assurance) toward some compromise which might appease the American government. Out of his anxiety in the matter, Walter Gordon sought assurances from Pearson and Sharp during their meeting on January 3 that there would be no retreat on either the Mercantile Bank or the prohibition on agencies of foreign banks.[24] He believed that these pledges had been given before he rejoined the Cabinet.

But press speculation and rumour about a Canadian retreat persisted after Gordon's return. On January 17 he met the Prime Minister and the Minister of Finance to review the case for firmness. The discussion was concerned largely with the agency question, and in the course of it Gordon gave Pearson and Sharp copies of a memorandum on the subject.[25] Gordon recommended that Sharp should instruct Herb Gray against any action by the House Committee on bank agencies, and gained "the clear impression" that this would be done.[26]

James S. Rockefeller and Robert MacFadden of Citibank and the Mercantile Bank testified before the House Committee on January 24, 1967. While they admitted under questioning, and tabled documentary evidence which proved, that they had indeed been informed by Walter Gordon before the purchase of the Mercantile Bank that it would be subject to all the provisions of the new Bank Act,[27] they continued to protest adamantly at the limitations contained in the Bill, and urged removal of the section tying the growth of Mercantile's assets to the proportion of foreign ownership in the bank.[28] They also refused to offer shares of the Mercantile Bank for sale on Canadian exchanges.

Citibank's defiance prompted one Liberal member of the House Committee, Bryce Mackasey, to seek terms for a mutually acceptable compromise in a visit to Citibank's New York head office.[29] Mackasey's visit to New York was approved by Pearson and Sharp in advance. His mediation resulted in contacts between Citibank and the Department of Finance, and an indication that Mercantile would be prepared to sell shares in Canada if it were allowed temporary exemption from the limitation on assets. On February 9 Pearson told Gordon that "Sharp wants to make a deal and to give them three years to sell stock to Canadians"[30] without restriction on the bank's growth during that period. Gordon opposed any concession, and "Mike said he would get Sharp and me together on this."

Gordon had arranged to be away from Ottawa for most of a three week period after mid-February (first on a speaking trip to western Canada and then on holiday in Jamaica). When he heard nothing from Mitchell Sharp, he wrote to the Prime Minister on February 15 to reiterate that "I can see no reason why the government should wish to make any changes in the present Bill."[31] Five days later Pearson telephoned him in Toronto.

> At the end of our conversation I said Sharp had not spoken to me about the Mercantile Bank and asked what was proposed. Mike replied that Sharp had decided not to do anything at all – certainly at this time. He might bring the matter up again later on but there will be no changes proposed in the present Bank Act revision. I repeated my concern about the matter and said I was pleased nothing was going to be done.[32]

With this assurance, Gordon flew to Calgary the next day. But he was sceptical of Mitchell Sharp's intent, and before leaving he asked Edgar Benson to hold a watching brief.

> ... I called Benson about the Mercantile Bank affair, reminded him that a condition of my returning to the Cabinet was that no concessions would be made, informed him of my various discussions with Mike, said I had had no word from Sharp but all the inspired stories in the press suggested a deal was in the making, said if this

happened in my absence I would have to resign and asked him to watch things for me. I also suggested he have a look at the letter I wrote to Mike on this subject a week ago.

Benson said Cabinet had decided there should be no deal & in his opinion Sharp could not make one without coming back to Cabinet. He agreed with the conditions I had mentioned in my letter to Mike i.e. that City Bank's interest should be reduced to ten percent not twenty-five percent – and said he would call me if anything came up.[33]

Gordon's uneasiness was well-founded. The next day, while he was in Winnipeg, an urgent telephone call from Bud Drury summoned him out of a meeting with students at United College.

Bud said Sharp had spoken to him about a proposed deal with Mercantile to be dealt with by the Committee on Finance, Trade and Economic Affairs that afternoon. Bud said he had urged Sharp to call me – and suggested I call Sharp. I told Bud the score (my conversations with Mike, etc.) and said I would resign if anything was done in my absence and without my approval. He said he would get Sharp to call me at the Fort Garry at 4:15 P.M. (Later Bud said he may have misunderstood and said 4:15 P.M. Ottawa time instead of Wpg. time.)

Shortly afterwards and following a press conference (I should think about 2:30 P.M. Wpg. time) I was able to call Sharp. I was told he could not leave the House to speak to me! – but would call me at the Fort Garry. I did nøt hear from him.[34]

As Drury had predicted, the parliamentary Committee amended the Bill that afternoon, granting Citibank five years in which to reduce its share in Mercantile to twenty-five percent without restriction on its expansion. Anthony Westell of the *Globe and Mail* reported "what appeared to be a well-planned manoeuvre by Mr. Sharp."[35] After reading a telegram to the Committee from Mercantile which promised a share offering to Canadians "when it is appropriate to make an attractive offering," Mr. Sharp "blandly asked the Committee if it was disposed to be sympathetic to Mercantile."

Mr. Sharp insisted that it was a matter for the judgment of the Committee and of Parliament whether the legislation should be enforced or amended to give the bank a better break.

But under questioning by MPs – mainly by Bryce Mackasey (L,

Verdun) – he allowed himself to be led into agreeing that Mercantile, which is not at present a profitable undertaking, would find it difficult to sell seventy-five percent of its shares at a reasonable price by the end of the year.

Gently prodded by Mr. Mackasey, Mr. Sharp ventured: "I am inclined to believe there is likely to be a more constructive outcome if this bank is given more time to get its affairs in order before they are required to sell shares."

It was a great advance, Mr. Sharp said, that the bank had changed its attitude to the extent where it now was willing to sell shares. He was eager that it should become a Canadian institution.

Mr. Sharp agreed with Mr. Mackasey that it would not alter the principle of the Bill and would appear reasonable to give the bank five years to sell seventy-five percent of its shares.

As the questioning continued, the Committee developed a consensus that five years would be a satisfactory grace period.

Chairman Herbert Gray (L, Essex West) asked if anyone wanted to move an amendment to that effect. Mr. Elderkin, sitting next to Mr. Sharp, reached into his briefcase and pulled out a draft amendment providing the five year extension.

It was promptly moved by Mr. Mackasey, seconded by New Democratic Party finance expert Colin Cameron (Nanaimo-Cowichan-The Islands) and approved without a dissenting voice.[36]

Gordon returned by air to Toronto that evening in an angry mood, and reached Mike Pearson on the telephone at about 11 P.M.

I asked Mike if he had shown Sharp my letter of last week. He said he had spoken to him about it. I reminded him of our telephone conversation on Monday – and said I felt I had been double-crossed. (I used that expression.) I said I would come to Ottawa for the Cabinet meeting this morning and that either Sharp would have to arrange matters in accordance with my letter to Mike of last week or I would have to resign. I suggested Mike should see both of us before Cabinet and that I would let him know when I got in. . . . [37]

He met the Prime Minister at 9 A.M. on Thursday, February 23, and Mitchell Sharp joined them soon afterwards. "Sharp was completely adamant that he would make no concessions to me whatever and I said that in these circumstances he or I would have to go."[38] The row exploded into Cabinet later in the morning. Mr. Sharp claimed that the Finance Committee had acted independently; but other ministers pointed out that "the responsible Minister must control the Committee dealing with his own legislation," and recalled that the Cabinet had previously decided against any change in policy without the Cabinet's express authority.[39] Eventually Walter Gordon spoke, reviewing his record of the case in detail. He concluded by warning that if the Cabinet supported the proposed changes in the Bank Act, he would be obliged to resign on the grounds that a firm commitment made to him when he rejoined the government had been repudiated, and that the concession to Citibank "would have a symbolic significance insofar as the whole foreign control issue is concerned."[40] Faced with this dangerous stalemate, the Prime Minister proposed that a group of six ministers – Gordon, Sharp, Winters, Marchand, Benson, and Martin – should meet with him at noon to seek a satisfactory settlement.[41]

> After a long discussion, it was agreed that an amendment would be made to the Bank Act to the effect that no bank in Canada would be permitted to increase its capital if any shareholder had or was about to have more than a ten percent interest in the bank. Mr. Benson was asked to get hold of Mr. Elderkin and draft an appropriate amendment, after which he is to discuss it with Sharp and myself. Presumably if we agree, there will be no need for further discussion. . . .
>
> I raised the question of agencies of foreign banks and explained why I would be opposed to allowing them in Canada. Sharp said that he disagreed with me in principle on this but that he had no thought at present of proposing any legislation that would permit such agencies to come into Canada. . . . It was reasonably clear that those present agreed with my position in this matter, but when Sharp said that he would take no initiative of any kind for at least twelve months, we all agreed to let the matter drop.[42]

The same evening Benson, Sharp and Gordon met in Benson's office to give form to the morning's agreement. Five possible variations on an amendment to the Bank Act were discussed, but Sharp was intransigent. Gordon wrote afterwards: "He argued the matter all over again and repudiated this morning's understandings. He was tired, tense and had not eaten. After about an hour he banged out of the office, angry and in a bad temper. Where do we go from here?"[43] Edgar Benson ended his independent account of the meeting by suggesting pessimistically that the House should not proceed with the legislation until the Cabinet had "somehow arrived at a consensus of opinion."[44]

A settlement was urgent, and Benson carried on his mediation among Sharp, Gordon and Pearson by telephone the same evening. Finally a formula was found: Benson would propose to Cabinet two amendments to the Bill, one prohibiting the acquisition of additional shares by any shareholder already possessing more than ten percent of a bank's shares, and the other providing that the waving of the limitation on assets would not be automatic, but would require a specific Cabinet order.[45] In addition, Benson would urge the Cabinet to adopt two resolutions, one "that no extension of time would be granted beyond 31 December 1967, unless prior to that date Citibank has given substantial evidence that it intends to sell seventy-five percent of its shares to Canadians"; the second "that the capital of Mercantile will not be increased until Citibank's interest has been reduced to ten percent."[46] Sharp accepted the two amendments but opposed the Cabinet resolutions; Benson was confident, however, "in view of all that has transpired, that a majority of the Cabinet" would favour the resolutions despite the opposition of the Minister of Finance.[47] Walter Gordon conveyed the terms of the compromise to the Prime Minister on February 25 before departing for his holiday in Jamaica. He also wrote to Robert Winters and Jean Marchand with the same information, and mentioned his belief that the matter would not be discussed in Cabinet until after his return.[48] Gordon now hoped for fourteen days of unworried relaxation in the sun.

Three days later the Cabinet acted. At its meeting on February 28, in Gordon's absence, it agreed to the amendments to the Bank Act, but postponed any decision on the resolutions until Gordon's return.[49] The Minister of Finance was impatient, however, and on March 2 Larry Pennell called Gordon in Jamaica to say that "Sharp now wants everything settled" before taking the legislation to the House. "In these circumstances, Larry advised me to come back for the Cabinet meeting next Tues. morning. He said Benson would be returning late Monday with Pickersgill. I asked him to let Mike know I would be back."[50] In other telephone conversations to Ottawa and Toronto Gordon learned that "Sharp's supporters were insisting he win this 'fight' otherwise his leadership hopes are dead."[51] To cap the day, two Toronto *Telegram* reporters in hot pursuit invaded Gordon's Jamaican retreat during a cocktail party.[52] Gordon arranged to fly back to Toronto on Sunday, March 5.

While he was publicly discreet about the dispute, Mitchell Sharp was not. Sharp told reporters from the three Toronto newspapers on March 4 that the government's policy was the one adopted by the House Finance Committee. "There will be no changes in principle . . . and I am the Minister of Finance."[53] "The only changes I have heard of," he said, "are changes in detail, not in principle."[54] An alteration in the percentage of shares Citibank would be required to sell would be a matter of principle, and that would not occur. Mr. Sharp's replies to questions did not quite bear on the points still at issue; but he implied that Cabinet policy was precisely established, that he was not seeking to alter it, and that anyone doing so would be guilty of overriding established principles. This was not a fair account of the dispute. The fundamental change in policy had occurred in Committee, when the Bill was altered to permit Mercantile five years' grace to acquire Canadian shareholders before imposing sanctions on its growth. The Cabinet's subsequent decisions on February 28 had moved it back from that concession by placing the period of grace at the discretion of the Cabinet and prohibiting the purchase of additional shares by Citibank; and these decisions could not be interpreted as anything but a measured rebuke to Mitchell Sharp. The semantic distinction between detail and principle was obscure; one man's detail was another man's principle. But given Mr. Sharp's role in promoting the original compromise with Mercantile, it was in his political interest to present any subsequent modifications as changes of detail.

The Cabinet met on March 7 in the shadow of the death of Governor General Georges Vanier, whose state funeral was to be held the next day. Even this could not dampen the Mercantile dispute.

> There was a flaming row in Cabinet on Tuesday, March 7. After reviewing the events of February 23 and 24, I stated what I believed to be the substance of the issue. Very simply, the problem was foreign control. The Mercantile question was symbolic for three reasons: Were we to give way to intensive pressures including those from the U.S. State Department? Were we to clear the way for the full scale entry into Canada of U.S. banks? Were the members of the Cabinet to be able to trust each other's commitments?[55]

No consensus was achieved, and that evening the Prime Minister, "desperately anxious for a settlement," met Benson, Marchand, Sharp, and Gordon.[56] The Prime Minister juggled with yet another formula for restricting the period of extension to Mercantile; and in response to Walter Gordon's reminder that he had returned to the Cabinet on condition that there would be no concessions, the Minister of Finance said that he did not consider the five year extension to be a concession. When Sharp departed after an hour there was still no agreement, but it was evident to Gordon that "the others were on my side," and that Benson and Marchand would join him in resignation if the Cabinet backed away from its existing position.[57]

Edgar Benson worked out a final accommodation between the two ministers the following day. It was spelled out in a memorandum providing that the two amendments to the Bank Act approved by the Cabinet would be introduced in the House by private members but supported by the government, "and no members of the Cabinet will in any way try to influence any changes or variations to the amendments as agreed upon by Cabinet."[58] The question of an increase in Mercantile's capital was to be left open until Mercantile actually made application for such an increase (which was not anticipated "for at least the next two or three years").[59]

The Cabinet's amendments were duly incorporated into the Bill at the report stage, and on March 21, 1967 the Bank Act received third reading in the House of Commons. The manoeuvring over technical detail had become increasingly arcane as the conflict progressed, and it was difficult for laymen to assess the outcome. The office of the Minister of Finance claimed that Mitchell Sharp had won a famous victory, and Walter Gordon did not contest that claim in public. (The ministers had agreed not to discuss the settlement publicly.) But the evidence does not sustain Sharp's claim. The result of the battle was at best a stalemate. By his presence in Cabinet Walter Gordon had maintained the essential restrictions on the Mercantile Bank contained in the original Bill; and he had prevented acceptance of the blanket five year extension of the period of grace arranged without his knowledge by the Minister of Finance. Walter Gordon and Edgar Benson had run very hard for three weeks to remain in the same place; they had fallen back a few paces after the coup in the House Finance Committee, but then recovered their position in Cabinet. They had a defensive victory, if nothing more. Mercantile did not receive the automatic concession it had reluctantly settled for, and in fact did not apply for any suspension of the ceiling on its assets after December 31, 1967.[60]

*

Gordon's understanding in January had been that he would become President of the Privy Council by the end of the month. The Prime Minister intended to appoint Guy Favreau to the Quebec Superior Court, but Favreau's illness persisted and Gordon agreed without reluctance that Favreau should not be disturbed until later in the spring. Gordon's other duties came somehow to be associated with his assumption of Favreau's title, and on February 9 he recorded this conversation with the Prime Minister:

> . . . I said I would be back from Jamaica on March 13th and would be asking Mike when I will be asked to take on the other responsibilities discussed when I returned to the Cabinet. Mike said

Favreau would be leaving by then – that I would be appointed to the Privy Council – and that the rest would follow.[61]

On April 4 Gordon succeeded Favreau as President of the Privy Council but the rest did not follow. Ten days later he wrote:

> I have had a number of short and rather confused conversations with Mike – since I was sworn in as Pres. of the Privy Council on 4th April about my responsibilities. He has had second thoughts about most of the matters outlined in his letter of January 4th or 5th. On the other hand he has been urging me to take responsibility for CMHC and (at Gordon Robertson's urging) of the Company of Young Canadians which I gather is in a mess.
> I have said on each occasion (we have probably had three or four brief conversations) that before I would agree to take on any additional assignments I must insist on having a base of operations i.e. responsibility for the Privy Council establishment.[62]

Gordon doubted whether he would ever assume the duties of "Deputy Prime Minister" – or general manager of Cabinet operations and chief of planning – that had been discussed in December. But he would not let his position go by default.

> In a brief conversation this afternoon I raised this point again. Mike said he had not understood the situation; that he assumed I would be in charge of the Privy Council office; and how else could I justify my salary. I told him this would need an Order-in-Council under the Transfer of Duties Act and we agreed I would ask Gordon Robertson to draft it.[63]

But when Gordon saw the clerk of the Privy Council, Robertson raised objections, and the Prime Minister told Gordon ingenuously a few days later that "he had not dreamed of all the problems until he had talked to Gordon Robertson" – which had not occurred until after Pearson had acknowledged the arrangement with Gordon on April 13.[64] They decided to meet Gordon Robertson together on April 26.

At this meeting Robertson argued firmly that the Privy Council office was part of the Prime Minister's establishment, that it could not function except in that relationship, and that Gordon was authorized to recruit his own aides as President of the Privy Council.[65]

> I reminded Mike that this was not the understanding when he

persuaded me to return to the Cabinet last December and asked me to take on the various responsibilities set out in our correspondence of early January. I also said it was neither his nor my understanding when we discussed the situation re the Privy Council office a few weeks ago. At that time we both agreed I would be responsible for the Privy Council staff, etc.

I said the various matters covered in our January correspondence could be handled best – or so we thought at the time – through the Privy Council office. I mentioned there was about to be quite a vacuum with LBP engaged with Expo visitors, with Robertson going to Quebec in Sept. for a year and with LBP thinking of a world tour, and then a Convention.[66]

Gordon proposed, as a compromise, that part of the Privy Council staff should be transferred to his jurisdiction, and asserted that, without this staff, he would still be, in effect, a Minister without portfolio holding an honorific title. "I said my alternative – if Pres. of the P.C. is to mean nothing – is to see through the white paper on foreign investment and then get out as soon as possible."[67]

When Gordon Robertson had left Pearson's office, the two politicians eased the tension amiably with another round of drinks and lunch, and ranged again over the Prime Minister's plans.

He insisted he would retire in the fall and go on a world tour in Nov.-Dec. but admitted he would be pressured to stay on. (However he thought Maryon would prevail.) We talked about the tour and his plans to write articles, to lecture and to write a book. . . . We talked about some of the members (he is not really interested) and about the leadership contenders. He is always changing his mind on this subject. At the moment he believes Hellyer & Sharp can't make it and that Turner should not run. He thought Martin could get in on a deal to stay for only a stipulated time. I referred to Marchand. He was interested but did not commit himself; I believe he could be persuaded to do so if well handled.

We had a pleasant easy lunch. I did not bring up my own problems again.[68]

The next day, however, Gordon wrote to Pearson to express his dissatisfaction at the failure of their agreement. The letter ended:

. . . I feel I should ask you now, without further delays, to implement the various proposals and understandings you made to me last January or, alternatively, to explain to me why you are not prepared to do so.[69]

When the Prime Minister replied after three weeks' interval on May 16, he countered with the suggestion that "my major commitment to you" to chair a Cabinet committee supervising a study of foreign ownership had been discharged. Pearson wrote that Gordon would be provided with adequate specialized staffs if he would agree to supervise the Central Mortgage and Housing Corporation, the Company of Young Canadians, the War on Poverty, a new study on problems of urbanization, a special study on space satellite communication, and a study of the usefulness of "the Royal Commission technique of enquiry." These duties, "to say nothing of others that might develop," would together make Gordon's position "an important one . . . far from being merely 'honorific'." That may have been true, but the Prime Minister knew that Gordon did not want these duties. Pearson rapped Gordon on the knuckles for engaging in public controversy about Cabinet policy on a number of subjects, but passed silently by the points of understanding set out in the January exchange of letters.[70] "It was obvious," Gordon concluded, "that the undertakings made to me when I rejoined the government were not going to be implemented, either because Pearson had changed his mind about them or because his own position was not strong enough to force them through."[71]

*

Walter Gordon felt frustrated on many grounds. Ever since the party had come to power in 1963, he had been critical of the Cabinet convention which left the elaboration and conduct of foreign policy to the Prime Minister and the Secretary of State for External Affairs. In 1967, he was particularly dissatisfied with Canada's muted response to the American role in the Vietnam war.

> I felt that Canada should protest more vigorously than it had done about what was going on in Vietnam, and I had said so in my book *A Choice for Canada*. . . . Since writing it, I had become increasingly concerned about the devastation and the terrible cruelties inflicted on the inhabitants of that country who had been involved in almost continuous war for several generations. Moreover, as a member of the Canadian government, I felt an urge to express my own horror and revulsion about the escalation of the war. I did not agree with Paul Martin's statements on the subject which, while

sometimes hard to interpret, seemed on the whole to support the policy and actions of the United States.[72]

Early in April, Prime Minister Pearson had spoken cautiously in a speech at the University of California in Santa Barbara in favour of suspending the American bombing of North Vietnam.[73] Pearson had spoken again of Canada's "worries and anxieties" about the war in the House of Commons on May 10.[74] Gordon knew that he would make no impression by raising the matter in Cabinet, and his general dissatisfaction inclined him to a certain defiance of convention on this issue of morality. With the advice of a few friends, he prepared a speech on Vietnam for mid-May.[75] On May 10 he mentioned his intention to the Prime Minister.[76]

The speech was delivered in Toronto on May 13. To demonstrate that he was no eccentric anti-American, Gordon built his case on extended quotations from the speeches and writings of American opponents of the war, and he claimed no original insights. He endorsed the recommendations of Senator George McGovern for a suspension of the bombing, an end to American offensive military operations in the South, an American statement of willingness to negotiate directly with the Vietcong, and an internationally supervised cease-fire and withdrawal of foreign troops. These appeals amounted to much more than the Canadian government had ever called for in public; and Gordon concluded with a conspicuous nudge at his Cabinet colleagues:

> I hope Canadians in all walks of life and in all political parties – including especially Mr. Pearson and Mr. Martin – will continue to do everything in their power to press the Americans to stop the bombing. If we fail to do this, we must be prepared to share the responsibility of those whose policies and actions are destroying a poor but determined people. We must share the responsibility of those whose policies involve the gravest risks for all mankind.[77]

Walter Gordon felt deeply about the evil of the war and spoke for many Canadians in expressing those feelings.[78] But the issues he raised were broader than they seemed. There was Canada's official position on the war, which did not satisfy him; there was the question of how she should express that position, through quiet diplomacy or public declamation; and there was the question of Cabinet solidarity. Gordon had disturbed the complacency of Mike Pearson and Paul Martin on all three counts, and he was not prepared to show remorse. The press seized predictably on his initiative, and awaited some statement of clarification from the Prime Minister.[79]

A special meeting of the Cabinet was hastily summoned for May 17 to deal with Gordon's indiscretion.[80] The Prime Minister read a prepared statement to the meeting which declared that Canadian policy was to seek – through diplomatic channels – an end to the bombing, an end to North Vietnamese infiltration, and the commencement of peace negotiations.[81] It was "wrong and unnecessary" to concentrate criticism on the United States, or normally "to publicly condemn or publicly proclaim"; and when criticism or advice were offered, they were to be delivered or approved by the Prime Minister or the Minister of External Affairs. The statement was severely critical of Gordon by implication, and Gordon judged that Mike Pearson was "tired and angry" in delivering it.[82] But it did contain an explicit request to the United States, "as the strongest of the warring parties," to end the bombing and enter negotiations. Gordon told the Cabinet that he could accept the statement because of this sentence.[83]

A number of ministers spoke critically of Gordon, and none came to his defence (although Jean Marchand said he agreed with what Gordon had said).[84] Gordon responded that he had no apologies to make, and that he would not resign – although the Prime Minister could, of course, dismiss him if he wished.[85] From this stormy meeting the ministers moved to the Liberal caucus, where Pearson delivered an even sharper rebuke to Gordon; and afterwards the Prime Minister told the press that the President of the Privy Council had been "criticized and disciplined."[86] The weight of ministerial disapproval had focussed on the issue of Cabinet solidarity rather than the substance of policy; but Walter Gordon was sceptical of that kind of criticism in a Cabinet which could keep no secrets from the press and which was openly divided on foreign investment policy.[87] Pearson's remarks in caucus and to the press (where Gordon could not properly respond) were a special source of anger and dismay to Gordon.

The conflict evaporated almost immediately. At the Cabinet meeting on May 23 Gordon noticed that "the atmosphere was very different," and speculated that this change was due to the predominantly favourable public response to his speech.[88] There was some discussion of a Cabinet resolution on the war, but the matter was dropped. The point was made forcibly that there were few occasions for general policy discussion in Cabinet such as Gordon's speech had provoked, and as a direct result the Prime Minister wrote to ministers on May 26 setting aside forty-five minutes each Thursday for this purpose.[89] That was progress of a kind, as was an invitation from Paul Martin to Gordon a few days later to attend the NATO Council meeting in Luxembourg in June.

Above all, the speech contributed to a moderate stiffening of Canada's critical posture on the war. It may even have influenced Paul Martin, who took the initiative at the Luxembourg meeting to promote a special private session on Vietnam, and alone among the foreign ministers spoke critically of United States policy in the war.[90] Gordon was impressed.

> It was an excellent presentation and took courage. Dean Rusk replied somewhat superciliously and proceeded to slap Paul down. In doing so he made it clear that, when it comes to foreign policy, the United States sees things in blacks and whites; there is nothing between, certainly no place for grey. Britain was dependent on the United States for the preservation of the pound and was therefore officially supporting U.S. policy in Southeast Asia. So George Brown remained silent, which was quite an unusual achievement for him. No one else said anything.[91]

Gordon's Vietnam speech and its repercussions were insignificant moments in the diplomacy of a barbaric war; but as a testament of decency it had some importance for Canadians in 1967.

Walter Gordon had grown suitably philosophic about his role as President of the Privy Council. He had no duties except the supervision of the Watkins Task Force, and would remain in the Cabinet only long enough to see that commitment through. He looked forward to retirement in the autumn, and in the meantime enjoyed a few unharassed months in office, attending official receptions, fishing with Robert Winters (a friend despite their disagreements), holidaying for a week in Europe after the NATO meeting, and visiting the Soviet Union, all in the charmed midsummer months of Canada's Centennial year.

15   Last Days

Canada was nearing the end of a regime.

By the end of the summer of 1967, it seemed improbable that Pearson would be able to carry on as Prime Minister much longer. He was over seventy and, except perhaps in physical terms, had aged noticeably in the past four years. He was disillusioned by his inability to obtain an over-all majority, and seemed to have lost the interest he once had in policy issues and political strategy. He was no longer able to control the Cabinet. He had been pre-occupied during the summer with the Centennial celebrations, including innumerable banquets and conversations with visiting heads of state. While exhausting, he seemed to enjoy these formal occasions. But in the main he gave the impression that he was just going through the motions and doing his best to avoid trouble by putting things off and not facing up to anything of importance.[1]

And yet there were urgent problems demanding the application of all the Cabinet's intelligence and political skill. The greatest of these was Quebec. The euphoric illusion of wellbeing which the Centennial and Expo had given to English-speaking Canada in the first months of 1967 was sensationally disturbed by President de Gaulle when he spoke the words "Vive le Québec! Vive le Québec libre!" from the balcony of Montreal City Hall on July 25. The rapid growth of the independence movement in Quebec was both marked and assisted by this signal of recognition from Le Grand Charles. The Quebec government of Daniel Johnson (which had come to power in June, 1966) had maintained the autonomist momentum of the previous Lesage administration. While the Johnson government sought "equality or independence" from Ottawa and the English-speaking provinces, the Quebec Liberal party moved along the same path toward the ambiguous goal of "special" or "associate" status. In a policy paper prepared for the Quebec Liberal Federation by Paul Gérin-Lajoie and published in August, 1967, the distinction between special status for Quebec and outright autonomy grew indistinct. At Montmorency Falls, in August, a "thinkers' conference" of the federal Progressive Conservative party agreed that Canada was made up of "deux nations" or "two founding peoples" – for whatever that might imply. On September 18 René Lévesque made his unequivocal declaration in favour of Quebec's independence to his constituents in Montreal Laurier, and urged the Quebec Liberal party to follow him in that crusade. The response of Jean Lesage and Pierre Laporte was veiled; among provincial Liberal leaders in Quebec, only Eric Kierans clearly repudiated Lévesque's position.

Ottawa's attitude to the autonomist pressures from Quebec, which had been sympathetic and conciliatory in the early years of the Pearson regime when a Liberal government faced it across the bargaining table, had grown more complex in 1966 and 1967. The reconciliation of Quebec had been the Prime Minister's most prominent domestic objective after 1963. His great efforts had gone into creating the Royal Commission on Bilingualism and Biculturalism, educating English-speaking Canada in his own generosity toward Quebec and the message of the Commission, and adjusting the federal tax balance in the hope of giving Quebec the financial means to satisfy its expanding ambitions. But the Pearson government's openness to Quebec had not satisfied those ambitions; and it had never been contained within a coherent constitutional strategy. ("Cooperative federalism" had never been more than a slogan to illustrate Ottawa's desire for accommodation.) When Quebec's claims took more explicit form in 1966 and 1967 as demands for the transfer of additional constitutional powers to "the state of Quebec," Ottawa had no comprehensive response. There were signs of a hardening in the federal bargaining position on the allocation of tax resources after Mitchell Sharp came to the Ministry of Finance, but in constitutional diplomacy there was a vacuum.[2]

The Lévesque speech startled Walter Gordon and some of his colleagues. Gordon consulted with Marchand, Trudeau and Benson, and when the Cabinet met on September 21 he proposed that it should examine the Quebec situation in the light, especially, of that event. The

Prime Minister agreed to do so later in the day, but the agenda stretched out until 4:30 P.M., which left time for only a brief discussion.[3] Gordon and a number of ministers expressed their anxiety, and "after considerable pressing" the Prime Minister consented "to arrange a meeting of Cabinet for Sunday afternoon to go into the matter further."[4]

The next day Gordon wrote to Pearson about Quebec. He told the Prime Minister that "I have often thought, and have often said publicly, that your understanding of Quebec and your efforts to hold the country together has been the single most important contribution you have made during your period as Prime Minister."[5] But now he feared "that if all this effort is not to be lost, a new and more positive stance will be called for." Gordon reviewed recent events in Quebec, and warned that unless there was a demonstration of fresh federal leadership, the English-speaking reaction might soon cease to be "quiet and moderate."

> It seems to me that in view of this confused situation and the vacuum that seems to exist at present, the federal government should be prepared to step into the breach and give a lead. Obviously the main burden would have to fall on Jean Marchand and the Quebec ministers, but they should know where they stand and that the rest of us are prepared to back them.[6]

Gordon mentioned a number of positive steps which should be considered by the Cabinet: first, the preparation of "a short memorandum written for a wide public audience indicating what could be the result for people in Quebec if Lévesque's separatist ideas were implemented" (Gordon could not foresee a calm and peaceful outcome); second, action to prevent the use of the CBC French network "to promote the separatists' cause"; and third, a possible referendum on Quebec's independence.

> Certainly this would be a dramatic way for the federal government to bring things to a head. While I would not advocate this course without being reasonably sure that the results would show an overwhelming majority of people in Quebec favoured the continuance of Confederation, it would not be too difficult to ascertain this fairly quickly. The federal ministers in Quebec could then engage in a battle they were reasonably sure of winning. Having done so, their standing and authority would be immeasurably improved.[7]

Gordon hoped that the Cabinet could meet on the weekend to adopt a position "so that everyone will speak with one voice when the House meets on Monday." But he recognized that the Prime Minister might be too busy to arrange it, and proposed as an alternative that Jean Marchand should chair a special meeting "to pull things together for your consideration."[8]

The Liberal caucus met the next morning in its regular pre-session assembly, and beforehand Pearson spoke to Gordon about his letter. He doubted that he could bring ministers together over the weekend, but "seemed to agree with me about the seriousness of the matter."[9]

> Later in his speech to the caucus he referred to the situation in Quebec, to the reaction in the rest of Canada and said it was the most serious situation to face us in the one hundred years of our existence. He raised the question of the possibility of our continued existence as a state.[10]

And he left caucus with the impression that he would stay on as Prime Minister to fight for the unity of Canada.

The confusion and disorganization of the Cabinet's work, which Walter Gordon now put down primarily to the Prime Minister's fatigue, had troubled Gordon since 1963. Now the deepening symptoms of "the dangerous situation in Quebec" gave new urgency to the need for Cabinet reorganization. What Gordon sought (as he had before) was somehow to inject force and direction into the Cabinet system in default of the Prime Minister's leadership. On October 3, 1967 he drafted a ten page memorandum for Mike Pearson on "The Position of the Government at the Present Time," and the next day he discussed it at length over lunch with the Prime Minister.[11]

"Canadians are deeply troubled," the paper began, "about the possible break-up of the country and are looking for strong leadership. This comes at a time when the government gives the impression of being weak and uncertain."[12] There were several sources of this impression: the government's minority position, the apparent rejuvenation of the Tory party under its new leader Robert Stanfield, the uncomfortable economic situation and the government's inability to deal with it,[13] the "deadening and unimaginative" domination of the Cabinet by its "more conservative elements," the frictions and suspicions arising from the "unofficial leadership race," the publicly demonstrated lack of Cabinet unity, and the resulting collapse of morale in the party caucus.

Gordon pointed above all to one basic difficulty:

By far the most important cause of the frustrations that exist at present is the confusion about areas of responsibility and authority and the way in which the time of busy ministers is wasted. The work of the Cabinet and Cabinet committees needs to be completely overhauled and the responsibilities of ministers more clearly defined.

Present frustrations and confusions are accentuated by overlapping authority and by reversals of and retreats from firmly agreed policy positions. The Prime Minister is the ablest member of the Cabinet, but his tendency to take on far more himself than any one man can handle is not an answer to the problem.[14]

Gordon believed that the party's confusion and depressed morale could bring defeat in the House of Commons "if we are not very careful." But he warned that "the Quebec situation and the constitutional issue" should be resolved before a federal election which would be likely to stimulate "all kinds of passions . . . and damaging statements." He therefore made a series of proposals to the Prime Minister. Lester Pearson should end the leadership race by announcing his firm intention to remain in office for at least one more year.

He should say that he plans to devote almost his whole attention and effort to helping Marchand with the Quebec situation and in negotiating new constitutional arrangements with the provinces. This should take precedence over everything else in an attempt to reach an agreement by next summer.[15]

In addition, "the work of the Cabinet should be reorganized in a way that will not flout all the elementary principles of organization":

There should be some division, or differentiation, according to rank and authority, and greater regularity in the way policies are developed and approved. In particular:

(a)   One senior Minister should be made responsible for organizing the work of the Cabinet, including a careful review of all proposals before they are presented. He should be chairman of the proposed Policy Committee (see below).

(b)   The present Cabinet committee system is time wasting and should be reduced to the following:

– A new Policy Committee (which, in effect, might become a sort of Inner Cabinet);

– A committee on the Quebec situation under Marchand;

– Treasury Board;

– Special Committee of Council to deal with routine matters;

– Legislation Committee – which should assume full and final responsibility for all Bills;

– ad hoc committees established from time to time to study particular problems.

(c)   Many of the matters now brought before Cabinet should be settled by the ministers themselves (in some cases, if they so wished, after consultation with the chairman of the Policy Committee) or by Treasury Board.

(d)   Three Deputy Prime Ministers should be designated in order to give them the necessary authority and standing. These should include Paul Martin, Jean Marchand and the chairman of the Policy Committee.

(e)   The Policy Committee which, in addition to the chairman and the Prime Minister, should include the Secretary of State for External Affairs, the leader of the Quebec caucus, the Minister of Finance, the president of the Treasury Board, the Minister of Justice and the House leader, should meet daily for an hour or an hour and a half – say, from 9:30 A.M. to 11 A.M. This Committee should deal with all questions involving policy.

If the principal ministers met together for a short time each day, they should soon begin to present a more united front to the House and to the public.

(f)   The full Cabinet should meet once a week only (say, at 11 A.M. on Tuesdays) and should devote most of its time to political matters rather than administration.

(g)   Concurrently with the other proposals, some important changes should be made in the composition of the Cabinet.[16]

In matters of policy, Gordon called for a number of early initiatives to draw attention away from the faltering economic situation. He suggested legislation on divorce, birth control, abortion, and capital punishment; foreign investment (including the Canadian Development Corporation and the forthcoming white paper); broadcasting; and the limitation of election expenses. He said that action was "vitally important" on Quebec and the constitution, housing policy ("Some Minister, preferably someone who knows something about the subject, should be placed in full charge with instructions to come up with a policy that will produce 200,000 starts in 1968 at substantially below present cost levels"), the reduction of interest rates, and . . . of government spending "so that next year's budget will be defensible."

Gordon concluded that "without a drastic reorganization along the lines suggested we are not likely to succeed in anything. It would be a case of waiting for the axe to fall which would not be a pleasant prospect."

Gordon's discussion with the Prime Minister the next day was genial but inconclusive. Pearson "could find no fault" with the memorandum, and agreed that if he stayed in office he would have to carry out the kind of reorganization that it proposed. But he told Gordon again that he wanted to retire, and would need a few days to consider Gordon's proposals.[17] Three weeks later, on October 23, Gordon raised the subject again, and the Prime Minister said "that he expected to make up his mind very soon, but left me with the clear impression that he intends to leave sooner rather than later and that he will probably announce this in early January."[18] Pearson felt he could not undertake the proposed reorganization if he planned to retire within a few months.[19] Gordon wrote later that "I interpreted this to mean that he was not up to the reorganization job and that he should be encouraged to say when he was proposing to retire."[20] The obvious alternative to Gordon's tentative plan of action was for a new leader of the party to fill the vacuum of authority as quickly as possible.

Meanwhile the urgency of the Quebec crisis seemed to ease somewhat, as the Quebec Liberal party rejected René Lévesque's separatism and put aside the Gérin-Lajoie paper, and as Daniel Johnson made his commitment to a renovated federal system. The Pearson government awaited with anxiety and scepticism the interprovincial "Confederation for Tomorrow" conference called by Premier John Robarts of Ontario for the end of November, and at last made clear that the next federal-provincial conference in February, 1968 would be broadened into the first of a series of constitutional reform. Walter Gordon's and Jean Marchand's inclination to support some kind of quick and decisive confrontation with Quebec nationalism (probably in the form of a referendum) was ignored by the Prime Minister in favour of less hurried diplomacy.[21]

*

At the request of Mitchell Sharp, the Cabinet turned in October and November to another subject of gloom and disagreement, the financial and economic situation. Walter Gordon had taken pride in his record as Minister of Finance in bringing government spending under control and reducing the annual deficit to a position of near-balance in 1965 and 1966. (Among other things, he had opposed separating the Treasury Board and its responsibility for the management of spending from the jurisdiction of the Minister of Finance, as the Glassco Commission on Government Organization had recommended. But after his resignation in 1965, the Treasury Board had been divided from Finance.) Mitchell Sharp's first budget, for the fiscal year 1966 – 1967, forecast a deficit of $150 million in spite of a major tax increase; and the actual deficit for the year was $428 million. In his budget speech for 1967 – 1968, Mr. Sharp forecast a moderate decline in the rate of economic growth, modest price inflation, and a budget deficit of $740 million. By the autumn he was warning the public about the drastic need for measures to control inflation and the budgetary deficit, and to offset the weakness of the Canadian dollar.

There was no disagreement in Cabinet in the fall of 1967 about the need to bring the government's finances under control. Everyone knew that the financial community was losing confidence and that it was becoming increasingly difficult for the government to sell its bonds. We were fully aware, also, that the Canadian dollar was under pressure. Some of us believed, however, that the lack of confidence in the government's fiscal measures was being aggravated by the kind of speeches Sharp was making, not to mention the very large deficit that had been forecast in the June budget. Quite apart from this there were differences of opinion respecting the nature and the timing of the corrective measures to be taken.[22]

Mitchell Sharp let it be known that he favoured a supplementary tax-raising budget before the end of the year, and the postponement of medicare beyond its scheduled starting date of July 1, 1968.[23] For his part, Walter Gordon told the Cabinet on October 24 that he believed the crisis was essentially political rather than financial and economic.[24] Economic prospects were in fact quite encouraging; but members of the government were themselves responsible for creating the fear of inflation and the mood of economic insecurity. The crisis was a crisis of confidence in the government, the result of the party's defeatism, its confusion on medicare, foreign investment, the Carter Report, and government spending, and uncertainty about the future leadership of the party. He recommended a series of measures aimed as much at the public mood as at the federal budget deficit: an immediate statement of reassurance that the complicated tax proposals of the Carter Report would not be adopted, but that taxes on the oil, mining and life insurance industries would be increased from January 1, 1968; a pledge to introduce the 1968 budget by February 1 (and a private Cabinet commitment to produce a balanced budget without increases in personal taxes); immediate action to reduce interest rates; the adoption of a floating exchange rate; a new housing policy; and the passage of legislation on the Canada Development Corporation and foreign investment policy.[25] Gordon also made indirect reference to the possibility of deferring a leadership convention for a year, and in the meantime agreeing that Mr. Pearson should pass the leadership of the government to a caretaker Prime Minister.

After a series of Cabinet meetings on the financial situation, Gordon wrote to the Prime Minister on November 7 to reiterate his case for a balanced budget in 1968 – 1969, and to make further suggestions for eliminating the estimated deficit (which now stood at $635 million).[26] Once again he opposed any increase in personal taxes and the proposal for an interim budget early in 1968. He knew that Edgar Benson shared these views.[27] Gordon repeated them in outline to Cabinet on November 9. [28] Nevertheless, during the month Mitchell Sharp gained the Cabinet's reluctant approval for a five percent surcharge on personal income taxes, to be introduced in a mini-budget on November 30.[29]

Walter Gordon had less and less doubt that the real problem of the government was Lester Pearson's failure of leadership. He knew, too, that the Prime Minister recognized the failure, but hesitated to make the final and irrevocable decision to retire. Once it was obvious that Mike Pearson could not face any major effort of reorganization, Gordon was ready to press the Prime Minister to make that decision. On November 8 Anthony Westell commemorated the second anniversary of the 1965 election with a devastating essay in the *Globe and Mail* on the disintegration of the government's morale, which tied its collapse not only to external circumstances but also to the likelihood of another year of Mr. Pearson's leadership.[30] "The Liberals are looking forward with dismay," Westell wrote, "to a further long period of uncertainty. Some have even conveyed to Mr. Pearson their feeling that he must remove the doubt by making known his intentions one way or the other, although they don't seem to know just what they themselves want him to do." Walter Gordon took Westell's article as his text in a conversation with Pearson the same day.

I had a straight talk with Mike in his office after the Orders of the Day. He was flushed, tired and unhappy. I said I had not felt like telling him at lunch on Sat. what was in my mind but wished to cover the following points:

(a) I said the Westell article in the *G & M* this morning is a fair reflection of the situation in my opinion – and the views expressed by members. Mike agreed.

(b) I said that six weeks ago I had given him a memo suggesting he stay on to try to resolve the constitutional issue – but it assumed a major reorganization of the govt. Mike admitted he is not up to this.

(c) In that event I urged him to get out as quickly as possible. He said he might do so immediately after he gets back from Europe about Dec. 6th. He doesn't want to before he goes. In fact he doesn't want to do so at all and mentioned he is hearing from Liberals all over Canada urging him to stay. He claims he is not impressed by these voices but. . . .

(d) He is worried about the period between an announcement of his intention to retire and the holding of a convention. I said there was an alternative he should consider and outlined the suggestion that Martin should take over for ten months or so – and the possible advantages in terms of the party. . . . Mike became quite intrigued (as he is with all new ideas). I suggested he think it over while he is in Europe – and if he thinks the idea has merit to act on it as soon as he gets back.

(e) I said if Mike did decide to turn things over to Paul M. for a short period that before doing so he should confer with a few of his Cabinet colleagues (who are not in the leadership race) and if they agreed to have them sit in on any discussion with Paul M.

(f) I told him I will be away for the next five weeks or so having an operation on my neck. I said my intention is to stay until I get the white paper before the Cabinet. If Cabinet rejects it I would resign – but I said it was my intention to leave the Cabinet very soon in any event. (Little comment from Mike except that he thought Cabinet should be able to deal with the matter before Xmas! He is thinking primarily if not entirely of his own situation and not really about anything else.)

(g) I referred very briefly to my letter to him about Sharp's proposals and said I doubted if I would lead much of a fight at tomorrow's Cabinet. I did say however that I had little confidence in Sharp.[31]

Gordon's pessimism about the state of the party was strengthened by separate discussions in the next few days with Benson, Pennell, Trudeau, Marchand, James Walker, Beland Honderich, Andrew Thompson, and John Nichol.[32] They all believed that the Prime Minister should announce his intention to retire.

Following a federal-provincial conference of Finance ministers on November 16 and 17 at which medicare was a prominent subject of discussion, Gordon received a message notifying him of an emergency

Cabinet meeting on Monday morning, November 20.[33] Mitchell Sharp was again reported publicly as opposing medicare, and on November 19 Benson told Gordon that "Sharp is against medicare and that it will be dead forever if deferred now."[34]

Gordon said to Cabinet the next day that he believed the collective decision on medicare must be respected and not undermined. He spoke once more against a mini-budget and tax increases, and in favour of an early and balanced budget in 1968. He ventured frankly onto the delicate ground of the Prime Minister's intentions, and hoped that Mr. Pearson would give the Cabinet a clear decision on his return from Europe in December.[35] The Prime Minister did not like this personal reference, and replied wryly that "it was certainly not something that could have been said in other governments under other Prime Ministers!"[36] Gordon noted that "he implied he would have hoped the matter I raised (about him) would not have been raised in Cabinet. I pointed out I had previously tried another approach." But Pearson did say that he would inform the Cabinet of his intentions on his return from Europe. The Minister of Finance's mini-budget was confirmed, but medicare was left intact.

Gordon returned to Toronto that day to enter hospital for the operation on the vertebrae of his neck, which would keep him away from Ottawa until after Christmas. Mike Pearson's generosity was not soured by the painful encounter in Cabinet that morning.

> Mike telephoned me this evening 5:45 P.M. (he thought I was still in Ottawa) to wish me luck with the operation. It was very nice of him in view of his annoyance at Cabinet. We joked & I wished him well in England. I suspect we both felt better. It was a nice gesture.[37]

In the aftermath of a successful but debilitating operation, Gordon reflected again on his frustrating year in Cabinet, and on the government's recent adoption of a financial policy which he heartily disapproved. On December 5 he drafted, but did not send, a letter of immediate resignation to Mike Pearson.[38] The report of the Watkins Task Force was now close to completion, and Gordon resigned himself to a few more weeks as a member of the government, until he could see the report through Cabinet.

On the morning of Thursday, December 14 Mike Pearson telephoned Gordon in Toronto to tell him that he would announce his intention to retire that day.

> I said I was sorry but felt he was making the right decision. I

added that I had not enjoyed the last few months. He said he hadn't either.[39]

Mr. Pearson informed the press of his choice the same afternoon. The great uncertainty was resolved. The Prime Minister had one final duty to perform, and he could do so in the disinterested role of retiring statesman. In February, he would preside over the first federal-provincial conference of constitutional review, and thus complete five years of constitutional diplomacy with a final act of reconciliation. But now the contest for the succession took centre stage.

On December 18 Pearson called Gordon to apologize for being unable to visit him in convalescence.

> We chatted pleasantly but rather coolly about the leadership candidates and about the months ahead. He said:
>
> (a)   Paul Martin can't make up his mind. I said we both knew he had been running for months – and might win if Marchand doesn't stand.
>
> (b)   He would favour a French Canadian (Marchand or Trudeau) especially at this time and having in mind the alternating principle. I said he had given Marchand the impression he favoured someone else. He said he had not meant to and would speak to Marchand tomorrow. . . .
>
> (c)   He was bothered by the next few months. I said the candidates would have to state their positions on policy otherwise it would be a farce.
>
> (d)   He said he would be away for the first week in Jan.; that the session would resume on Jan. 22nd; and that he thought the best plan would be to continue it – there are lots of items on the order paper – until the end of March and then adjourn.
> Note   One item on the order paper is the CDC. I should push hard for this as soon as Watkins report is in. . . . [40]

Walter Gordon's position in the progressive wing of the party meant that he had a natural (although peripheral) role in discussion about the succession. His interest centred on Jean Marchand, and in telephone conversations with Marchand, Lamontagne and Trudeau before Christmas he expressed his belief that Marchand should stand, and that he would announce his candidacy soon.[41] Gordon knew Marchand as a personal friend, but was not closely in touch with the sentiments of the Quebec wing of the Liberal party. Marchand was uncertain of himself, and Trudeau was reserved because (in Gordon's words) "Marchand has not had time to learn the ropes."[42] This reservation reflected doubts in the Quebec caucus about whether Marchand had the temperament, good health, or command of English appropriate to a Prime Minister.[43]

Late in the month Marchand spoke to Gordon again.

> He said he had not called before because he had not made up his mind about the leadership. He said his wife was much opposed and while this was not the only factor he had serious reservations about contesting it.
>
> He said the Quebecers seem to think some French Canadian should be a candidate and that Trudeau's (political) standing had improved & they might get behind him.
>
> He said he was going to Florida and would be thinking things over. He will get in touch with me as soon as he gets back – about Jan. 13th.
>
> My impression is that Marchand will not be a candidate. The longer he leaves it the more difficult it will be. People are getting committed.[44]

By early February Gordon was still not certain of Marchand's decision. In the meantime Pierre Trudeau's prospects had boomed as a result of the systematic activities of his advocates in the party and his impressive role alongside the Prime Minister at the constitutional conference.[45] From time to time Gordon kept in touch with Trudeau and his supporters, and on February 13, before he had announced his candidacy, Gordon spoke to him at length.[46] Gordon was concerned to judge Trudeau's views on foreign and defence policy, exchange policy, the foreign control issue and continentalism, election campaign funds, and the political situation in English-speaking Canada. If Trudeau decided to seek the leadership, Gordon urged him to concentrate on building his campaign organization and "clear policy statements of his position on the main issues." Gordon was not greatly reassured by Trudeau's responses, and wrote afterwards that "In effect I advised him not to run."[47]

*

On January 18, 1968 the Cabinet again reopened the unending debate on medicare. Some ministers argued that the scheme should be deferred because their constituents opposed it; others (including Mitchell Sharp) because it would be an additional charge on overloaded federal and provincial budgets; and others because the provinces would be jealously defending their constitutional authority over health at the forthcoming constitutional conference. Walter Gordon's response to all these claims was impatient: the policy had been adopted after due consideration, it was embodied in the law, and it should not be tampered with. To make a further retreat "would make everyone look ridiculous."[48] It was a familiar complaint. But the issue lingered on the agenda because it was one possible factor in the Cabinet's approach to the insecure financial and economic situation.

Toward the end of January international pressure on the Canadian dollar increased dangerously, in the wake of the devaluation of the pound and new American measures to bring the U.S. balance of payments under control. The Bank of Canada raised the bank rate from six percent to seven percent on January 21 in an effort to check the movement of short-term capital out of the country, and the Minister of Finance told the House that the government was determined to maintain the value of the Canadian dollar in the exchange market.[49] Walter Gordon was briefed on Ottawa's anxieties by Edgar Benson on January 26.

> Benson called me from Ottawa about 6:30 P.M. He said Mike had asked him to go out to Sussex ... to see him about the financial picture, that Sharp and Rasminsky had been to see Mike before that, and that everyone including Mike seemed to have the jitters.
>
> Mike was worried both by the financial situation and the exchange rate and about what he should say about medicare. He told Benson he had made a mistake about the latter subject.
>
> Mike was thoroughly upset – wondered if he should resign now and put Martin in – or whether he should defer or call off the leadership contest.
>
> Benson said Mike was thinking of calling me, Sharp and Benson in to discuss the situation (on grounds we are the only three who understand it).
>
> I said Rasminsky always gets the jitters and that this time we should let the exchange rate find its own level. I suggested that Ben call Mike back and urge him to have the meeting referred to above – but I bet he won't!
>
> Sharp's policies have been all wrong. I wonder if the chickens will come home to roost before April 4th?[50]

By the end of the month the immediate pressures on the dollar had eased in response to the actions of the Bank of Canada and the Minister; but the situation remained delicate. Mitchell Sharp reviewed it with the Cabinet on January 30, and the next day Gordon discussed the subject with the Prime Minister over lunch.

I said my main reason for wishing to speak to Mike was in connection with the exchange situation; that I thought Sharp had taken a great chance in speaking so openly at Cabinet on Tuesday (in view of leaks); and that we should know what action the govt. was going to take if there should be a crisis (as there well might be).

I said I felt there should be a prior discussion about the pros & cons of devaluation under IMF auspices & control vis-a-vis a floating rate. I reminded Mike of the 1962 situation when Rasminsky put it over him and said I could not accept a repetition of the same thing again.

Mike suggested a discussion some evening next week after the Constitutional Conference. We agreed that Sharp and Benson and I were the only Cabinet members who understood the situation. Also Rasminsky, Bryce and Arthur Smith (who has said publicly he favours a floating rate). . . .

Mike said he couldn't believe it made sense for twelve to fifteen central bankers to be able to tell govts. what to do. I agreed. He said however that Sharp would go along with Rasminsky. And I added that rather than face up to this Mike would go along with them. He agreed. I said in this case it would be preferable to have those who felt differently to resign before the crisis (if there is one) instead of during it. Mike agreed.

This should be interesting if it means that I (and Benson?) resign for no apparent reason *before* a possible crisis – but I want to get out anyway so what the hell. . . .

Mike is thinking only of getting out; of how to get the session over; and how to avoid trouble. . . . [51]

A few days later Walter Gordon was surprised to discover that the Prime Minister had held the private meeting he had proposed on the exchange situation on Sunday, February 4 without Gordon's knowledge. The subject was one that had concerned him from well before the day he took office as Minister of Finance in 1963, and he would not be ignored. He wrote to Pearson on February 8.

In the present disturbed conditions many people believe, and I am one of them, that Canada may well be faced with an exchange crisis within the next several months, perhaps within the next several weeks. I believe we should consider this well in advance so that we shall not be faced with taking a decision in a hurry at the time of a possible crisis.

I find it inconceivable that any member of the Cabinet who has raised this matter with you and who has views on the subject should be excluded from such consideration and discussion. It may well be that you do not, or would not, agree with me as to what should be done in such emergency. It may well be that Mr. Sharp and Mr. Rasminsky would not agree with me either. Nevertheless, I think it only reasonable to request an opportunity to express my opinions on what is obviously a matter of very considerable national importance.[52]

The Prime Minister telephoned Gordon on February 9 to say that "the meeting last Sunday was not the one we had been speaking about, . . . and that there had been no discussion of the alternatives to be considered in connection with the exchange rate."[53] That meeting, he told Gordon, would still have to take place. But Gordon had already learned that the Sunday meeting had indeed included "a long discussion about the exchange situation and the possibility that we would have to devalue. . . . There was a discussion about the alternatives of another pegged rate or adopting a floating rate."[54] Louis Rasminsky had apparently argued against floating the dollar on the ground that the United States would retaliate by cancelling Canadian exemptions under the interest equalization tax, which would deprive Canada of a large part of the annual capital inflow it needed to balance its current account deficit. Walter Gordon disputed this claim, but could only record his dissent in his own papers.[55]

Mitchell Sharp's unpopular finance Bill imposing a surtax on personal incomes had been one of the factors undermining the morale of the government. It had been disputed in Cabinet; it was widely disliked in caucus; and the Opposition suspected the existence of and shared Liberal distaste for the measure.[56] There was heavy absenteeism on the government benches when the Bill received second reading by a vote of 84 to 73 on February 6. Walter Gordon was in the House late on the afternoon of February 19 at the close of committee stage on the Bill.

I arrived in a half empty House at about 5:30 P.M. on Monday, February 19, to find the Bill was in committee. Someone ran over to ask me if I would speak in order to keep things going until the 6:00 P.M. adjournment, as we did not want to risk a vote. I agreed to this immediately, provided it would be satisfactory to Sharp if

I spoke about the financial and economic situation in general terms. I was not anxious to speak in favour of the proposed increase in personal income taxes, which I had opposed so strenuously in Cabinet. Sharp sent me a message that this would be quite in order and I made some notes for my speech. But I was not called upon to deliver it. Instead, to my surprise, at about 5:45 P.M. word was passed around that we had a comfortable majority and it had been decided to let the Bill go to a vote, which the Liberals won by only 65 to 62. It was a near thing, and a grave risk to have taken. But at 6:00 P.M. we adjourned assuming the danger was over until the Bill came up for third reading later in the week.

I was sitting in the parliamentary restaurant having dinner when the bells began to ring at about ten minutes after eight. This was perplexing, and I proceeded to the Chamber with other members to find out what was going on. We discovered that at 8.00 P.M., when the House was called to order, Sharp and Bernard Pilon, the government whip, had decided, against the advice and instructions of the House leader, Allan MacEachen, that it was safe to consent to having third reading of the contentious Bill called immediately. It was a fateful decision. The bells rang for well over an hour while the Opposition rounded up all the members they could find. Finally the vote was called, and the government was defeated 84 to 82. Later it turned out that two Liberal members, who were in Ottawa, refused to come to the House to vote, as they were opposed to the proposed tax increase.[57]

Because the Prime Minister was on holiday in Jamaica and Paul Martin was absent campaigning for the party leadership, Robert Winters was Acting Prime Minister. After the adjournment at 10 P.M. the Cabinet gathered in his office to consider its position. "No one displayed much leadership or initiative at the meeting," Gordon observed; but the Prime Minister was telephoned in Jamaica and agreed to return to Ottawa at once.[58] Another confused Cabinet meeting the next morning before his return ended with the understanding that "only the Prime Minister could decide what should be done."[59]

Members of the Cabinet were divided in their judgment of the defeat and their interpretation of its consequences. Since it had occurred over a major finance Bill, the vote could not be lightly passed over. The government (at least momentarily) had lost the confidence of the House; could it properly carry on in office without a dissolution of Parliament? If it chose to carry on and regained the House's majority support in another vote, what would be the status of the measures contained in the defeated Bill? What responsibility should the Minister of Finance bear for the government's defeat? (The situation was complicated by Lester Pearson's imminent retirement and the forthcoming leadership convention of the Liberal party from April 4 to 6.)

Mr. Pearson returned at midday, and met "most of the Cabinet" at 1:15 P.M. It was agreed almost immediately that the government should not resign or seek a dissolution, but instead should ask for a renewed vote of confidence. For a few days, the Cabinet would have to play for time – first, to draft a resolution commanding some minority party support; second, to allow the normal forty-eight hours' notice for a parliamentary resolution; and finally, to permit consideration of how to rescue the government's financial program once confidence had been restored. For three days the Cabinet avoided parliamentary embarrassments by moving the adjournment of the House at the opening of each session.[60] On the evening of February 20 the Prime Minister indicated his determination to fight in a belligerent television address to the nation in which he accused the Opposition of "trickery" in Monday's defeat.[61] And behind the scenes the Cabinet struggled over the substance of a confidence resolution and a new finance Bill.

At the Cabinet meeting subsequent to Monday night's defeat, there was at first insistence that the vote of confidence should include clauses which would, in effect, reinstate the Income Tax Bill. Pennell and I, in particular, urged that this was the wrong course to take; that we could not expect the Opposition parties to accept such a resolution which they would interpret as arrogance on our part; and that if we wanted to break the deadlock we would have to provide a means for at least a few of the Opposition members to save face. Our view was not accepted and on Tuesday afternoon Messrs. MacEachen, Trudeau and Pennell were asked to draft the resolution and see that it got on the order paper by six o'clock. This they failed to do.

They came back to Cabinet on Wednesday with a revised resolution which, while it did not go nearly as far, nevertheless tied in Bill 193 with the motion of confidence. Again some of us urged that this would make it very difficult for the Opposition and it was agreed that some modification of the language would be expected but that there would still be a reference to Bill 193.

This turned out to be a mistake as Opposition parties, when they saw the resolution, concluded that the government was trying to slip over a fast one. Subsequently it became obvious that if we were to get the backing of the Creditistes it would be necessary for the government to state categorically that Bill 193 was dead. In particular, it was agreed that the five percent personal surtax could not be introduced. At caucus on Friday morning, it became clear that it would also be necessary for the government to make it clear that those who have paid the five percent surtax since the first of January, or who have had it deducted from their wages, would be reimbursed.

In his speech this morning, the Prime Minister phrased it somewhat differently, but he did make it clear that Bill 193 would not be reintroduced and that those who had paid taxes under it "would not suffer."

Prior to the opening of the debate this morning, it seemed clear that (a) the public does not want an election; that the Creditistes group will not vote against the government; and that therefore we will win the vote of confidence.[62]

Debate on the government's confidence resolution[63] extended over four sitting days, and on February 28 the Cabinet was sustained, with Creditiste support, by a vote of 138 to 119.

For a few more days the Cabinet continued its acrimonious discussion of the finance Bill. Mitchell Sharp's influence in Cabinet had been shaken by the parliamentary fiasco, and in the end a new, compromise Bill was produced which included provision for a three percent surtax on personal and corporate incomes, a speed-up in corporation tax collections, further cuts in government spending, a freeze on civil service appointments, and the creation of a prices and wages review board.[64]

After more procedural setbacks, the revised Bill (described by the Conservative financial critic R. A. Bell as "the crumbling cornerstone of the government's tottering budgetary edifice")[65] was adopted by the House in March, 1968.[66] Walter Gordon reflected that the government's credibility had been destroyed in the parliamentary crisis, that its constitutional position was dubious, and that "if Robert Stanfield ... had felt more sure of his position, he could have forced a dissolution."[67]

*

The exchange position of the Canadian dollar remained precarious, and the crisis over the finance Bill did nothing to strengthen international confidence. On February 27 Mitchell Sharp again reviewed the record with Cabinet. (Gordon told the Prime Minister afterwards, as he had before, that he thought this kind of discussion in Cabinet "very dangerous" because of the likelihood of leaks to the press. Mike Pearson concurred.)[68] Later that day Gordon wrote to Pearson to repeat his request of the previous month that those concerned about the subject "should have an opportunity of laying our views before you. . . .[69] It would be inexcusable," Gordon suggested, "to allow ourselves to be suddenly confronted with an exchange crisis and then try to decide what should be done in a crisis atmosphere." Gordon listed the alternatives that had already been canvassed:

(a) We could appeal to the International Monetary Fund for help;
(b) We could ask the United States government to guarantee the present fixed rate of exchange;
(c) We could adopt a floating rate.[70]

Gordon opposed an appeal to the IMF because he believed that the Canadian economy was basically strong and did not require the medicine likely to be prescribed as the price of IMF support.[71] He opposed an appeal for American support "for more or less similar reasons."

The U.S. might refuse to do this and refer us to the IMF. If they acceded to our request they might insist on conditions we might not like. But quite apart from that, such a move would be another clear indication of our subservience or dependence on the U.S.A. I do not consider this to be either necessary or desirable.[72]

He was reassured that neither the Prime Minister nor the Minister of Finance favoured this alternative, although Paul Martin and Edgar Benson apparently did. In Gordon's view, "we should let nature take its course and say nothing to the IMF, the Federal Reserve Board, the U.S. Treasury, or anyone else": the dollar should be allowed to float within a wide range, "perhaps down as far as eighty-five cents U.S."[73]

On March 4 the Prime Minister accommodated Walter Gordon with a meeting to consider the alternatives if Canada were forced off the existing rate of exchange.[74] The dominant opinion was against floating and in favour of a fixed rate supported by the IMF. Gordon felt by the end of the evening, however, "that some of the dogmatism expressed at the beginning had weakened a little." But not much. The government's exchange rate policy was worked out in tandem with the new finance Bill, and taken together they made up a conventional package intended to attract international support for the dollar. After private consultations in Washington with the U.S. secretary of the Treasury, Henry Fowler, and an exchange of letters, the Minister of

Finance reasserted the government's intention to maintain the exchange value of the dollar, and announced agreements with the United States to assist Canada in its efforts.[75] In return for a full exemption from the recent American balance of payments measures affecting capital flows, the Canadian government undertook to invest its entire holdings of U.S. dollars in U.S. government securities constituting no liquid claim on the United States. While Mitchell Sharp told Henry Fowler that these agreements were evidence of "the close and mutually beneficial relationships between us," Walter Gordon commented that the "two letters will of course look like a deal": and so they were, negotiated on Canada's side under the duress of the American balance of payments measures.[76]

*

The Watkins Task Force *Report on the Structure of Canadian Industry* had meanwhile been completed and presented to the ministerial committee under Gordon's chairmanship in mid-January. Gordon had previously hoped that the *Report* would be endorsed by Cabinet, transformed into a white paper, and used as the basis for legislation across the whole range of foreign investment policy. He now recognized that the last hope was unrealistic, in view of the Cabinet's confusion and drift. But he had what he thought was an excellent *Report* sustaining his own position on the foreign investment issue, and expected, at worst, that the Cabinet would give it general endorsement and refer it to a House committee for debate. When the *Report* was discussed in Cabinet at the end of January, however, it became clear that the leadership contest and the financial crisis had reduced the government to complete immobility on the issue.[77] Robert Winters opposed publication of the *Report* because it might disturb the financial market; Mitchell Sharp held that the *Report* "was only the expression of the personal views of a group of professors and had no bearing on government policy."[78] The Prime Minister was tolerant but apathetic – and sensitive to the caution of the leadership candidates. Gordon was fortunate to gain Cabinet approval for publication of the document, without any public indication of the government's response to it. The Prime Minister insisted that the Minister's statement on tabling the *Report* should be approved by both the ministerial committee and the Cabinet before delivery.[79] (This review involved a number of niggling revisions to the statement just before its presentation to the House.) For the guidance of ministers, the Prime Minister distributed a statement indicating how to avoid any commitment on the substance of the *Report*.[80]

On February 15 Walter Gordon tabled the four hundred page *Report* in the House of Commons with a brief statement indicating that it was "an expression of the views of the members of the Task Force and not those of the government." The *Report* was to be referred to the House Committee on Finance, Trade and Economic Affairs.[81] For Gordon this was an ironic occasion.

> I had remained in the Cabinet in the hope that I could persuade the government to commit itself to the recommendations of the eight economists who comprised the Task Force. I had not succeeded. My only consolation was the knowledge that if I had not stayed on it would have been most unlikely that this important report and its very useful proposals would ever have been made public.[82]

Gordon wrote to the Prime Minister on February 19 to submit his resignation from the Cabinet, "to take effect as soon as may be convenient to you, but in any event, I would hope within the next two or three weeks."[83] The parliamentary crisis erupted the same evening, and Gordon told Pearson two days later that he did not wish to embarrass the government by insisting on his immediate departure.[84] On March 4 the two met to settle the formal date of resignation, and agreed that it should be the following Monday, March 11, 1968. The Prime Minister's letter of acceptance, delivered on March 5, thanked Gordon "most warmly for the fine contribution you have made to our work since your return," and concluded: "The fact that I will be leaving, myself, within a few weeks does not lessen my regret at your departure." It was signed simply: "Mike."[85]

On March 15 Walter Gordon became chairman of the board of Canadian Corporate Management Limited, the holding company he had founded twenty-three years earlier. He held his seat in the House of Commons until the parliamentary dissolution of April 23, 1968, and did not seek re-election.

Although it was disowned and ignored by the candidates for the succession in the Pearson Cabinet, the *Report* of the Watkins committee was neither revolutionary nor radical. It was a carefully argued extension of Walter Gordon's case for economic nationalism. The committee examined a wide range of implications and effects of unrestricted foreign investment in Canada, and concluded that the net economic benefit of foreign investment could not be precisely measured. Nevertheless, it demonstrated that there were tangible economic, social and political costs for Canada in the policy of the open door, and made a series of recommendations for reducing or eliminating those costs.

The committee noted that Canada's acceptance of foreign investment had not been completely without limit; there was already a core of generally accepted restrictive policies with a nationalist purpose.

> The most important point of a positive nature to emerge from the survey is that a clear Canadian policy at the level of the federal government has taken shape over the past decade to maintain Canadian ownership and control of federally-incorporated financial institutions, while the pre-existing policy of maintaining Canadian ownership and control of the media of communications has been strengthened. In general, this reflects the Canadian commitment, a liberal policy toward foreign investment notwithstanding, to protect Canadian business in these key sectors of the economy and the society. The rationale transcends narrowly economic considerations. Communications media lie at the heart of the technostructure of

modern societies. Canadian ownership and control facilitate the expression of Canadian points of view. Financial institutions, because of their pervasiveness and their potential as bases for influence and control, constitute the commanding heights of the economy. Canadian ownership and control facilitate the exercise of Canadian economic policies.[1]

The committee added that "The key sector commitment, and its variant, the key firm commitment, have not been extended, however, by the development of any policy instruments to deal with foreign takeovers outside these sectors."[2] Canadian national policy was incomplete, and in the absence of any general restrictions on foreign control, the alienation of the economy to foreign owners continued rapidly.

Just as exclusive control of the key sectors was intended to preserve Canadian independence and economic sovereignty, the Watkins committee argued for the further elaboration of federal policy in defence of the national interest. In particular, the committee recommended the creation of a special coordinating agency to gather and distribute information on the operations of foreign-owned firms, to examine licensing and marketing arrangements and taxation measures, and to promote international cooperation in the supervision of multinational corporations; new legislation to require full financial disclosure by all corporations, private or public, which carried on business in Canada; the amendment of anti-combines and tariff legislation to encourage greater efficiency and competitiveness in Canadian industry; new legislation to block the intrusion into Canada of American anti-trust and trade prohibition laws and balance of payment regulations; the creation of the Canada Development Corporation "as a large holding company with entrepreneurial and management functions to assume a leadership role in Canada's business and financial community"; and the provision of stronger tax incentives to large corporations to offer shares to Canadians.[3]

The Watkins committee emphasized that the problem of foreign investment reflected an absence of domestic policy:

The major deficiency in Canadian policy has not been its liberality toward foreign investment per se but the absence of an integrated set of policies, partly with respect to both foreign and domestic firms, partly with respect only to foreign firms, to ensure higher benefit and smaller costs for Canadians from the operations of multi-national corporations.[4]

In the postwar era of rapid technical change, free movement of international capital and rapacious exploitation of natural resources, Canadian politicians had apparently lost the capacity to perceive the national interest according to any measure beyond the crude scale of the gross national product. The Watkins committee reminded them that the national interest is potentially a more subtle concept than the GNP, that it should include the ability to shape economic and social policy within the country, and to provide the widest range of entrepreneurial, scientific and technical opportunities for Canadians in Canada. The committee made the defensive point – which was creative as well – that the Canadian nation-state is a natural and appropriate agent for the protection of collective interests, in countervailing balance against the interests of foreign-controlled corporations and foreign governments that attempt to impose their policies through those corporations. This formulation of the national interest is commonplace; but it was beyond the understanding of the Canadian Cabinet in February, 1968.

At the level of Parliament and the national parties, the spirit of C. D. Howe was still in the ascendant. Walter Gordon's assault upon it had accomplished marginal changes in policy, but they had been piecemeal rather than comprehensive. The consensus prevented more radical change. The questioning of Gordon's policy in his own party, the unwillingness and incapacity of the Opposition parties to offer him any effective support, and the absence of any strongly based nationalist sentiment in the country condemned his campaign to failure in the short run. But the Watkins *Report* itself was a sign of significant change. It was the unanimous work of eight economists, and marked the first substantial commitment from that profession to economic nationalism. Walter Gordon was no longer alone in his cause.

The public opinion polls also gave evidence of increasing general concern about the questions of foreign domination that Gordon had raised.[5] In 1969 and 1970 he was on constant call for speeches on the national question in Ontario, British Columbia, Alberta, Saskatchewan, and Quebec. More than ever before in his public career, Gordon had caught the public ear. But his direct political influence remained small.

Shortly before the Liberal leadership convention of April, 1968, Gordon announced his support for the candidacy of Pierre Elliott Trudeau, and expressed satisfaction that Mr. Trudeau was sympathetic to the objectives of the Watkins *Report*. (The strength of his commitment was not altogether clear, but in conversation with Gordon he had indicated general support both for the *Report* and for the views expressed in *A Choice for Canada*.) The issue of foreign ownership and control, however, was ignored at the leadership convention, and the new government came out of it – and the subsequent election – with no perceptible commitment to any program on foreign investment. The Canada Development Corporation was finally established in a low key in 1971, two foreign takeovers in the uranium and oil industries were arbitrarily prohibited by the Cabinet in 1969 and 1971, but no other steps were taken to implement the recommendations of the Watkins *Report*. The government's indifference reflected Prime Minister Trudeau's belief in the international free market and his rejection of nationalism (which had its origins in his Quebec experience and in a simplistic historical view of the evils of European nationalism); it coincided with the continuing influence of Mitchell Sharp and C. M. Drury in the Trudeau Cabinet, and the growing influence of John Turner.

With the accession of Pierre Trudeau, the Liberal government turned away from the open anarchy of the Pearson administration to a system of disciplined management dominated by the will of the Prime Minister. (The reorganization of the Cabinet and the Prime Minister's office reflected some of Walter Gordon's suggestions of 1967, but the infusion of will and the extremism of the transformation were the Prime Minister's alone.) In that austere atmosphere there was no room for the disorderly give and take that characterized the Pearson years. No strong advocate of a policy on foreign investment was left in the Cabinet after Gordon's departure, and if there had been he would have had slight chance of converting the ministry to his views. Liberals of nationalist instinct like Walter Gordon were willing, in any case, to give Pierre Trudeau the benefit of the doubt because he promised to deal decisively with the other great challenge to Canadian integrity, the independence movement in Quebec. They granted him a long period of grace; and Walter Gordon remained reasonably confident that the new Prime Minister could eventually be won by reason and political self-interest to the nationalist cause. But when the party met for intellectual nourishment at Harrison Hot Springs, B.C. in November, 1969, it was offered no taste of economic nationalism by its new guardians. Walter Gordon refused to attend the conference because the national question did not appear on the agenda. Instead, he participated immediately afterwards in a teach-in on Canadian nationalism at the University of Alberta where a large and passionate audience demonstrated its interest in what the Harrison meeting had ignored.[6]

In Winnipeg in October, 1969 the New Democratic Party moved toward a more emphatically nationalist position under pressure from the radical Waffle group, which had recently been created under the leadership, among others, of Melville Watkins – whose experience with the Watkins *Report* destroyed for him any lingering confidence that the Liberal party might confront the problems of foreign domination of the economy. In response to the evident growth of public interest in the subject, the government countered in the spring of 1970 with another temporizing study of foreign ownership and control, under the direction of a Minister without portfolio, Herb Gray. In August, 1970 the House of Commons Committee on External Affairs, with a Liberal majority under the chairmanship of Ian Wahn, produced a unanimous report endorsing a range of nationalist measures including legislation aimed at restoring predominant Canadian control in the economy.[7] The government ignored the report.

Meanwhile, Abraham Rotstein, another member of the Watkins Task Force, pursued its themes in the pages of the *Canadian Forum* (of which he was editor), and in 1970, with Peter C. Newman, Walter Gordon, Jack McClelland, Eddie Goodman, Mel Hurtig, and others, created the Committee for an Independent Canada.[8] Its purpose was to focus attention on the national question, and to maintain pressure on the federal Cabinet to act on the recommendations of the Gray enquiry. After a postponement resulting from the Quebec crisis of October, 1970, the Committee succeeded easily in gaining about 170,000 signatures (almost entirely in English Canada) supporting a petition to the federal Cabinet which was presented to Prime Minister Trudeau in June, 1971. He told the delegation (which included Walter Gordon) that he welcomed the Committee's vigilance about the "serious problem" of foreign domination, and insisted that his government's goals "are very close – though not identical" to those of the Committee. He blithely urged the Committee to remain in existence in order to offer public support for the government's forthcoming nationalist measures.

Richard Nixon's economic measures of August, 1971 demonstrated afresh Canada's vulnerability in the American embrace, and the absence of any Canadian strategy for confronting the relationship with the United States. Prime Minister Trudeau's utterances gave no indication of the government's definitive response; but gradually, as the months passed without action on the Gray *Report* (which had reached the Cabinet in draft in May, 1971), it became apparent that no assertive policy would emerge. The pale proposal for a screening agency limited to the review of new foreign takeovers, introduced in May, 1972, confirmed the most pessimistic of nationalist predictions. It was an innocuous piece of electoral window-dressing.

Walter Gordon testified to the House Committee on Finance, Trade and Economic Affairs during its hearings on the Bill on June 13, 1972. "This Bill," he said, "may encourage some people to pretend that something significant is being done to ensure Canada's future independence. But that something is so small it is almost meaningless."[9] The Bill's application would depend on the discretion of a Minister, and it would apply in potential to only about ten percent of the annual growth of foreign control in Canada. The Bill would entirely exempt from surveillance the extensions of foreign control achieved by the reinvestment of Canadian earnings (including depletion and capital cost allowances permitted under Canadian tax laws), and new developments financed from abroad. Gordon urged the committee either to broaden the Bill's application to match the recommendations of the Gray *Report*, or to reject it as inadequate. He was not disappointed when the measure died on the order paper at the dissolution of Parliament in September, 1972.

Gordon's disenchantment with the Trudeau government was now as complete as it had ever been with the Pearson government. But in 1972 there could be less reason for patience with the Cabinet's inaction; the evidence it possessed on the effects of unsupervised foreign investment on the Canadian scale was voluminous. Three major reports were in its hands. "But no government, including the present government," Gordon told the House committee, "has been willing to accept their recommendations. One is entitled to wonder why this should be so."

His next step was logical, although it had been long-considered and was made only tentatively. He wrote in the September, 1972 issue of *Maclean's* that "we seem destined to lose our independence and eventually become part of the United States. Most Canadians do not want this. But our leaders seem quite unable to comprehend the implications of trends that, if not soon reversed, will lead inevitably to the break-up of our country."[10] He offered his prescriptions for "some broad form of supervision over the activities of the very large business enterprises that are controlled by foreigners and over new foreign capital inflows for direct investment," and registered his disappointment at the inaction of Prime Minister Trudeau. He asked the party leaders, and particularly Mr. Trudeau, to explain their intentions on foreign investment policy. "Apart from everything else," Gordon declared, "this would resolve my personal dilemma as a longtime member of the Liberal party and perhaps that of others who may think as I do. . . . If Pierre Trudeau does not announce some major changes in his policies, I expect some of us will decide, on the day of the election, that we must put the future of the country first."[11]

The Prime Minister did not respond. But as the government and the Opposition parties reassessed their attitudes after the stalemate of October 30, 1972, the effect of this omission was critically canvassed in the Liberal party; and the NDP made the government's foreign investment policy one of the chief determinants of its conditional support for the minority government in 1973. The government therefore introduced a new Bill containing provision for wider surveillance of foreign investment when it met the new Parliament in January, 1973. The Bill was hedged with limitations which suggested that its purpose was only cosmetic; but its existence demonstrated that federal politicians could no longer ignore the subject. Gordon's long crusade had not yet failed.

*

By 1973 the independence movement in Canada had, in the judgment of a sceptic, "stopped dead in its tracks the traditional thrust of economic liberalism within Canada."[12] That was a substantial exaggeration. But it had at least created a self-conscious national lobby which cut across the divisions of party and class, and undermined the politicians' easy acceptance of a dependent role in the American economic empire. It was impossible to imagine that movement without the presence of Walter Gordon. He had given it his persistence, his moderation and his utter lack of stridency, and these had been indispensable qualities for confronting the contempt and disregard which typified the political response to Canadian nationalism in the 1960s. The anger and impatience born of the frustration of a reasonable cause led other nationalists beyond Gordon into the New Democratic Party, the Waffle movement and other more uncompromising splinter groups; but Gordon continued to speak gently to business, government and the middle class, appealing to their self-interest and self-respect, hoping that by doing so he could eventually convert them without the dislocations and excesses of a revolutionary reversal of national policy. This was a civilized and decent strategy, founded on a liberal faith in the reasonableness of his friends and his political opponents. The faith was not altogether justified, for English Canada was caught in the complex toils of rejecting its own survival as a mature and self-conscious community.

The great national debate which W. A. Wilson of the Montreal *Star* had predicted in 1963 as one product of the new government's reforming and interventionist program had never occurred. The political process was not that coherent. The response to Walter Gordon's nationalist measures, in particular, took the form of an irrational reflex of panic and alarm, an indication both of the insecure popular attachment to the postwar *status quo* and of the calculated obscurantism of various vested interests. Gordon's proposals were never given a fair public hearing during his political career.

This was only partly the result of weaknesses of presentation. It was true that Walter Gordon never offered a sufficiently full rational defence of his nationalist policies. He was impatient with complexity and detail, and almost always made his case in broad and general terms. In the early period of his public life, he probably underestimated the importance of documenting his case and arguing it in detail; he took too much for granted that the facts would speak for themselves to like-minded men. But the orthodoxy of the time contradicted him. He was nationalist, while the general faith was liberal internationalist and continentalist. But he did, nevertheless, offer solid questions about the economy and a program for critical analysis. He gained neither elaboration and intelligent support from his political friends (with rare exceptions like the Toronto *Star*), nor tolerant consideration from his antagonists. From the moment when Harry Johnson, among others, condemned the nationalist recommendations of the Gordon *Report* out-of-hand in 1958, the glib and dismissive response of liberal orthodoxy was established. It has largely taken the place of reasoned argument ever since, and has done nothing to distinguish the standard of Canadian public debate.[13] The prospects for calm discussion have improved since 1968 as moderate nationalism has attracted the adherence of more federal and provincial politicians and civil servants,[14] academics, journalists and occasional businessmen.[15] But the habits and states of mind which inhibit reasonable discussion of the issues remain deeply entrenched in the establishment of English-speaking Canada.

The endurance of Walter Gordon in pursuit of an independent Canadian economic policy was a sign of his own tenacity, resilience and good humour; and it was also a measure of the growing popular instinct for Canadian survival, which has remained alive below the level of politics and economic policy-making. In office, Gordon was reassured by the private support of his small band of advocates in the party. Out of power, he has been sustained more evidently by an undercurrent of shared feeling in English-speaking Canada. As the evidence for Gordon's concerns accumulated after 1968, and as Ottawa scornfully ignored it, the public sense of anxiety deepened and broadened, and was expressed more passionately in voices of indignation or outrage.[16] Finally the consensus was moving, as more and more Canadians realized that Gordon's targets were real and his instincts true. Nothing else can explain his prominent role in Canadian public life since 1968: not character, not rhetorical power, not fascination for the martyr.

His character is reserved, laconic and whimsical. He has never projected it easily on the public stage. The superficial impression he conveys to all but his intimates is typically one of stiffness, patrician aloofness and easy boredom. His range of expression and allusion on the platform is narrow, his use of language is dull, his humour is wry and ironic. His inability to invest words with emotion has been the despair of his political disciples. His public character and presence have been barriers, not aids, to his political cause. And yet, indisputably, his commitment has been recognized and echoed by audiences across the nation. No other retired politician in recent Canadian history (except Eric Kierans) has remained so prominent in the discussion of current public policy.

It would be dramatic to see Walter Gordon as a martyr now grate-fully acknowledged for his sacrifices. But it would be inappropriate. He is no tragic figure of pity and lament made victim to his cause. When the cause faltered Gordon had other sources of satisfaction to sustain him. His political commitment has always been measured, not fanatic, and that is one explanation of his extraordinary resilience.

Why was Gordon considered an extremist and a radical when his proposals, by comparison with the accepted policies of most other industrial countries, were almost all mild? Why was he rejected by his own business community and by his political colleagues in the federal Cabinet? Why has the country been so slow to recognize the force of Gordon's warnings?

Gordon's failure to convert his colleagues in power to the cause of economic nationalism requires several explanations. Political inexper-ience and accident were partly to blame: without the debacle of the 1963 budget, the story might have been different. Gordon himself attributes the failure to the uncertainty and loss of will that was a consequence of the first Pearson government's minority position in Parliament, and the exhaustion of Lester Pearson after 1965. The government's gradual loss of will and self-confidence in the face of John Diefenbaker's endless harassment was undoubted. But the government achieved much in the Parliament of 1963 – 1965 in spite of this. After the summer of 1963 the Conservative assault centred more frequently on the misadventures of some French-speaking members of the Cabinet than it did on Walter Gordon, and yet the Prime Minister's work of reconciliation with Quebec (carried on with the help of these ministers) proceeded nonetheless. The parliamentary timetable was often disrupted, and the government's program fell far behind schedule; but Gordon's measures suffered unduly in the delay. That could not be put down entirely to a general failure of will.

There were more complex forces at work. Walter Gordon knew that he could not count on the enthusiastic support of the Department of Finance and the Bank of Canada in his efforts to limit American economic influence, but he believed there was no similar problem within the Liberal party. Its conversion, however, which Gordon thought he had assured by 1962, was only superficial. It was one thing for the party to absorb the extension of the welfare state advocated by Maurice Lamontagne, Tom Kent and Gordon; that involved no radical break with recent habit and expectation. But Gordon's nationalist measures did. They implied a Canadian national interest distinct from and potentially in conflict with the American interest. But the conditioning of the wartime and postwar alliance, the casual absorption of American cultural and material values, the assumed benefits of economic growth and American capital investment together had smothered the very concept of a separate Canadian national interest.

To large elements of the Liberal party and the Canadian public it was more than heresy to advocate Canadian policies that might be at odds with those of the United States: it was literally inconceivable. The idea could not be grasped. This was probably the key to Lester Pearson's ambiguity. He saw himself as a Canadian nationalist, but his perspective was curious. He was a nationalist of the Washington variety, who believed that Canada could only properly move within limits established by American tolerance and the interests of the American alliance. For Pearson the Canadian national interest was subsumed under the American; and if he spoke critically and acted independently (as he sometimes did), he did so in what he conceived as the real interest of the United States, never in intentional conflict with it. There was a basic North American harmony of interests to be maintained, and it never seemed to occur to Pearson that in a direct conflict between the interests of the two nations the Canadian interest should legitimately be defended to the limit by Canadian politicians. He was prepared to back Gordon's policies only so long as they provoked no serious challenge. This was as much a basic tenet of his attitude toward the United States as it was a quality of his temperament.

Pearson's view of the relationship with the United States, although increasingly odd in retrospect, was orthodox. It was shared, with only minor shadings, not only by his colleagues in the Liberal party but by almost every federal politician of consequence (including John Diefenbaker, whose conflicts with the United States were personal and tactical rather than fundamental). It was shared above all by the old Liberal bureaucratic alliance of Cabinet ministers, senior civil servants and businessmen, who had entered wholeheartedly into the American embrace after the Second World War in the conviction of its benevolence and inevitability. What brought Walter Gordon down was not any broad public rejection of his policies (the public reaction, in the mid-sixties, rarely went beyond indifference or simple misunderstanding), but rejection by his own peers, whose assumptions he had set out to challenge. They had the sympathetic ear of Lester Pearson and the majority in his Cabinet, and in November, 1965 their influence told.

Walter Gordon had only gradually and partially freed himself from the conventional outlook; he too believed in the early 1960s that the adjustments he favoured could be accomplished with almost complete American tolerance and goodwill. The accelerating trend of American takeovers in Canada, Gordon's direct experience of government, and his disillusioned reflections on the Vietnam war gave him a progressively firmer grip on the realities of American power, and deepened his commitment to a distinctively Canadian destiny. But he still remained a moderate and liberal North American in many of his assumptions. That was one way of explaining the inadequacy of his argument: it was not thorough-going enough to strike a clear contrast between the America he rejected and the Canada he accepted. In a review of *A Choice for Canada* in 1966, Mel Watkins perceived that Walter Gordon often seemed "to retreat from the strength of his own convictions" because he "did not wish to offend the United States unnecessarily" and "admired and emulated" too much in the American way of life. While Gordon was

> ... suspicious of large corporations – they do not provide "the best training for future heroes" – ... he largely accepts the ideology of liberalism which permits them to thrive. His recommendations for reform run too heavily toward gimmickry – the usual failure of tax accountants – and not enough toward broad-gauged policies which are prepared to challenge the assumptions on which society both American and Canadian – operates.[17]

Walter Gordon was understandably cautious about where rigorous logic might lead him. He was setting off, almost alone, against the dominant beliefs of his own community. More thorough analysis would probably have confronted him with an irreconcilable conflict of values. He believed in central economic management, but always rejected the greater degree of public control advocated by those who passed beyond him into the left wing of the New Democratic Party; he was too much a liberal to trust that extent of radical change,[18] and too practical to believe that it would be publicly acceptable. For a Canadian nationalist facing the pervasive influence of the multinational corporations and American power, modest remedies may be inadequate; but Gordon did not allow himself to consider that possibility. And equally important, he remained too loyal to his friends in politics and business (however roughly they may have treated him) to contemplate a major break from them with any satisfaction.

If Walter Gordon had moved further in his economic and social analysis as Professor Watkins urged (and as Watkins himself later moved), he would not have taken the Liberal party with him, and he would not have remained in power as long as he did. He might have posed Canada's choices with greater clarity, but he would have achieved less. Instead, he remained a missionary to his own party, his own class and the moderate majority of the English Canadian electorate. This was a harder choice than his critics were usually prepared to allow. He held to a position in the political spectrum that made him vulnerable to criticism from both right and left, refusing the comforts either of right-wing complacency or of radical self-righteousness.

There is not much doubt that (barring some unforeseen and destructive upheaval) the achievement of a satisfactory degree of Canadian national independence will require the determined allegiance of a large part of the middle class to whom Walter Gordon made his reforming appeal. In 1960 the Liberal party, apparently open to new initiatives, was as reasonable a place as any to begin a nationalist campaign. For Walter Gordon it was the only possible place. John Diefenbaker's Conservative party made a show of nationalism, but in fact was lost in administrative and philosophic confusion. The NDP was more clearly nationalist but its popular appeal was marginal. The political views of Canadians were still dominated by American presuppositions, and these were not confined to any single political party. By entering the Liberal party under Lester Pearson where he had the opportunity, Walter Gordon took his program to the centre of power and made it one of the central issues of the decade. He did not transform the Liberal party or the Ottawa establishment, and he did not convert the business community, which became more fully integrated in and more blindly devoted to the American system during his decade in politics. Paradoxically, he began to achieve his success by doing what he had not set out to do. By 1973 Gordon could see the beginnings of a popular national movement – a political movement – which revealed itself in all the federal parties, in the universities and the periodical press, in royal commissions and government enquiries, in the Committee for an Independent Canada, in the trade unions, in the policies of provincial governments in Ontario, Manitoba and British Columbia, and very tentatively in a Liberal government in Ottawa. What he hoped to achieve directly at the centre will be accomplished instead, if it is accomplished at all, by slow and persistent democratic pressure. A politically acceptable set of nationalist policies was only beginning to emerge, and there was no certainty that they could successfully assert the independence lost so fecklessly over thirty uncomprehending years. But no one had done more than Walter Gordon to reveal to Canadians that there is such a thing as the national interest, and that its defence is a normal act of national self-respect.

*

Walter Gordon brought to politics the skills and deficiencies of a planner and consultant in management, along with the confidence and idealism of a genuinely decent man. He possessed a precise and rather clinical talent for setting objectives and creating the administrative machinery to achieve them, but he lacked interest in the more complex and wayward political processes by which democratic institutions actually live. What distinguished him in politics were his unusual purposes, his consistency, his integrity, his loyalty to friends, and his courage. These were all personal virtues of great strength which are not always political assets, but which are essential leavens in democratic politics.

His temperament, manner and background did not obviously suit him for political life, and he entered it with reluctance. While his business peers criticized him for betraying his own community, other critics mocked him always for being a member of it. When he came to office he found himself unprepared for the ruthlessness and ingratitude of the political game. He experienced its harshness in a particularly brutal and abrupt way. Thereafter he acted with caution, and concentrated on his role as adviser and chief-of-staff to the Prime Minister. This was more congenial to him, but it meant that, in the absence of a popular movement to sustain it, the success of his cause rested primarily on the conviction, determination and political influence of the Prime Minister.

The great advantage of Gordon's managerial style was that it emphasized planning. After 1958 the Liberal party lacked a program and an effective organization. Gordon guided it through three years of administrative reorganization and reassessment of policy, and as a result, when the party came to power in 1963 it possessed a program of remarkable fullness and coherence. The party's ability, in its years out of power, to stand back from the immediate political battle, to examine basic policy and to take a direction, was rare in Canadian politics. The legislative achievements of the next three years were almost all the products of this experience. Once the party was in office, it lost the ability to think ahead in an orderly way, or even to maintain direction; and by 1965 it was intellectually exhausted. This was not primarily the fault of Walter Gordon and his supporters, who urged through 1966 and 1967 that the party should undertake a new effort of policy-making, and an administrative reorganization in the Cabinet and Prime Minister's office to facilitate it. By this time, however, the Prime Minister had grown weary, Gordon's influence had declined, and the inertia of the more conservative elements in the Cabinet and senior civil service had reasserted its dominance. The conflict was between two managerial styles, one that accepted innovation and reform, the other that clung to cautious and familiar ways,

Not only was Walter Gordon personally unprepared for the bruises of politics, but his pattern of planning and organization was deficient, too, in its neglect of the political dimension. The government's early setbacks were partly the result of this failure to prepare the political ground by adequate consultation and persuasion, and Gordon's later frustrations in the party also owed something to his indifference to the political arts. He was inclined to rely too much upon formal commitments and the approval of policy in principle by his colleagues in the party leadership, and to neglect the need for broader bargaining and compromise on the way to his goals. His opponents in the party were more assiduous in their political efforts, and accomplished their tasks of blockade with relative ease.

The one source of lasting anguish in Walter Gordon's political career was the collapse of his friendship with Mike Pearson. Any political relationship of leader and chief-of-staff is bound to be tense and abrasive if the chief-of-staff is an independent man with his own objectives. This one was especially vulnerable because it began in personal friendship and was always seen in that light by Walter Gordon. He experienced Mike Pearson's irresolution, lack of organizing ability and occasional moral cowardice at close hand. Almost to the end of his political career, Gordon believed that Mike Pearson's will could be strengthened and his administrative habits reformed by criticism and friendly advice. This was too optimistic a judgment of Pearson and too simple an assessment of the forces that influenced the Prime Minister. The party was a loose and diverse coalition that could not be easily led in any direction. Given Pearson's pliability and indifference, Gordon's criticisms could only be seen by the Prime Minister as a series of irritating rebukes for being what he was and for leading an ideologically confused party. After 1965 Pearson lacked the spirit to offer leadership to his government, and Gordon's demands for it came more and more to imply the need for different leadership.

What eventually brought the friendship to an end, however, was not any dispute over policy and organization or any conflict of temperament. Gordon and Pearson knew each other too well, after thirty years, to let such things bring about a final break. The end came, for Walter Gordon, as the cumulative result of a series of acts and omissions by Mike Pearson. There was Pearson's failure to support Gordon in the controversy over the 1963 budget. There was the Prime Minister's breathtaking abandonment of Guy Favreau to his hostile critics in the autumn of 1964. There was Pearson's encouragement of Gordon to lead the 1965 campaign and to remain as Minister of Finance, followed by his private assurances to businessmen that Gordon would leave Finance after the election. There were the worthless undertakings made on Gordon's return to the Cabinet. And finally, there was Pearson's bitter castigation of Gordon in caucus and to the press over the Vietnam speech in May, 1967, after his much milder comments in Cabinet where Gordon could defend himself. Gordon never again trusted Pearson, and when he left the Cabinet in February, 1968 the long association ended. None of the friendships and accomplishments of Gordon's years in politics compensated him for the rupture of this close friendship with a man he had trusted and aided so loyally.

The two met formally once again, at Mike Pearson's house on November 28, 1972, a few weeks before Pearson's death. Shortly afterwards Walter Gordon recorded his reflections on that visit.

I had not seen Mike Pearson in the more than four years since I left Ottawa in March, 1968 – except casually at two or three large receptions and once on a plane trip. But in November, I began to hear stories that he had cancer and did not have long to live. At the end of the month, I went to Ottawa to see him and to say goodbye. He got out of bed, got dressed and came downstairs to greet me. He was witty as always and joked about having lost twenty-five pounds. As a matter of fact, he looked better (and younger) for it despite the gravity of his illness. He said in the short time left to him, he was trying to get down on paper, for the last volume of his memoirs – which as he said someone else would have to finish – his personal recollections of events and of some of the people involved during the years when he was Prime Minister. That morning, he had been writing about Judy LaMarsh and he said some kindly things about her. Later, in a serious vein, he said the two things that troubled him about the five years when he was leader of the government were the Favreau tragedy and the fact that, as he put it, "he and I had drifted apart." We did not pursue this.

I did not stay long as he soon began to tire and should have been in bed. When I left him, both of us knew we would not see one another again. He died one month later.

Mike Pearson was a much more complex character than the general public ever realized. He had his faults as we all do. But in retrospect I believe he will go down in history, not only as a witty, humorous, lovable human being, but as one of Canada's greatest men and certainly as one of her greatest public servants. He won the Nobel prize for peace in 1957 for his handling of the Suez affair, something no other Canadian has done. He was always at his best in a crisis and never lost his head. Late in life, he proved to be a courageous and resourceful political leader in the way he brought the Liberals back to power in five short years – following their devastating defeat in the 1958 election. Under his term of office as Prime Minister, Canadians obtained a respectable social security base on which to build. He, personally, directed the long drawn-out fight for the Canadian flag. With it all, he remained modest, unassuming and always very much a Canadian. Mike Pearson will be missed by all who knew him and especially by his host of friends.[19]

It was typical of the generosity of spirit of both men that Mike Pearson's last comments about his career to Walter Gordon should express regret that he had disappointed some of his colleagues, and that Walter Gordon's judgment of Pearson should in the end be benevolent and affectionate.

Lester Pearson was a more resourceful politician than Walter Gordon, with a more comprehensive grasp of the factors that required balancing in the Liberal party, and a more tenacious instinct for political survival. He gave the appearance of weakness, he was often a bad judge of mood and occasion, he had few basic commitments, and he recoiled from firm but unpleasant acts; but his leadership by indirection was more skilful than it appeared. His easy and personable manner created strong bonds of loyalty in all sections of the party when it had few other unifying ties; and he exploited this loyalty to maintain power and hold the party together. The impulses that drove him were transparently decent and humane, and he used his power in office to reconcile English- and French-speaking Canadians to a new and more equitable balance between them, and to promote the completion of a national welfare system. The gifts of a congenial personality were his chief political resource. Set against his dominant traits of openness and self-effacing affability, his faults were disguised or muted. The reactions among his closest associates to his retreats and failures of solidarity were always tempered by their loyal attachment to the man. Walter Gordon, who was unusually clear-sighted about Pearson's qualities as a political leader, nevertheless maintained his affection for him, and that affection was general. It was impossible to dislike Mike Pearson, even in disenchantment.

*

It is as well to step back, in conclusion, to remark on the circumstances of politicians. Democratic politics is a pitiless vocation which can expose and exaggerate every flaw in human character. But unblemished souls are no more frequent among the general population than they are among politicians; ours are only saved from public scrutiny by good fortune. Walter Gordon is a private man who was not easily drawn to politics and who suffered its wounds as much as any man. Through it all he retained his dignity, his integrity, his generosity, and his wit. He needs no other monument, although he will certainly have one.

Notes

Chapter One

1. The company traced its roots back to 1864. Its history is briefly recorded in A.J. Little, *The Story of the Firm, 1864–1964: Clarkson, Gordon & Co.* (University of Toronto Press, 1964, for Clarkson, Gordon & Co., privately printed and distributed).
2. The biographical details, unless otherwise located, are found in Little's *The Story of the Firm.*
3. Walter Cassels was knighted in 1917. A short biographical sketch appears in Allan Graydon, Q.C., *Some Reminiscences of Blakes* (privately printed, Toronto, 1970), 16.
4. Interview with Senator Keith Davey, November 25, 1971. The phrase was also applied to Gordon by Don McGillivray of Southam News Services, in an article on Gordon in the Ottawa *Citizen*, April 22, 1963.
5. Walter L. Gordon, *Memoir* (unpublished manuscript, 1969), I, 5. All references are to the revised draft of the manuscript, completed in the summer of 1969 and in Mr. Gordon's possession. The page numbers are those of the typed manuscript.
6. Gordon, *Memoir*, I, 10.
7. They have two daughters, Kyra and Jane, and a son, John.
8. See Donald Creighton, *Canada's First Century* (Macmillan of Canada, Toronto, 1970), 215-217.
9. Gordon, *Memoir*, I, 16.
10. Ibid., I, 13.
11. They were J.Y. Murdoch, K.C., president of Noranda Mines, and Arthur Purvis, president of Canadian Industries Limited.
12. Gordon, *Memoir*, I, 15. After the Second World War, Gordon and a number of associates, including J.Y. Murdoch, R.A. Laidlaw and Hartland Molson, organized Canadian Corporate Management Limited, with a much smaller capitalization. By this time British capital was unavailable, and seventy percent of the original investment was American. In 1969, eighty-five percent of the shares were held in Canada and fifteen percent in the United States.
13. Gordon was succeeded at the Foreign Exchange Control Board by Max Mackenzie, a Montreal chartered accountant who later became Deputy Minister of Trade and Commerce.
14. Gordon, *Memoir*, II, 33; Little, 39.

15. The Bank of Canada staff members on the committee were Alex Skelton and Dean Marble.
16. Gordon, *Memoir*, II, 38.
17. J.W. Pickersgill, *The Mackenzie King Record*, Vol. 1 (University of Toronto Press, Toronto, 1960), 155.
18. Ibid., 155.
19. Gordon, *Memoir*, II, 49.
20. Ibid., II, 43.
21. Ibid.
22. Ibid., II, 44.
23. Ibid., II, 45.
24. Ibid.
25. Pickersgill, 177.
26. Ibid.
27. W.L. Morton, *The Kingdom of Canada* (McClelland and Stewart, Toronto, second edition, 1969), 479-480.
28. Gordon, *Memoir*, II, 52, 53; Little, 60-61. The firm carried out studies for the Board until the end of 1943, when it reverted to its normal work of private management consultancy.
29. "Post-War Taxation," *The Canadian Chartered Accountant*, December, 1944.
30. Gordon, *Memoir*, II, 54.
31. Ibid., II, 55.
32. Gordon, *Memoir*, II, 56; *Report of the Royal Commission on Administrative Classifications in the Public Service* (The Queen's Printer, Ottawa, 1946), 23-28.
33. See Dale C. Thomson, *Louis St. Laurent: Canadian* (Macmillan of Canada, Toronto, 1967), 8; 169; 179; 184; 194-196; 211-213.
34. Gordon, *Memoir*, III, 1.
35. Thomson, 239.
36. Gordon, *Memoir*, III, 2.
37. See John R. Beal, *The Pearson Phenomenon* (Longmans Canada Limited, Toronto, 1964), 86; Rt. Hon. Lester B. Pearson, *Mike: Memoirs*, Vol. 1 (University of Toronto Press, Toronto, 1972), 202-285.
38. See Thomson, 196-207; 216-231; Patrick Nicholson, *Vision and Indecision* (Longmans Canada Limited, Toronto, 1968), 91.
39. Thomson, 217.
40. Ibid., 244; Beal, 88-89.
41. Gordon, *Memoir*, III, 4.
42. Thomson, 213, 216.
43. Gordon *Papers*, Memo, December 5, 1965.
44. Gordon, *Memoir*, III, 7-11. C.M. (Bud) Drury, who had been a member of the Department of External Affairs, was shortly chosen by Claxton as the Department's new Deputy Minister.
45. Ibid., III, 5.

46. Gordon *Papers*, Memo, December 5, 1965. Pearson wrote to Heeney on May 14, 1953 that the Cabinet had approved his move from Paris to Washington, and the public announcement of Heeney's appointment was made on June 10, 1953.
47. Gordon, *Memoir*, III, 14.
48. Ibid., III, 15.
49. Ibid.

Chapter Two

1. Gordon, *Memoir*, IV, 1.
2. Foreign long-term investment in Canada grew from $7 billion in 1945 to $17.4 billion in 1957. Direct American investment in equity ownership made up $2.3 billion of this total in 1945 and $8.4 billion in 1957; that is, almost sixty percent of the increase in foreign investment in the 1945–1957 period was made up of American direct investment, which was heavily concentrated in the secondary manufacturing, oil and gas, and mining and smelting industries (*Canada's International Investment Position, 1926 to 1967*, Statistics Canada, Ottawa, 1971, 25-40).
3. For this background, see, for example, Lester B. Pearson, "Canadian Foreign Policy in a Two-Power World," in his *Words and Occasions* (University of Toronto Press, Toronto, 1970), 101-108.
4. Gordon, *Memoir*, IV, 1.
5. The quarterly published by the Canadian Institute of International Affairs.
6. Gordon, *Memoir*, IV, 1.
7. Ibid., IV, 2.
8. See Dale C. Thomson, *Louis St. Laurent: Canadian* (Macmillan of Canada, Toronto, 1967),394-395, on the issue of negotiations for a trans-Canada gas pipeline.
9. Tom Kent, *Inside the Gordon Report* (Winnipeg *Free Press* Pamphlet No. 57, Winnipeg, June, 1958), 7. The articles in the pamphlet appeared first on the editorial page of the *Free Press* in April and May, 1958.
10. Ibid., 4, 5.
11. W.L. Morton, *The Kingdom of Canada* (McClelland and Stewart, Toronto, second edition, 1969), 512-513.
12. Lussier was a forestry engineer from Quebec City; A.E. (Del) Grauer was an economist and president of the B.C. Electric Company; Andrew Stewart was an agricultural economist and president of the University of Alberta; and Raymond Gushue was president of Memorial University in St. John's, Newfoundland.
13. Gordon, *Memoir*, IV, 3-4. Gordon had never met LePan, but had gained a high opinion of him through intermediaries. LePan was a poet with a literary education and interests, who was performing the work of minister counsellor in the Washington embassy. Gordon wrote that LePan had mastered economics on the side; LePan himself recalled that the knowledge of economics necessary for a diplomat in that position was not very great. When he came to the Royal Commission he had to educate himself in economics, and he found this, along with his major administrative duties, a trying task. (Interview with D.V. LePan, November 19, 1971.)
14. P.C. 1955-909. The terms of reference provided that the Commission should " . . . enquire into and report upon the long-term prospects of the Canadian economy, that is to say, upon the probable economic development of Canada and the problems to which such development appears likely to give rise, and without limiting the generality of the foregoing, to study and report upon:

  a) developments in the supply of raw materials and energy sources;

  b) the growth to be expected in the population of Canada and the changes in its distribution;

  c) prospects for the growth and change in domestic and external markets for Canadian production;

  d) trends in productivity and standards of living; and

  e) prospective requirements for industrial and social capital.

(Royal Commission on Canada's Economic Prospects, *Final Report* [The Queen's Printer, Ottawa, November, 1957], Appendix A, 471-472.)
15. Kent, 5.
16. Douglas LePan has said that Gordon was "the inspiration" of the Commission, and that its recommendations "were those that Walter Gordon wanted to produce, broadened, tempered and deepened by the very capable research staff which the Royal Commission engaged." (Interview with D.V. LePan, November 19, 1971.)
17. Gordon, *Memoir*, IV, 4-5.
18. Ibid., IV, 5.
19. Kent, 5. This criticism appeared to be centred in the prairies, and particularly in Manitoba. See the Winnipeg *Free Press*, November 12, 1955; Brandon *Sun*,

December 17, 1955; Winnipeg *Tribune*, December 21, 1955.
20. Gordon to author, February 24, 1972.
21. Ibid. Gordon's memorandum formed the basis for the *Preliminary Report*.
22. Thomson, 452-453.
23. Gordon, *Memoir*, IV, 21. Not all the recommendations of the proposed *Preliminary Report* were reviewed in the meeting. (Gordon to author, February 24, 1972.)
24. Gordon, *Memoir*, IV, 21.
25. Gordon to author, February 24, 1972.
26. Gordon, *Memoir*, IV, 21.
27. Kent, 8.
28. On the close relationship of Liberal Cabinet ministers and senior civil servants in policy-making, see John Meisel, "The Formulation of Liberal and Conservative Programmes in the 1957 Canadian General Election," *Canadian Journal of Economics and Political Science*, XXVI, No. 4, November, 1960, 565-574, and especially 565-567.
29. Jacob Viner, "The Gordon Commission Report," *Queen's Quarterly*, LXIV, No. 3, Autumn, 1957, 305.
30. Royal Commission on Canada's Economic Prospects, *Preliminary Report* (The Queen's Printer, Ottawa, 1956), 3, 4.
31. Viner, 306.
32. Ibid., 306-307.
33. See, for example, Thomson, 494.
34. *Debates*, January 17, 1957, 337-338.
35. *Preliminary Report*, chapter 14, 86-97.
36. Ibid., 89.
37. Ibid.
38. See, for example, Royal Commission on Canada's Economic Prospects, *Hearings*, January 30, 1956, 5554-5560. The Montreal *Star*, in a highly favourable editorial comment on the *Preliminary Report*, noted that "It is in some respects a pity that the report in its present form is a summary of more extended studies which will be published later. Its more controversial findings may suffer for lack of adequate documentation." (Montreal *Star*, January 14, 1957.)
39. *Preliminary Report*, 90.
40. Ibid., 90-93. Elsewhere in the *Report* the Commission urged complementary action to bring about greater processing of raw materials in Canada before export, greater Canadian participation in the oil and gas industry, and the creation of a national energy authority to coordinate all aspects of energy policy.
41. Montreal *Star*, January 15, 1957; Le *Devoir*, January 12, 1957. Paul Sauriol of Le

Devoir, in an article titled "The stimulating audacity of the Gordon Report," applied its nationalist lesson to Quebec: "In addition to any service it may render to the country as a whole, the Gordon Report . . . gives us by implication [in Quebec] advice that is most useful if we wish some day to achieve our economic autonomy."
42. *Debates*, January 11, 1957, 119.
43. Ibid.
44. Ibid., February 11, 1957, 1154.
45. Ibid., 1155.
46. Ibid.
47. Ibid.
48. Gordon, *Memoir*, IV, 8.
49. *Preliminary Report*, 99-100.
50. See the Cape Breton *Post* and the Charlottetown *Guardian*, January 12, 1957; Moncton *Transcript*, January 14, 1957; Fredericton *Daily Gleaner*, January 15, 1957. The Halifax *Chronicle*, almost alone in the Maritimes, attempted to place the paragraph fairly in context. (Halifax *Chronicle*, January 16 and 17, 1957.)
51. *Debates*, January 11, 1957, 159.
52. Viner, 310.
53. Harry G. Johnson, "Canada's Economic Prospects," *Canadian Journal of Economics and Political Science*, XXIV, No. 1, February, 1958, 109.
54. Grant Dexter in the Winnipeg *Free Press*, January 24, 1957.
55. Ibid.
56. Kent, 8.
57. *Debates*, January 11, 1957, 119.
58. Ibid., March 14, 1957, 2219.
59. Ibid. It was not in office to do so.
60. Kent, 6.
61. He returned to work for the Commission in the autumn. (*Debates*, October 23, 1957, 316-17.)
62. Kent, 10-11. H.F. Angus expressed a similar reservation in his review of the *Preliminary Report* in *The Canadian Banker* (Winter, 1958), 23-29.
63. Johnson, 104.
64. In a long and sympathetic review of the *Final Report* in *The American Economic Review* (June, 1959, 359-385), Professor Simon Kuznets of Johns Hopkins University praised the Commission's eighteen research studies as "a most valuable reference library on the past development, current structure, and prospective trends of Canadian industry," more competent and systematic than comparative industrial studies for any other country. He was critical, however, of the *Report's* failure to

analyze price movements and inflation, the distribution of income, the level of government revenues and expenditures, and the purpose of economic growth. These omissions, he suggested, coupled with the basic assumptions underlying the *Report*'s projections, left "an impression of a kind of 'problemlessness'" in the Canadian economy.

Kuznets described the *Report*'s treatment of Canada's economic relations with the United States as "cautious," and regretted that the references to non-economic considerations were "so general and vague that no firm ground for analysis and testable judgment is provided." The relevant factors in determining the appropriate economic relationship between Canada and the United States, Kuznets suggested, should be "cultural, socio-psychological, and political, rather than economic." He added: "Yet it is not impossible to note them explicitly, and even consider some uses of economic resources that could be expected to compensate by encouraging cultural and political leadership in Canada in respects and directions in which the United States may be deficient. Of course, the Commission, having been instructed to deal with economic prospects of Canada, may have considered itself barred from discussing these non-economic forces and factors. Yet in the case of international economic relations this limitation may be a serious disadvantage; and the refusal to deal more explicitly with the non-economic factors may encourage a greater unwillingness to accept the purely economic arguments than might otherwise be the case." (379-380)

This review by an American economist was the most comprehensive comment made on the *Final Report*, and almost the only one to treat the nationalist aspects of the *Report* with respect and understanding: an ironic and surely devastating commentary on Canadian indifference to the country's own situation in the 1950s.

Chapter Three

1. See, for example, John Meisel, "The Formulation of Liberal and Conservative Programmes in the 1957 Canadian General Election," *Canadian Journal of Economics and Political Science*, XXVI, No. 4, November, 1960, 566. General A. Bruce Matthews, who became president of the National

Liberal Federation in 1959, recalls that C.D. Howe's view of the party organization was that it should undertake no activity and spending until an election was in sight. As long as Howe remained in the Cabinet, no renovation of the party's structure was possible. (Interview with General Matthews, November 29, 1971.)
2. W.L. Morton, *The Kingdom of Canada* (McClelland and Stewart, Toronto, second edition, 1969), 509-510.
3. According to Patrick Nicholson, St. Laurent attempted to bring Harris back to Parliament in a safe Liberal seat. Two Ontario MPS were apparently ready to give up their seats for him, and the new Prime Minister respected Harris enough to suggest that he would try to assure Harris's acclamation if he chose to run in a by-election. But Harris would not do so. Patrick Nicholson, *Vision and Indecision* (Longmans Canada Limited, Toronto, 1968), 95.
4. Gordon, *Memoir*, V, 2.
5. Ibid., V, 3.
6. Interview with Senator Davey, November 25, 1971.
7. Gordon, *Memoir*, V, 3-4. In Canadian convention parlance, "hospitality" means booze.
8. Ibid., V, 4; Tom Axworthy, *Innovation and the Party System: An Examination of the Career of Walter L. Gordon and the Liberal Party* (M.A. thesis, Queen's University, May, 1970), 172-173.
9. Gordon, *Memoir*, V, 4-5.
10. Peter C. Newman, *Renegade in Power: The Diefenbaker Years* (McClelland and Stewart Limited, Toronto, 1963), 65.
11. Nicholson, 79.
12. Gordon, *Memoir*, V, 6.
13. The document came into the Prime Minister's hands through an intermediary, the journalist Patrick Nicholson, who gives his account in *Vision and Indecision*, 64-83. Mr. Sharp remained as Deputy Minister until the decisive results of the general election of March 31 were known, and then offered his resignation. See Denis Smith, "The Campaign in Eglinton," in John Meisel, ed., *Papers on the 1962 Election* (University of Toronto Press, Toronto, 1964), 89.
14. Gordon, *Memoir*, V, 6.
15. John G. Diefenbaker, quoted in J.M. Beck, *Pendulum of Power* (Prentice-Hall of Canada, Ltd., Scarborough, 1968), 316.
16. Gordon, *Memoir*, V, 6-7.

17. Ibid., V, 7-8.

18. Gordon *Papers*, W.L. Gordon to the Hon. L.B. Pearson, November 5, 1959.

19. See, for example, the generally flattering assessment of Pearson by Blair Fraser in April, 1951 in which Fraser noted among Lester Pearson's shortcomings that: "He isn't a good administrator. Pearson's interest is in policy, not organization. When he was under-secretary work tended to clog up among the few he knew and trusted most; others might be chafing for something to do. Also, in spite of his own talent for human relations, he isn't particularly good at putting the right men to work together." John Fraser and Graham Fraser, eds., *Blair Fraser Reports* (Macmillan of Canada, Toronto, 1969), 52.

20. Gordon *Papers*, Gordon to Pearson, November 5, 1959; Memorandum to the Hon. L.B. Pearson, November 5, 1959.

21. Ibid., November 5, 1959.

22. Ibid., "Summary of Proposed Budget and Present Expenditures."

23. Gordon *Papers*, Gordon to Pearson, November 5, 1959.

24. Gordon, *Memoir*, V, 12. The matter of an executive assistant to Pearson was not settled satisfactorily, and three months later Gordon returned to the problem, offering his good offices to replace the incumbent. (Gordon *Papers*, Gordon to Pearson, February 19, 1960.)

25. Gordon *Papers*, Gordon to Pearson, February 19, 1960.

26. Gordon, *Memoir*, V, 13.

27. Ibid., 13.

28. Walter L. Gordon, "Our Changing Economy" (Address to the Ontario Federation of Labour Weekend Educational Conference, February 13, 1960), 12.

29. Ibid., 17.

30. Ibid., 18-19.

31. Beland Honderich, the publisher of the Toronto *Star* (who was then financial editor of the *Star*), recalls that at this time he was starting to notice the nationalist question; and Walter Gordon's 1960 speeches marked him, in Honderich's view, as the only Canadian public figure who was applying himself seriously to the issues. (Interview with Beland Honderich, November 18, 1971.)

32. Toronto *Star*, February 13, 1960.

33. *Financial Post*, February 20, 1960.

34. Gordon *Papers*, Gordon to Pearson, March 9, 1960.

35. Gordon, *Memoir*, V, 22.

36. Gordon *Papers*, Gordon to Pearson, April 22, 1960; Gordon to Pearson, July 8, 1960. Interview with Senator Keith Davey, November 25, 1971.

37. Gordon *Papers*, Gordon to Pearson, July 8, 1960. Gordon acknowledged that "my own hesitations in this matter are well known to both of us."

38. Gordon *Papers*, Gordon to Pearson, July 8, 1960.

39. Gordon *Papers*, Gordon to Pearson, July 8, 1960. The Quebec Liberal party led by Jean Lesage defeated the Union Nationale government on June 22, 1960; and the New Brunswick Liberal party under Louis Robichaud defeated the incumbent Conservatives on June 27, 1960.

40. Gordon *Papers*, Gordon to Pearson, July 12, 1960.

41. Ibid. The August speech was titled "Whither Canada – Satellite or Independent Nation?"

42. Gordon, *Memoir*, V, 16.

Chapter Four

1. Walter L. Gordon, "Whither Canada – Satellite or Independent Nation?" (Remarks to the National Seminar, National Federation of Canadian University Students, at the University of British Columbia, August 29, 1960), 9.

2. Ibid., 10.

3. Ibid., 11.

4. James M. Minifie, *Peacemaker or Powdermonkey: Canada's Role in a Revolutionary World* (McClelland and Stewart, Toronto, 1960), 4.

5. Gordon, "Whither Canada," 11.

6. Ibid., 11.

7. Ibid., 15.

8. See, for example, Toronto *Star*, Montreal *La Presse*, Toronto *Telegram*, August 29, 1960; Vancouver *Province*, Edmonton *Journal*, August 30, 1960; Saskatoon *Star-Phoenix*, August 31, 1960; Peterborough *Examiner*, September 1, 1960. For editorial comment, see the Toronto *Star*, August 29, 30, 31, 1960; Toronto *Telegram*, August 30, 1960; Ottawa *Citizen*, Vancouver *Province*, Hamilton *Spectator*, August 31, 1960; Victoria *Daily Times*, September 9, 1960.

9. Toronto *Star*, August 29, 1960.

10. Victoria *Daily Times*, September 9, 1960.

11. Toronto *Telegram*, August 30, 1960.

12. Ottawa *Citizen*, August 31, 1960.

13. Hamilton *Spectator*, August 31, 1960.

14. Vancouver *Province*, August 31, 1960.

15. Quoted in Tom Axworthy, *Innovation and the Party System: An Examination of the Career of Walter L. Gordon and the Liberal Party* (M.A. thesis, Queen's University, May, 1970), 191. Sharp's use of the phrase "intelligent, liberally-minded Canadians" was no doubt intended to undermine the concurrent appeal being made to "liberally-minded Canadians" by the organizers of the New Party, whose founding convention in July, 1961 was to give birth to the New Democratic Party.

16. See Gordon, *Memoir*, V, 23; Maurice Lamontagne, "Growth, Stability and the Problem of Unemployment" in National Liberal Federation, *Study Conference on National Problems* (Kingston, Ontario, 1960), vol. 1; Tom Kent, *Social Policy for Canada* (Policy Press, Ottawa, 1962); Axworthy, 192-193.

17. The Foreword to Kent's essay acknowledges this influence, which is obvious throughout the paper.

18. Gordon, *Memoir*, V, 23; Michael Barkway, "Where are the Liberals going, Mr. Pearson?" *Executive*, December, 1961, 51; Interview with General A. Bruce Matthews, November 29, 1971. General Matthews described Lamontagne and Kent as "quasi-socialists. . . . These fellows," he said, "were not practical politicians; they were driving the thing very fast."

19. Montreal *Star*, September 15, 1960.

20. Gordon proposed: 1) that "the law respecting withholding taxes be changed so that a higher rather than a lower rate of tax be withheld on dividends paid by Canadian subsidiaries fifty-one percent (or if you like, seventy-five percent) of whose stock is held by a single foreign corporation or by a group of related foreign corporations. In other words, there should be an incentive rather than a disincentive to the owners of Canadian subsidiaries to sell part of their shares to Canadians." 2) That Pearson might mention in general terms the tax incentives proposed in the *Report* of the Gordon Commission. 3) That the Gordon Commission's recommendation for legislation prohibiting foreign control of Canadian chartered banks should be endorsed: "surely it would be wise to take whatever action might be necessary to prevent this in advance. Otherwise, it would be another case of locking the stable door after the horse has disappeared." 4) That the O'Leary Commission's proposals for aiding Canadian magazines against American competition should be embodied in legislation. 5) That Ottawa should use its influence with the provinces to bring about Canadian participation in mining and oil development. 6) That legislation should require companies to file financial statements with the Secretary of State for public inspection. (Gordon *Papers*, Memorandum, "Re: Speech about Foreign Investment," Gordon to Pearson, September 14, 1960.)

21. Gordon *Papers*, Gordon to Pearson, September 14, 1960.

22. Gordon *Papers*, Memorandum, Gordon to Pearson, September 14, 1960.

23. Ibid.

24. Montreal *Star*, October 20, 1960.

25. Gordon, *Memoir*, V, 24.

26. Ibid., V, 24. The papers were prepared by Tom Kent, Maurice Lamontagne, Robert Fowler, Maurice Sauvé, and Gordon, with specialist advice from other persons.

27. Ibid., V, 25.

28. This was a curiously inexact and misleading wording, for there was no existing requirement for a majority of Canadian board members in foreign-owned subsidiaries operating in the Canadian provinces. (The reference may have been to the federal requirements for Canadian participation in Arctic oil explorations.)

29. Gordon, *Memoir*, V, 26-27.

30. Ibid., V, 29. His enthusiasm was reflected in a speech to the Liberal Businessmen's Club of Toronto, "The Liberal Rally in Review," on January 19, 1961.

31. Ibid., V, 29.

32. "Not Right, Not Left, But Forward," *Canadian Forum*, February, 1961, 241-242.

33. Ibid.

34. Interview with Walter L. Gordon, November 22, 1971.

35. Gordon *Papers*, Gordon to Pearson, March 28, 1961.

36. Gordon, *Memoir*, VI, 1; Axworthy, 179-182; interview with Senator Davey, November 25, 1971; Peter C. Newman, *The Distemper of Our Times* (McClelland and Stewart, Toronto, 1968), 63-64.

37. Axworthy, 181.

38. For example, to arouse interest in the Toronto association Davey arranged a party on a Toronto Island ferryboat, and a u.s. election night party for five hundred persons. Using the slogan "Work or

Resign," Davey replaced ten of eighteen riding association presidents; and in January, 1961 he launched a Toronto membership campaign with the slogan "6 for 1 in '61" which resulted in a total membership of 10,000 persons in Toronto. A campaign college, the "School of Practical Politics," was organized in 1959 to convey basic information about campaign organization and tactics to candidates and party workers. This was the basis for the enlarged National Campaign College of 1962, directed by David Greenspan, which was active throughout the country before the general election. (Interview with Senator Davey, November 25, 1971; Axworthy, 181, 214-216.)

39. Quoted in Axworthy, 182.

40. Interview with Senator Davey, November 25, 1971.

41. Gordon, *Memoir*, VI, 1-2.

42. Interview with Senator Davey, November 25, 1971; Gordon, *Memoir*, V, 30; Gordon *Papers*, Gordon to Pearson, March 28, 1961. Pearson, for example, left Davey's salary and duties for discussion with Gordon. Following Davey's interview with Pearson, Davey visited the president of the National Liberal Federation, Senator John Connolly, and was surprised to have to inform Connolly for the first time of the appointment. (Interview with Senator Davey, November 25, 1971.)

43. The members of the committee were Pearson, Gordon, Davey, Pickersgill, Martin, Chevrier, Hellyer, General Matthews, Senator Connolly, and Pearson's three administrative aides, Maurice Lamontagne, Allan MacEachen and Richard O'Hagan. (Gordon, *Memoir*, VI, 1; interview with Senator Davey, November 25, 1971; Peter C. Newman, "Backstage," *Maclean's Magazine*, August 26, 1961, 50; Axworthy, 203-206.) Tom Axworthy notes the special nature of the Leader's Advisory Committee: "In early 1961, there was a strong move to make Walter Gordon president of the party, but Pearson had promised the job to Senator Connolly, in part, to keep the more traditional elements of the party satisfied. The Leader's Advisory Committee was really a device set up to ensure that Gordon would have control." (Axworthy, 203.)

44. Interview with Senator Davey, November 25, 1971; Axworthy, 204-205.

45. Lionel Chevrier was named joint chairman of the committee, but his role remained nominal. *Globe and Mail*, December 13, 1961; Axworthy, 207.)

46. Gordon, *Memoir*, VI, 2.

47. Axworthy, 207-208.

48. Walter Gordon, quoted in Axworthy, 207-208. The variations from province to province reflected varying states of party organization and degrees of entrenchment of local party magnates. In British Columbia, for example, Gordon and Davey succeeded in having Hugh Martin (who had lost his campaign for the provincial presidency) appointed to the committee against the protests of the incumbent president, William Gilmour. In Alberta, Manitoba, Ontario, New Brunswick, and Nova Scotia Gordon and Davey worked with campaign chairmen they had promoted. In Saskatchewan, however, the provincial Liberal leader, Ross Thatcher, was too powerful to be challenged in 1962; in Quebec, the 'old guard' remained in control of the campaign under Lionel Chevrier and the Quebec party treasurer Louis Gelinas; and in Newfoundland J.W. Pickersgill maintained his leading role with the support of Premier Smallwood. (Gordon, *Memoir*, VI, 2-3.)

49. Gordon, *Memoir*, VI, 3; Axworthy, 208.

50. Kent to author, July 10, 1973. The title, Kent recalled, "was a typically Pearsonian way of indicating importance, without using words, such as 'policy', that would increase the opposition of the 'establishment' wing of his party."

51. The members of this formal incarnation of "Cell 13" were Lang, Gordon, Davey, Frith, David Anderson, Richard Stanbury, David Greenspan, and Bruce Powe. (Gordon, *Memoir*, VI, 1.)

52. Gordon, *Memoir*, VI, 5-6.

53. Walter L. Gordon, "Where Do We Go from Here—Some Suggestions for the Budget" (Notes for remarks to the Rotary Club of Simcoe, Ontario, June 5, 1961; Notes for remarks to the Windsor Chamber of Commerce, June 8, 1961).

54. Ottawa *Citizen*, June 5, 1961.

55. Gordon, *Memoir*, VI, 6.

56. Windsor *Star*, June 8, 1961.

57. Gordon, *Memoir*, VI, 7.

58. For example, Peter C. Newman wrote of Gordon in August as "the brilliant Toronto chartered accountant who is Minister of Finance in the Liberal shadow cabinet." (*Maclean's Magazine*, August 26, 1961, 50.)

59. See, for example, the Windsor *Star*,

December 9, 1961, in which H.L. MacPherson identified the "common denominator" between Howe and Gordon as their similar approach to large national projects: "This needs doing. Let's do it."
60. Gordon, *Memoir*, VI, 8-9.
61. Ibid., VI, 9-10. Harris's Canadian company was known as Penetration Research Limited. From 1963, its operations were managed by Oliver Quayle and Company of New York, who carried out fourteen opinion studies for the Liberal party from February, 1963 to October, 1965. (Gordon *Papers*, Penetration Research Limited, Surveys.)
62. Interview with Walter L. Gordon, November 22, 1971; interview with Senator Davey, November 25, 1971. The question whether a public opinion adviser from another country might import alien and inappropriate assumptions and techniques did not arise, presumably because the party organizers, as philosophic liberals, assumed that what might be called 'electoral technology', like all technology, was without nationality and no respecter of frontiers. The technology would be imitated domestically if it proved efficient—or fascinating—abroad; the only significant question was, "who is the best supplier?" There are profound implications, deserving analysis, in this approach to political efficiency (which has become more common in Canadian political parties since 1961).
63. It was publicly revealed in 1963 by Peter Newman. (*Renegade in Power: The Diefenbaker Years* [McClelland and Stewart, Toronto, 1963], 267.) Newman's assertion that Harris used a pseudonym in Canada is denied by Gordon, Davey and Harris; but his suggestion that President Kennedy "gave his unofficial blessing" to the venture is tacitly conceded. Kennedy was Harris's major employer, and according to Harris, "it would have been natural to discuss the matter with Kennedy" before accepting the Canadian invitation. Newman's revelation was taken up by John Diefenbaker after 1963 as evidence of President Kennedy's plot to remove him from office, but the truth seems less melodramatic. Probably the most that can be said is that Gordon and Davey, having decided to seek Harris's assistance on the basis of his technical competence, discreetly ignored any broader political implications in the appointment. (The controversy was

reviewed by Arthur Blakely in the Montreal *Gazette*, September 9, 1971.)
64. Gordon, *Memoir*, VI, 10.
65. Ibid., VI, 10-11. Prime Minister Diefenbaker might have found it incredible to know that the alien pollster was actually advising the Liberal party to avoid personal attacks on himself.
66. Peter C. Newman, *Maclean's Magazine*, August 26, 1961, 50; interview with Senator Davey, November 25, 1971; interview with Walter Gordon, November 22, 1971; Gordon, *Memoir*, VI, 11; Axworthy, 213.
67. Gordon *Papers*, Gordon to Pearson, July 7, 1961.
68. Gordon, *Memoir*, VI, 12.
69. This concentration of focus upon central Canada remained one of the persistent characteristics of the Liberal party under the leadership of L.B. Pearson. It is an ironic bit of evidence to set against the charges often made against the Conservative party after 1957 for avoiding a major effort in Quebec in that campaign. See Newman, *Distemper*, 78-80; Axworthy, 210-212.
70. Gordon named the following new candidates as ones who "gave the necessary lead" to others by agreeing to stand in 1962: Captain David Groos (Victoria); Jack Nicholson and Jack Davis (Vancouver); Jim Coutts (Alberta); Hazen Argue (Saskatchewan); Fred Douglas and Margaret Konantz (Winnipeg); Sherwood Rideout and Jean-Eudes Dube (New Brunswick); Jack Lloyd and John Stewart (Nova Scotia); Maurice Lamontagne, Maurice Sauvé, Bud Drury, and John Turner (Quebec); and in Ontario, Edgar Benson (Kingston), Lloyd Francis (Ottawa), Lucien Lamoureux (Cornwall), Pauline Jewett (Northumberland-Durham), Larry Pennell (Brantford), John Munro (Hamilton), Herb Gray (Windsor), Eugene Whelan (Leamington), Jim McNulty (St. Catharines), Dr. Harry Harley (Oakville); Mitchell Sharp, "Red" Kelly, Donald Macdonald, James Walker, Maurice Moreau, and Ian Wahn (Metropolitan Toronto). Gordon, *Memoir*, VI, 12-13.
71. Walter L. Gordon, *Troubled Canada* (McClelland and Stewart, Toronto, 1961).
72. Ibid., 127.
73. Ibid., 133-134.
74. Montreal *Star*, November 16, 1971.
75. Regina *Leader-Post*, November 28, 1961; see also the Montreal *Gazette*, November 13, 1961.

76. Trenton *Trentonian*, November 24, 1961.
77. Gordon, *Memoir*, VI, 8.
78. Gordon, *Memoir*, VI, 19; Toronto *Star*, December 6, 1961, January 22, 1962.
79. Ottawa *Citizen*, January 24, 1962.
80. Toronto *Telegram*, December 7, 1961.

Chapter Five

1. Donald Creighton, *Canada's First Century* (Macmillan of Canada, Toronto, 1970), 311.
2. See Kari Levitt, *Silent Surrender* (Macmillan of Canada, Toronto, 1970), 58-70.
3. See, for example, J.M. Beck, *Pendulum of Power* (Prentice-Hall of Canada, Ltd., Scarborough, 1968), 329-347; *Canadian Annual Review for 1963* (University of Toronto Press, Toronto, 1963), 9-27.
4. *Globe and Mail*, August 12, 1960.
5. *Debates*, February 22, 1962, 1142. See also Peter Dempson, *Assignment Ottawa* (General Publishing, Toronto, 1968), 110-111; Peter C. Newman, *Renegade in Power: The Diefenbaker Years* (McClelland and Stewart Limited, Toronto, 1963), 252.
6. *Debates*, February 22, 1962, 1140-1141.
7. Dempson, 110.
8. See Dempson, 111. Cardin's overall majority increased from 2,492 in 1958 to 3,600 in 1962.
9. *Debates*, January 22, 1962, 40.
10. Ibid., 41.
11. Ibid., 57.
12. *Globe and Mail*, January 25, 1962.
13. *Debates*, January 23, 1962, 85.
14. *Globe and Mail*, January 25, 1962; Toronto *Star*, February 1, 1962.
15. *Debates*, January 23, 1962, 85-90.
16. Toronto *Star*, February 1, 1962.
17. This set of assumptions may help to explain why Mr. Diefenbaker and Mr. Fleming took so long to move against the independent acts of the governor of the Bank of Canada. The Prime Minister found it difficult to comprehend the need for coordinated economic policy, and had a bias against it. The confrontation with Mr. Coyne finally came over what was seen as his intolerable personal defiance of the government, rather than any intelligible differences about economic policy-making (although these did exist).
18. For analysis of the vote and the nature of the parties' appeal, see below and John Meisel, "The June 1962 Election: Break-up of Our Party System?" *Queen's Quarterly*,
LXIX, Autumn, 1962, 329-346.
19. Tom Kent later commented on the Liberal party's national advertising for the 1962 campaign: "Gordon made the decision to concentrate on Ontario and it was the right decision. We simply did not have the human resources to run several regional campaigns. We didn't have enough good people to write ads for the West or the Maritimes on separate policy for these areas. If anything, we should have concentrated on Ontario even more." (Quoted in Tom Axworthy, *Innovation and the Party System: An Examination of the Career of Walter L. Gordon and the Liberal Party* (M.A. thesis, Queen's University, May, 1970), 212.
20. Hamilton *Spectator*, January 29, 1962.
21. Ibid.
22. Peterborough *Examiner*, January 31, 1962.
23. *Canadian Annual Review for 1962* (University of Toronto Press, Toronto, 1963), 11.
24. Ibid., 10.
25. *Globe and Mail*, May 17, 1962.
26. Ibid.
27. This tactic took advantage of a latent resentment within the Liberal party itself. An observer writing early in 1962 quoted an unnamed "displaced veteran" of the party as saying that "today in the management of the Liberal party's affairs practical politicians have no place; only 'eggheads' are wanted." ("Nearing Dissolution," *Roundtable*, LII, March 1962, 203, quoted in Beck, 334.)
28. Creighton, 302.
29. Quoted in the *Canadian Annual Review for 1962*, 179.
30. Ibid., 180.
31. The program called for "appointment of a royal commission on taxation; updating measures of social justice to include portable pensions and a contributory health insurance plan; new government support for the modernization of secondary industries; production of foods now imported; construction within a reasonable time of an oil pipeline across Canada; start on a second trans-Canada highway; action to underwrite economic growth in all its phases; steps to keep Canada's credit facilities in line with the advantages available for foreign competitors; research into northern natural gas and resource possibilities; increased commuter facilities; more national development projects, such

as the causeway and new harbours and wharves; an integrated national plan for land and water use; ample credit for agriculture and a new policy for the movement of feed grains; an extension of the vocational training program to retired people; means to provide the small investor with a share in the development of Canada." (Quoted in *Canadian Annual Review for 1962, 14.*)

32. Ibid.

33. Ottawa *Journal*, May 14, 1962, quoted in Beck, 333.

34. Beck, 332, 337.

35. Quoted in *Canadian Annual Review for 1962*, 104.

36. Ibid., 16. The evidence does, indeed, suggest that the Diefenbaker government was regarded at best as a nuisance by the USSR and the USA. It mattered much more directly to Canada what the attitude of the latter government might be, and the question was one of great potential sensitivity in Canada. Walter Gordon was aware of the damage that might be done to the Liberal party by any overt intrusion into the campaign from Washington, and recalls that: "At one point, Jack Kennedy made some favourable comment about Mike Pearson which I thought could be dynamite to our side. Shortly afterwards Lou Harris was in my office and mentioned that he saw President Kennedy quite frequently and was there any message I would like to send along with him. I said that if he wanted Pearson to have a chance of being elected, to please keep his great big mouth shut on the subject of Pearson in particular and the Canadian election in general. I added that I thought Jack Kennedy, as a professional politician, should know better than to appear to be interfering in the politics of another country. I heard later from Jack Kennedy, long after the election, that Harris had relayed my message. Apart from that, I had no contact with Kennedy or any of his people during the course of the election." (Gordon to author, May 16, 1972.)

37. Gordon, *Memoir*, VI, 20.

38. Ibid., 22-23.

39. The results were:

Bell	(S.C.)	117
Clarke	(Comm.)	231
Gordon	(Lib.)	9,101
Morton	(P.C.)	6,713
Sefton	(N.D.P.)	5,181

(*Report of the Chief Electoral Officer*, Ottawa, 1962, 296.)

40. Social Credit took twenty-six seats in Quebec; the NDP took ten seats in B.C.

41. Gordon, *Memoir*, VI, 18.

42. See, for example, Blair Fraser's judgment that the Diefenbaker government "looks beaten, it feels beaten, and nobody is afraid of it any more." ("What Pearson Won by Losing," *Maclean's Magazine*, LXXXV, July 28, 1962, 39.)

43. Beck, 347.

Chapter Six

1. Interview with Walter L. Gordon, November 22, 1971. In the House of Commons on October 2, 1962, Prime Minister Diefenbaker said that "with my knowledge the governor of the Bank of Canada discussed this matter fully—I have a memorandum of what took place—with the leader of the Opposition. . . . " (*Debates*, October 2, 1962, 109.)

2. Interview with Walter L. Gordon, November 22, 1971.

3. Gordon, *Memoir*, VII, 3.

4. Ibid.

5. The dollar was floated again in 1970.

6. For a review of the course of the austerity program, see the *Canadian Annual Review for 1962* (University of Toronto Press, Toronto, 1962), 187-192.

7. Walter L. Gordon, "Financial and economic policy" (Address to the Kiwanis Club, London, Ontario, August 31, 1962).

8. Ibid.

9. Ibid.

10. This suggestion for substantial cuts in defence spending and the reorientation of defence policy, "almost casually thrown out," according to the Montreal *Star*, caused more comment than the general argument of the speech. Among others, the *Globe and Mail* (September 5, 1962), the Montreal *Star* (September 5, 1962), the Peterborough *Examiner* (September 4, 1962), and Professor Peyton V. Lyon in the *Canadian Commentator* (October, 1962) objected to the suggestion. The Toronto *Star* (September 1, 1962) approved. A common response of Gordon's critics was that his cavalier readiness to overturn Canadian defence policy neglected the complexities of Canada's role, and especially the symbolic importance of participation in the NATO alliance. The *Globe and Mail*, however, regretted the absence of information about the rationale

for defence policy, and criticized Gordon's position "because it is not based on the facts," which were known only to members of the Department of National Defence. The *Globe* wanted Canada to "receive value for the money we do spend" in the alliance, suspected that she did not get it, and concluded that "If Mr. Gordon wishes to be a useful member of the Opposition, he will endeavour to find out." Instead, Lester Pearson had assigned that task to Paul Hellyer and Judy LaMarsh, who toured Canada's NATO bases in November.

11. Gordon, "Financial and economic policy."

12. *Globe and Mail*, October 15, 1962. In an editorial the *Globe* commended Mr. Gordon for conceding the newspaper's repeated claim that "in the weeks before June 18 . . . the Liberals were going about the country making lavish promises to every section of the electorate without bothering to explain how they could pay for them." Arthur Blakely reported in the Montreal *Gazette* on October 19, 1962: "One thing was certain. In the next election campaign, Mr. Gordon said, the Liberals would unquestionably feed the voters a much heavier diet of facts and figures than they made available in the campaign earlier this year."

"Next time, for example, the Liberals intended to spell out much more clearly how they propose to cut down on unemployment. It was no longer enough for a party to promise that it would reduce unemployment to an irreducible minimum. The voters of today tended to adopt a sceptical attitude when confronted with such pledges. It was necessary to demonstrate clearly just how the party in question proposed to carry out its undertaking."

13. Moncton *Transcript*, September 21, 1962.

14. Interview with Rt. Hon. Lester B. Pearson, June 30, 1972.

15. Interview with Pauline Jewett, November 24, 1971.

16. Lester Pearson commented mordantly that McCutcheon, who had "served his country during the war in Ottawa with distinction and devotion, was one of Mr. C.D. Howe's wartime bureaucrats. He was one of those men who were trampling the liberties of the people under foot. . . .

"I wish I could remember what the Prime Minister used to say about them during the election campaigns [*sic*], but his adjectives are a little beyond me . . . .However, this particular appointment has purified some of my colleagues and I am grateful for that.

"The Prime Minister's reaction was an understandably happy one when the appointment was announced. He drew a parallel which, I confess, surprised me a little. He said: President Kennedy has his McNamara; I have my McCutcheon. When the Prime Minister said that, I thought we were at last going to get a defence policy." (*Debates*, October 1, 58-59.)

17. The *Canadian Annual Review for 1962* (34) summarized the speech in part: "The April 10 budget resolutions would be reintroduced, but "new budget measures . . . to provide further solutions to long-term problems" were promised. A host of old and new measures vied for position: the O'Leary recommendations, Senate reform, repatriation of the constitution, ratification of the Columbia River treaty, a federal-provincial conference to choose a national flag, an Atlantic development board, a national economic development board, a national medical research council, a national council of welfare, and drug control among them."

18. Walter L. Gordon, "Notes for Remarks" (Address to the Annual Meeting Luncheon, Ontario Women's Liberal Association, October 12, 1962).

19. Quoted in the *Canadian Annual Review for 1962*, 40.

20. Ottawa *Journal*, December 14, 1962.

21. Gordon, *Memoir*, VII, 5.

22. *Debates*, December 17, 1962, 2723.

23. Ibid., 2724.

24. *Le Devoir*, 19 decembre, 1962.

25. Almost ten years later, in June, 1972, Robert Fulford looked back in disenchantment: "There is a feeling abroad that *we* have done everything we could, that somehow *they* have betrayed us by failing to respond with enthusiasm. You need go no further than the middle ranges of the NDP to hear this view articulated; and in the Liberal and Conservative parties you can find it on all sides. . . . A sense emerges from all this that something important failed to work. Through all those years, after all, we were trying hard to get in touch with French Canada, to understand the Quebec point of view on a dozen national issues, and some of us had the idea that this would lead us to a form of understanding. . . . But it didn't work. As the years went by we came dimly to perceive two difficult and painful truths. The first was that there was seldom any possibility of dialogue.

You learned this when you discovered that the only way an English-speaking Canadian could establish his liberal credentials were [sic] to agree, in toto, with whatever radical position the French-speaking Canadian of the moment set forth. . . . The second truth was even more baffling. . . . French Canada became for us a spectator sport. French Canadians, it became clear, would play the game by themselves, and out of the game would come the final decision on their future—and ours." (*Saturday Night*, June, 1972, 9-10.)

26. Ibid., 7-8

27. Saskatoon *Star-Phoenix*, January 11, 1963.

28. These were, in Europe, the CF 104 strike-reconnaissance aircraft and the Honest John missile launcher; and in Canada, the Bomarc missile and the CF 101B interceptor. Sixty-four CF 101Bs were delivered to the RCAF for use in its NORAD squadrons in July, 1961. They were armed with conventional weapons, although before their transfer from the United States Air Force they had carried nuclear weapons.

29. For detailed accounts of the nuclear weapons crisis and the fall of the government, see Peyton V. Lyon, *Canada in World Affairs, 1961-1963* (Oxford University Press, Toronto, 1968), 76-222; Peter C. Newman, *Renegade in Power: The Diefenbaker Years* (McClelland and Stewart Limited, Toronto, 1963), 333-400.

30. Lyon, 108.

31. Ibid., 85. Lyon adds that "it should be noted that even before the decisive phase of the nuclear debate had begun, the Liberals were formally committed to a position which was far from total rejection. The impression left in the public mind was another matter. Mr. Pearson was widely believed to be more categorically opposed to the acquisition of nuclear ammunition than a reading of the fine print in his statements and the party resolutions would indicate." Pearson's relatively complicated position was elaborated in the House of Commons on September 14, 1961.

32. Ibid., 112.

33. Ibid., 123-124; Peter C. Newman, *The Distemper of Our Times* (McClelland and Stewart Limited, Toronto, 1968), 6, 473-477. Judy LaMarsh also recounts these events in her *Memoirs of a Bird in a Gilded Cage* (McClelland and Stewart, Toronto, 1969), 15-31.

34. The text of the memorandum is repro-

duced as an appendix to Newman's *Distemper*, 473-477.

35. Lyon, 124. Judy LaMarsh reports that Hellyer's speech was a kite-flying exercise which had been agreed to by Mr. Pearson in advance: "Paul suggested that it would be acceptable to him, if the leader wished, to disclaim this speech and disassociate himself and the party from it, if reaction was strong against it. In the event, that is what Pearson cravenly did." (LaMarsh, 26.)

36. *Debates*, December 14, 1962, 2683, quoted in Lyon, 125.

37. The transcript of the relevant part of the press conference appears in Lyon, 131-135.

38. There, Walter Gordon believes, Pearson discussed the nuclear question with his friend Adlai Stevenson, the American ambassador to the United Nations. John Diefenbaker made the visit into an ominous issue by suggesting in the House of Commons that Mr. Pearson had actually gone to New York to seek guidance from the U.S. government. According to Peyton Lyon, on the other hand, "there is no record of Mr. Pearson meeting with anyone during the week who might have been anxious to influence Canada's position on nuclear warheads. He himself, in conversation with the author, denied discussing the matter while in New York." The Hellyer memorandum, which Pearson followed closely in making his declaration of policy on January 12, presented the case for accepting nuclear weapons forcefully and succinctly, and appears to have been the key factor in Pearson's decision. (It is significant that Pearson apparently had no memorandum before him presenting the opposite case for his consideration.) In his memorandum, Hellyer argued that the military in NATO would soon bring Canada's indecision to the attention of the NATO Council "in a way which will bring the matter into the international political arena," and that continued failure to fulfill the agreements would mean that "the Americans are almost certain to reduce or terminate their production sharing arrangements with us." Peter Newman suggests that Pearson "checked the facts in the Hellyer memo with his own contacts at NATO by trans-Atlantic telephone," but does not mention the New York visit. Hellyer's and Norstad's suggestion that Canada's reputation in NATO was suffering through the default of her obligations was the kind of argument that appealed stron-

gly to Pearson's internationalist judgment; and the reference to the defence production sharing agreements may have struck him as realistic. Both of these arguments were indirect but clear expressions of American pressure; it seems unnecessary to search for any more conspiratorial explanation of Mr. Pearson's change of policy. While Mr. Pearson was inclined to respond sympathetically to such forceful representation of the American viewpoint, Mr. Diefenbaker was strongly inclined to balk at it. One considered it reasonable; the other considered it impudent defiance. (This note is based upon Lyon, 138; Newman, *Distemper*, 473-477; interviews with Walter L. Gordon, November 22, 1971; *Debates*, January 25, 1963, 3125.)

39. The speech appears in Lester B. Pearson, *Words and Occasions* (University of Toronto Press, Toronto, 1970), 198-206.

40. Saskatoon *Star-Phoenix*, January 12, 1963.

41. Pearson, *Words and Occasions*, 202-204.

42. Ibid., 204. The first two of these suggestions were, in effect, reassuring but essentially meaningless. "Genuine collective control" of some *strategic* nuclear weapons was being promoted by the Kennedy administration in its muddled plan for a multilateral nuclear force, but this project was doomed from the start by the opposition of the French and the coolness of other NATO members. The meaning of "genuine collective control" was in any case impenetrable, unless it meant unanimity in the NATO Council for any decision to use tactical nuclear weapons; but that prospect would not have satisfied the military and was never a realistic possibility. The warning against the acquisition of strategic nuclear arms was a red herring, since the matter was not in question; and it was also slightly disingenuous, because the distinction between tactical and strategic weapons – particularly in the case of those to be installed in the CF 104, whose role was one of "strike-reconnaissance" (that is, nuclear attack across the East European borders) – was dubious.

43. Lyon, 138.

44. Interview with the Rt. Hon. Lester B. Pearson, June 30, 1972.

45. Lyon, 139.

46. Winnipeg *Free Press*, January 14, 1963. The *Free Press* report did not draw attention to the shadings of Gordon's support for Mr. Pearson's statement, and simplified the account still more by heading the story "Canada Should Be True To Her Allies."

47. Gordon, *Memoir*, VII, 11.

48. Ibid., 11.

49. Ibid., 13-14.

50. Pearson, *Words and Occasions*, 201.

51. Lyon, 142.

52. Toronto *Star*, February 14, 1963.

53. Lyon, 146.

54. *Canadian Annual Review for 1963* (University of Toronto Press, Toronto, 1964), 13.

55. Newman, *Renegade*, 376-377.

56. Gordon, *Memoir*, VII, 17.

57. Ibid., 18. Davey and Gordon continued to exert their leadership in the National Campaign Committee by adjusting the membership after June, 1962. James Coutts (an unsuccessful Liberal candidate in 1962) replaced Earl Hastings as campaign chairman in Alberta; Otto Lang, the dean of Law at the University of Saskatchewan, was installed as Saskatchewan chairman in defiance of Ross Thatcher, the provincial leader; in Nova Scotia Allan MacEachen became co-chairman with Irving Barrow; in Quebec Robert Giguere assumed the campaign leadership. (Gordon, *Memoir*, VII, 17-18.)

58. Ibid., VII, 19.

59. J.M. Beck, *Pendulum of Power* (Prentice-Hall of Canada, Ltd., Scarborough, 1968), 355.

60. Gordon *Papers*, Penetration Research Limited, Surveys, January 10, March 22, 1963. These surveys were limited to Ontario and Quebec, although the lessons were applied nationally.

61. Gordon, *Memoir*, VII, 20.

62. *Globe and Mail*, March 1, 1963.

63. Montreal *Gazette*, March 5, 1963.

64. Gordon, *Memoir*, VII, 13.

65. Quoted in the *Canadian Annual Review for 1963*, 29.

66. Ibid., 30.

67. *Cité Libre*, avril, 1963. (Translation mine.)

68. Gordon, *Memoir*, VII, 28.

69. In four Quebec constituencies won by Social Credit in 1963 where Liberal candidates ran a close second, the NDP made gains greater than the margins between the leading candidates. Without the presence of the NDP candidates, or without the nuclear issue as their ammunition, it is likely that the Liberals would have won Quebec Montmorency, Rimouski,

Shefford, and Sherbrooke. Other things being equal, these four seats would have given the Liberal party its parliamentary majority.

70. See an article by Walter Gordon, "'We Must Buy Back Canada'," *Weekend Magazine*, March 2, 1963, reports in the Montreal *Star*, March 5, 1963, and the Windsor *Star*, March 7, 1963, and an interview with Gordon, "What would the Liberals do to get the economy moving?" Toronto *Star*, April 3, 1963.

71. Gordon, *Memoir*, VII, 28.

72. Ibid., 28-29.

73. Ibid., 29.

74. Ibid.

75. Ibid., 30.

76. *Canadian Annual Review for 1963*, 26.

77. Ibid.

78. Gordon, *Memoir*, VII, 30.

79. Ibid., VII, 30-31.

80. *Canadian Annual Review for 1963*, 27.

81. Vancouver *Sun*, April 1, 1963; Toronto *Telegram*, April 1, 1963.

82. Gordon *Memoir*, VII, 32.

Chapter Seven

1. Gordon *Papers*, Memorandum, Sunday, December 5, 1965. In his *Memoir* of 1968-69 Gordon dates this conversation differently, as "one afternoon in mid-April," shortly after the election.

2. Gordon, *Memoir*, VII, 35.

3. The full ministry is listed in appendix one. On his appointment, as he had planned, Gordon resigned his partnerships in Clarkson, Gordon & Company and Woods, Gordon and Company, the presidency of Canadian Corporate Management Limited, his membership on the Board of Governors of the University of Toronto, and placed his shareholdings under trusteeship.

4. Ottawa *Journal*, April 23, 1963.

5. Winnipeg *Free Press*, April 23, 1963.

6. Ottawa *Citizen*, April 23, 1963.

7. Quoted in the *Canadian Annual Review for 1963* (University of Toronto Press, Toronto, 1964), 48.

8. John Meisel, "Election Outcome: A Breather," *Canadian Forum*, May, 1963, 31.

9. Ibid.

10. Winnipeg *Free Press*, April 23, 1963.

11. Montreal *Star*, April 23, 1963.

12. Gordon, *Memoir*, VII, 36.

13. Montreal *Star*, *Globe and Mail*, May 18, 1963. Kent had been defeated by T.C. Douglas in the election.

14. See, for instance, the Ottawa *Citizen*, April 22, 1963; Toronto *Star*, April 25, 1963; Montreal *Star* and Toronto *Globe and Mail*, May 18, 1963.

15. "My recollection is that I had settled this with the Prime Minister some time between the date of the election, April 8, and the date when the government was formed, April 22." (Gordon, *Memoir*, VIII, 5.)

16. Ibid.

17. Ibid. Joseph Scanlon of the Toronto *Star* reported Gordon's confident self-deprecation as he assumed office: "Finance Minister Walter Gordon strolled through the lobby of the Confederation Building, got on the elevator, turned to the operator, and confessed, 'I don't know where I'm going.'

Someone volunteered, 'the Minister's office' and the elevator operator smilingly stopped at the second floor.

It was as simple as that when Mr. Gordon took over his duties as Minister of Finance in Canada's new Liberal government yesterday." (Toronto *Star*, April 23, 1963.)

18. Gordon, *Memoir*, VIII, 5.

19. Ibid., VIII, 6.

20. Ibid.

21. See, for example, Donald Creighton, *Canada's First Century* (Macmillan of Canada, Toronto, 1970), 333; Peter C. Newman, *Distemper of Our Times* (McClelland and Stewart Limited, Toronto, 1968), 8-9.

22. Kent to author, July 10, 1973; Newman, *Distemper*, 8-9. Kent did not, as Newman suggests, present "the broad outlines of Walter Gordon's first budget" to the civil servants at this meeting ("The group was too large for that to have been proper if I had been able to do it. I was not."), but rather, treated the budget briefly as a "housekeeping" item for the first sixty days. Kent suggested that a June budget should be "a fairly stand-pat budget," possibly to be followed by another in the autumn. Kent also rejects Newman's judgment that conflict developed at this meeting over the realism of the government's sixty day timetable for major legislation. The conflict, according to Kent, was a matter of "policy substance and power," not of "administrative feasibility" or timing. "Controversy developed when a few of the civil servants raised objections, particularly to the Canada Pension Plan, on grounds not of timing but of desirability."

Kent made it clear to the group that the Pearson government was committed to its major policies, and did not regard them simply as election promises to be treated cavalierly once in office and subject to the restraining advice of civil servants. This initial confrontation went to the root of the proper relationship between civil servants and politicians. In retrospect, apparently, some of the civil servants were inclined to interpret the dispute as essentially one of mechanics and timing; but it was clear to Kent at the time that more fundamental issues were involved.

23. In a letter to Gordon on April 16, 1963, Stanley mentioned a telephone conversation "a few days ago," and commented in detail on the professional qualities of a number of persons "whom we discussed" during that conversation. The list included the names of Martin O'Connell and Geoff Conway.

24. The speed with which Gordon acted in appointing these aides is illustrated by Conway's case. On April 13, 1963 Conway wrote from Boston to congratulate Gordon on his victory and to offer six pages of advice on foreign ownership and employment policy. He wrote in conclusion that "I would greatly appreciate being able to meet with you (in Ottawa or Toronto) as soon as possible to clarify in what ways I can be of greatest assistance over the forthcoming year." (Gordon *Papers*, Conway to Gordon, April 13, 1963.) Eight days later, on April 21, 1963, Conway began work as a special assistant to Gordon in Ottawa. (Newman, *Distemper*, 14.) Anderson was employed from May 7 to May 16 in statistical work; the other three remained throughout the budget process.

25. Peter Newman reported that their presence, along with Gordon's decision on May 15 to move his own budget work into his House of Commons office in the Centre Block, inadvertently added further tension to an already delicate situation: " . . . their presence in a place normally associated with authority, coupled with Gordon's physical separation from his officials, underlined the growing estrangement between Gordon and his department." (Newman, *Distemper*, 15.)

26. Newman, *Distemper*, 15-20; Interview with Brian Land, November 29, 1971; Gordon, *Memoir*, VIII, 7; Interview with Martin O'Connell, February 22, 1973.

27. Gordon recognized the policy differences, which were related frankly to him by the officials. Brian Land believes, however, that Gordon was never confronted directly with the more personal discontents. (Interview with Brian Land, November 29, 1971.)

28. The contact with Land was made through Keith Davey, who had attended school with Land. Land met Gordon for the first time in an interview arranged by Davey at Gordon's Wellington Street office in Toronto. Land told Gordon that he was not an active Liberal, not an economist, and that he had just had a promotion at the University of Toronto Library. Gordon nevertheless invited him to take the job, which he said involved liaison with his constituency and the press gallery, and generally "keeping me out of trouble." Land held the job until July, 1964 when he returned to the University of Toronto to become head of the Library School. (Interview with Brian Land, November 29, 1971.)

29. Miss Burpee had previously been Mitchell Sharp's secretary at Brazilian Traction in Toronto.

30. Toronto *Star*, April 23, 1963; Gordon, *Memoir*, VII, 39. Allan Donnelly, a reporter with the Ottawa office of the Canadian Press, succeeded Land as executive assistant in 1964. When Gordon rejoined the Cabinet in 1967, David Smith, president of the National Federation of Young Liberals, became his executive assistant. In the autumn of 1965 (when Nancy Burpee left the office to become director of Admissions in the Graduate School at the University of Toronto), Barbara Hunter became Gordon's private secretary. She remained in this position while Gordon was a private member in 1966, and on his return to the Cabinet in 1967. Muriel Mersey also rejoined the staff as special assistant when Gordon returned to the Cabinet in 1967.

31. Gordon, *Memoir*, VII, 39.

32. Newman, *Distemper*, 15.

33. Interview with Rt. Hon. Lester B. Pearson, June 30, 1972.

34. Creighton, 334.

35. Newman, *Distemper*, 12.

36. Ottawa *Citizen*, May 17, 1963.

37. Montreal *Star*, May 17, 1963.

38. *Debates*, May 17, 1963, 23-24. Maurice Lamontagne also emphasized the coherence of the government's program of social and economic planning in his speech during the budget debate on June 25.

39. Ibid., May 29, 1963, 431.
40. Ibid., 432.
41. Ibid.
42. Montreal *Star*, May 18, 1963.
43. Ibid.
44. Gordon, *Memoir*, VIII, 1.
45. Gordon *Papers*, "Notes for Davenport Meeting, Earlscourt School," April 3, 1963.
46. Montreal *Star*, May 4, 1963.
47. Ibid.
48. There was comment among press gallery correspondents after the budget, for example, that the presence of the three aides to Gordon produced an attitude among some permanent officials that, since their advice was not wanted, they would not extend themselves to produce a workable budget. At the extreme, it was suggested that some technical weaknesses in the budget proposals were purposely inserted to trip the Minister up. Gordon himself commented on the removal of the sales tax exemption on building and production materials (which he regarded with reserve) that "It was not until long afterwards that I discovered that this latter measure had been discussed on a previous occasion, and that certain officials in the Department of National Revenue (not the top ones) had prepared a memorandum which anticipated practically all difficulties that this measure later encountered in the House." (Gordon, *Memoir*, VIII, 8.) This failure to brief the Minister adequately seemed to imply a serious lapse of efficiency, and perhaps also of impartiality. See also Peter Newman's account of budget preparations in his *Distemper*, 15-19.
49. Gordon, *Memoir*, VIII, 7. The meeting is dated, and its membership recounted, in Newman, *Distemper*, 16.
50. Gordon, *Memoir*, VIII, 8.
51. Ibid., VIII, 7.
52. Newman, *Distemper*, 16.
53. Gordon *Papers*, Conway to Gordon, April 13, 1963.
54. Ibid.
55. Ibid. Conway went on in the next paragraph to suggest an alternative that has historic interest: "A better solution would be to pass legislation requiring government approval of any sale of equity stock to a non-resident. Again small sales would be exempted and also sales if at least seventy-five percent of the equity remained in the hands of residents, or if the value of the company did not exceed a certain amount. Public statements would emphasize that sales would be approved as a matter of course if Canadian capital was not available or if there was some specific benefit to the economy that would result from foreign control. If such legislation is constitutional, it should be possible to present it in a manner that is not too frightening to the potential foreign investor." The proposal does not seem to have been pursued.
56. Newman, *Distemper*, 16-17. Gordon supports the essentials of this account in his *Memoir*, VIII, 8.
57. Gordon, *Memoir*, VIII, 8.
58. Newman, *Distemper*, 18.
59. Ibid. Gordon writes less specifically that the officials "expressed their criticism to me both singly and as a group" over "some of the new ideas that were proposed." (*Memoir*, VIII, 7.)
60. Gordon, *Memoir*, VIII, 9.
61. Ibid.
62. Ibid. In retrospect, Pearson felt that Rasminsky's objections had not been expressed with great strength, and had not made a deep impression on him. Pearson was surprised after the presentation of the budget to learn that Rasminsky's concerns were stronger than they had seemed during the interview on May 31. (Interview with Rt. Hon. Lester B. Pearson, June 30, 1972.)
63. Gordon, *Memoir*, VIII, 9.
64. Ibid. Pearson himself could not recall this incident. (Interview with Rt. Hon. Lester B. Pearson, June 30, 1972.)
65. Gordon, *Memoir*, VIII, 9-10.
66. There was probably a quite natural element of rationalization in this judgment. It implied either that wider preliminary discussion would have brought changes in the budget, or a stronger collective commitment to defend it as it stood; and that in either case the Minister might have emerged from the budget controversy with less political harm than he actually suffered. There is a possibility that strong criticism from Kent or other ministers might have led to alterations in the budget; but this assumption perhaps gives insufficient weight to the confidence and prestige of Pearson and Gordon as they approached budget day. Their political position in the party was strong, and they were determined to act decisively. In this atmosphere their colleagues were in a mood to grant them deference (at least as long as their policies paid political dividends). If there had been wider discussion

and the budget had not been changed before its presentation, it does not necessarily follow that there would have been a more effective defence of it or the Minister in Cabinet or the House.

67. *Debates*, June 13, 1963, 996.

68. Ibid., 997.

69. Gordon, *Memoir*, VIII, 10.

70. Donald Forster reported, for example, that "Most newspapers agreed that Mr. Gordon had to deal with more than his share of . . . problems, faced with conflicting demands for a balanced budget, a cut in personal and corporate income tax rates, higher or lower government expenditures depending on the source of the advice, measures to deal with unemployment, the current account deficit, and the 'problem' of foreign control." (*Canadian Annual Review for 1963*, 195.)

71. Gordon's review of these measures occurs in the budget speech, *Debates*, June 13, 1963, 997-998, 1004.

72. These included directions to officials to tighten their review of expense account deductions; a limitation on the tax deductible allowance for company automobiles; limitations on "dividend stripping"; changes in lease-option arrangements to prevent the avoidance of tax; restrictions on the application of company losses against the taxable income of other companies; and certain changes in excise and sales taxes. (*Debates*, June 13, 1963, 1004-1005.)

73. The Minister estimated that this change would result in approximately $220 million in non-recurrent additional tax revenue in 1964–1965 and 1965–1966. (*Debates*, June 13, 1963, 1007-1008.)

74. Ibid., 1006-1007.

75. Ibid., 1008.

76. Ibid., 1006.

77. Ibid., 1001.

78. Ibid., 1006.

79. Gordon wrote of the budget that "this was a lot of ground for any government to cover within two months of its formation and, quite frankly, I was well pleased with it. . . . In retrospect, I believe the substantive proposals contained in the budget . . . were sound. The main proposals for stimulating the economy and thus providing more jobs, for plugging blatant loopholes in the tax laws and for bringing the national finances under control were remarkably successful." (Gordon, *Memoir*, VIII, 16, 18.)

80. *Debates*, June 13, 1963, 1030.

81. Ibid., 1032.

82. *Globe and Mail*, June 14, 1963.

83. Toronto *Star*, June 14, 1963.

84. Winnipeg *Free Press*, June 14, 1963.

Chapter Eight

1. *Debates*, June 14, 1963, 1169. Clive Baxter's article of May 18, 1963 had already revealed that three temporary assistants were helping Gordon in the preparation of the budget, and Fisher, who was a friend of Gordon's executive assistant, Brian Land, had seen them in the company of Land during the previous month. (Interview with Brian Land, November 29, 1971.)

2. *Debates*, June 14, 1963, 1169.

3. Ibid. Peter Newman reported that J.W. Pickersgill, sitting beside Gordon in the House, had whispered "Don't answer!" to him. (Peter C. Newman, *The Distemper of Our Times* (McClelland and Stewart Limited, Toronto, 1968), 19.

4. *Debates*, June 14, 1963, 1170.

5. Ibid.

6. Ibid.

7. Ibid., 1171.

8. Ibid., 1198-1199.

9. Ibid., 1199.

10. Ibid.

11. Ibid., 1199-1200.

12. Ibid., 1200.

13. Ibid.

14. Ibid., 1201. It was ironic that, aside from Gordon's use of the special consultants, the Prime Minister held scrupulously to the conventional practices that Mr. Diefenbaker outlined.

15. *Debates*, June 14, 1963, 1201.

16. Ibid.

17. Ibid. In the light of the budget's content and its fate, Douglas's concluding quip was probably the most outlandish and misleading comment of any made upon it.

18. Ottawa *Journal*, June 17, 1963.

19. Ibid.

20. *Debates*, June 17, 1963, 1209.

21. Ibid., 1211; Gordon, *Memoir*, VIII, 22-24. When the Minister of Finance attempted to read the telegram to the House, the Opposition refused unanimous consent for him to do so. He was permitted to make his statement when Gilles Gregoire, the Creditiste member for Lapointe, asked him a leading question because, he said, "I believe that the Minister of Finance, after having raised a

question of personal privilege, should have the right to speak."

22. *Debates*, June 17, 1963, 1235.

23. The vote was 97-64, with the Social Credit party supporting the government and the Conservative and New Democratic parties opposed. (*Debates*, June 17, 1963, 1239-1241.)

24. *Globe and Mail*, June 17, 1963.

25. Montreal *Star*, June 18, 1963.

26. The questions arising from the appointment of the advisers multiplied to the point of absurdity, and the original, apparently simple question of whether it was acceptable constitutional practice to involve temporary staff in the preparation of budgets (which seemed, on balance, to have been answered in the affirmative) was soon lost in the undergrowth. Were the advisers appointed properly, by Order-in-Council, Treasury Board minute, or service contract? Were they "engaged" or "appointed"? Were they sworn to secrecy? Did they take precedence over the senior permanent officials of the Department? Did they have access to the budget speech before its presentation? Was it appropriate for their employers to continue paying their salaries? Did they communicate budget information to anyone before Gordon's speech? Were they Canadian citizens? Were they informed of the withdrawal of the takeover tax before its announcement in the House? Did they take advantage of this knowledge on the stock market? Was the Minister intentionally misleading the House? The only one of these questions which seems to bear any weight is the prudential one of whether the consultants should have been paid by their firms while in temporary government service. Gordon conceded the strength of this point in the House on June 24. There was no evidence presented to the House of any impropriety in the acts of the advisers, and after his first hesitation, Gordon sought to be entirely open with the House in his answers to questions about the matter. (See the *Debates*, June 17, 1963, 1235-1244; June 18, 1963, 1273-1276; June 19, 1963, 1341-1342; June 20, 1963, 1373; June 24, 1963, 1496-1497; July 5, 1963, 1873-74; July 8, 1963, 1925; July 11, 1963, 2067.)

27. Gordon, *Memoir*, VIII, 25; *Debates*, June 18, 1963, 1276-1277; June 19, 1963, 1321. One of the stories that sustained the morale of the Minister's office during this period

of onslaught was the reply that Gordon's private secretary, Nancy Burpee, was said to have given on the telephone to an angry businessman who said he wished to come to Ottawa to shoot the Minister: "You will just have to stand in line and take your turn like everybody else." (Gordon, *Memoir*, VII, 39-40.)

28. Gordon, *Memoir*, VIII, 25. Donald Forster summarized the "immense administrative problems" of the budget's proposals on foreign ownership as follows: "the difficulty of identifying the beneficial or real owner of shares, the problem of preventing sales through foreign exchanges or the spreading out of buying to avoid the tax, "dummy listings," lack of incentives for Canadians to take up shares offered in foreign-controlled companies, and so on." (*Canadian Annual Review for 1963*, [University of Toronto Press, Toronto, 1964], 201.)

29. *Debates*, June 18, 1963, 1277.

30. Gordon, *Memoir*, VIII, 25. Gordon told the House that Senator Louis Gelinas, the Liberal fundraiser and Montreal investment broker, was a member of the delegation. (*Debates*, June 20, 1963, 1372.)

31. *Debates*, June 19, 1963, Appendix "A," 1366.

32. Gordon, *Memoir*, VIII, 25.

33. Gordon *Papers*, Appointments calendar, 1963; *Debates*, June 20, 1963, 1373; Newman, *Distemper*, 20-21.

34. *Debates*, June 19, 1963, 1321.

35. Ibid.

36. Newman, *Distemper*, 21. Kierans' views on foreign investment have since then changed dramatically.

37. *Debates*, June 19, 1963, 1350.

38. The Winnipeg *Free Press* echoed the *Globe's* demand in an editorial on Saturday, June 22.

39. This account relies upon Gordon, *Memoir*, VIII, 26; Newman, *Distemper*, 21-23; Interview with the Rt. Hon. Lester B. Pearson, June 30, 1972. Peter Newman reported that the discussion was interrupted and extended over an hour, and that in the interval Pearson consulted "key colleagues" and invited Mitchell Sharp to assume the Finance portfolio if Gordon resigned.

40. When questioned by reporters, Pearson denied that Gordon had offered to resign, and in subsequent conversation Gordon too agreed to say the same thing, since the offer had not been made "in a formal way or in writing."

41. Ottawa *Journal*, June 24, 1963.

42. *Debates*, June 24, 1963, 1515-1518.

43. Davis, the parliamentary secretary to the Prime Minister, spoke on June 20 and Benson on June 25. (*Debates*, June 20, 1963, 1407-1411; June 25, 1963, 1569-1572.)

44. Gordon *Papers*, W.L. Gordon to Willson Woodside, July 1, 1963.

45. *Debates*, June 21, 1963, 1424.

46. Gordon *Papers*, Memorandum, Sunday, December 5, 1965; Interview with Brian Land, November 29, 1971; Interview with Rt. Hon. Lester B. Pearson, June 30, 1972.

47. *Debates*, June 21, 1963, 1427.

48. *Debates*, June 20, 1963, 1390.

49. Ibid., 1391.

50. *Debates*, June 24, 1963, 1520. Russell B. Irvine, the director of research for the New Democratic Party, repeated this theme in an article which described the budget as "In some ways . . . an even more backward budget than those of Mr. Nowlan and Mr. Fleming. They were merely pre-Keynesian; Mr. Gordon is almost pre-Cambrian." (*Canadian Forum*, July, 1963, 75.)

51. *Debates*, June 20, 1963, 1393.

52. *Debates*, June 24, 1963, 1497.

53. *Debates*, June 25, 1963, 1571.

54. *Debates*, June 20, 1963, 1411.

55. The Prime Minister's illness is one aspect of the budget crisis, the influence of which is extremely difficult to assess. Mr. Pearson offers it as one reason why he did not come forthrightly to Gordon's defence, even though he was present in the House until the conclusion of the budget debate and entered hospital on the next day, June 27. It may indeed be that his uncertainty about the nature of the illness affected the Prime Minister's role in the House in the previous days. This would not, however, explain the reticence of his Cabinet colleagues. After June 27 the Prime Minister's absence may have been a positive demoralizing factor.

56. Gordon, *Memoir*, VIII, 30.

57. Ibid., VIII, 31.

58. Judy LaMarsh, *Memoirs of a Bird in a Gilded Cage* (McClelland and Stewart, Toronto, 1969), 65.

59. *Debates*, July 4, 1963, 1821; July 5, 1963, 1872.

60. Ottawa *Citizen*, July 6, 1963.

61. Ibid. This latter suggestion was not quite true. Gordon's statement on July 8 was made "on motions," which allowed for short responses from the financial critics of the Opposition parties but no general debate, while the budget speech and debate took place on a resolution for the House to go into committee of ways and means. Opposition critics pointed out that a statement "on motions" did not allow the Minister of Finance to substitute his new budget resolutions for the old ones as he intended, and this procedural difficulty had to be sorted out afterwards by agreement among the parties. (*Debates*, July 8, 1963, 1961–1962.)

62. This was especially evident in George Nowlan's attempt to shift responsibility for the budget from Gordon to Prime Minister Pearson: "There is another reason, too, why we on this side of the House welcome his return to this chamber this evening. Some of us have felt that possibly the Minister of Finance (Mr. Gordon) has been blamed unduly and unjustly for many of the provisions contained in the budget which he presented to this House. We are, therefore, happy to see the Prime Minister back here tonight to accept responsibility, on behalf of the government, for the budget." (*Debates*, July 8, 1963, 1953.)

63. *Debates*, July 8, 1963, 1950.

64. The new definition of Canadian ownership provided that "the requirement that twenty-five percent of the company's directors shall be Canadians will not come into effect until 1965 and will be broadened to include resident officers of the corporation"; that status would be determined by the ownership of shares in the sixty days preceding the beginning of the taxation year; and that the twenty-five percent Canadian ownership requirement could be satisfied by offering twenty-five percent of stock for sale on Canadian stock exchanges. The other major modifications in the budget resolutions included exemptions from the sales tax for the printing and graphic arts industries, and schools, universities and similar educational institutions; the clarification of definitions and the extension of the deadline for exemption under fixed-price contracts; and the establishment of a statutory right of appeal to the Exchequer Court in cases of "dividend stripping" and the use of associated companies to reduce tax. (*Debates*, July 8, 1963, 1950–1953.)

65. *Debates*, July 8, 1963, 1952.

66. Ibid., 1960.

67. See, for example, editorials in the Toronto *Globe and Mail*, Toronto *Telegram*, Montreal *Star*, and Winnipeg *Free Press*,

July 9, 1963.

68. For accounts of the interest equalization tax negotiations, see the *Canadian Annual Review for 1963*, 204-210; Newman *Distemper*, 26-30. In the account that follows, I am chiefly grateful to Gerald Wright of the Donner Canadian Foundation for the use of his unpublished memorandum on the U.S. interest equalization tax, prepared in the course of research on Canadian independence and the economic relationship with the United States.

69. The group consisted of Plumptre, J.R. Beattie (the deputy governor of the Bank of Canada), Trued, and Linville. (Gordon, *Memoir*, IX, 1.)

70. Gordon, *Memoir*, IX, 2.

71. *Debates*, July 18, 1963, 2329.

72. Gordon, *Memoir*, IX, 3.

73. Gerald Wright, "The Interest Equalization Tax," 6. This does not mean, however, that the inclusion of Canada within the general application of the tax had occurred without thought. For discussion of this point, see below.

74. Wright, 6; Gordon, *Memoir*, IX, 3.

75. Wright, 6.

76. Newman, *Distemper*, 28; Wright, 7. The Canadian delegation also included Charles Ritchie, the Canadian ambassador.

77. Wright, 10.

78. The Treasury apparently did not accept the Canadian assurance that Canadian interest rates would not be allowed to rise too far above U.S. rates in an effort to maintain the attractions of investment in Canada despite the tax; they believed in any case that the Canadians were exaggerating the inhibiting effects of the tax on the level of investment in Canada; and they did not accept that there was any simple one-to-one relationship between the level of capital movements and the trade balance. They were thus inclined to consider that the real Canadian case was the overriding present danger to Canadian economic stability, and to bargain hard for an American advantage in the negotiations. (Wright, 9-10.)

79. *Debates*, July 22, 1963. Appendix, "Statement agreed on 21st July, 1963 between representatives of Canada and the United States," 2500. There was no exemption granted for the purchase of existing Canadian securities.

80. Ibid.

81. *Debates*, July 22, 1963, 2438. Mr. Diefenbaker went on to express, uncon-

sciously, one of the enduring dilemmas of Canadian-American relations. On the one hand, he demanded the full exercise of Canada's sovereign authority; on the other hand he insisted that there should be "consultation beforehand" in cases of this kind, which implied an even greater measure of intimacy and integration between the economic policies of the two countries. It was evident that the United States would not engage in "consultation in the true sense of the word"—meaning the joint elaboration of policy—without at the same time enlarging its own ability to influence Canadian economic policy to its own advantage.

82. George Nowlan raised this question following Gordon's initial statement in the House on July 18. (See the *Debates*, July 18, 1963, 2329-2331.)

83. *Debates*, July 22, 1963, 2437.

84. Wright, 3. He adds: "Those possessing a benign image of the bilateral relationship have managed to keep it intact by pointing to the fact that the tax was given a general, and not a particular, application. That the net should have been spread so wide is preferred as a consolation for the fish."

85. The logician may respond that, by the same reasoning, the Canadian government either knew what it was getting into with the takeover tax, or was equally incompetent and guileless in its action. In both cases, I believe, the truth is probably more complicated than this.

86. A.E. Safarian, in "Retaliation: The Price of Independence," in Stephen Clarkson, ed., *An Independent Foreign Policy For Canada* (McClelland and Stewart Limited, Toronto, 1968), 49-50.

87. Wright, 4.

88. Ibid., 4-5.

89. The evidence of Merlyn Trued's visit to Ottawa reinforces this hypothesis. Prime Minister Pearson told the House of Commons that President Kennedy did not send a special emissary to any other of the twenty-two governments affected by the tax. (*Debates*, July 18, 1963, 2331.) While Pearson offered this as evidence of the harmony between the two countries, it also suggests a high degree of calculation in the decision not to exempt Canada. In his press conference announcing the tax, Secretary Dillon stated that it would affect Canada more severely than any other country.

The weakness in this explanation is, perhaps, that it appears to ignore the

Canadian government's retreat from the intentions of the June 13 budget, and the stock market disorder that the budget created. But the government's announced intention remained. Even taking the retreat into account, it remains plausible that the experience would lead the u.s. Treasury to treat Canada with less sensitivity than before. Wright admits that "In their own minds, [the Treasury officials] probably could not tell whether this was a *post hoc* justification for a punitive action or a rational calculation of a new policy approach." (Wright, 5.) In either case the action was not thoughtless.
90. *Debates*, June 20, 1963, 1390.

Chapter Nine

1. William MacEachen in the Toronto *Star*, Charles Lynch in the Ottawa *Citizen*, Tim Creery in the Ottawa *Citizen*, August 3, 1963.
2. Winnipeg *Free Press*, August 10, 1963. The editorial writers were less generous than the reporters, as some editorial titles made clear: "Shaky Performance," "An Uncertain Lead," "A Disappointing Session," "The Shambling Session," "Sadder and Wiser." These appeared, respectively, in the Toronto *Telegram* (August 7, 1963), the *Globe and Mail* (August 5, 1963), the Toronto *Star* (August 3, 1963), the Montreal *Gazette* (August 7, 1963), and the Winnipeg *Free Press* (August 6, 1963).
3. Judy LaMarsh, *Memoirs of a Bird in a Gilded Cage* (McClelland and Stewart, Toronto, 1969), 66.
4. See John Bird's article, "Where does Pearson stand? Aim so far is dead centre," Toronto *Star*, June 19, 1963.
5. Ibid.
6. Gordon, *Memoir*, X, 1. Edgar Benson, Gordon's parliamentary secretary, was also a close colleague. He joined the Cabinet on Gordon's recommendation as Minister of National Revenue following the death of J.R. Garland in 1964. Larry Pennell, another close associate, became Solicitor General in July, 1965.
7. LaMarsh, 66. This is not, I believe, an entirely fair assessment of the Prime Minister's sense of direction, as should emerge in the course of the narrative.
8. Gordon, *Memoir*, X, 3.
9. Ibid., LaMarsh, 76. Judy LaMarsh wrote that Walter Gordon "will always be a great guy for me, for he took the time in Cabinet to write me funny notes, and laugh in appreciation at my sallies."
10. Gordon, *Memoir*, IX, 5.
11. Vancouver *Sun*, August 27, 1963.
12. Gordon, *Memoir*, IX, 5-6.
13. Ibid., IX, 6.
14. Ibid.
15. George Ball, *The Discipline of Power* (Atlantic-Little Brown, Boston, 1968), 113. Walter Gordon's experience of relations with Washington convinced him that this dazzlingly simple bit of prophecy accurately represents the "decidedly imperialistic views about Canada" of "at least the more junior people in the State and Treasury Departments." (Gordon, *Memoir*, IX, 12.)
16. Gordon, *Memoir*, IX, 7-9; *Canadian Annual Review for 1963* (University of Toronto Press, Toronto, 1964), 207. The American delegates were Dean Rusk (secretary of State), Douglas Dillon, George Ball, Orville Freeman (secretary of Agriculture), Luther Hodges (secretary of Commerce), John Kelly (assistant secretary of the Interior), Walter Heller (chairman of the President's Council of Economic Advisers), Christian Herter (special representative for trade negotiations), Frank Coffin (deputy administrator of the Agency for Economic Development), and Walton Butterworth (U.S. ambassador to Canada).
17. Gordon, *Memoir*, IX, 7.
18. Ibid., IX, 9.
19. *Debates*, June 11, 1963, 888-889.
20. *Canadian Annual Review for 1963*, 67-68.
21. Gordon, *Memoir*, X, 9.
22. For a vivid account of the pension plan's birth, see Judy LaMarsh's *Memoirs*, 77-99.
23. Ibid., 84.
24. Gordon *Papers*, Memorandum to Mr. Pearson, August 8, 1963.
25. These considerations, among others, are discussed in Gordon's memorandum to Pearson of August 8, 1963.
26. Ibid.
27. LaMarsh, 84.
28. Ibid.
29. Ibid., 45.
30. Gordon *Papers*, Memorandum to Mr. Pearson, August 8, 1963.
31. Ottawa *Journal*, October 1, 1963; *Canadian Annual Review for 1963*, 82. The caucus meetings resulted in the creation of a system of caucus policy committees which the government pledged itself to consult

regularly.

32. Ottawa *Journal*, October 1, 1963. Walter Gordon attended the first caucus sessions on Friday evening and Saturday morning, but was absent in Washington for the remainder of the meetings and for the Cabinet meeting of September 30.

33. Toronto *Star*, October 10, 1963.

34. Gordon, *Memoir*, X, 5-6.

35. Montreal *Star*, October 5, 1963.

36. *La Presse*, 28 novembre 1963.

37. See, for example, Marcel Gingras's article referred to above, and the text of a CTV News commentary by Baden Langton, December 3, 1963.

38. Toronto *Star*, December 31, 1963.

39. Toronto *Telegram*, January 4, 1964.

40. Toronto *Star*, January 21, 1964. The remaining changes did not appear to affect the balance of forces in the Cabinet. J.W. Pickersgill became Minister of Transport, and George McIlraith took the new post of president of the Treasury Board.

41. Gordon was in Washington for meetings of the International Monetary Fund from September 28 to October 2, and in Paris from November 16 to 20 at O.E.C.D. meetings.

42. Gordon *Papers*, Gordon to Pearson, September 4, 1963.

43. Gordon *Papers*, Memorandum to the Prime Minister "Re: Control of Expenditures," August 6, 1963.

44. In the period from October 1 to December 31, 1963, Gordon attended twenty-four meetings of the Treasury Board, eleven meetings of the Cabinet committee on economic policy, and twenty-five meetings of the Cabinet. (Gordon *Papers*, Appointments calendar, 1963.) Some of the results of these meetings were reflected in the government's financial proposals to the federal-provincial conferences of November, 1963 and March–April, 1964 discussed below.

45. Gordon *Papers*, Memorandum to Mr. Pearson, November 4, 1963.

46. Gordon *Papers*, Memorandum to the Rt. Hon. L.B. Pearson "Re: Draft White Paper on Defence," February 12, 1964.

47. Ibid.

48. Gordon *Papers*, Memorandum to the Prime Minister "Re: Proposed Budget of the Department of National Defence," November 21, 1964.

49. Gordon *Papers*, Note to Mr. Pearson "Re: Supervision of Expenditures," August 6, 1963.

50. Gordon *Papers*, Memorandum to the Prime Minister "Re: Reorganization of the Department of Finance and Control of Expenditures," January 2, 1964.

51. Ibid.

52. The committees were concerned with external affairs and defence; legislation and sessional; finance and economic policy; trade and resources; communications and works; social security and labour; agriculture, forestry, and fisheries; culture and related matters; federal-provincial relations.

53. *Canadian Annual Review for 1964* (University of Toronto Press, Toronto, 1965), 6.

54. Ibid., 13.

55. On the previous day Gordon had sent a few draft notes to the Prime Minister for possible use in his speech, and these had included the following sentence: "The government has certain provisional plans for financial legislation, both for new legislation such as would be required for the establishment of the Canada Development Corporation and also for amendments of existing Acts of Parliament, including the Bank Act and the Bank of Canada Act." The Prime Minister did not use this reference. (Gordon *Papers*, Gordon to Pearson, February 19, 1964.)

56. In the Ottawa *Journal*, March 2, 1964; Toronto *Telegram*, March 13, 1964; Toronto *Star*, March 14, 1964.

57. Ottawa *Journal*, March 2, 1964.

58. *Debates*, March 16, 1964, 969-987. Gordon began his speech by paying tribute to the late Minister of National Revenue, J.R. Garland, who had died suddenly over the weekend.

59. Calgary *Herald*, March 17. 1964.

60. Peterborough *Examiner*, March 18, 1964.

61. Gordon, *Memoir*, X, 6.

62. *Le Soleil*, 17 mars 1964.

63. Gordon *Papers*, Memorandum, Sunday, December 5, 1965.

64. Gordon, *Memoir*, X, 11-12.

65. Ibid., X, 12.

66. Gordon, *Memoir*, X, 12-15; *Canadian Annual Review for 1964*, 62-73; Richard Simeon, *Federal-Provincial Diplomacy* (University of Toronto Press, Toronto, 1972), 43-65.

67. Gordon, *Memoir*, X, 15.

68. Toronto *Star*, May 25, 1964.

69. For a useful comment on this subject, see Stanley Westall's "Will the Real Pearson Stand Up?" *Globe and Mail*, June 11, 1964.

70. Toronto *Star*, May 25, 1964; *Debates*, May 19, 1964, 3336-3339.

71. See, for example, the report of the Gallup poll of Canada, "Walter Gordon in comeback, fifty-one percent like his work," Toronto *Star*, July 22, 1964; and Blair Fraser's column in *Maclean's*, July 25, 1964.

72. Gordon, *Memoir*, X, 17.

73. Gordon *Papers*, Memorandum to Mr. Pearson, July 16, 1964.

74. Ibid.

75. Ibid.

76. Ibid.

77. Ibid.

78. Ibid.

79. Gordon, *Memoir*, X, 19. On August 10, 1964 the Prime Minister submitted an outline of the proposed study of Canada's economic unity to Gordon, McIlraith, Sharp, and Drury for their comments. The paper, he said, "should give guidance and encouragement to people who are looking for a 'positive Canadianism', and provide a counterweight to divisive tendencies not so much by arguing against them as by showing positively what unity means." It would seek to counter the "defeatist trend" of opinion that accepted the gradual drifting apart of the regions of Canada. Pearson proposed Kent as chairman of the study committee, Simon Reisman (the Deputy Minister of Industry) as vice-chairman, and A.W. Johnson (Assistant Deputy Minister of Finance), W.R. Dymond (Assistant Deputy Minister of Labour), and J.E.G. Hardy (of the Privy Council office) as members. "If all goes well," wrote the Prime Minister, "the result will be a substantial White Paper published about a year hence." On August 27 Gordon commented in a letter to Pearson that the memorandum "strikes just the right note." (Gordon *Papers*, Gordon to Pearson, August 27, 1964.)

This committee met intermittently over the following nine months, and presented an interim report which was tabled in Parliament on May 7, 1965. The report emphasized the need for adequate federal-provincial fiscal arrangements to overcome persistent regional inequalities, and proposed that the economic relations of the regions should be one aspect of further studies by the Tax Structure Committee. The "unity study" thus discharged the Prime Minister's potentially dangerous proposal for a study of the economic effects of Quebec's separation into the broader field of federal economic policy toward the regions. For Tom Kent, the creation of the committee helped to release him from "my involvement in tactical trivia," and led him into new policy-making activities over the winter of 1964–1965 in manpower, regional incentive grants, rural economic development, the Canada Assistance Plan, and medicare. (Kent to author, July 10, 1973.)

80. Gordon *Papers*, Memo to the Prime Minister "Re: The Flag Issue," August 31, 1964. The Queen was to visit Charlottetown for the centennial of the Charlottetown Conference in September, and Quebec City for the centennial of the Quebec Conference in October.

81. There were seven candidates for the leadership, including Charles Templeton, Robert F. Nixon and Joe Greene, the federal MP for Arnprior. Thompson won the contest on the seventh ballot. (Toronto *Telegram*, September 21, 1964, November 7, 1964; Toronto *Star*, October 20, 1964; *Canadian Annual Review for 1964*, 115-116.) Both Ron Collister of the *Telegram* and Peter Newman of the *Star* speculated after the Ontario convention that Gordon's resilience, his effective leadership of the party organization, and his strong base of support in Ontario made him a key figure in the succession to Prime Minister Pearson. Collister raised the prospect of Gordon as leader, and Newman predicted that he "may very well have the power to secure the succession for the candidate of his choice."

82. *Debates*, November 23, 1964, 10378-10389. The best account of the affair and the government's trials of the autumn is Richard Gwyn's *The Shape of Scandal* (Clarke, Irwin and Company, Toronto, 1965).

83. *Debates*, November 23, 1964, 10392. Favreau had been warned several days before that Nielsen intended to reveal the case in the House, but had confidently failed to prepare any defence against Nielsen's charges of ineptitude. (Gwyn, 18-21.)

84. *Debates*, November 23, 1964, 10392.

85. Gwyn, 27.

86. Ibid.

87. *Debates*, November 24, 1964, 10423.

88. Ibid.

89. Ibid., 10424.

90. Ibid., 10425.

91. Ibid., 10429.

92. Gordon, *Memoir*, X, 28.
93. Gwyn, 38.
94. Gordon, *Memoir*, X, 29.
95. *Debates*, November 26, 1964, 10572.
96. Ibid., 10575-10576.
97. Gwyn, 38.
98. Ibid., 53.
99. LaMarsh, 153.
100. Gordon *Papers*, Favreau to Gordon, December 30, 1964.

Chapter Ten

1. Quoted in Richard Gwyn, *The Shape of Scandal* (Clarke, Irwin and Company, Toronto, 1965), 86.
2. Gwyn, 88; Gordon *Papers*, Gordon to Pearson, January 5, 1965.
3. Gordon wrote pointedly to Davey on February 24, 1964, with a copy to Pearson, declining an invitation to attend a meeting of the National Campaign Committee on March 6, 1964. Gordon noted that some provincial chairmen still regarded him as National Chairman, and that this confusion might be perpetuated if he attended. "In order to avoid any crossing of wires and confusion from now on, you should explain to them that this is not the case." (Gordon *Papers*, Gordon to Davey, February 24, 1964.)
4. Gordon *Papers*, Memorandum, Sunday, December 5, 1965.
5. Gordon *Papers*, Minutes of Meeting, National Campaign Committee, Liberal Federation of Canada, January 5, 1965.
6. Ibid.
7. Gordon *Papers*, Gordon to Pearson, January 5, 1965.
8. Ibid.
9. Ibid.
10. Gordon *Papers*, Minutes of Meeting, National Campaign Committee, Liberal Federation of Canada, January 5, 1965.
11. Ibid. Both these pieces of advice were recommended to Gordon in Davey's preparatory memorandum on the meeting. (Gordon *Papers*, Memorandum, Davey to Gordon, January 4, 1965.)
12. Gordon *Papers*, Minutes of Meeting, National Campaign Committee, National Liberal Federation of Canada, January 5, 1965.
13. Gordon *Papers*, Gordon to Pearson, January 5, 1965.
14. *Canadian Annual Review for 1965* (University of Toronto Press, Toronto, 1966), 9.

15. For accounts of the Conservative party's bloodletting, see Peter C. Newman, *The Distemper of Our Times* (McClelland and Stewart Limited, Toronto, 1968), 102-122; *Canadian Annual Review for 1965*, 7-14.
16. Gordon reported to the National Campaign Committee that the latest party survey in December pointed to a Liberal majority; the Gallup poll on January 13 reported public preferences as forty-seven percent Liberal, thirty-two percent Conservative, twelve percent NDP, and nine percent other.
17. *Debates*, February 16, 1965, 11365.
18. Ibid., March 3, 1965, 11940.
19. See the *Debates*, March 3, 1965, 11931-11957; March 10, 1965, 12188-12192.
20. Gordon *Papers*, Pearson to Gordon, January 27, 1965.
21. Gordon *Papers*, Pearson to Gordon, January 27, 1965 (2).
22. Ibid.
23. Ibid.
24. Ibid.
25. Gordon *Papers*, Gordon to Pearson, February 1, 1965.
26. Gordon *Papers*, Gordon to Pearson, March 16, 1965. Gordon also hoped that two of the Prime Minister's schemes, the "Canada Work and Opportunity Plan" and the "Canada Youth Corps," could be given more attractive titles. (They were.)
27. Ibid. Gordon's memory about the 1964 throne speech was wrong. It had not made reference to the Corporation, although the first speech in May, 1963 had done so.
28. Toronto *Star*, April 16, 1965.
29. Hugh Whalen, "Speech from the Throne, Trends and Portents," *Canadian Forum*, May, 1965, 27. Whalen went on to reflect on the curiously inadequate public response to the Liberal program. "Initial public reaction to the speech from the throne . . . illustrates with dramatic force the prevailing unrest, uncertainty and bitterness in the national temper. Thus far, at any rate, neither in Parliament nor in the press has there been much rational commentary on the Liberal initiative, whether in terms of its objects or its methods. Most of the 'feedback,' that is to say, is distorted by the tensions, strains and blockages now afflicting the political system. No doubt some may say that the debate will become more rational as particular measures are introduced by the government. But surely it is necessary to consider the Liberal package as a whole,

since treatment of specifics ought not to proceed without clear perception of the general policy tendency. . . . Hopefully, the program could stimulate and provide a sense of direction, thus siphoning off destructive energy from the channels of regional, ethnic and cultural cleavage. Given the perils of our present journey toward national self-discovery, however, Liberal intentions might equally exhaust our limited political leadership resources and strain our parliamentary institutions to the breaking point." (Ibid., 28-29.)

30. *Debates*, April 6, 1965, 37.

31. Ibid., 43.

32. Gordon wrote that it was also "designed in part to give relief to the middle income group of managers and professional men in an attempt to stop the brain drain to the United States." (Gordon, *Memoir*, XI, 1.)

33. Gordon *Papers*, Gordon to Pearson, February 9, 1965.

34. Ibid. See also the *Globe and Mail*, Montreal *Gazette* and Winnipeg *Free Press*, January 5, 1965; *Globe and Mail*, February 13, 1965.

35. Gordon *Papers*, Gordon to Pearson, March 26, 1965.

36. Gordon, *Memoir*, XI, 2.

37. *Debates*, April 26, 1965, 427-428.

38. Ibid., 429. Gordon used this comparison, not because of a high level of unemployment, but as the primary argument for pursuing an expansionist policy which would keep unemployment low. The government of Prime Minister Trudeau later put the same estimate to a more apologetic use.

39. *Canadian Annual Review for 1965*, 20.

40. Walter L. Gordon, *Troubled Canada* (McClelland and Stewart Limited, Toronto, 1961), 127.

41. *Debates*, April 26, 1965, 434.

42. Ibid., 434-435.

43. Gordon *Papers*, Memorandum to the Cabinet from the Hon. Walter L. Gordon, April 27, 1963.

44. *Debates*, April 26, 1965, 435.

45. Gordon *Papers*, Memorandum to the Cabinet from the Hon. Walter L. Gordon, April 27, 1963.

46. It was prepared by the Minister's temporary special assistant, David Stanley, who had been working informally on the project for some time before the party came to power.

47. Gordon *Papers*, Memorandum April 27, 1963.

48. Ibid.

49. Gordon *Papers*, Canadian Development Corporation, Notes and Suggestions Made at the Meeting of May 1, 1963; May 3, 1963.

50. Gordon *Papers*, Draft of May 13, 1963, Canada Development Corporation.

51. This memorandum was also prepared by David Stanley. (Gordon *Papers*, Bryce to Gordon, June 13, 1963.)

52. Gordon *Papers*, Canada Development Corporation, November 22, 1963.

53. Ibid. Canadian Oil Companies had been acquired by the Royal Dutch Shell Group in 1962.

54. Ibid.

55. This timetable is mentioned by Gordon in a number of letters to business and financial persons written on August 13, 1965. (Gordon *Papers*.)

56. The negotiations with Strong can be traced in correspondence in the Gordon *Papers*, commencing in April, 1965.

57. Gordon *Papers*, Strong to Gordon, June 4, 1965; Strong to Gordon, August 31, 1965.

58. One of the more alarmist attacks on the Corporation was made by G. Arnold Hart, the chairman and president of the Bank of Montreal, in a speech to the annual meeting of the Canadian Manufacturers' Association on June 7, 1965. He said:

Whatever merit the over-all aims of the Canada Development Corporation may have, it is extremely doubtful that they warrant a far-reaching intrusion of government into the savings and investment process. While this billion dollar corporation is to be financed largely through the sale of shares to the public, it is virtually certain that an important measure of control will remain with the government, or that at the very least the government will have a dominant influence on policy. Once established, the existence of such a corporation on this scale places in the hands of the government of the day enormous control over the allocation of financial resources. Coupled with the new pension plans, the ground is laid for a massive shift in the control over savings from the private to the public sector. Such a pronounced move in the direction of state socialism can only be viewed with considerable alarm by those who believe, as I do, that dynamic expansion of the private sector of the economy is the best assurance of future growth and prosperity for all Canadians.

59. Gordon *Papers*, (Address by the Hon. Walter L. Gordon to the Canadian Institute of Actuaries, Ottawa, September 20, 1965). In June he had addressed the Canadian Textiles Institute on the same subject.

60. *Report of the Royal Commission on Publications* (The Queen's Printer, Ottawa, May, 1961). The Commission recommended, among other things, the disallowance for tax purposes of advertising expenditures in foreign periodicals directed at the Canadian market, and the prohibition of entry into Canada of periodicals from abroad containing advertising directed specifically at the Canadian market.

61. *Debates*, February 20, 1964, 57-58.

62. Ibid.

63. Ibid.

64. See, for example, the comments of Barry Mather, the NDP member for New Westminster, in the *Debates*, March 2, 1964, 436-437.

65. Judy LaMarsh wrote that "There was a long period of lobbying for both sides. Neither side forgot to lobby the private members of our caucus and the ministers, most of whom had taken sides." (Judy LaMarsh, *Memoirs of a Bird in a Gilded Cage* [McClelland and Stewart Limited, Toronto, 1969], 69.) A brief from *Weekend Magazine/Perspectives* of November 20, 1963, which urged the adoption of the measures later outlined by the Prime Minister, but without any exemptions, concluded that "What perhaps was not said in the formal presentations before the O'Leary Commission is that no magazines could be more obviously foreign than *Time* and *Reader's Digest*, no magazines could be more commercial in the rationale of their strong Canadian roots, yet both have not hesitated to use the American government to fight their battles for them."

66. Gordon *Papers*, Kent to Gordon, undated.

67. Gordon *Papers*, "The Preservation of Canadian Magazines," April 27, 1964.

68. Gordon was the recipient of advice on the subject from a number of Canadian newspaper publishers; and he sought legal opinions on various legislative approaches to the problem. He was assisted in his study by the parliamentary secretary to the Minister of Justice, Donald S. Macdonald, MP, who prepared two memoranda on the legal and practical aspects of the question in April and May, 1964. (Gordon *Papers*.)

69. Gordon *Papers*, Memorandum, "The Magazine Problem: A Possible Solution," Kent to the Prime Minister, May 11, 1964.

70. Ibid.

71. Ibid.

72. Ibid.

73. Publishing companies did not require federal charters, and it was arguable that ownership fell under several categories of jurisdiction allocated to the provinces under the BNA Act.

74. Gordon *Papers*, "Re: Magazines," Kent to Gordon, May 24, 1964.

75. Gordon, *Memoir*, XI, 5.

76. Ibid.

77. *Debates*, June 22, 1965, 2786.

78. *The Uncertain Mirror: Report of the Special Senate Committee on Mass Media*, Volume I (The Queen's Printer, Ottawa, 1970), 162; Interview with Senator Davey, November 25, 1971; Interview with Walter L. Gordon, November 22, 1971; Interview with the Rt. Hon. Lester B. Pearson, June 30, 1972.

79. *Maclean's* and *Saturday Night* told the Committee, however, that they no longer opposed the exemption because they now benefited from the attractiveness to advertisers of *Time* and *Reader's Digest* by sharing in a cooperative advertising scheme. This scheme, the Magazine Advertising Bureau, was created at the initiative of the two American magazines, and in 1970 its members were *Time*, *Reader's Digest*, *Maclean's*, *Le Magazine Maclean*, *Chatelaine* and *Miss Chatelaine*, the *United Church Observer*, *Actualité*, *TV Hebdo*, and *Saturday Night*. (Davey *Report*, 159.)

80. Resolution adopted by the Canadian Daily Newspaper Publishers Association at its Forty-Sixth Annual Meeting held in Toronto April 29, 1965.

81. Gordon noted that "The Winnipeg *Free Press* in an article on June 19, 1965, printed my picture with those of Adolf Hitler, Joseph Stalin, Fidel Castro, King George III, Benito Mussolini and Juan Peron, all of whom, it was claimed, had interfered with the freedom of the press." (Gordon, *Memoir*, XI, 6.)

82. Gordon, *Memoir*, XI, 6.

83. Gordon *Papers*, Gordon to Pearson, May 14, 1965.

84. Basil Dean, the publisher of the Edmonton *Journal*, one of those present at the meeting, reversed his position in a signed editorial on May 8, 1965.

85. Gordon, *Memoir*, XI, 7.

86. *Debates*, June 22, 1965, 2787. Richard A. Graybiel, the president of the C.D.N.P.A., protested in a public statement on June 23, 1965 that the government had not given the publishers sufficient time to prepare alternative proposals. In response, Pearson and Gordon repeated the pledge to substitute any alternative legislation which the publishers might request, providing it could achieve the government's purposes in a manner acceptable to it. By this time the publishers were seriously divided on the Association's tactics, and Graybiel lacked the broad support he had possessed after the budget speech. The Association did not offer any substitute proposals.

87. The Thomson organization, fearing the prospect of retaliatory legislation affecting its ownership of newspapers abroad, maintained its opposition to the legislation. In addition, the Inter-American Press Association censured the Canadian government in 1965, 1966, 1968, and 1970 for violating section four of the Association's charter, which asserts that "Prohibitions, restrictions or permits to exercise it, whether they affect owners, editors, publishers, contributors or employees of a publication, violate freedom of the press." (This censure was supported at the annual meetings of the Association in 1965 and 1966 by the representatives of Thomson newspapers.) In 1970 the Association adopted a code of free press guidelines which included one clause mentioning restricted ownership or taxes on advertising and circulation, and under this definition the Association "for the first time officially recognized that there are fifteen countries in the hemisphere which have restrictions relating to the foreign ownership of newspapers." The Association has never sought to distinguish with any precision between restrictions on foreign ownership and restrictions on "freedom of the press." This curious history is reviewed in "'Freedom of the Press' and Foreign Ownership," *Canadian Forum*, September, 1972, 4-5.

88. Gordon *Papers*, Memorandum, Sunday, December 5, 1965.

89. Gordon, *Memoir*, IX, 18.

90. Under the agreement, Canada permitted free importation by participating producers of autos and auto parts from all countries, conditional on commitments from the Canadian manufacturers to increase their production according to certain formulae; and the United States undertook to eliminate tariffs on autos and auto parts imported from Canada. Ratification of the agreement occurred by Order-in-Council in Canada, and was followed by the adoption of supporting resolutions in the House of Commons and Senate. In the United States legislation was required, which was adopted after months of hesitation in Congress in October, 1965.

91. See the *Debates*, May 10, 1965, 1125-1132; *Senate Debates*, June 1, 1966, 616-622; Gordon, *Memoir*, IX, 18-20. The Minister of Industry also foresaw that the retail price differential between Canadian and United States cars would be progressively lessened in favour of Canadian consumers.

92. Gordon, *Memoir*, IX 18-19. The Big Three were General Motors, Ford and Chrysler.

93. Ibid., IX, 19.

94. In the period from 1964 to 1968, the number of vehicles manufactured in Canada almost doubled, the number of employees in the Canadian industry increased by 20,000, the Canadian share of North American production increased from four percent to six percent, and the deficit in the Canadian balance of trade in cars and parts with the United States fell from $714 million in 1965 to $343 million in 1968. Nevertheless Canada still retained a substantial automotive trade deficit throughout the period up to 1972.

95. Gordon noted later in *A Choice For Canada* that "The eight chartered banks taken together held seventy percent of all deposits or deposit-type liabilities at the end of 1964. The three largest of the chartered banks held almost one half of all deposits or deposit-type liabilities in Canada." (See Walter L. Gordon, *A Choice for Canada* [McClelland and Stewart Limited, Toronto, 1966], 58-59.)

96. Gordon, *Memoir*, XI, 9-10.

97. *Debates*, May 6, 1965, 987.

98. Gordon, *Memoir*, XI, 10-11.

99. Gordon, *Memoir*, XI, 11; *Debates*, September 22, 1964, 8316.

100. Gordon, *Memoir*, XI, 11.

101. When the hearings on the revisions to the Act were held in 1967, Mercantile sought exemption, and contested Gordon's account of the negotiations preceding the purchase. The controversy caused a public sensation and anxious moments in the Liberal Cabinet and caucus. For this further episode, see chapter 14.

102. The Winnipeg *Free Press*, for example, which was by this time a crusading opponent of the Minister of Finance, called the measure "discrimination of the worst sort" on June 24.

103. Gordon, *Memoir*, XI, 12-13.

104. Gordon *Papers*, Memorandum, Sunday, December 5, 1965.

105. *Canada and the United States: Principles for Partnership* (Ottawa, June 28, 1965), 49.

106. Gordon, *Memoir*, IX, 25.

107. Heeney was disappointed that Gordon shared what he regarded as the general misunderstanding of the report in Canada, but noted Gordon's generous personal remarks.

108. Newman, *Distemper*, 337.

109. Gordon, *Memoir*, X, 32.

110. Gwyn, 225.

111. Ibid., 223-231. (Favreau subsequently became President of the Privy Council.)

112. Gordon, *Memoir*, X, 32-33.

113. In particular, the commissioner challenged the judgment of Guy Favreau and the RCMP Commissioner in matters of political discretion which were not the normal concern of a judicial enquiry; and misinterpreted evidence presented to the commission to suggest that the Prime Minister had learned of the involvement of Guy Rouleau, his parliamentary secretary, more than two months earlier than he had in fact learned of it. Chief Justice Dorion took the unusual step of altering his *Report* after publication to correct the statement about the Prime Minister, following angry public denials from Pearson and Favreau. But the gratuitous political judgments remained. There is a strong case that the Minister's actions (apart from the strictly legal aspect of the case) should never have been made the subject of a judicial enquiry. That initial error was made by the Cabinet in establishing the terms of the investigation. Once the commissioner had been charged with what was in part a political task, it was perhaps inevitable that his conclusions would lack the appropriate discretion.

114. *Debates*, June 30, 1965, 3110.

Chapter Eleven

1. Gordon *Papers*, Memo to Pearson, "Re: Strategy," December 30, 1964. The Redistribution Act, which provided for the creation of independent redistribution commissions in the provinces and regular decennial redistribution of parliamentary seats after each census, was passed in November, 1964. The Carter Royal Commission on Taxation had been appointed by the Diefenbaker government and was expected to report late in 1965.

In the same memorandum Gordon proposed interim action to limit election expenses and campaign contributions, pending the report of the Committee on Election Expenses which had been appointed previously by the Pearson government. (The advice was ignored.) Gordon also suggested that Mitchell Sharp (a native of Manitoba) should be encouraged to run in Winnipeg in order to take the lead in recreating a base of support in the prairies for the Liberal party. Gordon considered Sharp's decision to remain in his constituency of Toronto Eglinton "a serious political mistake." (Gordon, *Memoir*, XII, 3-4.)

2. *Canadian Annual Review for 1965* (University of Toronto Press, Toronto, 1966), 66.

3. Ibid., 66-67.

4. Toronto *Star*, March 30, 1965.

5. Gordon *Papers*, Gordon to Pearson, March 31, 1965.

6. These developments can be traced in the memoranda produced for party officials by the national organizer, Keith Davey, in the spring of 1965.

7. John Nichol had succeeded Senator John J. Connolly as president of the National Liberal Federation in 1964, and in March, 1965 he also became communications chairman of the National Campaign Committee.

8. Gordon *Papers*, Liberal Party of Canada, To: Key Liberals Across Canada, May 11, 1965.

9. Peter C. Newman, *The Distemper of Our Times* (McClelland and Stewart Limited, Toronto, 1968), 342; Gordon *Papers*, Penetration Research Limited, Survey, April, 1965. In March, Quayle had also written informally to Gordon and Davey expressing caution, in view of the increased strength of the minor parties and the February Gallup poll figure of thirty-three percent undecided. On this basis, he estimated Liberal gains of nine or ten seats. (Gordon *Papers*, To Keith Davey and Walter Gordon from Olly, March 19, 1965.)

10. Gordon refers to this in his letter to Pearson of June 30, 1965 in the Gordon *Papers*.

11. Gordon *Papers*, Memorandum to Mr. Pearson, June 25, 1965.

12. Ibid. The "firm and fast action," in the event that Favreau and Tremblay were cleared by the Dorion Commission, was suggested as "an important Cabinet shuffle" and an announcement that Guy Rouleau, Yvon Dupuis and Eddie Asselin would not be Liberal candidates in the next election.

13. Gordon *Papers*, Gordon to Pearson, June 30, 1965. After the election, however, one MP reported to Gordon that the Prime Minister had referred the question of an election to the provincial and regional caucuses of the parliamentary party, and that the Ontario caucus had "voted one-hundred percent against it." (Gordon *Papers*, Dr. W.M. McMillan to Gordon, November 17, 1965.)

14. Ibid. This case about the timetable for redistribution was phrased imprecisely, and Gordon undoubtedly attempted to make too much of it in his enthusiasm for a general election. But his hypothetical timetable appeared plausible at this time. The key factor in the case was whether administrative arrangements for an election under the new redistribution scheme could be completed to allow for the possibility of an election by the autumn of 1966; there was general agreement that one would be undesirable in the first six to eight months of Centennial year, 1967. The question was pursued later by the Prime Minister (see below).

15. Ibid.

16. Gordon referred to this decline in good relations in his memorandum of Sunday, December 5, 1965. This failure of a friendship was probably one reason for Gordon's faith in the healing powers of a general election victory. He was optimistically inclined to put the failure down to the severe pressures on the minority Cabinet and the ministry's weariness, rather than to any basic conflict of personalities, and to hope that the removal of pressure would restore the relationship.

17. *Globe and Mail*, July 27, 1965.

18. The memorandum is reproduced in full in Peter Newman's *Distemper*, Appendix G, 503-508.

19. Ibid., 503-504.

20. Ibid., 504-505. Payne suggested that the undecided portion in the opinion polls, which was as high as thirty percent, offered proof that the government could not win "anything other than a minority government or a very narrow majority." (Newman, *Distemper*, 506.)

21. Ibid., 505.

22. Ibid., 505-506.

23. The memorandum is reproduced in full in Newman's *Distemper*, Appendix F, 498-500.

24. Ibid., 341.

25. This was an extraordinary omission. In the circumstances, it seems likely that Pearson followed his diplomatic habit, in situations of conflict, of avoiding direct confrontation. This was especially likely in the case of potential disagreement with a friend.

26. Gordon *Papers*, Gordon to Pearson, August 13, 1965.

27. Ibid. The same day, in Winnipeg, Judy LaMarsh said that a majority of the Cabinet favoured an election, and that the only source of delay was the Prime Minister's lack of opportunity to make a firm decision. (*Canadian Annual Review for 1965*, 69.)

28. Newman, *Distemper*, 340.

29. Pearson made the same claim in Ottawa before departing for the West on August 19. (*Canadian Annual Review for 1965*, 70.)

30. Newman, *Distemper*, 340.

31. Gordon, *Memoir*, XII, 11: Gordon *Papers*, "Memo of conversation with Mike re the election decision," September 12, 1965.

32. Among those expressing preferences, forty-three percent favoured the Liberal party as compared with forty-one percent in April, and thirty percent favoured the Conservative party as compared with thirty-two percent in April. (Newman, *Distemper*, 342; Gordon *Papers*, Penetration Research Limited, Survey, August, 1965.)

33. Newman, *Distemper*, 343.

34. Gordon *Papers*, Penetration Research Limited, Survey, August, 1965.

35. Newman, *Distemper*, 343.

36. Gordon *Papers*, Memorandum to the Prime Minister "Re: The Quayle Report," August 31, 1965.

37. Ibid.

38. Ibid.

39. Gordon recorded his account of this meeting in two memoranda, one handwritten the same day, and one typed

on September 12, 1965.

40. Gordon *Papers*, "Note of conversation with Mike Pearson this morning," August 31, 1965.

41. Gordon *Papers*, "Memo of conversation with Mike re the election decision," September 12, 1965.

42. Gordon *Papers*, Note of conversation..., August 31, 1965. (Gordon still assumed that Maurice Strong would become president of the CDC.)

43. Gordon *Papers*, Memo of conversation ..., September 12, 1965.

44. Gordon *Papers*, Note of conversation..., August 31, 1965.

45. Gordon *Papers*, Memo of conversation ..., September 12, 1965.

46. Ibid.

47. Ibid. Gordon noted that some member of the Cabinet had leaked an accurate account of the discussion to Peter Newman, who reported it in his column the next day. (The account appears in summary in Newman's *Distemper*, 343.)

48. Gordon *Papers*, Memo of conversation ..., September 12, 1965.

49. The correspondence is reproduced in Newman, *Distemper*, Appendix F, 501.

50. In his television address on September 7 the Prime Minister conceded that an election could occur under the redistribution by October, 1966, but said that "officials agree that a more realistic date for the earliest possible election under the new distribution of seats would be early in 1967." (*Canadian Annual Review for 1965*, 70.) There was some confusion in this smudging of the distinction between the "earliest possible" and the "more realistic" dates.

51. Gordon *Papers*, Memo from office of the Prime Minister, September 2, 1965; Newman, *Distemper*, 343. Mrs. Pearson was also present.

52. Newman, *Distemper*, 344.

53. *Canadian Annual Review for 1965*, 70-71.

54. Quoted in Newman, *Distemper*, 346.

55. Ibid., 504.

56. Jean Marchand was president of the Confederation of National Trade Unions and a member of the Royal Commission on Bilingualism and Biculturalism; Gérard Pelletier was a columnist with *Le Devoir*; and Pierre Elliott Trudeau was editor of *Cité Libre* and a professor of Law at the University of Montreal.

57. Gordon, *Memoir*, XII, 15.

58. Ibid., XII, 15-16.

59. Arthur Blakely mentioned this prospect in the Montreal *Gazette*, September 21, 1965.

60. Newman, *Distemper*, 373-375.

61. Gordon, *Memoir*, XII, 16-17.

62. George Hees and Davie Fulton returned as parliamentary candidates; Dalton Camp and Eddie Goodman directed the campaign as national president and campaign chairman respectively; and the Conservative provincial premiers Robert Stanfield, John Robarts and Duff Roblin gave their public support to John Diefenbaker's campaign.

63. Gordon *Papers*, Memorandum to the Prime Minister "Re: Latest Survey," October 18, 1965; Gordon, *Memoir*, XII, 17-18.

64. Gordon *Papers*, Memorandum to the Prime Minister "Re: Latest Survey," October 18, 1965.

65. Ibid.

66. J.M. Beck, *Pendulum of Power* (Prentice-Hall of Canada, Ltd., Scarborough, 1968), 380.

67. Toronto *Telegram*, September 20, 1965.

68. Gordon, *Memoir*, XII, 19-20; Montreal *Gazette*, Toronto *Globe and Mail*, September 30, 1965.

69. *Globe and Mail*, September 30, 1965.

70. Toronto *Star*, October 14, 1965.

71. Montreal *Gazette*, October 25, 1965.

72. The rumour was mentioned, for example, in the Toronto *Star* on October 27, 1965 and in the *Globe and Mail* and Montreal *Gazette* on October 29, 1965.

73. Gordon, *Memoir*, XII, 20; Toronto *Star*, October 27, 1965; *Globe and Mail*, October 28, 1965. Gordon sensed that the promise was a spontaneous response to the audience's enthusiasm rather than a calculated effort to deny the rumour: Mike Pearson did not seem to think ahead that way.

74. Gordon, *Memoir*, XII, 20.

75. *Globe and Mail*, October 29, 1965.

76. Ibid.

77. Toronto *Telegram*, October 30, 1965.

78. Gordon, *Memoir*, XII, 20-21.

79. See the *Canadian Annual Review for 1965*, 95. Liberal party officials in Toronto suspected that the public address system had been deliberately sabotaged.

80. Gordon, *Memoir*, XII, 21; see also the *Canadian Annual Review for 1965*, 94; Beck, 379.

81. Gordon, *Memoir*, XII, 24; Gordon *Papers*, Estimated Campaign Budget. The budget for the election was $12,300, and less than this was actually spent. Joe Grittani,

Gordon's former campaign manager, had been appointed to the Board of Broadcast Governors and was replaced by the president of the constituency association, Lex Thomson.

82. Toronto *Telegram*, October 30, 1965.

83. Gordon, *Memoir*, XII, 22.

84. Gordon, *Memoir*, XII, 24-25; see also *Time (Canada)*, November 19, 1965.

85. On election night, reported the Toronto *Star*, Gordon had "dismissed suggestions he might be switched from the Finance post, stating 'I expect to return to Finance where there is lots of hard work to do.'" (Toronto *Star*, November 9, 1965.)

86. Pearson said afterwards that "if I had told him he simply *had* to remain, I think he would have done so." (Interview with the Rt. Hon. Lester B. Pearson, June 30, 1972.)

87. Gordon, *Memoir*, XII, 25-26.

88. Gordon *Papers*, Memorandum, Sunday, December 5, 1965.

89. Gordon *Papers*, Gordon to Pearson, November 9, 1965.

90. Gordon *Papers*, Pearson to Gordon, November 11, 1965.

91. *CBC Transcript*, Walter Gordon interview at VIP lounge, undated.

Chapter Twelve

1. The remaining changes were as follows: Jean Marchand, Minister of Citizenship and Immigration; J.J. Greene, Minister of Agriculture; Jean-Pierre Côté, Postmaster General; John Turner, Minister without portfolio; Arthur Laing, Minister of Northern Affairs and Indian Affairs; Allan MacEachen, Minister of Health and Welfare; Judy LaMarsh, Secretary of State; John R. Nicholson, Minister of Labour; Maurice Sauvé, Minister of Rural Development and Forestry; Edgar Benson, Minister of National Revenue and President of the Treasury Board; Jean-Luc Pepin, Minister of Resources and Energy. A number of these appointments involved the reallocation of responsibilities among departments, and the creation of new departments, by legislation at the forthcoming session. (*Globe and Mail*, December 18, 1965.)

2. Gordon *Papers*, Memorandum, Sunday, December 5, 1965; interview with Walter L. Gordon, November 22, 1971.

3. Gordon, *Memoir*, XIII, 1.

4. In passing Pearson expressed annoyance to Gordon that Winters had held him to his promise of Trade and Commerce. (Gordon *Papers*, Memo of conversation with Pearson, 10 A.M., January 15, at Sussex Drive.)

5. In particular, Gordon would have nothing to do with the Toronto *Star's* intention to examine the story critically early in 1966, and told Beland Honderich that its publication might lead to his own resignation from the House. (Gordon *Papers*, Memorandum, January 26, 1966.)

6. Gordon, *Memoir*, XIII, 1.

7. Ibid., XIII, 2.

8. Gordon *Papers*, Gordon to Sharp, January 5, 1966.

9. Ibid.

10. Gordon *Papers*, Gordon to Pearson, January 5, 1966.

11. Gordon *Papers*, Memo of conversation with Pearson 10 A.M., January 15, at Sussex Drive.

12. The usual leaks from caucus occurred, and the discussion was widely reported in the press. (See, for example, the Toronto *Telegram*, February 2, 1966; *Globe and Mail*, February 15, 1966.)

13. Gordon *Papers*, "Notes for remarks to the Caucus about the future of the Liberal Party and the Bank Act," January 26, 1966.

14. Ibid.

15. Ibid.

16. Toronto *Star*, February 3, 1966.

17. Gordon *Papers*, Conversation with Pearson, June 27, 1966; Gordon, *Memoir*, XIII, 4-5; Peter C. Newman, *The Distemper of Our Times* (McClelland and Stewart Limited, Toronto, 1968), 410; *Canadian Annual Review for 1966* (University of Toronto Press, Toronto, 1967), 25-27.

18. Gordon recorded meetings with Pearson on January 15, January 26, March 15, March 30, June 9, June 14, and June 27, 1966. (Gordon *Papers*.)

19. Toronto *Star*, February 3, 1966.

20. Gordon *Papers*, Memo of conversation with Pearson, 10 A.M., January 15, at Sussex Drive.

21. Ibid.

22. Ibid.

23. Gordon discussed the matter in his memoranda of March 15 and March 30, 1966. (Gordon *Papers*.)

24. Peter Newman reported on this coincidence in his column of February 15, 1966, and commented sympathetically: "After a lifetime spent in the service of his country, Pearson could hardly be expected to leave

his office before that date. Which is yet another good reason why the betting in Ottawa is that Lester Pearson's retirement is at least fourteen months away." (Montreal *Star*, February 15, 1966.)

25. Gordon *Papers*, Memorandum, January 26, 1966.

26. Gordon *Papers*, Memorandum, March 15, 1966.

27. Gordon *Papers*, Lunch with Pearson, March 30, 1966.

28. *Debates*, February 23, 1966, 1682.

29. *Debates*, March 4, 1966, 2204-2209.

30. Ibid., 2205.

31. Ibid., 2210.

32. Ibid., 2211.

33. Ibid.

34. Gordon, *Memoir*, XIII, 8.

35. Gordon, *Memoir*, XIII, 8-9.

36. Gordon *Papers*, Memorandum, March 15, 1966. Pearson told Gordon that he had not intended to introduce the Munsinger case to public debate, but that Cardin had done so spontaneously.

37. Montreal *Star*, March 24, 1966.

38. Ibid.

39. *Financial Post*, March 26, 1966.

40. Ottawa *Citizen*, May 6, 1966.

41. See the *Globe and Mail*, May 5, May 6, 1966; Toronto *Telegram*, May 6, 1966; Ottawa *Citizen*, May 6, May 7, 1966; *Financial Post*, May 7, 1966.

42. Toronto *Star*, May 6, 1966.

43. *Globe and Mail*, May 6, 1966.

44. Gordon made reference in particular to the 1963 budget and the takeover tax; the interest equalization tax; the magazine legislation, *Time* and the Auto Pact; and the Bank Act and Mercantile Bank affair.

45. Walter L. Gordon, *A Choice for Canada* (McClelland and Stewart Limited, Toronto, 1966), 124.

46. Ibid., xix.

47. Ibid., 124.

48. Ibid., 93.

49. See the Toronto *Star* and *Globe and Mail*, May 5, 1966; Winnipeg *Free Press*, May 6, 1966.

50. Vancouver *Sun*, Ottawa *Journal*, May 6, May 7, 1966.

51. Ottawa *Citizen*, May 6, 1966.

52. *Le Devoir*, 20 mai 1966.

53. Montreal *Star*, May 14, 1966.

54. The Toronto *Star* was Gordon's outspoken advocate, with milder support from the Calgary *Herald* and the *Financial Post*. The *Globe and Mail*, Montreal *Star*, Montreal *Gazette*, Hamilton *Spectator*, Saskatoon *Star-Phoenix*, Winnipeg *Free Press*, Edmonton *Journal*, and Vancouver *Sun*, among others, were his familiar adversaries.

55. Toronto *Telegram*, May 10, 1966.

56. Gordon *Papers*, "Where is the Liberal Party Heading?" (Notes for Remarks by the Hon. Walter L. Gordon to the Liberal Party of Ontario Annual Meeting, Toronto, Saturday, May 7, 1966).

57. Regina *Leader-Post*, Ottawa *Citizen*, May 30, 1966.

58. See the Winnipeg *Free Press*, May 30, 1966; Saskatoon *Star-Phoenix*, June 1, 1966; Vancouver *Sun*, June 2, 1966; and a speech by Ray Perrault reprinted in *The Young Liberal Voice* (Vancouver, June, 1966), 1-3.

59. Gordon *Papers*, Memorandum, Lunch with Pearson, June 9, 1966.

60. Ibid.

61. Gordon *Papers*, Memorandum, June 14, 1966.

62. Ibid.

63. Gordon, *Memoir*, XIII, 17.

64. Ibid.

65. Ibid., XIII, 18.

66. Gordon *Papers* (Address by the Hon. Walter L. Gordon to the Women's Canadian Club in Edmonton, Alberta, Tuesday, September 13, 1966).

67. Ibid.

68. Gordon *Papers* (Notes for Remarks by the Hon. Walter L. Gordon to the Young Liberals of Calgary, Alberta, in Calgary, September 13, 1966).

69. Ibid.

70. Ibid. The proposal had been made by Professor Clarence Barber of the University of Manitoba.

71. Gordon *Papers* (Notes for Remarks by the Hon. Walter L. Gordon to the Canadian Clubs of Port Arthur and Fort William at Port Arthur, Ontario, Thursday, September 15, 1966).

72. Gordon *Papers* (Notes for Remarks by the Hon. Walter L. Gordon to the students of Simon Fraser University and the University of British Columbia, Vancouver, September 26, 1966).

73. See, for example, the Winnipeg *Free Press*, September 24, 1966; Ottawa *Journal*, September 28, 1966; Toronto *Telegram*, September 28, 1966; *Globe and Mail*, October 10, 1966.

74. Andrew Thompson, who had promised to organize the Ontario delegates for Gordon over the summer, had failed to do so as the result of illness, but had not dele-

gated the task or informed Gordon's other supporters of his inability to do so. (Gordon, *Memoir*, XIII, 23.)

75. Gordon, *Memoir*, XIII, 24-25.
76. Quoted in the *Canadian Annual Review for 1966*, 40.
77. Gordon *Papers*, Memorandum, October 29, [1966]. Gordon had no interest in the appointment, but deferred his reply out of courtesy to Pearson.
78. Gordon *Papers* (Notes for Remarks by the Hon. Walter L. Gordon to the Advertising & Sales Club of Toronto, Tuesday, October 25, 1966).
79. Ibid.

Chapter Thirteen

1. Gordon *Papers*, Memorandum, November 28, 1966; Memorandum, November 30, 1966. Pearson told Gordon on November 25 that most of the members of the Ontario caucus had sought "to persuade him to persuade me not to resign my seat." (See below.)
2. Gordon *Papers*, Memorandum, November 10, 1966.
3. Interview with Senator Davey, November 25, 1971.
4. Pearson told Gordon this on November 30.
5. Gordon *Papers*, Memorandum, November 10, 1966.
6. Pearson's strongest fear was that the split would develop over the issue of medicare, which was still in danger of further postponement. "I had to bring Gordon back in to avoid it," he recalled; and one result of Gordon's return, in Pearson's view, was that the medicare dispute was settled according to Gordon's wishes, and against those of "the Winters crowd." (Interview with the Rt. Hon. Lester B. Pearson, June 30, 1972.)
7. For an account of the CBC's troubles in 1966 and 1967 from the Minister responsible, and of the Prime Minister's efforts to find "a lid for the whole mess"—often pursued without the knowledge of the Minister—see Judy LaMarsh's *Memoirs of a Bird in a Gilded Cage* (McClelland and Stewart Limited, Toronto, 1969), 229-274.
8. Gordon *Papers*, Memorandum, November 10, 1966.
9. Peter C. Newman in the Toronto *Star*, November 19, 1966.
10. Gordon *Papers*, Memorandum, November 30, 1966.

11. Gordon *Papers*, Hon. Maurice Lamontagne, "The Federal Liberal Party," December 12, 1966.
12. Ibid.
13. Gordon *Papers*, Notes for telephone conversations with Messrs. Benson and Lamontagne, December 15, 1966.
14. Gordon *Papers*, Memorandum, December 15, 1966.
15. Gordon *Papers*, Memorandum, December 20, 1966.
16. Ibid.
17. Ibid.
18. Ibid. Guy Favreau, the incumbent President of the Privy Council, had been seriously ill during the autumn and had informed the Prime Minister of his intention to resign during the winter.
19. Interview with Senator Davey, November 25, 1971. Davey commented on his role as an intermediary in the negotiations: "I played a big part in bringing Walter back into the Cabinet, and I must say that I was dishonest to both of them in doing it. I would see Pearson in Ottawa and he would say, 'Well, yes, I suppose I could get along with Walter back in the Cabinet. But if he comes back, it will only be on my terms'. Then I would rush off to Toronto to see Walter and tell him that Pearson was desperate to get him back into the Cabinet. Walter would say, 'Well, yes, I suppose I could go back in, but if I do it will only be on my terms', and then I would rush back to Ottawa and say to Mike, 'Walter is eager to get back into the Cabinet'. I was indulging my wishes rather than being honest about it."
20. Gordon *Papers*, Memorandum, December 22, 1966.
21. Gordon *Papers*, Memorandum, December 29, 1966.
22. Ibid.
23. Ibid.
24. Ibid. Gordon immediately briefed Larry Pennell and Edgar Benson on his conversation with the Prime Minister.
25. Gordon *Papers*, Gordon to Pearson, December 29, 1966.
26. Gordon *Papers*, Memorandum, "Re: The Foreign Control Issue," December 29, 1966.
27. Ibid.
28. Gordon knew in general what he wanted. More than half of the seven page memorandum was taken up with a summary of "the kind of conclusions that might be incorporated in the proposed

white paper, whose emphasis should be on the control and supervision of monopolies rather than on foreign investment per se." His proposals were: 1. That a new monopolies commission should exercise general supervision over "all large corporations (or possibly just all large corporations that are foreign controlled)." Its jurisdiction would apply to about 500 companies with net worth of more than $25 million. The commission should "lay down and ... enforce guidelines for foreign controlled companies respecting such matters as export policies, purchasing policies, pricing policies, etc." 2. There should be no restrictions on capital imports for five years, after which capital should be encouraged in the form of fixed term securities or direct investment in partnership with Canadian capital. 3. Closely held large companies should be required, over a period of twenty-five or thirty years, to make up to seventy-five percent of their shares available on the Canadian stock exchanges. The purpose would be "to break the present parent-subsidiary structure"; but the policy would not discriminate against foreign companies since it would apply to Canadian companies as well. The proposal was not, Gordon noted, to "buy back" control of subsidiaries, but to give Canadians an opportunity to invest in Canadian enterprises that was presently denied them. It would not affect "the vast majority of small and medium-sized companies." 4. As an alternative to a takeover tax, there should be a capital gains tax on the sale of certain types of assets such as large blocks of shares, perhaps not to be applied to Canadian residents. 5. There should be a large resource development fund which would serve the purpose of regional assistance anywhere in Canada, as well as associating Canadian capital with foreign capital in joint ventures when this was desirable (for example, when foreign interests could provide markets). Gordon concluded that these were tentative suggestions which "no doubt would be revised quite considerably and perhaps radically as the work on the white paper progressed."

29. Gordon *Papers*, Gordon to Thomson, January 2, 1967. The original, unsigned and undelivered copy of this letter is in the file. An earlier draft of the letter is dated December 29, 1966.

30. An unsigned notice of resignation to the Speaker of the House of Commons dated December 27, 1966 is filed with the draft letters of resignation.

31. Gordon *Papers*, Memorandum, January 4, 1967, 10:30 A.M.

32. Ibid.

33. Ibid.

34. Ibid. In another interview with Pearson on January 4, Gordon dwelt upon three potential sources of disagreement with Sharp: Gordon's expansionism versus Sharp's fear of inflation; Gordon's opposition to agencies of foreign banks; and the likelihood of conflict over Gordon's proposals on foreign investment. (Gordon *Papers*, Memorandum, Thursday, January 5, 1967, 10:00 A.M.)

35. Gordon *Papers*, Memorandum, January 4, 1967, 2:30 P.M.

36. Gordon *Papers*, Memorandum, Thursday, January 5, 1967, 10:00 A.M.

37. Gordon *Papers*, Draft, Pearson to Gordon, January 3, 1967.

38. Gordon *Papers*, Transcript, the Prime Minister's Press Conference, January 4, 1967.

39. Gordon *Papers*, Draft, Pearson to Gordon, January 3, 1967.

40. Gordon, *Memoir*, XIV, 9.

41. Ibid., XIV, 9-10; Gordon *Papers*, Memorandum, December 20, 1966.

42. Gordon, *Memoir*, XIV, 12.

43. Gordon *Papers*, Pearson to Gordon, January 5, 1967.

44. Gordon *Papers*, Gordon to Pearson, January 9, 1967.

Chapter Fourteen

1. Winnipeg *Free Press*, January 5, 1967. The Conservative Winnipeg *Tribune* took the unusual step of reprinting the editorial of its rival as its own statement, and it was widely quoted elsewhere.

2. Montreal *Star*, January 5, 1967.

3. Toronto *Star*, January 9, 1967; Ottawa *Citizen*, January 10, 1967.

4. Toronto *Star*, January 9, 1967; *Globe and Mail*, January 13, 1967.

5. *Globe and Mail*, January 13, 1967.

6. Gordon, *Memoir*, XIV, 12; Gordon *Papers*, Memorandum, January 17, 1967.

7. Gordon, *Memoir*, XIV, 16.

8. Ibid., XIV, 12; Gordon *Papers*, Memorandum, January 17, 1967.

9. Gordon *Papers*, Gordon to Pearson, January 16, 1967. On the pledge to give Gordon responsibility for organizing

Cabinet business, Gordon suggested the same day that this could be left until his appointment as President of the Privy Council, when the role "would be easily understood." (Gordon *Papers*, Memorandum, January 17, 1967.)

10. Gordon *Papers*, Memorandum, January 18, 1967.

11. Ibid.

12. Gordon, *Memoir*, XIV, 16-17; Gordon *Papers*, Statement by the Prime Minister, January 23, 1967.

13. Gordon, *Memoir*, XIV, 17.

14. Gordon *Papers*, Memorandum, January 18, 1967.

15. Gordon *Papers*, Statement by the Prime Minister, January 23, 1967.

16. Besides Professor Watkins, the members appointed then and shortly afterwards were: Bernard Bonin (University of Montreal), Stephen Hymer (Yale University), Claude Masson (Laval University), Gideon Rosenbluth (UBC), Abraham Rotstein (University of Toronto), Ed Safarian (University of Toronto), and William Woodfine (St. Francis Xavier University).

17. Pearson had mentioned his desire to do so to Gordon several times in the course of their meetings in December, and had said so to Lamontagne himself in the hearing of reporters. On January 4, 1967, Pearson expressed doubt to Gordon about the possibility of Lamontagne's return, and Gordon wrote to Pearson urging strongly that the commitment should be fulfilled. Lamontagne, wrote Gordon, "has a knowledge of economics and sometimes a useful scepticism of official thought that is not matched by anyone in the Cabinet. He is an original thinker and his assistance would be invaluable in the work you have asked me to supervise in connection with a long term program for the Liberal party. I believe it was Maurice who suggested that this work should be undertaken in the first place." Gordon offered to stand aside from the presidency of the Privy Council if another suitable portfolio could not be found for Lamontagne, and insisted that it would be a "serious injustice" to fail to bring Lamontagne in. (Gordon *Papers*, Gordon to Pearson, January 4, 1967.) Lamontagne was not reappointed, but on Gordon's urging he was later appointed to the Senate.

18. Gordon, *Memoir*, XIV, 14-16.

19. The note is reproduced in Appendix I of Peter C. Newman's *Distemper of Our Times* (McClelland and Stewart Limited, Toronto, 1968), 511.

20. The text of this note also appears in Appendix I of Newman's *Distemper*, 512-514.

21. These terms restricted the share holdings of any person or associated group to ten percent and the holdings of all non-residents in a single bank to twenty-five percent; and limited the assets of any bank in which more than twenty-five percent of the shares were held by one shareholder to not more than twenty times its authorized capital. The effect on the Mercantile Bank was to place a limit of $200 million on its assets for as long as the First National City Bank of New York held more than twenty-five percent of its shares. (*Debates*, July 5, 1966, 7237; Gordon, *Memoir*, XIV, 19-20; Newman, *Distemper*, 419.)

22. The text appears in Newman, *Distemper*, Appendix I, 515-518. The claim of retroactivity rested on acceptance by the State Department of James S. Rockefeller's claim, challenging the record of Walter Gordon and his officials, that he had told Gordon during their interview in Gordon's office on July 18, 1963 that the purchase had been completed, and that he had not been warned clearly of the consequences of the purchase.

23. *Debates*, December 2, 1966, 10663-10664.

24. Gordon *Papers*, Memorandum, January 4, 1967, 10:30 A.M.

25. Gordon *Papers*, "Re: Agencies of Foreign Banks," January 16, 1967. The memo argued that agencies of foreign banks, with U.S. dollar assets, would not be subject to the normal monetary restraints of the Bank of Canada and might act in conflict with Bank of Canada policy; that agencies operating in most of the provinces and carrying on business with Canadian subsidiaries of American companies would occupy an unfair competitive position against their Canadian competitors; that the situation in New York State, where foreign agencies are permitted, is not parallel to the Canadian situation because New York is the financial capital of the world; that American threats of retaliation against Canadian bank agencies were probably hollow, in light of the divided jurisdiction over banking in the USA; that some American banks would prefer Canada not to open its doors to their

399

operations; and that a policy permitting agencies, once introduced, could not be reversed.

26. Gordon *Papers*, Memorandum, January 18, 1967.

27. *Proceedings of the Standing Committee on Finance, Trade, and Economic Affairs*, January 24, 1967, 1347-1459.

28. Gordon *Papers*, "A Submission to the Standing Committee on Finance, Trade and Economic Affairs by the Mercantile Bank of Canada," 1-10.

29. Mackasey's odyssey is reviewed in Newman's *Distemper*, 421-422; and in a retrospective account of the affair by Anthony Westell in the Toronto *Star*, January 23, 1971.

30. Gordon *Papers*, Memorandum, Conversation with LBP, February 9, 1967, 3:30 P.M.

31. Gordon *Papers*, Gordon to Pearson, February 15, 1967. If any bargain with Mercantile was contemplated, Gordon insisted that it should at least include a requirement that over the period Citibank should reduce its interest in Mercantile to ten percent rather than twenty-five percent, to put it on an equal footing with all other chartered banks.

32. Gordon *Papers*, Memorandum, Monday, February 20, 1967.

33. Gordon *Papers*, Memorandum, Thursday, February 23, 1967, 7:30 A.M. en route to Ottawa.

34. Ibid.

35. *Globe and Mail*, February 23, 1967.

36. Ibid.

37. Gordon *Papers*, Memorandum, Thursday, February 23, 1967, 7:30 A.M. en route to Ottawa.

38. Gordon *Papers*, Memorandum, February 24, 1967.

39. Ibid.

40. Ibid.

41. Ibid., Gordon *Papers*, Memorandum of discussion in the Prime Minister's office at 12 noon today, February 24, 1967. The Cabinet dispute was also widely reported in the press, which appeared to have almost open access to Cabinet proceedings by this time.

42. Ibid.

43. Gordon *Papers*, Memorandum, February 24, 1967, 10:00 P.M. Gordon sent copies of this memo to Edgar Benson and the Prime Minister, accompanied by a longer account of the meeting dictated by Benson.

44. Gordon *Papers*, Memorandum, Dictated by the Hon. E.J. Benson in Mr. Gordon's office, February 24, 1967.

45. Gordon *Papers*, Gordon to Benson, February 25, 1967.

46. Ibid. (An increase in authorized capital, granted by Order-in-Council, would permit Citibank to increase its assets beyond $200 million in spite of the rule limiting its assets to twenty times the authorized capital of $10 million.)

47. Ibid.

48. Gordon *Papers*, Gordon to Winters, Gordon to Marchand, February 25, 1967.

49. The Cabinet's action was relayed by telephone and letter to Gordon by his secretary, Barbara Hunter, and in a letter from the Solicitor General, Larry Pennell. It was also leaked to Ron Collister of the Toronto *Telegram*, who reported the decisions accurately on March 1, 1967. (Gordon *Papers*, Hunter to Gordon, Pennell to Gordon, March 1, 1967; Toronto *Telegram*, March 1, 1967.)

50. Gordon *Papers*, Memorandum, Friday, March 3, 10:00 A.M.

51. Ibid.

52. Gordon refused to comment or to give them the names of the other guests, but appeased them by posing for a photograph.

53. Toronto *Telegram*, March 6, 1967.

54. *Globe and Mail*, March 6, 1967.

55. Gordon, *Memoir*, XIV, 29.

56. Gordon *Papers*, Memorandum, March 9, 1967.

57. Ibid.

58. Gordon *Papers*, Memorandum concerning discussion relating to amendments to the Bank Act, March 9, 1967.

59. Ibid.

60. Whether the Bank Act restrictions will successfully achieve Walter Gordon's long-term objective of preventing Citibank from retaining effective control of the Mercantile Bank is more doubtful. Mercantile reduced its assets to less than the $200 million limit before December 31, 1967, and did not offer shares to the public for three years. In 1970, it was granted permission by the Cabinet to increase its authorized capital to $40 million by the sale of $30 million in new shares. Under the amended act, these shares must be sold to Canadian buyers, and the government holds them in trusteeship until 1980 to guarantee that this occurs. But once the shares have been sold, Citibank's interest in Mercantile will have fallen to its statutory limit of twenty-five percent, and the

ceiling on its independent expansion will be lifted. With twenty-five percent of outstanding shares, it will retain effective control of the bank. Citibank's permanent presence in Canada will probably lead to renewed pressure for the entry of other American banks on the grounds of equity. If the general policy of reserving banking to Canadian ownership is to be sustained, the case for bringing Mercantile under the ten percent ownership rule applying to all other chartered banks at the next decennial revision of the Bank Act will be strong. (See Anthony Westell's review of the case in the Toronto *Star*, January 23, 1971.)

61. Gordon *Papers*, Memorandum, Conversation with LBP, February 9, 1967, 3:30 P.M.

62. Gordon *Papers*, Memorandum, April 13, 1967.

63. Ibid.

64. Gordon *Papers*, Memorandum, Monday, April 17, 1967. (The memo is erroneously dated March 17th and later corrected.)

65. Gordon *Papers*, Memorandum, Wednesday, April 26, 1967.

66. Ibid. The question of a formal transfer of jurisdiction over the Privy Council office had not, apparently, been discussed in December, but only arose in March and April. But Gordon had certainly anticipated a *de facto* supervisory role over the Prime Minister's staff and the PCO, which Pearson did not, perhaps, appreciate.

67. Ibid.

68. Ibid.

69. Gordon *Papers*, Gordon to Pearson, April 27, 1967.

70. Gordon *Papers*, Pearson to Gordon, May 16, 1967.

71. Gordon, *Memoir*, XIV, 34.

72. Gordon, *Memoir*, XV, 5. Canada's representative on the International Control Commission in Indochina was also engaged, at this time, in activities which marked Canada virtually as an agent of the United States government (according to the *Pentagon Papers*). But Gordon was unaware of this role.

73. *Globe and Mail*, April 3, April 4, 1967. Two years before, at Temple University in Philadelphia, Prime Minister Pearson had been notably more outspoken, and had been personally chastised for his words by President Johnson.

74. *Debates*, May 10, 1967, 57.

75. He was provided with background material by Professor James Steele of

Carleton University and Professor Abraham Rotstein of the University of Toronto.

76. Gordon *Papers*, Memorandum, May 11, 1967.

77. Gordon *Papers*, "Notes for Remarks by the Hon. Walter L. Gordon to the Sixth Arts of Management Conference," Toronto, Ontario, Saturday, May 13, 1967.

78. His mail on the speech was greater than he had received on any other single occasion during his political career, and it was almost entirely favourable; he wrote more than one thousand letters of acknowledgment.

79. See, for example, editorials in the Ottawa *Citizen, Globe and Mail*, Toronto *Star*, and Montreal *Star*, May 16, 1967.

80. The notice of meeting informed ministers that the Prime Minister requested their "special effort" to attend both the Cabinet and the caucus which followed.

81. Gordon *Papers*, Memorandum, "Our policy toward the Vietnam conflict . . . ," May 17, 1967.

82. Gordon *Papers*, Memorandum, May 23, 1967.

83. Gordon *Papers*, Memorandum, May 17, 1967.

84. Ibid., Gordon *Papers*, Memorandum, May 23, 1967.

85. Ibid.

86. Gordon *Papers*, Memorandum, May 23, 1967; *Globe and Mail*, May 18, 1967.

87. The problem of Cabinet secrecy was a subject of continuing fascination and no action. On one occasion, Gordon remembered, Joe Greene proposed that a sentence of five years in the penitentiary for one Cabinet colleague would solve the problem. On another occasion Walter Gordon offered a helpful suggestion: "One morning before Cabinet began, several ministers commented on an article by Peter Newman which had appeared . . . the previous day. Newman . . . had quoted with remarkable accuracy what was said by a number of ministers at a recent Cabinet meeting. This was still the topic of conversation when the Prime Minister arrived. I asked him if it would not be a kindness to give Newman a chair on the grounds that it was most uncomfortable for him to have to crouch for several hours under the table while Cabinet meetings were in session. I was delighted to notice two ministers looking surreptitiously under the table to see if Peter was really there." (Gordon,

Memoir, XV, 13.)
88. Gordon *Papers*, Memorandum, May 23, 1967.
89. Gordon *Papers*, Pearson to Gordon, May 26, 1967.
90. Gordon *Papers*, Memorandum, June 7, 1967.
91. Gordon, *Memoir*, XV, 15.

Chapter Fifteen

1. Gordon, *Memoir*, XVI, 1.
2. The Prime Minister told the House of Commons on September 25, 1967 that a special branch in the Department of Justice was "studying the question" of Canada's constitutional future, but that until it completed its work the government had no position to take. (*Debates*, September 25, 1967, 2429.)
3. Gordon *Papers*, Memorandum, "Re: Quebec Situation," September 21, 1967; Gordon, *Memoir*, XVI, 3.
4. Gordon *Papers*, Memorandum, "Re: Quebec Situation," September 21, 1967.
5. Gordon *Papers*, Gordon to Pearson, September 22, 1967.
6. Ibid.
7. Ibid.
8. Ibid.
9. Gordon *Papers*, Memorandum, September 23, 1967.
10. Ibid.
11. Gordon *Papers*, Memorandum, October 4, 1967, 2:45 P.M.
12. Gordon *Papers*, Memorandum, "The Position of the Government at the Present Time," October 3, 1967.
13. Gordon cited as evidence, in particular, rising living costs and the high level of taxes, Ottawa's lack of control over public spending, the fear of inflation and the self-fulfilling capacity of ministerial speeches about inflation, the housing crisis, rising interest rates, and public uncertainty about the Carter Report on taxation.
14. Ibid.
15. Ibid. Gordon proposed that Marchand should be relieved of his departmental duties to concentrate on Quebec.
16. Ibid. On October 2, Robert Winters also wrote to the Prime Minister pointing out the need for a regrouping of federal functions and responsibilities, and urging him to give Walter Gordon the task of reviewing "the overall administration of government." Winters promised his full cooperation if Gordon were to be offered

this assignment. (Gordon *Papers*, Copy, Winters to Pearson, October 2, 1967.)
17. Gordon *Papers*, Memorandum, October 4, 1967, 2:45 P.M.
18. Gordon *Papers*, Memorandum, October 23, 1967.
19. Ibid.
20. Gordon, *Memoir*, XVI, 8.
21. Gordon recorded a long discussion at the Prime Minister's house on October 10 in which he and Marchand argued for a referendum while Pearson successfully advocated caution and delay. (Gordon *Papers*, Memorandum, October 10, 1967.)
22. Gordon, *Memoir*, XVI, 21.
23. *Globe and Mail*, October 25, 1967.
24. Gordon *Papers*, Memorandum, October 24, 1967.
25. Ibid. Gordon had previously reopened the question of a floating exchange rate in a letter to the Prime Minister on June 1, 1967.
26. Gordon *Papers*, Gordon to Pearson, November 7, 1967.
27. Gordon, *Memoir*, XVI, 24-25.
28. Gordon *Papers*, Memorandum, November 9, 1967.
29. Gordon, *Memoir*, XVI, 26.
30. "A not-so-happy Liberal anniversary," *Globe and Mail*, November 8, 1967.
31. Gordon *Papers*, Memorandum, Wednesday, November 8, 1967.
32. Gordon *Papers*, Memorandum, November 17, 1967. Honderich and Thompson were apparently hopeful that Pearson might agree to make Gordon caretaker Prime Minister, but Gordon could not believe this would happen. Honderich told Gordon that he intended to write to Pearson about his retirement and to request an interview. Honderich did so on November 20, 1967 but did not meet Pearson before the announcement of his decision to retire. (Interview with Beland Honderich, November 18, 1971.)
33. Gordon *Papers*, Memorandum, November 19, 1967.
34. Ibid.
35. Gordon *Papers*, Memorandum, "Medicare," November 20, 1967.
36. Gordon *Papers*, Memorandum, November 20, 1967.
37. Ibid.
38. Gordon *Papers*, Draft, December 5, 1967, not sent.
39. Gordon *Papers*, Memorandum, December 14, 1967.
40. Gordon *Papers*, Memorandum,

December 18, 1967, 6:00 P.M.

41. Gordon *Papers*, Memorandum, December 19, 1967.

42. Ibid.

43. See Martin Sullivan, *Mandate '68* (Doubleday Canada Limited, Toronto, 1968), 147. Sullivan reported that these doubts made it unlikely that Marchand could win if he did contest the leadership. This was a potent consideration weighing more heavily with the Quebec caucus than it did with supporters of the English-speaking candidates. "So there was considerable risk that if he did decide to be a candidate he would not do too well – a loss of face that the reformed Quebec caucus felt it could not afford."

44. Gordon *Papers*, Memorandum, December 28 or 29, 1967. (The memorandum appears to have been dated, and perhaps written, a few days later.)

45. Sullivan, 273-306; Peter C. Newman, *The Distemper of Our Times* (McClelland and Stewart Limited, Toronto, 1968), 435-451; Donald Peacock, *Journey to Power* (The Ryerson Press, Toronto, 1968), 156-233.

46. Gordon *Papers*, Memorandum, Conversation with PET, February 13, 1968. In his manuscript *Memoir*, Gordon also recalled "a pleasant personal conversation" with Trudeau in late January, before the constitutional conference. In this conversation Gordon explained his support for Marchand, and said that if Marchand won the leadership "I would feel obligated to stay with him and to run in the next election, despite the fact that I was not at all sure my health was up to it." Gordon added that if Marchand would not run, and if Trudeau did so, "I would support him to the best of my ability. However, I said that in these circumstances I did not wish to obligate myself to run in the next election, primarily because after my operation it was very difficult for me to work as hard as I was used to. In the course of the conversation, I said I was not certain that Trudeau could win the nomination. (How wrong I was!) At that time, he was not nearly as well known as Marchand. However, I said I was inclined to agree with Marchand's opinion that if Trudeau did win he might very well make the better Prime Minister." (Gordon, *Memoir*, XVI, 15-16.)

Gordon's special concern for policy was reflected in his later meeting with Trudeau on February 13. The apparent inconsistency between the two accounts seems merely to echo the uncertainty of the situation and the very tentative nature of the judgments expressed by Gordon about the succession during this period of uncertainty.

47. Ibid. Trudeau announced his candidacy four days later.

48. Gordon's views are contained in a handwritten draft letter to the Prime Minister of January 19, 1968, which was not sent. (Gordon *Papers*.)

49. *Debates*, January 22, 1968, 5761-5762.

50. Gordon *Papers*, Memorandum, Toronto, Friday, January 26, 1968.

51. Gordon *Papers*, Memorandum, January 31, 1968.

52. Gordon *Papers*, Gordon to Pearson, February 8, 1968.

53. Gordon *Papers*, Memorandum, Friday, February 9, 1968, 10:55 A.M.

54. Ibid.

55. Gordon wrote: "I do not accept Rasminsky's argument about the interest equalization tax. If we were under pressure – or preferably before we come under pressure – we should discuss the problem in Washington and explain why we are in difficulties; i.e., because of generally upsetting conditions in the world which are primarily due to Vietnam and because of the large number of Canadian subsidiaries of American corporations who are in a position to cause a financial crisis in Canada at any time. We should explain that we are not anxious to introduce exchange controls or to subject Canadian subsidiary companies to any form of harassment. Instead we have concluded that the best course is for us to adopt a floating rate before a crisis occurs and to support that rate to the best of our ability. We should argue that this would be in everyone's best interests and in the circumstances that naturally we would expect the exemption under the interest equalization tax to be continued." (Gordon *Papers*, Memorandum, Friday, February 9, 1968, 10:55 A.M.) When the Canadian dollar was floated in 1970 the United States maintained Canada's exemptions under the interest equalization tax, as Gordon had expected.

56. *Debates*, February 6, 1968, 6424-6451.

57. Gordon, *Memoir*, XVI, 26-27.

58. Gordon *Papers*, "Notes Re: Defeat in the House in February, 1968," February 21, 1968.

59. Ibid.

60. *Debates*, February 20, 1968, 6901; February 21, 1968, 6907-6908; February 22, 1968, 6920. (On Wednesday, February 21, 1968 the Prime Minister sought unanimous consent to waive the rule requiring forty-eight hours' notice of resolution, but when this was not granted he successfully moved the adjournment.)

61. *Globe and Mail*, February 21, 1968.

62. Gordon *Papers*, Memorandum, "Re: Defeat on Income Tax Bill and Subsequent Crisis," February 23, 1968. Gordon was also told that Sharp had offered his resignation on February 20, "but was told this would not help." Two days later, however, he recorded this account of a conversation with the Prime Minister: "He said he would say tomorrow that the Income Tax Bill is dead. He added he did not know what Sharp would do and that he would be very 'neutral' meaning he would let Sharp resign if he wants to.

I said it was obvious the Income Tax Bill—or at least the personal income surtax—couldn't pass and mentioned that many of our side are and always have been against it." (Gordon *Papers*, "Notes Re: Defeat in the House in February, 1968," February 21, 1968; Memorandum, Thursday, February 22, 1968; 6:20 P.M.)

63. The resolution read: "That this house does not regard its vote on February 19th in connection with third reading of Bill C-193, which had carried in all previous stages, as a vote of non-confidence in the government." (*Debates*, February 23, 1968, 6921.)

64. The negotiations leading to the Bill are discussed in the Gordon *Papers*, Memorandum, "Re: New Financial Proposals," February 23, 1968; Memorandum, "Where do we go from here?" February 22 or 23, 1968; Memorandum, February 27, 1968; Memorandum, "Re: The Parliamentary Crisis," February 28, 1968; Gordon, *Memoir*, XVI, 27-28.

65. *Debates*, March 12, 1968, 7540.

66. Mr. Sharp was required by the Speaker to withdraw his first revised Bill on March 11, 1968, on the ground that it contained four clauses identical with clauses in the previously defeated Bill. He did so, and introduced a third version the following day. (*Debates*, March 11, 1968, 7471-7481; 7493-7496.)

67. Gordon, *Memoir*, XVI, 27.

68. Gordon *Papers*, Memorandum, Febru-

ary 27, 1968.

69. Gordon *Papers*, Gordon to Pearson, February 27, 1968.

70. Ibid.

71. He put the threat to the dollar down to "the uncertain world situation," to President Johnson's balance of payments policy, and to "our inherently vulnerable position in respect of sudden withdrawals of funds by U.S. corporations from their Canadian subsidiaries," and only partly to increased Canadian costs of production.

72. Ibid.

73. Once again he argued that the U.S. would be unlikely to retaliate by cancelling Canada's exemption under the interest equalization tax. "Conceivably the U.S. Treasury people might threaten to do this if we consulted them beforehand. But if our dollar were to slip under pressure, then it would surely be inconceivable for the U.S. to threaten us with a withdrawal of the exemption under the Interest Equalization Tax. Inevitably any such move would drive the Canadian dollar lower which would not be in the best interests of the USA. I believe it would be much more likely that, having gone off the fixed rate, the U.S. would allow us to borrow in the New York market in order to re-establish our reserve position."

74. Gordon *Papers*, Memorandum, March 4, 1968, 10:00 P.M. Those present were Rasminsky and Beattie (of the Bank of Canada), Bryce (of the Department of Finance), Marshall Crowe (of the Prime Minister's Office), Stoner (of the Privy Council Office), Arthur Smith (chairman of the Economic Council of Canada), Sharp, Benson, Drury, Pearson, and Gordon.

75. *Debates*, March 6, 1968, 7332-7334; March 7, 1968, 7379-7380.

76. Gordon *Papers*, undated memorandum, 1968.

77. The *Report* was distributed to members of the Cabinet by January 17, 1968, and discussed at Cabinet meetings on January 30 and February 1. It is doubtful whether the Cabinet gave serious consideration to the *Report* in this period of distraction. Pierre Trudeau, the Minister of Justice, admitted to reporters when he announced his candidacy for the party leadership on February 16 "that he had not had time to read the task force report." Nevertheless he asserted confidently that "no trading nation should practise" the economic nationalism advocated by his Cabinet

colleague Walter Gordon. (Toronto *Star*, February 16, 1968.) For further discussion of the *Report*, see chapter 16.

78. Gordon, *Memoir*, XVI, 33. Peter Newman also referred to their opposition in the Toronto *Star* on February 16.

79. Gordon *Papers*, Pearson to "My dear Colleague," January 31, 1968.

80. Gordon *Papers*, "Text of Statement which should be used in any Comment by a Member of the Government on the Report of the Task Force on the Structure of Canadian Industry," February 12, 1968.

81. *Debates*, February 15, 1968, 6749.

82. Gordon, *Memoir*, XVI, 33.

83. Gordon *Papers*, Gordon to Pearson, February 19, 1968.

84. Gordon *Papers*, Memorandum, February 21, 1968, 4:15 P.M.

85. Gordon *Papers*, Pearson to Gordon, March 4, 1968. The original draft of the Prime Minister's letter contained the words "I know that you returned to the government at my earnest request for certain specific purposes. I hope you feel that they have been achieved . . . ," but these were removed at Walter Gordon's suggestion, "as, if they were included, I would have to reply in no uncertain language." In one final compromise, the Prime Minister agreed to defer a Cabinet decision extending the NORAD agreement until after Walter Gordon left the Cabinet, because Gordon had indicated he would oppose renewal of the agreement without "a full public debate." (Gordon *Papers*, Memorandum, March 4, 1968; Gordon, *Memoir*, XVI, 33-34.)

Chapter Sixteen

1. *Foreign Ownership and the Structure of Canadian Industry: Report of the Task Force on the Structure of Canadian Industry* (Privy Council Office, Ottawa, 1968), 389.

2. Ibid., 389-390.

3. Ibid., 395-413.

4. Ibid., 392.

5. *Brief to the Prime Minister of Canada and Members of the Cabinet by the Committee for an Independent Canada* (Toronto, June, 1971), Appendix B, 12-14; Toronto *Star*, August 20, 1972.

6. See Dave Godfrey and Mel Watkins, eds., *Gordon to Watkins to You* (New Press, Toronto, 1970), 119-132.

7. *Eleventh Report of the Standing Committee of Defence and External Affairs Respecting Canada-U.S. Relations* (The Queen's Printer, Ottawa, 1970).

8. Toronto *Star*, July 3, 1971.

9. Gordon *Papers*, "Submission by the Hon. Walter L. Gordon to the Standing Committee on Finance, Trade and Economic Affairs Respecting Bill C-201." June 13, 1972.

10. Walter L. Gordon, "Last Chance for Canada," *Maclean's*, September, 1972, 38.

11. Ibid., 72.

12. Alan Heisey, in the *Globe and Mail*, March 17, 1973.

13. The kind of alarmist treatment which neglects and makes difficult any careful analysis of the issues was typified by Lester Pearson's careless remark in the mid-sixties that a policy of economic nationalism would mean a twenty-five percent fall in Canadian living standards; by Pierre Trudeau's assertion that no government should ever assume that its citizens might be willing to accept such a cut in living standards "for the mere pleasure of seeing a national middle class replacing a foreign one at the helm of various enterprises"; and by the comment of Alan Heisey in 1973 in a review of Abraham Rotstein's *The Precarious Homestead* that "For the Scarborough family man, bringing home what's left from $8,500 a year, struggling with mortgages, clothes for the kids and a rusting chariot," Canadian economic independence has nothing to offer. The assumption that anti-nationalists have a monopoly on concern for the Canadian wage-earner is arrogant and unwarranted. In fact the unfettered dominance of the multinational corporations in Canada reduces the ability of the Canadian government to stabilize the economy for the benefit of Canadians, and makes Canada unusually vulnerable to unemployment generated by American policy and the American economic climate. Anti-nationalists who put their faith in the rationality of the international free market cannot assume any greater benevolence for themselves than for their nationalist opponent; their case must be argued rather than dogmatically asserted.

14. *The Report of the Interdepartmental Task Force on Foreign Investment* published by the Ontario government in November, 1971, is an example, like the Watkins *Report*, of calm and analytical study of the issues. It concludes that "a high level of foreign ownership and control in many sectors of Canada's economic and cultural life has

recently lessened national self-confidence and created problems which are generally not common to countries relying predominantly on their own domestic capital and their own entrepreneurial and technological resources," and recommends that Ontario should "espouse the philosophy of moderate Canadian nationalism as the basic framework for policy formulation." (*Report*, 51-52.)

15. There is some reason to believe that experience in the management of multinational subsidiaries in Canada has made more than a few nationalists within their ranks; but the restraints of corporate solidarity and the Canadian businessman's traditional avoidance of political controversy tend to conceal this useful source of evidence for the nationalist cause.

16. One expression of the changing spirit was the decision by the editorial board of the *Canadian Forum* in November, 1971 to publish extracts from the Gray Report without authorization (the *Report* had been withheld from publication for months by the Cabinet), in the hope of moving the government to action. Public interest in the *Forum*'s initiative was wide and generally sympathetic.

By the early 1970s there was also an extensive nationalist literature in English Canada, including especially Godfrey and Watkins, *Gordon to Watkins to You*; Kari Levitt, *Silent Surrender: The Multinational Corporation in Canada* (Macmillan of Canada, Toronto, 1970); and Ian Lumsden, ed., *Close the 49th Parallel: The Americanization of Canada* (University of Toronto Press, 1970).

17. "Is Gordon's Game Worth the Candle?" *Canadian Forum*, July 1966, 78.

18. It is significant that a philosophic conservative like Donald Creighton can more easily admit the necessity of a socialist strategy for national independence than Walter Gordon can.

19. Gordon *Papers*, Memorandum, February 1, 1973.

APPENDIX ONE

The Pearson Cabinet
22 April 1963 to 18 December 1965

Prime Minister	Rt. Hon. Lester B. Pearson	22 Apr. 1963 – 18 Dec. 1965
Minister of Agriculture	Hon. Harry W. Hays	22 Apr. 1963 – 18 Dec. 1965
Minister of Citizenship and Immigration	Hon. Guy Favreau	22 Apr. 1963 – 2 Feb. 1964
	Hon. René Tremblay	3 Feb. 1964 – 14 Feb. 1965
	Hon. John R. Nicholson	15 Feb. 1965 – 18 Dec. 1965
Minister of Defence Production	Hon. Charles M. Drury	22 Apr. 1963 – 18 Dec. 1965
Secretary of State for External Affairs	Hon. Paul J.J. Martin	22 Apr. 1963 – 18 Dec. 1965
Minister of Finance and Receiver General	Hon. Walter L. Gordon	22 Apr. 1963 – 10 Nov. 1965
Minister of Fisheries	Hon. Hedard Robichaud	22 Apr. 1963 – 18 Dec. 1965
Minister of Forestry	Hon. John R. Nicholson	22 Apr. 1963 – 2 Feb. 1964
	Hon. Maurice Sauvé	3 Feb. 1964 – 18 Dec. 1965
Minister of Industry	Hon. Charles M. Drury	25 July 1963 – 18 Dec. 1965
Minister of Justice and Attorney General	Hon. Lionel Chevrier	22 Apr. 1963 – 2 Feb. 1964
	Hon. Guy Favreau	3 Feb. 1964 – 29 June 1965
	Hon. Lucien Cardin	7 July 1965 – 18 Dec. 1965
Minister of Labour	Hon. Allan J. MacEachen	22 Apr. 1963 – 18 Dec. 1965
Minister of Mines and Technical Surveys	Hon. William M. Benidickson	22 Apr. 1963 – 6 July 1965
	Hon. John Watson MacNaught	7 July 1965 – 18 Dec. 1965
Minister of National Defence	Hon. Paul T. Hellyer	22 Apr. 1963 – 18 Dec. 1965
Associate Minister of National Defence	Hon. Lucien Cardin	22 Apr. 1963 – 14 Feb. 1965
	Hon. Leo A.J. Cadieux	15 Feb. 1965 – 18 Dec. 1965
Minister of National Health and Welfare	Hon. Julia V. LaMarsh	22 Apr. 1963 – 18 Dec. 1965
Minister of National Revenue	Hon. John R. Garland	22 Apr. 1963 – 13 Mar. 1964
	Hon. Edgar J. Benson	29 June 1964 – 18 Dec. 1965
Minister of Northern Affairs and Natural Resources	Hon. Arthur Laing	22 Apr. 1963 – 18 Dec. 1965
Postmaster General	Hon. Azellus Denis	22 Apr. 1963 – 2 Feb. 1964
	Hon. John R. Nicholson	3 Feb. 1964 – 14 Feb. 1965
	Hon. René Tremblay	15 Feb. 1965 – 18 Dec. 1965
President of the Privy Council	Hon. Maurice Lamontagne	22 Apr. 1963 – 2 Feb. 1964
	Hon. George J. McIlraith	3 Feb. 1964 – 6 July 1965
	Hon. Guy Favreau	7 July 1965 – 18 Dec. 1965
Minister of Public Works	Hon. Jean Paul Deschatelets	22 Apr. 1963 – 11 Feb. 1965
	Hon. Lucien Cardin	15 Feb. 1965 – 6 July 1965
	Hon. George J. McIlraith	7 July 1965 – 18 Dec. 1965
Secretary of State of Canada	Hon. John W. Pickersgill	22 Apr. 1963 – 2 Feb. 1964
	Hon. Maurice Lamontagne	3 Feb. 1964 – 18 Dec. 1965

Solicitor General	Hon. John Watson MacNaught	22 Apr. 1963 – 6 July 1965
of Canada	Hon. Lawrence Pennell	7 July 1965 – 18 Dec. 1965
Minister of Trade	Hon. Mitchell Sharp	22 Apr. 1963 – 18 Dec. 1965
and Commerce		
Minister of Transport	Hon. George J. McIlraith	22 Apr. 1963 – 2 Feb. 1964
	Hon. John W. Pickersgill	3 Feb. 1964 – 18 Dec. 1965
Minister of Veterans	Hon. Roger J. Teillet	22 Apr. 1963 – 18 Dec. 1965
Affairs		
Minister without	Hon. W. Ross Macdonald	22 Apr. 1963 – 3 Feb. 1964
Portfolio	(Senator)	
	Hon. John Watson MacNaught	22 Apr. 1963 – 6 July 1965
	Hon. René Tremblay	22 Apr. 1963 – 2 Feb. 1964
	Hon. John J. Connolly	3 Feb. 1964 – 18 Dec. 1965
	(Senator)	3 Feb. 1964 – 21 Jan. 1965
	Hon. Yvon Dupuis	7 July 1965 – 18 Dec. 1965
	Hon. Lawrence Pennell	7 July 1965 – 18 Dec. 1965
	Hon. Jean-Luc Pepin	

APPENDIX TWO

The Pearson Cabinet
18 December 1965 to 6 July 1968

Prime Minister	Rt. Hon. Lester B. Pearson	18 Dec. 1965 – 20 Apr. 1968
	Rt. Hon. Pierre Elliott Trudeau	20 Apr. 1968 – 6 July 1968
Minister of Agriculture	Hon. John J. Greene	18 Dec. 1965 – 6 July 1968
Minister of Citizenship		
and Immigration	Hon. Jean Marchand	18 Dec. 1965 – 30 Sept. 1966
Minister of Consumer and		
Corporate Affairs	Hon. John N. Turner	21 Dec. 1967 – 6 July 1968
Minister of Defence		
Production	Hon. Charles M. Drury	18 Dec. 1965 – 6 July 1968
Minister of Energy, Mines		
and Resources	Hon. Jean-Luc Pepin	1 Oct. 1966 – 6 July 1968
Secretary of State for		
External Affairs	Hon. Paul J.J. Martin	18 Dec. 1965 – 20 Apr. 1968
	Hon. Mitchell Sharp	20 Apr. 1968 – 6 July 1968
Minister of Finance and		
Receiver General	Hon. Mitchell Sharp	18 Dec. 1965 – 20 Apr. 1968
	Hon. Edgar J. Benson	20 Apr. 1968 – 6 July 1968
Minister of Fisheries	Hon. Hedard Robichaud	18 Dec. 1965 – 6 July 1968
Minister of Forestry	Hon. Maurice Sauvé	18 Dec. 1965 – 30 Sept. 1966
Minister of Forestry and		
Rural Development	Hon. Maurice Sauvé	1 Oct. 1966 – 6 July 1968
Minister of Indian Affairs		
and Northern Development	Hon. Arthur Laing	1 Oct. 1966 – 6 July 1968
Minister of Industry	Hon. Charles M. Drury	18 Dec. 1965 – 6 July 1968
Minister of Justice and		
Attorney General	Hon. Lucien Cardin	18 Dec. 1965 – 3 Apr. 1967
	Hon. Pierre Elliott Trudeau	4 Apr. 1967 – 6 July 1968
Minister of Labour	Hon. John R. Nicholson	18 Dec. 1965 – 20 Apr. 1968
	Hon. Jean-Luc Pepin	20 Apr. 1968 – 6 July 1968

Minister of Manpower and Immigration	Hon. Jean Marchand	1 Oct. 1966– 6 July 1968
Minister of Mines and Technical Surveys	Hon. Jean-Luc Pepin	18 Dec. 1965–30 Sept. 1966
Minister of National Defence	Hon. Paul T. Hellyer	18 Dec. 1965–18 Sept. 1967
	Hon. Leo A.J. Cadieux	19 Sept. 1967– 6 July 1968
Associate Minister of National Defence	Hon. Leo A.J. Cadieux	18 Dec. 1965–18 Sept. 1967
Minister of National Health and Welfare	Hon. Allan J. MacEachen	18 Dec. 1965– 6 July 1968
Minister of National Revenue	Hon. Edgar J. Benson	18 Dec. 1965–17 Jan. 1968
	Hon. Jean Chretien	18 Jan. 1968– 6 July 1968
Minister of Northern Affairs and Natural Resources	Hon. Arthur Laing	18 Dec. 1965–30 Sept. 1966
Postmaster General	Hon. Jean-Pierre Côté	18 Dec. 1965– 6 July 1968
President of the Privy Council	Hon. Guy Favreau	18 Dec. 1965– 3 Apr. 1967
	Hon. Walter L. Gordon	4 Apr. 1967–11 Mar. 1968
Minister of Public Works	Hon. George J. McIlraith	18 Dec. 1965– 6 July 1968
Registrar General of Canada	Hon. Guy Favreau	18 Dec. 1965– 3 Apr. 1967
	Hon. John N. Turner	4 Apr. 1967–20 Dec. 1967
Secretary of State of Canada	Hon. Julia V. LaMarsh	18 Dec. 1965– 9 Apr. 1968
	Hon. Jean Marchand	20 Apr. 1968– 6 July 1968
Solicitor General of Canada	Hon. Lawrence Pennell	18 Dec. 1965–19 Apr. 1968
	Hon. John N. Turner	20 Apr. 1968– 6 July 1968
Minister of Trade and Commerce	Hon. Mitchell Sharp	18 Dec. 1965– 3 Jan. 1966
	Hon. Robert H. Winters	4 Jan. 1966–29 Mar. 1968
	Hon. Charles M. Drury	20 Apr. 1968– 6 July 1968
Minister of Transport	Hon. John W. Pickersgill	18 Dec. 1965–18 Sept. 1967
	Hon. Paul T. Hellyer	19 Sept. 1967– 6 July 1968
President of the Treasury Board	Hon. Edgar J. Benson	1 Oct. 1966– 6 July 1968
Minister of Veterans Affairs	Hon. Roger J. Teillet	18 Dec. 1965– 6 July 1968
Minister without Portfolio	Hon. John J. Connolly (Senator)	18 Dec. 1965–20 Apr. 1968
	Hon. Lawrence Pennell	18 Dec. 1965–30 Sept. 1966
	Hon. John N. Turner	18 Dec. 1965– 3 Apr. 1967
	Hon. Walter L. Gordon	9 Jan. 1967– 3 Apr. 1967
	Hon. Jean Chretien	4 Apr. 1967–17 Jan. 1968
	Hon. Charles R. Granger	25 Sept. 1967– 6 July 1968
	Hon. Bryce S. Mackasey	9 Feb. 1968– 6 July 1968
	Hon. Paul J.J. Martin (Senator)	20 Apr. 1968– 6 July 1968
	Hon. Donald S. Macdonald	20 Apr. 1968– 6 July 1968
	Hon. John C. Munro	20 Apr. 1968– 6 July 1968
	Hon. Gerard Pelletier	20 Apr. 1968– 6 July 1968
	Hon. Jack Davis	26 Apr. 1968– 6 July 1968

Index

Aberhart, William, 22
Advertising and Sales Club of Toronto, 293
Aird, John, 68
Anderson, David, 81
Anderson, Rod, 139
Andras, Robert, 294
Atlantic Development Board, 181, 222
Auto Pact, 214, 217, 234-235, 391n
Axworthy, Tom, 371n

Balcer, Leon, 213
Balfour, St. Clair, 233
Ball, George, 174, 183-185
Bank Act, 214, 218, 235-238, 270-273, 311-319, 391n, 399n, 400-401n
Bank of Canada, 10, 11, 20, 21, 61-62, 103, 107-108, 109, 149-150, 175, 339-340, 357; relations with government, 61-62, 95-96
Bank of England, 108
Bank of Montreal, 389n
Banks, Hal, 205
Barkway, Michael, 76
Barrie, Vincent, 85
Barron's Magazine, 103
Barrow, Irving, 377n
Baxter, Clive, 139
Bay Street, 10, 123
Beck, Murray, 106, 123, 259
Bell, R.A., 344
Benson, Edgar, 139, 166, 168, 268, 297-304, 307, 313-314, 316-319, 327, 335, 339-341
Berry, Adrian, 283
Bird, John, 99, 181, 192, 278
Blake, Anglin & Cassels, 16
Blakely, Arthur, 372n
Board of Broadcast Governors, 94
Brazilian Traction, Light and Power, 76
Bryce, R.B., 21, 137-318, 146, 193, 340
Buckwold, Sidney, 123
budget, and role of special assistants, 155-162; and secrecy, 150; mini-budget of 1967, 332-334; of 1963, 136-172; of 1964, 196-197; of 1965, 219-221; revisions to, 1963, 162-172
Burnaby Coquitlam, 123
Burpee, Nancy, 140
Butterworth, W. Walton, 173, 312

CCF, 54
Cabinet, balance of opinions in, 1963, 135-136, 142-143, 181-182; organization of, 195-196, 200-203, 329-332; selection of, 1963, 135
Calgary, Alberta, 288-289
Calgary Herald, 196
Cameron, Colin, 167-168, 171, 177, 315
Camp, Dalton, 213

Canada Development Corporation, 90-91, 191, 196, 203, 214, 215, 217-218, 221-226, 252, 291, 298, 300, 306, 331, 334, 349, 351, 386n, 389n
Canada Student Loan Bill, 204
Canadian-American joint cabinet committee on trade and economic affairs, 184-185
Canadian Broadcasting Corporation, 295
Canadian Corporate Management Limited, 347, 365n
Canadian Daily Newspaper Publishers' Association, 232-233
Canadian Forum, 80, 135-136, 352
Canadian Institute of Actuaries, 226
Canadian Institute of International Affairs, 52
Canadian Legion, 199, 201
Canadian Mounted Rifle Regiment, 17
Canadian Oil Co., 224
Canadian Overseas Telecommunications Corporation, 225
Canadiana Motor Hotel, Scarborough, 117
Cardin, Lucien, 97-98, 275-277
Cardin, P.J.A., 24
Cassels, Kathleen Hamilton, 16
Cassels, Sir Walter, 16, 365n
Castonguay, Nelson, 254-255
"Cell 13," 81-82, 372n
Central Mortgage and Housing Corporation, 305, 322
Chase Manhattan Bank, 237-238
Chatham, Ontario, 85
Chelmsford, Ontario, 105
Chevrier, Lionel, 57, 123, 135, 181, 192
Churchill, Gordon, 156, 241
Cité Libre, 126
Clark, Dr. W.C. (Clifford), 21-26, 137
Clarkson & Cross, 16
Clarkson, G.T., 19
Clarkson, Gordon & Co., 17-21, 139, 160-161
Clarkson, Gordon & Dilworth, 15, 16, 17, 18
Claxton, Brooke, 28
Committee for an Independent Canada, 352
Commonwealth Prime Ministers' Conference, 239, 271
Company of Young Canadians, 218, 322
Connolly, Senator John, 308, 311
Conway, Geoffrey, 139, 147-148, 157, 379n, 380n
Cook, Ramsay, 80-81
Cooper Brothers & Co., London, 16
Cooperative federalism, 141, 219
Counsell, J.L., Q.C., 18
Coutts, James, 377n
Coyne, James, 61-62, 95-96
Creighton, Donald, 93, 103, 140, 406n
Cuban crisis, 116

Dalton, Hugh, 157
Davenport constituency, 91-92, 205, 260, 263
Davey, Senator Keith, 136, 190-191, 294-295, 298, 304, 370-371n, 397n; and "Cell 13," 81-82; and general elections of 1962, 1963, 1965, 86-88, 90, 105, 122-133, 211-213, 245, 250; and Leader's Advisory Committee, 83; and Liberal revival, 84; and National Campaign Committee, 83, 122, 211-212; and selection of L.B. Pearson as party leader, 53; appointment as National Director, 82-83; resignation and Senate appointment, 265, 268, 269
Davis, Jack, 166, 168-169
Defence Department, 28
Defence Production Sharing Agreements, 94, 124
Defence White Paper, 194
De Gaulle, President Charles, 326-327
Denis, Azellus, 192
Denis, Raymond, 239
Deutsch, John, 21, 60
Devoir, Le, 42, 114, 126, 282
Dewar, Gordon, 160
Dexter, Grant, 45
Diefenbaker, Rt. Hon. John G., 40; and Avro Arrow, 94; and Bomarc missiles, 94; and cabinet crisis of 1962-63, 115-116, 121-122; and Canadian nationalism, 42-44, 48, 93-95; and Lucien Cardin, 97-98, 275-278; and defence policy, 93-95, 115-122; and Defence Production Sharing Agreements, 94; and economic policy, 94-96, 99-100, 107-112; and general election of 1957, 12, 51-52; and general election of 1958, 55-56; and general election of 1962, 86-88, 98-100, 103-106; and general election of 1963, 123-133; and general election of 1965, 242-245, 394n; and Liberal party, 98-100, 104-105; and 1963 budget, 156-161; and nuclear arms, 115-119, 121-122; and Quebec, 94-95, 96; and trade policy, 93-94; as Prime Minister, 12-13, 93-100; at United Nations, 96; becomes Prime Minister, 12; challenge to leadership of, 213-214; parliamentary defeat of, 121-122
Dillon, Douglas, 172-175, 182-183
dollar, devaluation and floating rate, 62, 344-346; devaluation of 1962, 103-104, 110
Dominion-provincial conference, of 1941, 22-23
Donnelly, Allan, 379n
Dorion, Chief Justice Frederic, 209, 239-241, 245, 392n
Douglas, T.C., 123, 125-126, 157, 159-160, 167-168, 191, 205, 206

Drury, Charles M. (Bud), 99, 116, 135, 181, 184, 234, 246, 314, 351, 365n
Duplessis, Maurice, 22
Dupuis, Yvon, 192-193, 205, 209-210, 247

Eaton's (T. Eaton Company), 18
Economic Council of Canada, 180
Economist, The, 103
Edmonton, Alberta, 131, 287
Eldorado Mining and Refining Co. Ltd., 225
European Common Market, 93-94, 98
Export-Import Bank, U.S., 108
External Affairs Department, 58

Favreau, Guy, 123, 135, 181, 192-193, 196, 202, 205-209, 210, 214-215, 239-241, 243, 246, 268, 319-320, 362, 363
Federal-provincial conferences, 197-199, 247
Federal Reserve Bank, U.S., 108
Finance Department, 11, 21-25, 33, 38, 137-140, 175, 193, 225, 357
Financial Post, 63, 139, 278-279
Financial Times, 225
First National City Bank of New York (Citibank), 172, 237, 311-319
Fisher, Douglas, 142, 155-158, 190-191, 192, 193, 282
flag debate, 199-200, 202-203, 204, 245
Fleming, Donald, 85, 97, 101, 103-104, 112, 139
Foreign Exchange Control Board, 20
foreign investment in Canada, and Royal Commission on Canada's Economic Prospects, 40-44; Task Force on Foreign Ownership, 325, 336, 346-347, 348-350, 397-398n, 404n
Fowler, Robert, 53
Foy, Walter, 294
Fraser, Blair, 369n
Frith, Royce, 81, 82, 129
Frost, Leslie, 56
Fulford, Robert, 375-376n
Fullerton, Douglas, 225

Galbraith, J.K., 76
Gallup Poll, 115, 128-129
Gardiner, James G., 27, 45
Garland, J.R., 169
Gelinas, Louis, 68
general election, of 1957, 12, 51-52; of 1958, 55-56; of 1962, 93-106; of 1963, 122-133; of 1965, 242-267; of 1968, 351; of 1972, 353-354
Gerin-Lajoie, Paul, 327, 332
Giguere, Robert, 377n
Gillis, Clarie, 45
Gingras, Marcel, 191
Glassco, J. Grant, 19, 20
Goodman, Eddie, 352
Gordon, Donald, 25

Gordon, Duncan, 17
Gordon, Harry Duncan Lockhart, 16-17
Gordon, Hon. Walter L., *A Choice for Canada*, 279-282, 358; administrative talents of, 26; and article for *International Journal*, 32; and austerity measures of June, 1962, 107-108; and Canada Development Corporation, 221-226; and Canadian economic independence, 11, 40-44, 62-67, 71-75, 76-77, 78, 354-360; and "Cell 13," 82; and Committee on the organization of government in Ontario, 56-57; advises 1965 general election, 202, 212-213, 242-255; and cabinet reorganization, 195-196, 200-204, 329-332; and defence policy, 65-66, 72-73, 78-79, 110, 119-121, 194-195; and economic emergency of 1962, 107-108, 109-111; and economic union with U.S., 63-66, 293; and Foreign Exchange Control Board, 20; and Keith Davey, 81-83; and Leader's Advisory Committee, 83; and Louis St. Laurent, 27-30, 37, 38, 46, 49-50; and Mercantile Bank, 237, 311-319, 391n, 400-401n; and National Liberal Rally, 77-81; and party leadership, 274-275, 278-279, 402n; and Presidency of Privy Council, 319-325; and reorganization of Department of National Defence, 28; and review of federal-provincial fiscal arrangements, 29; and review of Liberal party organization, 1959, 57-59; and revision of senior civil service salaries, 29; and Royal Commission on Administrative Classifications in the Public Service, 25-26; and Royal Commission on Canada's Economic Prospects, 31-50; and selection of L.B. Pearson as party leader, 53-54; and "Sixty days of decision," 129-132, 134-154, 177-178; and U.S. Interest Equalization Tax, 172-177; and wartime tax rental agreements, 21-25; as architect of Liberal renewal and reorganization, 9, 12-14, 57-70; as articled student, 15, 17; as chartered accountant and management consultant, 15-26; as member of business elite, 11; as Minister of Finance, 64, 68, 131-132, 134-267; as opposition financial critic, 112; as partner in Clarkson, Gordon & Co., 15; as Special Assistant to the Deputy Minister of Finance, 21-25; Chairman of National Campaign Committee, 83, 122, 211-212, 243, 245-246, 252, 265; criticisms of Diefenbaker government, 61-64, 90-91, 107, 109-111; defence of Guy Favreau, 207-209, 210; entrepreneurial talents of, 9-11, 15-16, 19-20, 26, 360-361; family

of, 16-18; friendship with L.B. Pearson, 13, 19, 252, 264-267, 273, 361-364, 393n; illness, 336; in 1958 general election, 56; in 1962 general election, 86-90, 101-106; in 1963 general election, 122-133; in 1965 general election, 256-267; 1954 invitation to join cabinet, 11-12; 1963 budget, 136-179, 191, 380n, 381n, 382n, 383n; 1964 budget, 196-197; 1965 budget, 219-221; 1965 resignation, 252, 254, 264-267, 268-270; nomination for Davenport constituency, 91-92; on salaries and perquisites of M.P.s, 88-90; proposed retirement, 292-293, 294-300; retirement, 1968, 347; return to Cabinet, 1967, 283-285, 294-306, 397n; speeches of, 61-64, 71-75, 85, 105, 107, 109-111, 119, 283, 286-291, 293; *Troubled Canada*, 90-91; Vietnam speech, 322-325; vision of Canada, 288; youth of, 15-18
Gordon, Elizabeth (née Counsell), 18
Gordon, Hugh, 17
Gordon, Isabelle, 17
Gordon, Jane, 365n
Gordon, John, 365n
Gordon, Kathleen, 17
Gordon, Kyra, 365n
Gordon, W.H. Lockhart, 16
Graham, Gen. Howard, 162
Grauer, A.E., 34, 366n
Gray, Herb, 294, 312, 315, 352
Graybiel, Richard A., 391n
Green, Howard, 79
Greene, J.J., 123
Greenspan, David, 81
Grittani, Joe, 105
Gushue, Raymond, 34, 366n
Gwyn, Richard, 208

Hahn, David, 256
Halifax, Nova Scotia, 129, 131
Hamilton, Ontario, 130
Hamilton *Spectator*, 75
Harkness, Douglas, 160, 206
Harley, Harry, 294
Harrington Lake, 169, 255
Harris, Louis, 86-88, 96-97, 124, 245, 372n
Harris, Sam, 86-87
Harris, Walter, 33-34, 46-47, 52, 368n
Harris and Partners, 139
Hart, G. Arnold, 389n
Hastings, Earl, 377n
Hays, Harry, 123, 135, 169, 181, 184, 196, 254
Heeney, Arnold, 29, 239, 366n
Hees, George, 39, 122
Heisey, Alan, 405n
Hellyer, Paul, 77, 92, 116-117, 135, 254, 258, 278, 286, 310-311
Hepburn, Mitchell, 22-24
Honderich, Beland, 335, 369n

House of Commons, Committee on
   Defence, 181; Committee on Finance,
   Trade and Economic Affairs, 300, 312,
   314-316, 317-318, 347, 353; Committee
   on Price Spreads and Mass Buying,
   18-19
Howe, C.D., 9, 27, 29-34, 37-50, 52, 54,
   80, 85-86, 134, 257, 261, 350
Hunter, Barbara, 140
Hurtig, Mel, 352
Hutchison, Bruce, 180, 250
Hyannis Port, 140, 176

Iannuzzi, Dan, 263
Ilsley, Hon. J.L., 21, 24
Industry, Department of, 180
Industrial Development Bank, 222
Inter-American Press Association, 391n
Interdepartmental Task Force on Foreign
   Investment (Ontario), 405-406n
Interest Equalization Tax, U.S., 172-177,
   182-183, 185, 384n, 385n, 403n, 404n
International Monetary Fund, 103,
   107-108, 109, 204, 340, 345-346
Investment Dealers' Association of
   Canada, 162
Isbister, Claude, 138, 145, 146, 149

Jewett, Pauline, 141
Johnson, Daniel, 327, 332
Johnson, Harry, 45, 49, 355
Johnson, Lyndon B., 239
Justice Department, 249, 255

Katzenbach, Nicholas, 312
Kelly, Leonard (Red), 256
Kennedy, John F., 80, 86-87, 88, 100, 117,
   124, 126, 127, 140-141, 172, 175, 372n,
   374n
Kent, Tom, 33-38, 48-49, 76, 80, 84, 87,
   99, 123, 136, 139, 142, 150, 186, 196,
   200-203, 205, 228-230, 250, 253, 255,
   257, 265, 268, 269, 357, 378-379n, 387n
Keynes, J.M., 62; Keynesian policy, 10,
   62, 167-168
Kierans, Eric, 162-165, 176, 179, 327, 356
King, W.L. Mackenzie, 9, 21-28, 81, 90,
   166
Kingston, Ontario, 131
Knowles, Stanley, 159, 166, 170
Kuznets, Simon, 367-368n

Laidlaw, R.A., 365n
LaMarsh, Judy, 135, 169-170, 181, 182,
   186, 188-189, 198-199, 209, 268, 311,
   363
Laing, Arthur, 254, 311
Lamontagne, Maurice, 57, 76, 80, 99, 114,
   135, 142, 169, 181, 192, 193, 196, 205,
   209, 249, 265, 268, 269, 271-272,
   277-278, 291, 292, 295, 296-297, 337,
   357, 399n

Lang, Daniel, 81, 84, 90, 129
Lang, Otto E., 377n
Land, Brian, 139, 379n
Laporte, Pierre, 327
Laurendeau, André, 114
Leamington, Ontario, 85
LePan, Douglas V., 35-36, 366n
Lesage, Jean, 126, 185-186, 198-199, 258,
   263, 273, 327
Lévesque, René, 327-329, 332
Lewis, David, 190, 276
Liberal party, 31-34, 357-360; finances
   and fund-raising, 59, 68; Kingston
   Conference, 75-77; leadership
   convention of January, 1958, 52-54;
   National Campaign Committee, 83,
   100-101, 122, 211-212, 213, 243, 252,
   377n, 388n; National Liberal
   Conference, 1966, 274, 291; National
   Liberal Federation, 27, 250; National
   Liberal Rally, 1961, 77-81, 91;
   1945-1957, under King and St. Laurent,
   26-50; of Ontario, 81; Ontario
   Campaign Committee, 84; Quebec
   Liberal Federation, 68, 278;
   reorganization of, 1959-1960, 57-70;
   Western Liberal Conference, 1966, 291
Linville, Francis, 172
London, Ontario, 85
Luce, Henry, 231-232
Lussier, Omer, 34, 366n
Lynch, Charles, 170
Lyon, Peyton, 115-116, 121

Macdonald, Donald S., 256, 291, 292
Macdonald, Mary, 53, 59
MacEachen, Allan, 57, 135, 181, 190, 192,
   196, 243, 268, 297, 303, 304, 307, 311,
   342, 343, 377n
MacFadden, Robert, 312-313
Mackasey, Bryce, 313, 314-315
Mackenzie, Max, 365n
Mackintosh, W.A., 21, 34
Maclaren Advertising, 86
Maclean's, 226, 353
Macmillan, Harold, 117, 140
MacTavish, Duncan, 27, 59
Marble, Dean, 365n
Marchand, Jean, 120, 254, 256, 268,
   272-273, 276, 277, 279, 297, 307, 309,
   311, 316, 317, 327, 329, 330, 331, 335,
   337-338, 394n
Maritime provinces, 44-45, 47
Martin, Paul, 52, 53, 57, 85-86, 112, 135,
   173, 181, 182, 184, 202, 207, 243, 252,
   253, 254, 273, 278, 285, 286, 310, 316,
   323-325, 331, 342
Mass Media, Special Senate Committee
   on, 232
Massey, Vincent, 76
Matthews, General A. Bruce, 59, 68, 368n
McCabe, Mike, 292

413

McClelland, Jack, 352
McCutcheon, Wallace, 113, 259-260, 375n
McGovern, George, 323
McIlraith, George, 135, 181, 195, 205, 308, 311
McLeod, John T., 135
medicare, 216, 247, 335-336, 338-339
Meisel, John, 135-136
Mercantile Bank, 237, 311-319, 391n, 399n, 400-401n
Merchant, Livingston, 239
Mersey, Muriel, 140
Minifie, James M., 72-73
Mississauga Horse, 17
Molgat, Gil, 283
Molson, Hartland, 365n
Montreal, Quebec, 131
Montreal *Gazette*, 124-125
Montreal *Star*, 42, 91, 136, 141, 142-143, 161, 243-244, 307, 354
Montreal Stock Exchange, 162-165, 173
Morton, M. Douglas, 92, 105
Morton, W.L., 24, 34, 51
Municipal Development and Loan Fund, 180-181, 185-186, 222
Munro, John, 294
Munsinger, Gerda, 276-278
Murdoch, J.Y., 365n

Napoleon's Hundred Days, 130
Nassau conference, 117
National Campaign Committee (see Liberal party)
National House Builders' Association, 169
National Liberal Federation (see Liberal party)
NATO, 72-73, 78, 116-119, 194-195
NATO Council, 116, 121, 324-325
NATO Parliamentary Association, 116
NDP, 112, 115, 123, 132, 169, 218, 244, 248, 351-352, 354, 359; and American investment in Canada, 125-126, 351-352; and support for Liberals, 190-191; in Davenport riding, 105; policy on nuclear weapons, 125-126
Newman, Peter C., 54, 146, 239, 278, 352
Newspaper and magazine legislation, 214, 215, 218, 226-234, 390-391n
Newsweek, 124
Niagara Falls, Ontario, 86
Nichol, John, 245, 250, 335
Nicholson, Patrick, 368n
Nielsen, Erik, 205, 207
Nixon, Richard, 352
Nobel Prize for Peace, 52, 97, 120, 363
NORAD agreement, 72-73, 79, 93, 116-122
Norstad, General Lauris, 116, 117, 123, 124, 126
Nova Scotian Hotel, Halifax, 129
Nowlan, George, 113, 137, 140, 165
nuclear weapons, for Canadian forces,

72-73, 78-79, 115-122

O'Connell, Martin, 139, 157, 161
O'Hagan, Richard, 167
O'Leary, Grattan, 94
Ontario Campaign Committee (see Liberal party)
Ontario Federation of Labour, 61, 63
Ontario Institute of Chartered Accountants, 16, 17
Ontario Liberal party (see Liberal party)
Ottawa *Citizen*, 75, 85, 135
Ottawa *Journal*, 135, 160, 166

Paul, Remi, 213
Payne, John de B., 248, 255-256
Pearson, Rt. Hon. Lester B., 13, 14, 19; and Cabinet organization, 195-196, 200-203, 329-332; and Canadian flag, 199-200, 203, 204, 363; and Dorion enquiry, 239-241; and economic emergency of 1962, 107-108; and Gordon's offer of resignation, 1965, 252, 254, 264-267, 268-270; and Gordon's return to Cabinet, 294-306, 397n; and John G. Diefenbaker, 95, 96-97, 98; and Kingston Conference, 75-77; and Leader's Advisory Committee, 83, 371n; and NATO, 27, 58, 117-119; and 1963 budget, 148-150, 165-172, 383n; and 1965 general election, 242-267; and non-confidence motion, January, 1958, 54-55; and nuclear weapons for Canada, 78-79, 115-122, 127-128, 376-377n; and party organization, 57-61, 68-70, 81, 82-83; and renewal of Liberal party, 13-14, 57-70, 81, 90, 363; and Rivard affair, 205-209, 239-241; and Royal Commission on Bilingualism and Biculturalism, 327; and standards of ministerial conduct, 209; and "Pearson Team," 88, 97, 169-170; and "Sixty days of decision," 129-132, 134-154, 177-178; and United Nations, 27, 58; and Vietnam war, 323-325, 401n; anxiety over financial security, 28; as administrator, 58, 369n; as Canadian Ambassador to Washington, 27; as party leader, 52-55, 57-59; as Prime Minister, 133, 134-347; as Secretary of State for External Affairs, 27-28, 52; as secretary to Royal Commission on Price Spreads, 19; as Under-secretary of State for External Affairs, 27-28; awarded Nobel Prize for Peace, 52; defeat of government, February, 1968, 338-344; in House of Commons, 28, 121-122; in 1958 general election, 55-56; in 1962 general election, 87-88, 101-106; in 1963 general election, 122-133; Quebec policy, 114-115, 128,

219, 326-332; retirement, 273-275, 334-337, 340, 395-396n; seat for Algoma East, 28; selection as party leader, 52-54; speech on Quebec and Confederation, December, 1962, 114-115; succession to, 278, 284-286, 337-338

Pearson, Maryon, 134

Pelletier, Gérard, 254, 256, 394n

Penetration Research Limited, 372n

Pennell, Larry, 268, 276, 294, 301, 303, 304, 307, 311, 317, 335, 343

Pension Plan, 185-189, 191, 194, 197-199, 202-203, 214, 245

Pepin, Jean-Luc, 123, 192

Perrault, Ray, 283

Peterborough Examiner, 101

Peterborough, Ontario, 86

Pickersgill, J.W., 54, 57, 112, 135, 142, 156, 181, 182, 196, 240, 243, 254, 311

Plumptre, A.F.W., 137-138, 145, 148-149, 172, 173

Polymer Corporation, 225

Port Arthur, Ontario, 290

Powe, Bruce, 81, 85

Power, C.G., 27

Power Corporation, 226

Presse, La, 116, 126, 191

Price Spreads and Mass Buying, House Committee (later Royal Commission) on, 18-19

Progressive Conservative party, 115, 160, 213-214; Association, 121; Montmorency Conference, 327

Purvis, Arthur, 365n

Quayle, Oliver, 245, 250-251, 253, 258-259, 372n

Quebec, 250-251

Quebec government (see Lesage, Jean and Johnson, Daniel)

Rasminsky, Louis, 107, 146, 149, 173, 174, 185, 193-194, 339-341

RCMP, 205, 207, 210

Reader's Digest, 227-232

Regina, Saskatchewan, 131

Reisman, Simon, 138, 145, 146, 149

Rideau Club, 172

Rideau Hall, 135, 136, 137

Ridgetown, Ontario, 85

Ritchie, Charles, 183, 184

Ritchie, A.E., 173, 312

Rivard, Lucien, 205-209, 214, 239-241

Robarts, John, 186-189, 332

Robertson, Gordon, 306, 320-321

Rockefeller, David, 237-238

Rockefeller, James S., 172, 312-313

Roosa, Robert, 174

Roosevelt, Franklin D., 130

Rotary Club, of Ottawa, 283; of St. John's, 287; of Saskatoon, 286-287; of Simcoe, 85

Rotstein, Abraham, 310, 352

Rouleau, Guy, 192-193, 205-206

Rowell-Sirois Commission, 22-24

Royal Commission on Administrative Classifications in the Public Service, 25-26

Royal Commission on Banking and Finance, 235-237

Royal Commission on Bilingualism and Biculturalism, 181, 327

Royal Commission on Canada's Economic Prospects, 12, 31-50, 61, 355; and cabinet, 31-34; commentary on, 38-50; *Final Report*, 48-50; members and staff, 34-35; on foreign investment in Canada, 40-44; on the Atlantic provinces, 44-45; planning, 35-38; political implications of, 42-50; *Preliminary Report*, 37-48; public hearings, 36; recommendations of, 38-50; research studies, 35-36; terms of reference, 366n

Royal Commission on Customs and Excise, 17-18

Royal Commission on Government Organization, 195

Royal Commission on Publications, 94, 226-227

Royal Commission on Taxation, 243

Royal Military College at Kingston, 16, 17

Ryan, Claude, 282

Safarian, A.E., 176

St. James' Anglican Cathedral, 17

St. James Street, 10

St. John of Jerusalem, Order of, 17

St. Laurent, Louis, as leader of Liberal party and Prime Minister, 9, 26-30, 37, 48, 46, 52, 54, 90; as Secretary of State for External Affairs, 26-27; invitations to Gordon, 11-12, 29-31, 34

St. Thomas, Ontario, 85

Sales tax, on building and production materials, of 1963, 152, 162, 169-171

Saskatoon, Saskatchewan, 115, 125

Sauvé, Maurice, 80, 181, 192-193, 254

Saywell, John, 122, 185-186

Scott, James, 59, 68, 82

Sefton, William, 105

Sharp, Mitchell, 21, 55, 60, 76, 99, 101, 107, 135, 142, 166, 169, 170, 181, 184, 196, 258, 260, 261, 268, 269, 270-273, 278, 279-280, 286, 292, 294, 296, 299, 301-305, 307-319, 327, 332-334, 335-336, 338-345, 351, 368n, 392n, 404n

Simcoe, Ontario, 85

Skelton, Alex, 365n

Smallwood, Joseph, 200

Smith, Arthur, 340

Smith, David, 379n

Smith, I. Norman, 166

Social Credit party, 105, 132, 133, 169,

343-344, 377n; and defeat of
Diefenbaker government, 112, 121-122;
schism, 1963, 133, 190
Soleil, le, 197
Southam Press, 141, 233
Southwestern Ontario Liberal
Association, 85
Spencer, George Victor, 275-278
Stanbury, Richard, 81
Stanbury, Robert, 294
Stanfield, Robert, 329, 344
Stanley, David, 139, 147-149, 157, 161,
224
State Department, u.s., 121, 123, 126, 318
Steele, G.G.E., 138, 145
Stevenson, Adlai, 376n
Stewart, Andrew, 34, 366n
Strong, Maurice F., 226
Surrey, Stanley, 174

Takeover tax, of 1963, 146-148, 153-154
tariff surcharges, 1962, 108-109
Taylor, K.W., 33, 137-138, 145, 149, 159
Teillet, Roger, 309
Thatcher, Ross, 283, 291, 377n
Thompson, Andrew, 91-92, 105, 204-205,
291, 335
Thomson, Dale, 27
Thomson, Lex, 300
Tillsonburg, Ontario, 85
Time, 227-232
Times, The, 103
Toronto and York Liberal Association,
81
Toronto Board of Trade, 81
Toronto *Globe and Mail*, 95, 101-103, 113,
124, 154, 161, 165, 188, 233, 247-248,
258, 260, 280, 314-315, 334
Toronto *Star*, 63, 74, 76, 99, 121, 135, 154,
190, 218, 260, 355
Toronto Stock Exchange, 162-163, 173
Toronto *Telegram*, 75, 92, 282, 317
Toronto, University of, 289
Towers, Graham, 20, 34
Trade and Commerce Department, 37-38,
55
Trail, b.c., 105
Trans-Canada pipeline, 37
Treasury Board, 140, 157, 193, 195, 331,
332-333
Treasury Department, u.s., 172-177
Tremblay, René, 123, 193, 205, 209, 265,
268
Troubled Canada, 90-91, 141, 221
Trudeau, Pierre Elliott, 120, 126, 254, 256,

311, 327, 335, 337-338, 343, 350-354,
394n, 403n, 404n
Trued, Merlyn, 172-173
"Truth Squad," 129
Turner, John, 273, 279, 309, 351

Union Nationale party, 185
United College, Winnipeg, 314
United States (see State Department, u.s.,
Interest Equalization Tax, u.s., etc.)
Upper Canada College, 16, 17

Vancouver, b.c., 105, 131, 132, 250, 290
Vancouver *Province*, 75
Vancouver Stock Exchange, 162
Vanier, Governor-General George C.,
135, 255, 318
Victoria, b.c., 131
Victoria *Times*, 74-75
Vietnam war, 323-325
Viner, Jacob, 38-39, 45

Waffle group, 351-352
Wallaceburg, Ontario, 261
Walker, James, 272, 294, 335
Walker, John R., 141
war on poverty, 218-219, 322
Waring, Gerald, 112, 182-183
Wartime Prices and Trade Board, 25
Watkins, Melville, 310, 346-347, 348-350,
358, 404n
Weekend Magazine, 390n
Westell, Anthony, 314-315, 334
Whalen, Hugh, 218, 388-389n
White, Theodore, 86-87
Wilson, J.R.M., 160-161
Wilson, W.A., 142-144, 191, 243-244, 354
Windsor Chamber of Commerce, 85
Windsor, Ontario, 85
Winnipeg *Free Press*, 99, 135-136, 233, 307
Winnipeg, Manitoba, 115, 131
Wintermeyer, John, 187-188
Winters, Robert H., 52, 86, 256-257,
260-262, 268, 269, 273, 278, 286,
308-311, 316, 317, 325, 342
withholding tax on dividends, 1963
alternations, 146, 153
Wood, Gundy and Company, 139
Woods, J.D., and Gordon Ltd., 25
World Bank, 204
Wright, Gerald, 173, 176-177

York-Scarborough Liberal Association,
117-119